EXPERIENTIAL LEARNING

Experience as the Source of Learning and Development

Second Edition

EXPERIENTIAL LEARNING

Experience as the Source of Learning and Development

Second Edition

DAVID A. KOLB

EXPERIENCE BASED LEARNING SYSTEMS, INC.

Editor-in-Chief: Amy Neidlinger
Executive Editor: Jeanne Glasser Levine
Operations Specialist: Jodi Kemper
Cover Designer: Chuti Prasertsith
Managing Editor: Kristy Hart
Project Editor: AndyBeaster
Copy Editor: Crystal Bullen
Proofreader: Audrey Jacobs
Indexer: Margaret Hentz
Compositor: codeMantra
Manufacturing Buyer: Dan Uhrig

Upper Saddle River, New Jersey 07458

For information about buying this title in bulk quantities, or for special sales opportunities (which may include electronic versions; custom cover designs; and content particular to your business, training goals, marketing focus, or branding interests), please contact our corporate sales department at corpsales@pearsoned.com or (800) 382-3419.

For government sales inquiries, please contact governmentsales@pearsoned.com.

For questions about sales outside the U.S., please contact international@pearsoned.com.

Company and product names mentioned herein are the trademarks or registered trademarks of their respective owners.

Printed in the United States of America

Second Printing: July 2015

ISBN-10: 0-13-389240-9
ISBN-13: 978-0-13-389240-6

Pearson Education LTD.
Pearson Education Australia PTY, Limited.
Pearson Education Singapore, Pte. Ltd.
Pearson Education Asia, Ltd.
Pearson Education Canada, Ltd.
Pearson Educación de Mexico, S.A. de C.V.
Pearson Education—Japan
Pearson Education Malaysia, Pte. Ltd.

Library of Congress Control Number: 2014952293

For Alice

Contents

Part II   The Structure of Learning and Knowledge

Foreword

This is a very special and important book. I say that at the outset because the book is written with such grace and gentleness, with such clarity and directness, that you will know that David Kolb has written an excellent treatise on learning theory, certainly for educators and quite possibly for Educated Persons, whatever that means. But as you read on—as *I* read on, I had to catch my breath every once in a while, wondering if the velocity of my excitement would ever cease.

Kolb has written a wonderful book, one I've been waiting for—without quite realizing it—for a long time. It's a book (I'm only guessing here) that he took a very, *very* long time to write, since it is crafted so carefully and is so deeply nuanced that you are certain that it's been filtered and re-set and redrafted many times, like a precious stone, turned and polished into a lapidary's gem.

Why this excitement? Well, the hyper-ventilation I alluded to above is based on Kolb's achievement in providing the missing link between theory and practice, between the abstract generalization and the concrete instance, between the affective and cognitive domains. By this BIG achievement he demonstrates conclusively—and is the first to do so—that learning is a social process based on carefully cultivated experience which challenges every precept and concept of what nowadays passes for "teaching." And with this major achievement he knowingly shifts the ecology of learning away from the exclusivity of the classroom (and its companion, the Lecture) to the workplace, the family, the carpool, the community, or wherever we gather to work or play or love.

The significance for educators is profound because, among other things, Kolb leads us (again, so gently) away from the traditional concerns of credit hours and calendar time toward competence, working knowledge, and information truly pertinent to jobs, families, and communities.

The book is no "piece of cake." Despite its graceful aesthetic and illuminating diagrams, from mandalas to tight-lipped 2 × 2 tables that management professors love to show on the overhead screen, the author takes us on a fascinating but densely written journey in and around some of the most seminal thinkers who laid the foundations of "experience-based learning"—great minds such as Dewey, Lewin, and Piaget. Nor does he neglect other auxiliary players like Maslow, Rogers, and Erikson. Aside from creating a framework that removes whatever residual guilt those of us have felt or feel when using experience-based learning within the formal classroom boundaries, Kolb provides a thick texture of understanding by building his framework on the wonderful armatures of that trinity: Dewey, Lewin and Piaget.

As I say, this is an important book, one the field has been waiting for, worth every ounce of energy it takes to read. But, because of its revolutionary undertones, read it at your own risk. For each reader must take the risk of creating a life of his or her own. When you think about it, you are the thread that holds the events of your life together. That's what Kolb gets us to understand.

Warren Bennis, 1925–2014

In fond remembrance of Warren,
my mentor and friend.

About the Author

David Kolb is the Chairman of Experience Based Learning Systems (EBLS), an organization that he founded in 1980 to advance research and practice on experiential learning. EBLS conducts basic research on Experiential Learning Theory and has developed many experiential exercises and self-assessment instruments including the latest Kolb Learning Style Inventory 4.0. The EBLS program of research on experiential learning is ongoing in collaboration with an international network of researchers, practitioners and learning partners.

He received his BA in psychology, philosophy, and religion at Knox College and his Ph.D. in Social Psychology from Harvard University. He was a professor of organizational behavior and management at the MIT Sloan School of Management and at the Weatherhead School of Management, Case Western Reserve University, where he is currently Emeritus Professor of Organizational Behavior.

He is best known for his research on experiential learning and learning styles described in this book, *Experiential Learning: Experience as the Source of Learning and Development*. Other books include *Conversational Learning: An Experiential Approach to Knowledge Creation, Innovation in Professional Education: Steps on a Journey from Teaching to Learning*, and *Organizational Behavior: An Experiential Approach*. In addition, he has authored many journal articles and book chapters on experiential learning. David Kolb has received several research recognition awards and four honorary degrees recognizing his contributions to experiential learning in higher education.

For more information about his work, go to www.learningfromexperience.com.

Preface

To the Revised Edition

This revised edition of *Experiential Learning* is the most comprehensive and up to date statement of experiential learning theory (ELT), a work that marks the centerpiece of my 50-year academic career. My involvement with experiential learning has been one of the most stimulating and rewarding associations of my adult life. As I described in the 1st edition, I didn't create experiential learning theory, but discovered it in the works of prominent twentieth-century scholars who gave experience a central role in their theories of human learning and development—notably John Dewey, Kurt Lewin, Jean Piaget, Lev Vygotsky, William James, Carl Jung, Paulo Freire, Carl Rogers, and Mary Parker Follett. The rewards of this long involvement have been multifaceted, ranging from the discovery of an intellectual perspective on human learning and development that is at once pragmatic and humanistic, to techniques of experience-based education that have added vitality to my teaching and to a perspective on adult development that has influenced my own personal growth and development as well as others.

I have been sustained and inspired in my work by a growing network of thousands of colleagues in over 30 academic disciplines from all over the world who share my excitement about experiential learning. Each year I have the pleasure of reviewing 300–400 research articles that have cited *Experiential Learning* and other ELT-related research papers for inclusion in the Experiential Learning Theory Bibliography (Kolb and Kolb, 2014). The scope of this work is broad and innovative, making immeasurable contributions to experiential learning theory research and practice. More personally, it is a source of endless inspiration for my own work. Even deeper satisfaction has come from supervising well over a hundred theses and Ph.D. dissertations at MIT and Case Western Reserve University and consulting with many other similar scholars at institutions around the world. I am filled with gratitude and admiration for the multiyear commitment they have made to advancing experiential learning theory. Engaging in the "nitty gritty" of ELT research as part of the dissertation process has given us the opportunity to explore theoretical, methodological, and practical issues in great depth and has produced lifelong friendships as well. Some of these scholars have carried research work on experiential learning forward into their own distinguished careers.

The Plan for This Revised Edition

I have chosen to keep the text of the first edition intact and add research updates and reflections at the end of each chapter. In this way the original text and theoretical statement of *Experiential Learning* is preserved and differentiated from the contemporary additions. The Update and Reflections (U&R) sections of the chapters include developments in experiential learning theory research and theory since the publication of the first edition of *Experiential Learning* as well as my reflections on critical reviews of experiential learning theory and on theoretical issues raised by other research since the 1984 book.

Part I, "Experience and Learning," begins in Chapter 1 with a review of the history of experiential learning as it emerged in the works of Dewey, Lewin, and Piaget. It includes an analysis of the contemporary applications of experiential learning theory in education, organization development, management development, and adult development. The Chapter 1 Update and Reflections adds other foundational scholars of experiential learning and their particular contributions to experiential learning theory. The communalities among these scholars in their theories, methods, and careers are examined.

Chapter 2 compares the learning models of Dewey, Lewin, and Piaget and identifies the common themes that characterize the experiential learning process. The Chapter 2 Update and Reflections examines the process aspects of experiential learning with particular focus on the learning cycle. It explores the connections between learning and life in the concept of "autopoesis" developed by Maturana and Varela. Parallels between this spiral of life and the spiral of learning from experience are examined. Misunderstandings and critiques of the learning cycle and its application are also examined.

Part II, "The Structure of Learning and Knowledge," begins in Chapter 3 with a structured model of the learning process depicting two basic dimensions—a prehension or "grasping" dimension and a transformation dimension. Philosophical, physiological, and psychological evidence for this model are reviewed. The Chapter 3 Update and Reflections examines recent research on the brain and its links with the learning cycle, with particular emphasis on the work of James Zull.

Chapter 4 focuses on individuality in learning with the development of a typology of learning styles based on the structural model of learning presented in Chapter 3. Assessment of individual learning styles with the Learning Style Inventory is described. Data are presented relating individual learning styles to personality type, educational specialization, professional career, current job, and adaptive competencies. In the Chapter 4 Update and Reflections, the latest Kolb Learning Style Inventory 4.0 with nine learning styles and the assessment of learning flexibility will be examined in the context of the concept of conceptions of the self and individuality.

Chapter 5 presents a typology of social knowledge structures—formism, contextualism, mechanism, and organicism—and relates these knowledge structures to academic fields of study and career paths. The Chapter 5 Update and Reflections examines research on the spiral of knowledge creation with particular emphasis on tacit knowledge. The latest research on Pepper's world hypotheses is examined with its implications for disciplinary learning spaces.

Part III, "Learning and Development," begins in Chapter 6 with a statement of the experiential learning theory of development wherein adult development is portrayed in three stages—acquisition, specialization, and integration. The chapter describes how conscious experience changes through these developmental stages via higher levels of learning. The Chapter 6 Update and Reflections examines the latest research on adult development and its implication for ELT development theory.

Chapter 7 documents specialization as the major developmental process in higher education. It describes the knowledge structures of different fields of study and the consequences of matches and mismatches between student learning styles. Relationships between professional education and later career adaptation are also examined. The section called "managing the learning process" describes applications of experiential learning theory to teaching and administration. The Chapter 7 Update and Reflections describes our latest research on learning spaces and educator roles involved in teaching around the learning cycle and the assessment and development of learning skills.

Chapter 8 describes the challenges of integrative development in adulthood by examining the life structures of integrated and adaptively flexible individuals. Integrity is posed as the pinnacle of development, conceived as the highest form of learning. The Chapter 8 Update and Reflections focuses on lifelong learning and the learning way; describing how learners can use practices of deliberate experiential learning to respond to a changing world where lifelong learning is the norm.

David A. Kolb
Kaunakakai, Hawaii

Introduction

To the Second Edition

Pleasure is the state of being
Brought about by what you
Learn.
Learning is the process of
Entering into the experience of this
Kind of pleasure.
No pleasure, no learning.
No learning, no pleasure.

—Wang Ken, Song of Joy

Revisiting *Experiential Learning* after 30 years to prepare this second edition is a great pleasure for me. The book has been the centerpiece of my career as a scholar. Try as I might to escape it, inquiry about experiential learning has continued to inspire and fascinate, always drawing me back to explore new questions and ideas. Heidegger said that any thinker has but one central thought in life, one essential intuition, and I guess experiential learning is mine.

I still remember vividly the experience that gave rise to my intuition about the power of experience in learning. It was in the summer of 1966 at a two week T-group at the National Training Laboratory in Bethel, Maine. Early in the morning that began the second week, I was standing on the porch of the old Victorian house where we held our meetings. The sun was rising through the trees bringing its warmth to the morning chill. Its light bathed the woods in a golden glow that seemed to emanate from everything it struck. The surreal vividness of the scene was matched by the intensity of my emotions as I marveled at the closeness I felt to my group members who only a week before had been total strangers. We had shared our life stories with one another, but more powerfully had experienced one another deeply in the here-and-now. I had experienced a transformation in myself and witnessed transformation in others flowing from the contact. I was so eager to begin our next week together. The scene before me became blurred and sparkled like crystal as my eyes teared up in the sun. Fully experiencing such intense emotion was not typical for me, and it highlighted my sense that there was magic in the sensitivity training model of group dynamics that Kurt Lewin and his associates had created (see Chapter 1, p. 10).

I resolved to learn more and thus began a lifetime of inquiry into experiential learning. That fall my colleagues and I began experimenting with T-groups in our introductory course on Organizational Behavior at MIT's Sloan School of Management. Later we used them in our Peace Corps training programs. In both cases, these efforts met with mixed results in spite of our persistent attempts. While some students and trainees "got it" and were as profoundly influenced by their experience as I was, for many it was more about "emotional intelligence" than they were ready for. The lack of structure and deviation from the traditional classroom learning process they were accustomed to was too confusing for them to get much from the unstructured groups.

These difficulties spurred us to reflect more deeply in a search for a way to extract the "active experiential learning ingredient" that made these groups so powerful, and harness it to produce a more effective learning process. What we extracted was the experiential learning cycle based on Lewin's laboratory method. T-groups were typically introduced by saying, "We are going to share *experiences* together, *reflect* and share their meaning for us and together *think* about the implications for or group. From this understanding we can *act* to create the kind of group we want." We ask ourselves if this learning cycle might be a way to structure learning experiences.

For me this marked the beginning of my research based on the works of those who I have come to call the Foundational Scholars of Experiential Learning—William James, Kurt Lewin, John Dewey, Jean Piaget, Lev Vygotsky, Carl Jung, Carl Rogers, Paulo Freire, and Mary Parker Follett. I chose the word "experiential" to describe a particular perspective on the learning process that originated in the work of these scholars of experiential learning (see Chapter 1 Update and Reflections). Some have suggested that the term experiential learning is redundant since learning itself is generally conceived to be the result of experience as opposed to genetics, biological development, or instinct (e.g., Fenwick, 2003). However, the behaviorist approaches to the study of learning that dominated psychology in the first half of the twentieth century reduced objective experience to reinforcements and denied any role for subjective conscious experience in learning. The foundational scholars all stood at the margins of this dominant tradition placing subjective, conscious, and intentional experiencing at the center of the learning process.

In *Experiential Learning,* I developed Experiential Learning Theory (ELT) to integrate the common themes in their work into a systematic framework that can address twenty-first century problems of learning and education. My intention was to describe a theoretical perspective on the individual learning process that applied in all situations and arenas of life. Experiential learning theory was developed following Lewin's plan for the creation of scientific knowledge by conceptualizing phenomena through formal, explicit, testable theory. In his approach, "before a system can be fully useful the concepts in it have to be defined in a way that (1) permits the treatment of both the qualitative and quantitative aspects of phenomena in a single system, (2) adequately represents the conditional-genetic (or causal) attributes of phenomena, (3) facilitates the measurement (or operational definition) of these attributes, and (4) allows both generalization to universal laws and concrete treatment of the individual case" (Cartwright, 1951, p. ix).

Having studied experiential learning for nearly 50 years, my views have evolved and deepened but not changed substantially. In many ways I have moved forward by moving backward, studying more deeply the works of the foundational scholars, recalling the line of T. S. Eliot at the beginning of Chapter 2, "We shall not cease from exploration. And the end of all our exploring. Will be to arrive where we started. And know the place for the first time." In revisiting *Experiential Learning* for this second edition, I cannot say that I know it definitively, but I can see that countless cycles through the learning spiral have deepened and expanded my views about learning and development.

What Is Experiential Learning?

The most important of these spirals of learning was a continuing inquiry into the nature of experience and the process of learning from it. The research literature on experiential learning contains much confusion and debate about its meaning. My inquiry took me back to William James' (1912) creation of the philosophy of radical empiricism in a search for an epistemological perspective that would help explain the ELT meaning of experiential learning and clarify the differences with other uses of the term. If I were to rewrite *Experiential Learning* today, I would promote James to equal status with Dewey, Lewin, and Piaget in the book. My further study of his work (James, 1912; Taylor and Wozniak, 1996) after its publication revealed in radical empiricism an epistemological foundation for experiential learning theory and a detailed analysis of the role of experience in learning. His description of the learning cycle (see Chapter 1 Update and Reflections, page 24) may well have been the first.

Experiential Learning as an Educational Technique or Type of Learning

A common usage of the term "experiential learning" defines it as a particular form of learning from life experience; often contrasted it with lecture and classroom learning. Keeton and Tate (1978) offered this definition, "Learning in which the learner is directly in touch with the realities being studied. It is contrasted with the learner who only reads about, hears about, talks about, or writes about these realities but never comes into contact with them as part of the learning process." In this view of experiential learning, the emphasis is often on direct sense experience and in-context action as the primary source of learning, often down-playing a role for thinking, analysis, and academic knowledge. Many educational institutions offer experiential education programs such as internships, field projects, and classroom experiential learning exercises to add a direct experience component to their traditional academic studies. Here it is thought of as an educational technique like service learning, problem-based learning, action learning, or team learning. Lifelong learning is often conceived as a process of learning from direct life experiences that is controlled by the individual.

Buchmann and Schwille (1983) argue against education based on this type of experiential learning and further propose that the purpose of formal education is to overcome the biases inherent in the process of learning from ongoing life experience. They cite numerous sources of error in judgments based on experience such as Tversky and Kahneman's (1973) availability heuristic where the availability of objects and events in memory such as those experienced firsthand tend to be overused. Similarly vivid experiences tend to be weighted more highly than objective data. One's experience is necessarily influenced by their political and social context and thus is biased in judging social and political issues from other perspectives in the social order. They argue that reading is in some ways superior to reflection on personal experience because it broadens possibilities and perspectives. Secondhand knowledge is more generalizable and can go beyond what is known from experience. They conclude, "The measure of education is the degree to which it allows all people to access the objective contents of thought, to theoretical systems, problems and ideas with a range of implications not yet known" (1973, p. 46).

In a series of experiments examining performance after repeated decision making with outcome feedback called action-based or experiential learning, Eisenstein and Hutchinson (2006) conclude that "managers and consumers should increase their use of objective analyses and decrease reliance on experience or intuition" (2006, p. 256). Their studies showed that learning from experience was dependent on learning goals. "Some goals direct attention toward information that results in learning that transfers across situations, but other goals result in learning that is distorted by the characteristics of the stimuli that were considered most goal relevant. Contrary to popular wisdom, we found that reliance on this type of experiential learning is likely to be a risky proposition because it can be either accurate and efficient or errorful and biased" (2006, p. 257).

Brehmer (1980) cites studies showing that experienced experts are often no better than novices at making clinical judgments; for example, a study that compared clinical psychologists' and secretaries' ability to diagnose brain damage showed no difference between these two groups. He also describes studies that show that people have a number of biases that prevent them from using the information that experience provides. He concludes that experience does not necessarily lead to better judgment and decisions "because it stems from an untenable conception of the nature of experience, a conception that assumes that truth is manifest and does not have to be inferred . . . if we do not learn from experience, this is largely because experience often gives us little information to learn from" (1980, pp. 239–240).

In *The Ambiguities of Experience* the great organizational theorist James March contrasts his definition of experiential knowledge, "lessons extracted from the ordinary course of life and work," with academic knowledge "generated by systematic observation and analysis by expert and transmitted by authorities" (2010, p. 9). He attributes the problems and pitfalls of learning from experience to the incomprehensible nature of experience. "Experience is rooted in a complicated causal system that can be described adequately by a description that is too complex for the human mind" (2010, p. 47). "As a result, the lessons derived from experiential learning are rife with unjustified conclusions, superstitious associations, misleading correlations, tautological generalizations, and systematic biases" (2010, p. 107).

When experiential learning is defined as a naturalistic ongoing process of direct learning from life experiences contrasted with the systematic learning of formal science and education, the picture that emerges is that experiential learning is haphazard, unreliable, and misleading, and it must be corrected by academic knowledge. The characterization of experiential learning conjures images of the ordinary persons blindly groping their way through daily experiences while academic knowledge is created by extraordinary persons who are presumably immune to the biases of learning from ordinary experience. For all humans, experience does not yield reliable knowledge easily. The experiential learning biases described above apply in the scientific laboratory as well as on the street. Scientists also learn from experience and are equally challenged by the difficulties of overcoming the biases involved. What the above cost/benefit analyses of experiential and academic knowledge fail to consider are the biases and limitations of generalized academic knowledge. Judgments and decisions based on "objective" knowledge can also be incorrect and unreliable because of unjustified assumptions in the analysis of data, professional tunnel vision that reinforces an availability heuristic in judgment, and many of the other problems cited above that are associated with learning in the course of ordinary life. Further, the context-free nature of generalized knowledge which is often considered its strength can become a liability in practice through the misapplication of generalized knowledge to a specific context. The first chapter of Mary Parker Follett's *Creative Experience* offers an excellent analysis of the limitations of the expert's generalized knowledge and the process through it is applied: "The social process is not, first, scientific investigation, then some method of persuading the people to abandon their own experience and thought, and lastly an acclaiming populace. The social process is a process of cooperating experience. But for this every one of us must acquire the scientific attitude of mind. This will not make us professional experts; it will enable us to work with professional experts and to find our place in a society which needs the experience of all, to build up a society which shall embody the experience of all" (1924, p. 30).

Experiential Learning in ELT

The above definition of experiential learning as in-context experiencing and action is not the meaning of experiential learning as defined in ELT. My intention in using the term "experiential" was to describe a theoretical perspective on the individual learning process that applied in all situations and arenas of life, a holistic process of learning that can aid in overcoming the difficulties of learning from experience enumerated above.

The aim of ELT is to create, through a synthesis of the works of the foundational scholars, a theory that helps explain how experience is transformed into learning and reliable knowledge. Truth is not manifest in experience; it must be inferred by a process of learning that questions preconceptions of direct experience, tempers the vividness and emotion of experience with critical reflection, and extracts the correct lessons from the consequences of action.

Dewey, himself, struggled with the incomprehensibility of experience to the point that, in preparing a new introduction to his master philosophical work *Experience and Nature* (1988/1925), he considered changing the title. In his 1951 draft for a new introduction, he wrote, "Were I to write (or rewrite) *Experience and Nature* today I would entitle the book *Culture and Nature* and the treatment of specific subject-matters would be correspondingly modified. I would abandon the term 'experience' because of my growing realization that the historical obstacles which prevented understanding of my use of 'experience' are, for all practical purposes, insurmountable. I would substitute the term 'culture' because with its meanings as now firmly established it can fully and freely carry my philosophy of experience." In this respect, he may have been influenced by the work of Vygotsky who emphasized the powerful influence of cultural artifacts and tools such as language on experience.

Dewey came to the realization that most experience is culturally mediated by many previous trips around the learning cycle:

> Experience is already overlaid and saturated with the products of the reflection of past generations and by-gone ages. It is filled with interpretations, classifications, due to sophisticated thought, which have become incorporated into what seems to be fresh naïve empirical material. It would take more wisdom than is possessed by the wisest historical scholar to track all off these absorbed borrowings to their original sources. [Dewey, 1925, p. 40]

He called this "empirical experience" which was conservative, tradition bound, and prone to conformity and dogmatism. He emphasized that this traditional flow of experience must be interrupted to initiate reflection and learning. While he argued that it was necessary to reflect on experience in order to draw out the meaning in it and to use that meaning as a guide in future experiences, he observed that the reflective process seemed to be initiated only when we are "stuck" with a problem or difficulty or "struck" by the strangeness of something outside of our usual experience (Dewey, 1933). Paulo Freire made a similar point arguing that an intense direct experience, such as a majestic sunrise, which he called "espanto" or shock, was necessary for deep learning.

In this formulation, Dewey echoes his collaborator William James, whose radical empiricism was foundational for the later development of the philosophy of pragmatism. James proposed radical empiricism as a new philosophy of reality and mind, which resolved the conflicts between nineteenth-century rationalism and empiricism as expressed in the philosophies of idealism and materialism. Speaking of "tangles" created by philosophical and psychological inquiry in his time, he succinctly describes the central principles of both philosophies: "It seems to me that if radical empiricism be good for anything, it ought, with its pragmatic method and principle of pure experience, be able to avoid such tangles, or at least simplify them somewhat. The pragmatic method starts from the postulate that there is no difference of truth that doesn't make a difference of fact somewhere; and it seeks to determine the meaning of all differences of opinion by making the discussion as soon as possible hinge on some practical or particular issue. The principle of pure experience is also a methodological postulate. . . . Everything real must be experiencable somewhere, and every kind of thing experienced must be somewhere real" (1943, pp. 159–160).

For James, everything begins and ends in the continuous flux and flow of experience. In short, experience is all there is—"we start with the supposition that there is only one primal stuff or material in the world, a stuff of which everything is composed . . . we call that stuff 'pure experience'" (1943, p. 4). In this formulation, the duality between the mind (thought) and physical world (thing) is resolved since both are experienced but with different characteristics. Thought is the concrete here-and-now experience "redoubled" in reflection—"If it be the self-same piece of pure experience taken twice over that serves now as thought and now as thing . . . how comes it that its attributes should differ so fundamentally in the two takings? As thing, the experience is extended; as thought, it occupies no space or place. As thing, it is red, hard, and heavy; but who ever heard of a red, hard, or heavy thought" (1943, pp. 27–28).

James was influenced in this view by Husserl's phenomenological view of experience which Calvin Scrhag in *Experience and Being* says, "conveys the unity of insight and action, perception and conception, knowledge and valuation, theory and practice. Experience has to do with seeing into a situation and acting within it. It includes in its range perceptual acts and the anticipation of concepts. It involves both the knowledge and evaluation of objects, events, and situations. Thus experience in its primitive presence lies beyond any conflict between theory and practice, subject and object, intellect and will" (cited in Hopkins, 1993, p. 53). Dewey set forth the postulate of immediate empiricism to describe radical empiricism. He argued that the significance of the principle is that of a philosophical method of analysis, "If you wish to find out what subjective, objective, physical, mental, cosmic, psychic, cause, substance, purpose, activity, evil, being, quantity—any philosophical term, in short—means go to experience and see what it is experienced *as*" (1905, p. 399).

The implication of the philosophy of radical empiricism for experiential learning theory and the experiential learning cycle is that it is not only the Concrete Experience mode of learning that is experiential, all modes of the learning cycle (see Figure 2.5, p. 51) are included in experience. Both modes of grasping experience—Concrete Experience (CE) and Abstract Conceptualization (AC)—and both modes of transforming experience—Reflective Observation (RO) and Active Experimentation (AE)—are part of the experiential learning process. Many use the term experiential learning to refer to exercises and games used to involve students in the learning process. However, a classroom lecture may be an abstract experience, but it is also a concrete one, when, for example, a learner admires and imitates the lecturer. Likewise a learner may work hard to create an abstract model in order to make sense of an internship experience or experiential exercise. From the learner's perspective, solitary reflection can be an intensely emotional concrete experience, and the action of programming a computer can be a highly abstract experience.

Returning to my vivid sunrise experience in Bethel, Maine, for Dewey I was struck, for Freire it was a shock, for James it was a pure experience. It was, of course, not totally a pure experience, being surrounded by many thoughts. I had read about Lewin's laboratory method and Rogers, emphasis on experiencing in the change process. But the experience had the effect of focusing my attention and drawing me more deeply into a commitment to explore it more deeply. As Dewey said, I was provoked by it into critical reflection, a reflection that led to an idea (the learning cycle) which we tried out in action, the consequences of which provided new stuckness (e.g., student and Peace Corps volunteer resistance) and other trips around the learning cycle. All of these were experiences—the concrete "pure experience," the critical reflection, thinking about ideas, and the process of implementing actions. The critics of learning from direct experience cited above describe how the vividness of a personal experience can cause it to have undue weight in decisions and judgments. Whether it was undue or not, I certainly gave it a lot of weight. It captured my interest and attention and thus created a continuity of selected experiences that continues to this day, following James interest–attention–selection cycle.

James in *The Principles of Psychology* describes how attention plays its focus "like a spotlight" across the field of consciousness in a way that is sometimes involuntary, as when the shock of pure experience "captures" our attention, but is often voluntary. James defines the voluntary process as a spiral of interest–attention–selection that creates a continuous ongoing flow of experience summarized in the pithy statement: "My experience is what I agree to attend to" (1890, p. 403). He defines interest as an "intelligible perspective" that directs attention and ultimately selection of some experiences over others. Selection feeds back to refine and integrate a person's intelligible perspective serving as "the very keel on which our mental ship is built" (James cited in Leary, 1992, p. 157).

Experiential Learning Theory Research Today

The most gratifying and motivating result of experiential learning theory for me has been in the way it has stimulated and focused a scholarly research conversation about experiential learning. Experience Based Learning Systems was created in 1980 to facilitate experiential learning theory research and communication among researchers and practitioners of experiential learning through its website www.learningfromexperience.com.

Since its first statement in 1971 (Kolb, 1971; Kolb, Rubin, and McIntyre, 1971), there have been many studies using experiential learning theory to advance the theory and practice of experiential learning. Since experiential learning theory is a holistic theory of learning that identifies learning style differences among different academic specialties, it is not surprising to see that experiential learning theory research is highly interdisciplinary, addressing learning and educational issues in many fields. An analysis of the 1,004 entries in the 1999 bibliography (Kolb, Boyatzis, and Mainemelis, 2001) shows 207 studies in management, 430 in education, 104 in information science, 101 in psychology, 72 in medicine, 63 in nursing, 22 in accounting, and 5 in law. About 55 percent of this research has appeared in refereed journal articles, 20 percent appeared in doctoral dissertations, 10 percent appeared in books and book chapters, and 15 percent appeared in conference proceedings, research reports, and others.

Since 2000 experiential learning theory research in these fields around the world has more than quadrupled. A 2013 review of management education research (Arbaugh, Dearmond, and Rau) showed that 27 percent of the top cited articles in management education journals were about experiential learning and learning styles. Research in engineering, computer science, and health care has increased substantially. The current experiential learning theory bibliographies include nearly 4,000 entries from 1971–2014. Kolb and Kolb (2013) have summarized selected studies of the experiential learning method and the Learning Style Inventory (LSI) applied in 30 different professions and academic disciplines. The studies cover a broad range of applications using experiential learning theory and the Learning Style Inventory. Some studies have used the LSI and the experiential learning cycle to understand and manage differences between students and faculty learning styles. Some educators have used an experimental design to compare the effectiveness of an experiential learning method with a more traditional course format, whereas others have developed and implemented instructional methods using the experiential learning model as a framework.

Included are research studies from every region of the world with many contributions coming from the United States, Canada, Brazil, the United Kingdom, China, India, Australia, Japan, Norway, Finland, Sweden, the Netherlands, and Thailand. These studies support the cross-cultural validity of experiential learning theory and the Kolb Learning Style Inventory (KLSI) and also support practical applicability across cultures. The KLSI has been translated into many languages including English, Spanish, French, Portuguese, Arabic, Russian, Dutch, German, Swedish, Chinese, Romanian, Persian, Thai, and Japanese. The value of the holistic ELT framework for understanding cultural differences has been show in a number of studies on cross-cultural management (Kayes, Kayes, and Yamazaki, 2005; Kayes, Kayes, and Yamazaki, 2006; Yamazaki, and Kayes, 2004; Yamazaki and Kayes, 2007).

There have been two comprehensive reviews of the experiential learning theory literature, one qualitative and one quantitative. In 1991, Hickox extensively reviewed the theoretical origins of experiential learning theory and qualitatively analyzed 81 studies that focused on the application of the experiential learning theory model as well as on the application of the concept of learning style in accounting and business education, helping professions, medical professions, post-secondary education, and teacher education. She concluded that, overall, 61.7 percent of the studies supported experiential learning theory, 16.1 percent showed mixed support, and 22.2 percent did not support experiential learning theory. In 1994, Iliff conducted a meta-analysis of 101 quantitative LSI studies culled from 275 dissertations and 624 articles that were qualitative, theoretical, and quantitative studies of ELT and the KLSI (LSI, Kolb, 1971, 1985, 1999a, 2005). Using Hickox's evaluation format, he found that 49 studies showed strong support for the LSI, 40 showed mixed support, and 12 studies showed no support. About half of the 101 studies reported sufficient data on the LSI scales to compute effect sizes via meta-analysis. Most studies reported correlations that fell in the .2 to .5 range for the LSI scales. In conclusion, Iliff suggested that the magnitude of these statistics is not sufficient to meet standards of predictive validity, while noting that the LSI was not intended to be a predictive psychological test like IQ, GRE, or GMAT. The LSI was originally developed as a self-assessment exercise and a means for construct validation of experiential learning theory.

Judged by the standards of construct validity, experiential learning theory has been widely accepted as a useful framework for learning-centered educational innovation, including instructional design, curriculum development, and life-long learning. Academic field and job classification studies viewed as a whole also show a pattern of results consistent with the experiential learning theory structure of knowledge theory. Most of the debate and critique in the ELT/LSI literature has centered on the psychometric properties of the LSI. Results from this research have been of great value in revising the LSI in 1985, 1999, 2005, and most recently in 2011. The Kolb Learning Style Inventory 4.0 (Kolb and Kolb, 2011; see Chapter 4 Update and Reflections). Recent critique (see Chapter 2 Update and Reflections) has been more focused on the theory than the instrument examining the intellectual origins and underlying assumptions of experiential learning theory from what might be called a critical theory perspective where the theory is seen as individualistic, cognitivist, and technological (e.g., Vince, 1997; Holman, 1997; Hopkins, 1993). Kayes (2002) has reviewed these and other critics of experiential learning theory and offered his own critique of the critics. He suggests that critics have overlooked the role of Vygotsky's social constructivist learning theory in the experiential learning theory of development and the role of personal knowledge and social knowledge in experiential learning. He proposes an extension of experiential learning theory based on Lacan's post-structuralist analysis that elaborates the fracture between personal and social knowledge and the role that language plays in shaping experience.

1

The Foundations of Contemporary Approaches to Experiential Learning

The modern discovery of inner experience, of a realm of purely personal events that are always at the individual's command and that are his exclusively as well as inexpensively for refuge, consolidation and thrill, is also a great and liberating discovery. It implies a new worth and sense of dignity in human individuality, a sense that an individual is not merely a property of nature, set in place according to a scheme independent of him . . . but that he adds something, that he makes a contribution. It is the counterpart of what distinguishes modern science, experimental hypothetical, a logic of discovery having therefore opportunity for individual temperament, ingenuity, invention. It is the counterpart of modern politics, art, religion and industry where individuality is given room and movement, in contrast to the ancient scheme of experience, which held individuals tightly within a given order subordinate to its structure and patterns.

—John Dewey, Experience and Nature

Human beings are unique among all living organisms in that their primary adaptive specialization lies not in some particular physical form or skill or fit in an ecological niche, but rather in identification with the process of adaptation itself—in the process of learning. We are thus the learning species, and our survival depends on our ability to adapt not only in the reactive sense of fitting into the physical and social worlds, but in the proactive sense of creating and shaping those worlds.

Our species long ago left the harmony of a nonreflective union with the "natural" order to embark on an adaptive journey of its own choosing. With this choosing has come responsibility for a world that is increasingly of our own creation—a world paved in concrete, girded in steel, wrapped in plastic, and positively awash in symbolic communications.

From those first few shards of clay recording inventories of ancient commerce has sprung a symbol store that is exploding at exponential rates, and that has been growing thus for hundreds of years. On paper, through wires and glass, on cables into our homes—even in the invisible air around us, our world is filled with songs and stories, news and commerce interlaced on precisely encoded radio waves and microwaves.

The risks and rewards of mankind's fateful choice have become increasingly apparent to us all as our transforming and creative capacities shower us with the bounty of technology and haunt us with the nightmare of a world that ends with the final countdown, "... three, two, one, *zero*." This is civilization on the high wire, where one misstep can send us cascading into oblivion. We cannot go back, for the processes we have initiated now have their own momentum. Machines have begun talking to machines, and we grow accustomed to obeying their conclusions. We cannot step off—"drop out"—for the safety net of the natural order has been torn and weakened by our aggressive creativity. We can only go forward on this path—nature's "human" experiment in survival.

We have cast our lot with learning, and learning will pull us through. But this learning process must be reimbued with the texture and feeling of human experiences shared and interpreted through dialogue with one another. In the over-eager embrace of the rational, scientific, and technological, our concept of the learning process itself was distorted first by rationalism and later by behaviorism. We lost touch with our own experience as the source of personal learning and development and, in the process, lost that experiential centeredness necessary to counterbalance the loss of "scientific" centeredness that has been progressively slipping away since Copernicus.

That learning is an increasing preoccupation for everyone is not surprising. The emerging "global village," where events in places we have barely heard of quickly disrupt our daily lives, the dizzying rate of change, and the exponential growth of knowledge all generate nearly overwhelming needs to learn just to survive. Indeed, it might well be said that learning is an increasing *occupation* for us all; for in every aspect of our life and work, to stay abreast of events and to keep our skills up to the "state of the art" requires more and more of our time and energy. For individuals and organizations alike, learning to adapt to new "rules of the game" is becoming as critical as performing well under the old rules. In moving toward what some are optimistically heralding as "the future learning society," some monumental problems and challenges are before us. According to some observers, we are on the brink of a revolution in the educational system—sparked by wrenching economic and demographic forces and fueled by rapid social and technological changes that render a "frontloaded" educational strategy obsolete. New challenges for social justice and equal opportunity are arising, based on Supreme Court decisions affirming the individual's right of access to education and work based on proven ability to perform; these decisions challenge the validity of traditional diplomas and tests as measures of that ability. Organizations need new ways to renew and revitalize themselves and to forestall obsolescence for the organization and the people in it. But perhaps most of all, the future learning society represents a personal challenge for millions of adults who find learning is no longer "for kids" but a central lifelong task essential for personal development and career success.

Some specifics help to underscore dimensions of this personal challenge:

- Between 80 and 90 percent of the adult population will carry out at least one learning project this year, and the typical adult will spend 500 hours during the year learning new things (Tough, 1977).

- Department of Labor statistics estimate that the average American will change jobs seven times and careers three times during his or her lifetime. A 1978 study estimated that 40 million Americans are in a state of job or career transition, and over half these people plan additional education (Arbeiter et al., 1978).

- A study by the American College Testing Program (1982) shows that credit given in colleges and universities for prior learning experience has grown steadily from 1973–74 to 1980–82. In 1980–82, 1¼ million quarter credit hours were awarded for prior learning experience. That learning is a lifelong process is increasingly being recognized by the traditional credit/degree structure of higher education.

People do learn from their experience, and the results of that learning can be reliably assessed and certified for college credit. At the same time, programs of sponsored experiential learning are on the increase in higher education. Internships, field placements, work/study assignments, structured exercises and role plays, gaming simulations, and other forms of experience-based education are playing a larger role in the curricula of undergraduate and professional programs. For many so-called nontraditional students—minorities, the poor, and mature adults—experiential learning has become the method of choice for learning and personal development. Experience-based education has become widely accepted as a method of instruction in colleges and universities across the nation.

Yet in spite of its increasingly widespread use and acceptance, experiential learning has its critics and skeptics. Some see it as gimmicky and faddish, more concerned with technique and process than content and substance. It often appears too thoroughly pragmatic for the academic mind, dangerously associated with the disturbing anti-intellectual and vocationalist trends in American society. This book is in one sense addressed to the concerns of these critics and skeptics, for without guiding theory and principles, experiential learning can well become another educational fad—just new techniques for the educator's bag of tricks. Experiential learning theory offers something more substantial and enduring. It offers the foundation for an approach to education and learning as a lifelong process that is soundly based in intellectual traditions of social psychology, philosophy, and cognitive psychology. The experiential learning model pursues a framework for examining and strengthening the critical linkages among education,

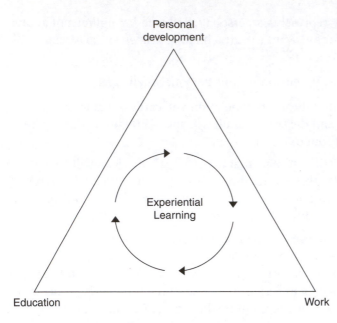

Figure 1.1 Experiential Learning as the Process that Links Education, Work, and Personal Development

work, and personal development. See Figure 1.1. It offers a system of competencies for describing job demands and corresponding educational objectives, and it emphasizes the critical linkages that can be developed between the classroom and the "real world" with experiential learning methods. It pictures the workplace as a learning environment that can enhance and supplement formal education and can foster personal development through meaningful work and career-development opportunities. And it stresses the role of formal education in lifelong learning and the development of individuals to their full potential as citizens, family members, and human beings.

In this chapter, we will examine the major traditions of experiential learning, exploring the dimensions of current practice and their intellectual origins. By understanding and articulating the themes of these traditions, we will be far more capable of shaping and guiding the development of the exciting new educational programs based on experiential learning. As Kurt Lewin, one of the founders of experiential learning, said in his most famous remark, "There is nothing so practical as a good theory."

Experiential Learning in Higher Education: The Legacy of John Dewey

In the field of higher education, there is a growing group of educators—faculty, administrators, and interested outsiders—who see experiential education as a way to revitalize the university curriculum and to cope with many of the changes facing higher education today. Although this movement is attributed to the educational philosophy of John Dewey, its source is in reality a diverse group spanning several generations. At a conference of the National Society for Internships and Experiential Education (NSIEE), a speaker remarked that there were three identifiable generations in the room: the older generation of Deweyite progressive educators, the now middle-aged children of the 1960s' Peace Corps and civil-rights movement, and Vietnam political activists of the 1970s. Yet it is the work of Dewey, without doubt the most influential educational theorist of the twentieth century, that best articulates the guiding principles for programs of experiential learning in higher education. In 1938, Dewey wrote *Experience and Education* in an attempt to bring some understanding to the growing conflict between "traditional" education and his "progressive" approach. In it, he outlined the directions for change implied in his approach:

> If one attempts to formulate the philosophy of education implicit in the practices of the new education, we may, I think, discover certain common principles. . . To imposition from above is opposed expression and cultivation of individuality; to external discipline is opposed free activity; to learning from texts and teachers, learning through experience; to acquisition of isolated skills and techniques by drill is opposed acquisition of them as means of attaining ends which make direct vital appeal; to preparation for a more or less remote future is opposed making the most of the opportunities of present life; to static aims and materials is opposed acquaintance with a changing world. . . .

> I take it that the fundamental unity of the newer philosophy is found in the idea that there is an intimate and necessary relation between the processes of actual experience and education. [Dewey, 1938, pp. 19, 20]

In the last 40 years, many of Dewey's ideas have found their way into "traditional" educational programs, but the challenges his approaches were developed to meet, those of coping with change and lifelong learning, have increased even more dramatically. It is to meeting these challenges that experiential educators in higher education have addressed themselves—not in the polarized spirit of what Arthur Chickering (1977) calls "either/orneriness," but in a spirit of cooperative innovation that integrates the best of the traditional and the experiential. The tools for this work involve many traditional methods that are as old as, or in some cases older than, the formal education system itself. These methods include apprenticeships, internships, work/study programs, cooperative education, studio arts, laboratory studies, and field projects. In all these methods, learning is experiential, in the sense that:

> . . . the learner is directly in touch with the realities being studied. . . . It involves direct encounter with the phenomenon being studied rather than merely thinking about the encounter or only considering the possibility of doing something with it. [Keeton and Tate, 1978, p. 2]

In higher education today, these "traditional" experiential learning methods are receiving renewed interest and attention, owing in large measure to the changing educational environment in this country. As universities have moved through open-enrollment programs and so on, to expand educational opportunities for the poor and minorities, there has been a corresponding need for educational methods that can translate the abstract ideas of academia into the concrete practical realities of these people's lives. Many of these new students have not been rigorously socialized into the classroom/textbook way of learning but have developed their own distinctive approach to learning, sometimes characterized as "survival skills" or "street wisdom." For these, the field placement or work/study program is an empowering experience that allows them to capitalize on their practical strengths while testing the application of ideas discussed in the classroom.

Similarly, as the population in general grows older and the frequency of adult career change continues to increase, the "action" in higher education will be centered around adult learners who demand that the relevance and application of ideas be demonstrated and tested against their own accumulated experience and wisdom. Many now approach education and midlife with a sense of fear ("I've forgotten how to study") and resentment based on unpleasant memories of their childhood schooling. As Rita Weathersby has pointed out, "adults' learning interests are embedded in their personal histories, in their visions of who they are in the world and in what they can do and want to do" (1978, p. 19). For these adults, learning methods that combine work and study, theory and practice provide a more familiar and therefore more productive arena for learning.

Finally, there is a marked trend toward vocationalism in higher education, spurred on by a group of often angry and hostile critics—students who feel cheated because the career expectations created in college have not been met, and employers who feel that the graduates they recruit into their organizations are woefully unprepared. Something has clearly gone awry in the supposed link between education and work, resulting in strong demands that higher education "shape up" and make itself relevant. There are in my view dangerous currents of anti-intellectualism in this movement, based on reactionary and counterproductive views of learning and development; but a real problem has been identified here. Experiential learning offers some avenues for solving it constructively.

For another group of educators, experiential learning is not a set of educational methods; it is a statement of fact: People *do learn* from their experiences. The emphasis of this group is on assessment of prior experience-based learning in order to grant academic credit for degree programs or certification for licensing in trades and professions. The granting of credit for prior experience is viewed by some as a movement of great promise:

> The great significance of systematic recognition of prior learning is the linkage it provides between formal education and adult life; that is, a mechanism for integrating education and work, for recognizing the validity of all learning that is relevant to a college degree and for actively fostering recurrent education. [Willingham et al., 1977, p. 60]

Yet it has also raised great concern, primarily about the maintenance of quality, since such assessment procedures might easily be abused by "degree mills" or mail-order diploma operations. To respond to both these opportunities and these concerns, in 1973 the Cooperative Assessment of Experiential Learning (CAEL) project was established in cooperation with the Educational Testing Service to create and implement practical and valid methodologies for assessing what people have learned from their prior work and life experience.[1]

As might be expected, researchers and practitioners in this area are more concerned with *what* people learn—the identifiable knowledge and skill outcomes of learning from accumulated experience—than they are with *how* learning takes place, the process of experiential learning. This emphasis on the outcomes of learning and their reliable assessment is critical to the establishment of effective links between education and work, since this linkage depends on the accurate identification and matching of personal skills with job demands. Since the Supreme Court's *Griggs v. Duke Power* decision, establishing an equitable and valid matching process has become a top priority in our nation's efforts toward equal employment opportunity. In that case, Griggs, an applicant for a janitorial job, sued to challenge a requirement that applicants have a high school diploma. In supporting Griggs, the court ruled that no test, certificate, or other procedure can be used to limit access to a job unless it is shown to be a valid predictor of performance on that job. This ruling, which has since been extended and supported by other high-court rulings, has set forth a great challenge to educators, behavioral scientists, and employers—to develop competence-based methods of instruction and assessment that are meaningfully related to the world of work.

Taken together, the renewed emphasis on "traditional" experiential learning methods and the emphasis on competence-based methods of education, assessment, and certification signal significant changes in the structure of higher education. Arthur Chickering sees it this way:

> . . . there is no question that issues raised by experiential learning go to the heart of the academic enterprise. Experiential learning leads us to question the assumptions and conventions underlying many of our practices. It turns us away from credit hours and calendar time toward competence, working knowledge, and information pertinent to jobs, family relationships, community responsibilities, and broad social concerns. It reminds us that higher education can do more than develop verbal skills and deposit information in those storage banks between the ears. It can contribute to more complex kinds of intellectual development and to more pervasive dimensions of human development required for effective citizenship. It can help students cope with shifting developmental tasks imposed by the life cycle and rapid social change.

---

1. CAEL has since changed its name to the Council for the Advancement of Experiential Learning to reflect its broader interests in experiential learning methods as well as assessment.

If these potentials are to be realized, major changes in the current structures, processes, and content of higher education will be required. The campus will no longer be the sole location for learning, the professor no longer the sole source of wisdom. Instead, campus facilities and professional expertise will be resources linked to a wide range of educational settings, to practitioners, field supervisors, and adjunct faculty. This linking together will be achieved through systematic relationships with cultural organizations, businesses, social agencies, museums, and political and governmental operations. We no longer will bind ourselves completely to the procrustean beds of fixed time units set by semester, trimester, or quarter systems, which stretch some learning to the point of transparency and lop off other learning at the head or foot. Instead, such systems will be supplemented by flexible scheduling options that tailor time to the requirements for learning and to the working realities of various experiential opportunities. Educational standards and credentials will increasingly rest on demonstrated levels of knowledge and competence as well as on actual gains made by students and the value added by college programs. We will recognize the key significance of differences among students, not only in verbal skills and academic preparation but also in learning styles, capacity for independent work, self-understanding, social awareness and human values. Batch processing of large groups will be supplemented by personalized instruction and contract learning.

The academy and the professoriat will continue to carry major responsibility for research activities, for generating new knowledge, and for supplying the perspectives necessary to cope with the major social problems rushing toward us. That work will be enriched and strengthened by more broad-based faculty and student participation and by its wide-ranging links to ongoing experiential settings. [Chickering, 1977, pp. 86–87]

Experiential Learning in Training and Organization Development: The Contributions of Kurt Lewin

Another tradition of experiential learning, larger in numbers of participants and perhaps wider in its scope of influence, stems from the research on group dynamics by the founder of American social psychology, Kurt Lewin. Lewin's work has had a profound influence on the discipline of social psychology and on its practical counterpart, the field of organizational behavior. His innovative research methods and theories, coupled with the personal charisma of his intellectual leadership, have been felt through three generations of scholars and practitioners in both fields. Although the scope of his work has been vast, ranging from leadership and management style to mathematical contributions to social-science field theory, it is his work on group dynamics and the methodology of action research that have had the most far-reaching practical significance. From these studies came the laboratory-training method and T-groups (T = training), one of the most potent educational innovations in this century. The action-research method has proved a useful approach to planned-change interventions in small groups and large complex organizations and community systems. Today this methodology forms the cornerstone of most organization development efforts. The consistent theme in all Lewin's work was his concern for the integration of theory and practice, stimulated if not created by his experience as a refugee to the United States from Nazi Germany. His classic studies on authoritarian, democratic, and *laissez faire* leadership styles were his attempt to understand in a practical way the psychological dynamics of dictatorship and democracy. His best-known quotation, "There is nothing so practical as a good theory," symbolizes his commitment to the integration of scientific inquiry and social problem solving. His approach is illustrated no better than in the actual historical event that spawned the "discovery" of the T-group (see Marrow, 1969). In the summer of 1946, Lewin and his colleagues, most notably Ronnald Lippitt, Leland Bradford, and Kenneth Benne, set out to design a new approach to leadership and group-dynamics training for the Connecticut State Interracial Commission. The two-week training program began with an experimental emphasis encouraging group discussion and decision making in an atmosphere where staff and participants treated one another as peers. In addition, the research and training staff collected extensive observations and recordings of the groups' activities. When the participants went home at night, the research staff gathered together to report and analyze the data collected during the day. Most of the staff felt that trainees should not be involved in these analytical sessions where their experiences and behavior were being discussed, for fear that the discussions might be harmful to them. Lewin was receptive, however, when a small group of participants asked to join in these discussions. One of the men who was there, Ronald Lippitt, describes what happened in the discussion meeting that three trainees attended:

> Sometime during the evening, an observer made some remarks about the behavior of one of the three persons who were sitting in—a woman trainee. She broke in to disagree with the observation and described it from her point of view. For a while there was quite an active dialogue between the research observer, the trainer, and the trainee about the interpretation of the event, with Kurt an active prober, obviously enjoying this different source of data that had to be coped with and integrated.

> At the end of the evening the trainees asked if they could come back for the next meeting at which their behavior would be evaluated. Kurt, feeling that it had been a valuable contribution rather than an intrusion, enthusiastically agreed to their return. The next night at least half of the 50 or 60 participants were there as a result of the grapevine reporting of the activity by the three delegates.

> The evening session from then on became the significant learning experience of the day, with the focus on actual behavioral events and with active dialogue

about differences of interpretation and observation of the events by those who had participated in them. [Lippitt, 1949]

Thus the discovery was made that learning is best facilitated in an environment where there is dialectic tension and conflict between immediate, concrete experience and analytic detachment. By bringing together the immediate experiences of the trainees and the conceptual models of the staff in an open atmosphere where inputs from each perspective could challenge and stimulate the other, a learning environment occurred with remarkable vitality and creativity.

Although Lewin was to die in 1947, the power of the educational process he had discovered was not lost on the other staff who were there. In the summer of 1947, they continued development of the insights they had gained in a three-week program for change agents, this time in Bethel, Maine. It was here that the basic outlines of T-group theory and the laboratory method began to take shape. It is important to note that even in these early beginnings, the struggle between the "here-and-now" experiential orientation and the "there-and-then" theoretical orientation that has continued to plague the movement was in evidence:

> There resulted a competition between discussing here-and-now happenings, which of necessity focused on the personal, interpersonal and group levels; and discussing outside case materials. This sometimes resulted in the rejection of any serious consideration of the observer's report of behavioral data. More often it led eventually to rejection of outside problems as less involving and fascinating. [Benne, 1964, p. 86]

Later, in the early years of the National Training Laboratories,[2] this conflict expressed itself in intense debates among staff as to how conceptual material should be integrated into the "basic encounter" process of the T-group. And still later, in the 1960s, on the waves of youth culture, acid rock, and Eastern mysticism, the movement was to be virtually split apart into "West Coast" existential factions and "East Coast" traditionalists (Argyris, 1970). As we shall see later in our inquiry, this conflict between experience and theory is not unique to the laboratory-training process but is, in fact, a central dynamic in the process of experiential learning itself.

In its continuing struggle, debate, and innovation around this and other issues, the laboratory-training movement has had a profound influence on the practice of adult education, training, and organization development. In particular, it was the spawning ground for two streams of development that are of central importance to experiential learning, one of values and one of technology. T-groups and the so-called laboratory method on which they were based gave central focus to the value of subjective personal experience in learning, an emphasis that at the time stood in sharp contrast to

---

2. Now known as the NTL Institute for Applied Behavioral Sciences.

the "empty-organism" behaviorist theories of learning and classical physical-science definitions of knowledge acquisition as an impersonal, totally logical process based on detached, objective observation. This emphasis on subjective experience has developed into a strong commitment in the practice of experiential learning to existential values of personal involvement, and responsibility and humanistic values emphasizing that feelings as well as thoughts are facts.

To the leaders of the movement, these values, coupled with the basic values of a humanistic scientific process—a spirit of inquiry, expanded consciousness and choice, and authenticity in relationships—offered new hope-filled ideals for the conduct of human relationships and the management of organizations (Schein and Bennis, 1965). More than any other single source, it was this set of core values that stimulated the modern participative-management philosophies (variously called Theory Y management, 9.9 management, System 4 management, Theory Z, and so on) so widely practiced in this country and increasingly around the world. In addition, these values have formed the guiding principles for the field of organization development and the practice of planned change in organizations, groups, and communities. The most recent and comprehensive statement of the relationship between laboratory-training values and experiential learning is the work of Argyris and Schon (1974, 1978). They maintain that learning from experience is essential for individual and organizational effectiveness and that this learning can occur only in situations where personal values and organizational norms support action based on valid information, free and informed choice, and internal commitment.

Equally important, there has emerged from the early work in sensitivity training a rapidly expanding applied technology for experiential learning. Beginning with small tasks (such as a decision-making problem) that were used in T-groups to focus the group's experience on a particular issue (for example, processes of group decision making), there has developed an immense variety of tasks, structured exercises, simulations, cases, games, observation tools, role plays, skill-practice routines, and so on. The common core of these technologies is a simulated situation designed to create personal experiences for learners that serve to initiate their own process of inquiry and understanding. These technologies have had a profound effect on education, particularly for adult learners. The training and development field has experienced a virtual revolution in its methodology, moving from a "dog and pony show" approach that was only a fancy imitation of the traditional lecture method to a complex educational technology that relies heavily on experience-based simulations and self-directed learning designs (Knowles, 1970). Indeed, there are many who share the view of Harold Hodskinson, a former director of the National Institute for Education and the current president of the NTL Institute, that these private-sector innovations in educational technology are challenging the ability of the formal educational establishment to compete in an open market. Along with the American Society for Training and Development (ASTD), specialized associations of academics and training and development practitioners have been formed to extend experiential approaches that were initially focused on the human-relationship issues emphasized in T-groups to other content areas, such as finance, marketing, and planning through the use of computer-aided instruction, video recording, structured role-play cases, and other software and hardware techniques. In addition, there are countless small and relatively large organizations specializing in the various educational technologies that have grown to support the $50 billion training and development industry in the United States. Although the laboratory-training movement has not been responsible for all these developments, it has had an undeniable influence on many of them.

Jean Piaget and the Cognitive-Development Tradition of Experiential Learning

The Dewey and Lewin traditions of experiential learning represent external challenges to the idealist or, as James (1907) terms them, rationalist philosophies that have dominated thinking about learning and education since the Middle Ages; Dewey from the philosophical perspective of pragmatism, and Lewin from the phenomenological perspective of Gestalt psychology. The third tradition of experiential learning represents more of a challenge from within the rationalist perspective, stemming as it does from the work of the French developmental psychologist and genetic epistemologist Jean Piaget. His work on child development must stand on a par with that of Freud; but whereas Freud placed his emphasis on the socioemotional processes of development, Piaget's focus is on cognitive-development processes—on the nature of intelligence and how it develops. Throughout his work, Piaget is as much an epistemological philosopher as he is a psychologist. In fact, he sees in his studies of the development of cognitive processes in childhood the key to understanding the nature of human knowledge itself.

It was in Piaget's first psychological studies that he came across the insight that was to make him world-famous. He began to work as a student of Alfred Binet, the creator of the first intelligence test, standardizing test items for use in IQ and aptitude tests. During this work, Piaget's interests began to diverge sharply from the traditional testing approach. He found himself much less interested in whether the answers that children gave to test problems were correct or not than he was in the process of reasoning that children used to arrive at the answers. He began to discover age-related regularities in these reasoning processes. Children at certain ages not only gave wrong answers but also showed qualitatively different ways of arriving at them. Younger children were not "dumber" than older children; they merely thought about things in an entirely different way. In the 50 years that followed this discovery, these ideas were to be developed and explored in thousands of studies by Piaget and his co-workers.

Stated most simply, Piaget's theory describes how intelligence is shaped by experience. Intelligence is not an innate internal characteristic of the individual but arises as a product of the interaction between the person and his or her environment. And for Piaget, action is the key. He has shown, in careful descriptive studies of children from infants to teenagers, that abstract reasoning and the power to manipulate symbols arise from the infant's actions in exploring and coping with the immediate concrete environment. The growing child's system of knowing changes qualitatively in successively identifiable stages, moving from an enactive stage, where knowledge is represented in concrete actions and is not separable from the experiences that spawn it, to an ikonic stage, where knowledge is represented in images that have an increasingly autonomous status from the experiences they represent, to stages of concrete and formal operations, where knowledge is represented in symbolic terms, symbols capable of being manipulated internally with complete independence from experiential reality.

In spite of its scope and the initial flurry of interest in his work in the late 1920s, Piaget's research did not receive wide recognition in this country until the 1960s. Stemming as it did from the French rationalist tradition, Piaget's work was not readily acceptable to the empirical tradition of American psychology, particularly since his clinical methods did not seem to meet the rigorous experimental standards that characterized the behaviorist research programs that dominated American psychology from 1920 to 1960. In addition, Piaget's interests were more descriptive than practical. He viewed with some disdain the pragmatic orientation of American researchers and educators who sought to speed up or facilitate the development of the cognitive stages he had identified, referring to these interests in planned change and development as the "American question."

Piaget's ultimate recognition in America was due in no small part to the parallel work of the most prominent American cognitive psychologist, Jerome Bruner. Bruner saw in the growing knowledge of cognitive developmental processes the scientific foundations for a theory of instruction. Knowledge of cognitive developmental stages would make it possible to design curricula in any field in such a way that subject matter could be taught respectably to learners at any age or stage of cognitive development. This idea became at once a guiding objective and a great challenge to educators. A new movement in curriculum development and teaching emerged around this idea, a movement focused on the design of experience-based educational programs using the principles of cognitive-development theory. Most of these curriculum-development efforts were addressed to the subject matters of science and mathematics for elementary and secondary students, although related efforts have been made in other subject areas, such as social studies, and such experience-based curricula can be found in some freshman and sophomore college-level courses. The major task addressed by these programs was the translation of the abstract symbolic principles of science and mathematics into modes of representation that could be grasped by people at more concrete stages of cognitive development. Typically, this representation takes the form of concrete objects that can be manipulated and experimented with by the learner to discover the scientific principle involved. Many of these were modifications of Piaget's original experiments—for example, allowing children to pour water back and forth from tall, thin beakers to short, fat ones to discover the principle of conservation.

When introduced in the proper climate, these experience-based curricula had the same exhilarating effect on the learning process as Lewin's discovery of the T-group. Children were freed from the lockstep pace of memorizing (or ignoring) watered-down presentations of scientific and mathematical principles that in some cases actually made learning more advanced principles more difficult; for example, to spend years learning to count only in base 10 makes learning base 2, 3, and so on, much more difficult. Learning became individualized, concrete, and self-directed. Moreover, the child was learning about the process of discovering knowledge, not just the content. Children became "little scientists," exploring, experimenting, and drawing their own conclusions. These classrooms buzzed with the excitement and energy of intrinsically motivated learning activity. These experience-based learning programs changed the educational process in two ways. First, they altered the *content* of curriculum, providing new ways of teaching subjects that were formerly thought to be too advanced and sophisticated for youngsters; and second, they altered the learning *process*, the way that students went about learning these subjects.

Even though in many quarters these innovations met an enthusiastic reception and eventual successful implementation, they also provoked strong reaction and criticism. Some of these criticisms were justified. This new way of learning required a new approach to teaching. In some cases, teachers managed the learning process well, and intrinsically motivated learning was the result. In others, the climate for learning was somehow different; students did not learn the principle of conservation by experimenting with the water jars, they just learned how to pour water back and forth. Other criticisms seem to me less valid. Some have blamed the decline on SAT scores on the new math and other self-directed curricula that made learning appear to be fun and lacking in disciplined practice of the basics. In spirit, these debates are strongly reminiscent of the controversy surrounding Dewey's progressive-education movement and the experience/theory conflicts concerning T-groups.

The cognitive-development tradition has had a less direct but equally powerful effect on adult learning. Although Piaget's stages of cognitive development terminated in adolescence, the idea that there are identifiable regularities in the development process has been extended into later adulthood by a number of researchers. In method and conceptual structure, these approaches owe a great deal to the Piagetian scheme. One of the first such approaches was Lawrence Kohlberg's extension of Piaget's early work on moral development (see Kurtines and Greif, 1974). Kohlberg began his research on schoolchildren but soon found that only the early stages of moral judgment that he had identified were actually achieved in childhood and that for many adults, the challenges of the later stages of moral judgment still lay before them. William Perry, in his outstanding book, *Forms of Intellectual and Ethical Development in the College Years* (1970), found similar patterns in the way Harvard students' systems of knowledge evolved through the college years, moving from absolutist, authority-centered, right/wrong views of knowledge in early college years, through stages of extreme relativism and, in their later college years, toward higher stages of personal commitment within relativism. Perry also found that these higher stages of development were not achieved by all students during college but, for many, posed developmental challenges that extended into their later lives. Jane Loevinger (1976) has attempted to integrate these and other cognitive developmental theories (for instance, Harvey, Hunt, and Schroder, 1961) with the socioemotional developmental theories of Erikson and others (described below) under the general rubric of ego development. Her six stages of ego development—impulsive, self-protective, conformist, conscientious, autonomous, and finally, integrated—clearly identify learning and development as a lifelong process.

The effects of these new conceptions of adult development are only now beginning to be felt. With the recognition that learning and development are lifelong processes, there comes a corresponding responsibility for social institutions and organizations to conduct their affairs in such a way that adults have experiences that facilitate their personal learning and development. One application of Kohlberg's work in moral development, for example, has been in prison reform (Hickey and Scharf, 1980), attempting in the management of prisons to build a climate that fosters development toward higher moral stages through the creation of a "just community" within the prison society. Although perhaps not as dramatic and obvious, there is a corresponding need in many public and private organizations to improve the climate for learning and development. It is not just in prisons that people feel they must adopt self-protective and conformist postures in order to survive, seeing little reward for conscientious, autonomous, and integrated behavior.

Other Contributions to Experiential Learning Theory

Dewey, Lewin, and Piaget must stand as the foremost intellectual ancestors of experiential learning theory; however, there are other, related streams of thought that will contribute substantially to this inquiry. First among these are the therapeutic psychologies, stemming chiefly from psychoanalysis and reflected most particularly in the work of Carl Jung, although also including Erik Erikson, the humanistic traditions of Carl Rogers's client-centered therapy, Fritz Perls's gestalt therapy, and the self-actualization psychology of Abraham Maslow.

This school of thought brings two important dimensions to experiential learning. First is the concept of adaptation, which gives a central role to affective experience. The notion that healthy adaptation requires the effective integration of cognitive and affective processes is of course central to the practice of nearly all forms of psychotherapy. The second contribution of the therapeutic psychologies is the conception of socioemotional development throughout the life cycle. The developmental schemes of Erik Erikson, Carl Rogers, and Abraham Maslow give a consistent and articulated picture of the challenges of adult development, a picture that fits well with the cognitive schemes just discussed. Taken together, these socioemotional and cognitive-development models provide a holistic framework for describing the adult development process and the learning challenges it poses. It is Jung's theory, however, with its concept of psychological types representing different modes of adapting to the world, and his developmental theory of individuation that will be most useful for understanding learning from experience.

A second line of contribution to experiential learning theory comes from what might be called the radical educators—in particular, the work of Brazilian educator and revolutionary Paulo Freire (1973, 1974), and of Ivan Illich (1972), whose critique of Western education and plan to "deschool" society concretely applies many of Freire's ideas to contemporary American social problems. The core of these men's arguments is that the educational system is primarily an agency of social control, a control that is ultimately oppressive and conservative of the capitalist system of class discrimination. The means for changing this system is by instilling in the population what Freire calls "critical consciousness," the active exploration of the personal, experiential meaning of abstract concepts through dialogue among equals. If views of education and learning are to be cast on a political spectrum, then this viewpoint must be seen as the revolutionary extension of the liberal, humanistic perspective characteristic of the Deweyite progressive educators and laboratory-training practitioners. As such, these views serve to highlight the central role of the dialectic between abstract concepts and subjective personal experience in educational/political conflicts between the right, which places priority on maintenance of the social order, and the left, which values more highly individual freedom and expression.

Two further perspectives will be central to an inquiry helping to unravel the relationships between learning and knowledge. The first is the very active area of brain research, which is attempting to identify relationships between brain functioning and consciousness. Most relevant for our purpose is that line of research that seeks to identify and describe differences in cognitive functioning associated with the left and right hemispheres of the brain (Levy, 1980). The relevance of this work for experiential learning theory lies in the fact that the modes of knowing associated with the left and right hemispheres correspond directly with the distinction between concrete experiential and abstract cognitive approaches to learning. Thus, in his review of this literature, Corballis concludes:

> Such evidence may be taken as support for the idea that the left hemisphere is the more specialized for abstract or symbolic representation, in which the symbols need bear no physical resemblance to the objects they represent, while the right hemisphere maintains representations that are isomorphic with reality itself. . . . [Corballis, 1980, p. 288]

The implication here is that these two modes of knowing or grasping the world stand as equal and complementary processes. This position stands in sharp contrast to that of Piaget and other cognitive theorists, who consider concrete, experience-oriented forms of knowing as lower developmental manifestations of true knowledge, represented by abstract propositional reasoning.

A full exploration of this issue requires examination of the philosophical literature, particularly the domains of metaphysics and epistemology. Here also, the scientific rational traditions have been dominant, even though challenged since the early years of this century by the pragmatism of Dewey, James, and others, and certain scientists and mathematicians like Michael Polanyi and Albert Einstein, who in their own work came upon the limitations of rational scientific inquiry. Of special relevance is the work of the philosopher and metaphysician Stephen Pepper (1966, 1942), who developed a system of world hypotheses on which he bases a typology of knowledge systems. With this framework as a guide, we shall be able to explore the relationships between the learning process and the knowledge systems that flow from it.

Figure 1.2 summarizes seven themes that offer guidance and direction for programs of experiential learning. These themes stem from the work of Dewey, Lewin, and Piaget. From Kurt Lewin and his followers comes the theory and technology of T-groups and action research. The articulation of the democratic values guiding experiential learning is to be found in both Lewin's work and the educational philosophy of John Dewey. Dewey's pragmatism forms the philosophical rationale for the primary role of personal experience in experiential learning. Common to all three traditions of experiential learning is the emphasis on development toward a life of purpose and self-direction as the organizing principle for education. Piaget's distinctive contributions to experiential learning are his description of the learning process as a dialectic between assimilating experience into concepts and accommodating concepts to experience, and his work on epistemology—the relationship between the structure of knowledge and how it is learned.

These themes suggest guiding principles for current and emerging applications of experiential learning theory. In the case of social policy and action, experiential learning can be the basis for constructive efforts to promote access to and influence on the dominant technological/symbolic culture for those who have previously been excluded: minorities, the poor, workers, women, people in developing countries, and those in the arts. In competence-based education, experiential learning offers the theory of learning most appropriate for the assessment of prior learning and for the design of competence-centered curricula. Lifelong learning and career-development programs can find in experiential learning theory a conceptual rationale and guiding philosophy as well as practical educational tools. Finally, experiential learning suggests the principles for the conduct of experiential education in its many forms and for the design of curricula implementing Bruner's manifesto: "Any subject can be respectably taught at any level."

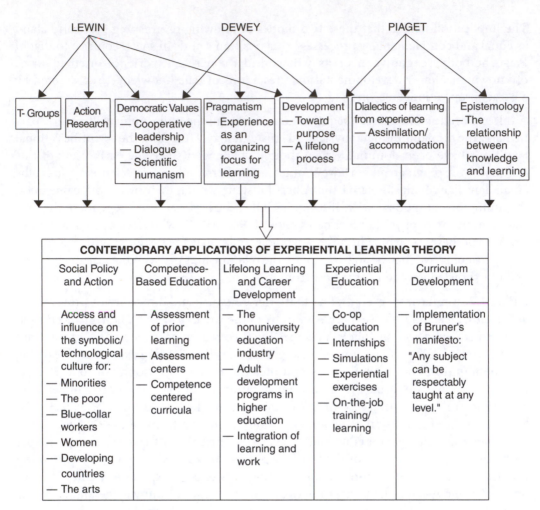

Figure 1.2 Three Traditions of Experiential Learning

In all these applications it is important to recognize that experiential learning is not a series of techniques to be applied in current practice but a program for profoundly re-creating our personal lives and social systems. William Torbert puts the issue this way:

> In seeking to organize experiential learning, we must recognize that we are stepping beyond the personally, institutionally, and epistemologically preconstituted universe and that we deeply resist this initiative, no matter how often we have returned to it. We must recognize too that the art of organizing through living inquiry—the art of continually exploring beyond pre-constituted universes and continually constructing and enacting universes in concert with others—is as yet a publicly undiscovered art. To treat the dilemma of organizing experiential

learning on any lesser scale is to doom ourselves to frustration, isolation or failure. [1979, p. 42]

The Dewey, Lewin, and Piagetian traditions of experiential learning have produced a remarkable variety of vital and innovative programs. In their brief histories, these traditions have had a profound effect on education and the learning process. The influence of these ideas has been felt in formal education at all levels, in public and private organizations in this country and around the world, and in the personal lives of countless adult learners. Yet the future holds even greater challenges and opportunities. For these challenges to be successfully met, it is essential that these traditions learn from one another and cooperate to create a sound theoretical base from which to govern practice. Although in practice these traditions can appear very different—a student internship, a business simulation, a sensitivity training group, an action research project, a discovery curriculum in elementary science study—there is an underlying unity in the nature of the learning process on which they are based. It is to an examination of that process that we now turn.

Update and Reflections
Foundational Scholars of Experiential Learning Theory

nanos gigantum humeris insidentes
If I have seen further it is by standing on the shoulders of giants.

—Isaac Newton

Chapter 1 described the conceptual foundations of experiential learning theory (ELT) with particular emphasis on the works of John Dewey, Kurt Lewin, and Jean Piaget who at the time were the particular scholars who informed my research on experiential learning and learning style. I also included other scholars—William James, Carl Rogers, Paulo Freire, Lev Vygotsky and Carl Jung—who influenced the development of other parts of the theory. I discovered Mary Parker Follett some time after the book was published and have used her work ever since. From their varied professions and cultural perspectives, these great Western scholars have had a profound impact on our thinking about learning and development, challenging and inspiring us to better ways of learning and growing as human beings. Their contributions span 100 years beginning at the end of the nineteenth century with William James, John Dewey, and Mary Parker Follett and ending at the end of the twentieth century with the deaths of Carl Rogers and Paulo Freire (refer to Figure 1.3 on page 29). In spite of the Western origins of their work, their influence today is global; East and West, North and South. Their approaches were in many respects more consistent with the East Asian Confucian and

Taoist spiritual traditions that were shaped by the 5,000-year-old Chinese text *Yijing* (易經—the Book of Changes (Trinh and Kolb, 2011). Jung in particular was influenced in his later years by Hinduism, Buddhism, and Taoism, concluding that development toward integration and individuation is central to all religions. James also studied Eastern thought and his radical empiricism became a central focus for the Japanese philosopher Kitaro Nishida (1911).

Liminal Scholars

I was first attracted to the *ideas* of these scholars, delighted in discovering one piece after another of the puzzle of learning from experience. Their work opened my eyes to things that had never occurred to me. Later, as I explored how they lived and did their work, I found much to be inspired by and emulate. A remarkable similarity among these nine scholars, aside from their shared view of the importance of experience in learning, is that they all are what I call liminal scholars, standing at the boundaries of the mainstream establishment of their fields and working from theoretical and methodical perspectives that ran counter to the prevailing scientific norms of their time. As a result, it is only in recent years that their ideas have reemerged to influence learning, education, and development.

Mary Parker Follett, 1868–1933, for example, was awarded a Lifetime Achievement Award by the International Leadership Association in 2011—78 years after her death. She graduated 'summa cum laude' from Radcliff College but was not allowed to pursue a Ph.D. because she was a woman. She was a broad thinker who spanned disciplines and schools of thought, challenging her academic colleagues to think outside their disciplinary boxes. True to her theory of relations, she refused to identify with any particular school of thought but stood in "the space between" drawing insights from both perspectives. For example, while many see her as a Gestalt theorist along with Lewin, she drew from both Gestalt theory and the opposing school of behaviorism in creating her approach. While she was a popular lecturer and writer in her day, Peter Drucker observed that "she gradually became 'non-person'" after her death in 1933. Her radical circular theory of power that emphasized cooperation and humanistic ideas about management and organizations was foreign to the culture of management in the 1930s and 40s. Today she has gained new recognition as a foundational figure. According to Warren Bennis, "Just about everything written today about leadership and organizations comes from Mary Parker Follett's writings and lectures" (Smith, 2002).

William James also found himself outside of the mainstream of behaviorist psychology with examination of conscious experience in his two-volume magnum opus *The Principles of Psychology*. He devotes the last two thirds of the work to what he called the "study of the mind from within" (James, 1890, p. 225). Today, "his ideas about consciousness have been resurrected by modern neuroscientists such as Karl Pribram and Roger Sperry who drew on James' work for their own formulations. The geneticist Francis Crick, reviewing the philosophical implications of biological advances in our understanding of consciousness, has invoked James as a guiding philosopher who had said it all a hundred years ago" (Taylor and Wozniak, 1996, p. xxxii). His examination of the role of attention in conscious experience and his ideo-motor theory of action, addressing how consciousness of one's learning process can be used to intentionally improve learning, were foundational for the later work on metacognition and deliberate experiential learning described in the Chapter 8 Update and Reflections. He is also recognized as the founder of the contemporary concept of dual processing theories (Evans, 2008) derived from his dual knowledge concepts of apprehension and comprehension.

Lev Vygotsky, whose prodigious brilliantly creative career was ended prematurely by his death from tuberculosis at age 38, was called the Mozart of psychology by Stephen Toulmin. This is in spite of the fact that he never had any formal training in psychology, being interested in literature, poetry, and philosophy when he was young. The Soviet authorities of his time kept him under pressure to toe the ideological Marxist line in his theories, and after his death the government repudiated his ideas. Today, however, his work is hugely influential in education around the world (Tharpe and Gallimore, 1988), and his ideas about the role of culture in the development of thought are widely cited as foundational for liberation ideologies, social constructionism, and activity theory (Bruner, 1986; Holman, Pavlica, and Thorpe, 1997).

These scholars not only studied experiential learning; they lived it. They approached their scientific inquiry as learning from experience, examining their own personal experience, using careful observation, building sophisticated and creative theoretical systems, bringing a passionate advocacy for their ideas for the betterment of humanity. I suspect they would all subscribe to Carl Rogers' description of his approach to research, "I have come to see both research and theory as being aimed toward the inward ordering of significant experience. Thus research is not something esoteric, nor an activity in which one engages to gain professional kudos. It is the persistent, disciplined effort to make sense and order out of the phenomena of subjective experience. Such effort is justified because it is satisfying to perceive the world as having order and because rewarding results often ensue when one understands the orderly relationships which appear to exist in nature. One of these rewarding results is that the ordering of one segment of experience in a theory immediately opens up new vistas of inquiry, research, and thought, thus leading one continually forward. (I have, at times, carried on research for purposes other than the above to satisfy others, to convince opponents and sceptics, to gain prestige, and for other unsavory reasons. These errors in judgment and activity have only deepened the above positive conviction.)" (1959, p. 188).

Most, like Rogers, also chaffed at the confines of conventional disciplinary inquiry methods, "In the invitation to participate in the APA study, I have been asked to cast our theoretical thinking in the terminology of the independent-intervening-dependent variable, in so far as this is feasible. I regret that I find this terminology somehow uncongenial.

I cannot justify my negative reaction very adequately, and perhaps it is an irrational one, for the logic behind these terms seems unassailable. But to me the terms seem static, they seem to deny the restless, dynamic, searching, changing aspects of scientific movement . . . The terms also seem to me to smack too much of the laboratory, where one undertakes an experiment de novo, with everything under control, rather than of a science which is endeavoring to wrest from the phenomena of experience the inherent order which they contain" (1959, p. 189).

Jean Piaget, for example, ignored sample sizes, statistical tests, and experimental and control groups in the creation of his theories. He focused instead on observations of his children, presenting them with cleverly designed puzzles and problems to understand the process of how they solved them. Unlike Binet, his mentor, and other intelligence researchers, he was less interested in correct answers than how children arrived at these answers. Not surprisingly, his successive case study technique was not well received in American psychology when it was introduced in 1926. However, by the 1950s with the rise of cognitive psychology and, particularly, Jerome Bruner's generous advocacy for his approach, his ideas and methods gained widespread acceptance and influence in education.

Another inspiration for me was the passionate advocacy of many to the scholars for the betterment of the world through learning. The leadership provided by John Dewey and Mary Parker Follett to the Progressive Movement of the 1920s focused the profound insights of their thinking on democracy, social justice, education, and advocacy for the needy.

Paulo Freire was first a social activist where he developed his theories based on this work. His work on literacy campaigns in Brazil, later extended to other countries in South America and Africa, used what he called culture circles based on his theory of conscientiziation, the ability to problematize and take transformative action on the social, political, economic, and cultural realities that shape us. Culture circles in their process were much like Lewin's T-groups where group participants were active participants in creating the topics to be explored through dialogue with the help of a coordinator. They differed from the T-group, however, in that their focus was on actively shaping the reality of the participants' lives, exploring topics such as the vote for illiterates, nationalism, political revolution in Brazilian democracy, and freedom. "The first experiments with the method began in 1962 involving 300 rural farmers who were taught how to read and write in 45 days. In 1964, 20,000 culture circles were planned to be set up. However, the military coup in that year interrupted Freire's work. He was jailed for 70 days and later went into exile in Chile" (Nyirenda, 1996, p. 4).

Kurt Lewin's commitment to solving social problems and conflicts was born out of his marginalization growing up as a Jew in the strongly anti-Semitic culture of East Prussia. It continued throughout his life culminating in his creation of the Center for Group Dynamics at MIT and his leadership in the Commission on Community Interrelations (CCI), which conducted many action research projects, including The Connecticut State

Interracial Commission to combat racial and religious prejudice that led to the creation of the T-Group (see Chapter 1, pp. 8–12). His development of the action research methodology in these projects has had a great continuing influence.

Often described as the founder of social psychology, Lewin's influence in the field is so pervasive that it is hard to define. Warren Bennis said simply, ". . . we are all Lewinians." John Thibaut, one of Lewin's research assistants at MIT, said, ". . . it is not so difficult to understand why he was influential. He had an uncanny intuition about what problems were important and what kinds of concepts and research situations were necessary to study them. And though he was obsessed with theory, he was not satisfied with the attainment of theoretical closures but demanded of the theory that its implications for human life be pursued with equal patience and zeal" (cited in Marrow, 1969, p. 189). Yet, paradoxically, he too was a liminal scholar, working for the most part outside the psychological establishment. "No prestigious university offered him an appointment. (His significant work was done in odd settings, such as the Cornell School of Home Economics and the Iowa Child Welfare Research Station.) The American Psychological Association never selected him for any assignment or appointed him to any important committee. . . ." (Marrow, 1969, p. 227).

My deep admiration for Lewin stems from the many students and colleagues he nurtured and developed to become outstanding scholars in their own right. His influence in the field came not so much from his published works, which can be hard to find, but from those who worked with him. He consistently put their names forward in publications. Jerome Frank, a graduate student of Lewin's, describes how he accomplished this, "Each new idea or problem seemed to arouse him, and he was able to share his feelings with colleagues and juniors. . . . Seminars were held in his home, and it was hard to distinguish the influence of his ideas from the influence of his personality. Because Lewin could be critical without hurting, he stimulated creativity in all those around him. . . . He seemed to enjoy all kinds of human beings and, open and free as he was, shared his ideas immediately—even if they were half-formed—eager for comments and reactions while the original idea was still being developed" (cited in Marrow, 1969, p. 54).

Contributions to Experiential Learning

The following summary of the key contributions of the foundational scholars to experiential learning can only highlight the influence of their work in experiential learning theory. Their respective approaches will be elaborated on in subsequent chapters.

William James (1841–1910)

In the introduction, I have already described how James, among the foundational scholars, is the originator of experiential learning theory in his philosophy of radical empiricism and the dual knowledge theory, knowing by apprehension (CE) and comprehension

(AC) (see Chapter 3, pp. 69–77). James proposed radical empiricism as a new philosophy of reality and mind that resolved the conflicts between nineteenth century rationalism and empiricism and integrated both sensation and thought in experience. His concept of pure experience helps elucidate the dual knowledge idea of concrete experience as present-oriented experiencing free from conceptual interpretation.

James, description of the primacy of the direct perception of Concrete Experience and how it is altered by transformation through the other learning modes is the first description of the experiential learning cycle I have found: "The instant field of the present is at all times what I call 'pure experience.' It is only virtually or potentially either object or subject as yet. For the time being it is plain, unqualified actuality, or existence, a simple *that* (CE). In this naïf immediacy it is of course valid; it is *there*, we *act* upon it (AE); and the doubling of it in retrospection into a state of mind and a reality intended thereby (RO), is just one of the acts. The 'state of mind' first treated explicitly as such in retrospection will stand corrected or confirmed (AC), and the retrospective experience in its turn will get a similar treatment; but the immediate experience in its passing is always 'truth,' practical truth, something *to act on*, at its own moment. If the world were then and there to go out like a candle, it would remain truth absolute and objective, for it would be the 'last word,' would have no critic, and no one would ever oppose the thought in it to the reality intended" (1912, pp. 23–24).

John Dewey (1859–1952)

Dewey (1905) supported James in his theory of radical empiricism and pure experience against his other contemporary critics. Their ideas were foundational for the later development of the philosophy of pragmatism with C. S. Peirce.

In *Art as Experience* he also embraced a version of James, dual knowledge theory where self and environment are mutually transformed through a dialectic between rational controlled doing and what he called receptive undergoing, "Perception of relationship between what is done and what is undergone constitutes the work of intelligence . . . (1934, p. 45). Until the artist is satisfied in perception with what he is doing, he continues shaping and re-shaping. The making comes to an end when its result is experienced as good—and the experience comes not by mere intellectual and outside judgment but in direct perception" (1934, p. 49).

Dewey's contribution to experiential education began in the progressive education movement he founded by establishing the laboratory schools at the University of Chicago in 1896. The following excerpts from his article "My Pedagogic Creed" (1897) describe key propositions of experiential learning:

1. ". . . education must be conceived as a continuing reconstruction of experience: . . . the process and goal of education are one and the same thing." (13)

2. "I believe that education is a process of living and not a preparation for future living." (7)

3. "I believe that education which does not occur through forms of life that are worth living for their own sake is always a poor substitute for genuine reality and tends to cramp and to deaden." (7)

4. "I believe that interests are the signs and symptoms of growing power. I believe they represent dawning capacities. I believe that only through the continual and sympathetic observation of childhood's interests can the adult enter into the child's life and see what it is ready for." (15)

Mary Parker Follett (1868–1933)

For Follett the keys to creativity, will, and power lie in deep experiencing. Like Dewey's "undergoing," surrendering the totality of one's self to each new experience, Follett describes, "All that I am, all that life has made me, every past experience that I have had—woven into the tissue of my life—I must give to the new experience. . . . We integrate our experience, and then the richer human being that we are goes into the new experience; again we give our self and always by giving rise above the old self" (1924, pp. 136–137).

True to her Gestalt influence, she saw everything in relation. Anticipating Norbert Weiner's discovery of cybernetics by many years, she described how we co-create one another in relationship by circular response. Through circular response transactions we create each other. In this co-creation, she describes how we can meet together in experience to evoke learning and development in one another: ". . . the essence of experience, the law of relation, is reciprocal freeing: here is the 'rock and the substance of the human spirit.' This is the truth of stimulus and response: evocation. We are all rooted in that great unknown in which are the infinite latents of humanity. And these latents are evoked, called forth into visibility, summoned, by the action and reaction of one on the other. All human interaction should be the evocation by each from the other of new forms undreamed of before, and all intercourse that is not evocation should be eschewed. Release, evocation—evocation by release, release by evocation—this is the fundamental law of the universe. . . . To free the energies of the human spirit is the high potentiality of all human association." Mary Parker Follett along with Carl Rogers, Lev Vygotsky, and Paulo Freire all gave a central place to the relationship between educator and learner in their theories (see Chapter 7 Update and Reflections).

Kurt Lewin (1890–1947)

I have described Lewin's major practical contributions to experiential learning, the T-Group laboratory method, and action research in EL Chapter 1. Lewin's concept of the life space that describes subjective experience as a holistic field of forces is the most systematic framework for describing experience even to this day. Based on his field theory using mathematical concepts of topography, he describes the life space as the totality of the situation as the person experiences it at a moment in time. The life space is a field of interdependent forces including needs, goals, memories, as well as events in the environment, barriers, and pathways. Lewin believed that behavior was shaped by contemporary causation. Only those forces present in the here-and-now influenced behavior. The life space conception was inspirational for the experiential learning theory concept of learning spaces described in the Chapter 7 Update and Reflections.

Jean Piaget (1896–1980)

Piaget's constructivism describes the child's development from less to more complex discrete stages of thinking driven by the dialectic tension between previous information acquired through the process of assimilation and the accommodation of existing cognitive structures to new information. While his account portrays a linear developmental continuum with stages roughly equivalent to the child's age (as described in Chapter 2, pp. 54–55), I modified his scheme in its incorporation into experiential learning theory to depict it within the learning cycle (see Figure 2.3) to indicate that development beyond adolescence involves the integration of abstract cognitive frameworks with experience (see Chapter 6, pp. 201–205 and Update and Reflections).

The educational implications of constructivism, that learning is best facilitated by a process that draws out the students' beliefs and ideas about a topic so that they can be examined, tested, and integrated with new, more refined ideas, has had a profound impact on education at all levels all over the world (see Chapter 3 Update and Reflections). In addition, his stage theory has formed the foundation of nearly all theories of adult development (see Chapter 6 Update and Reflections).

Lev Vygotsky (1896–1934)

While much attention has been given to the origins of experiential learning in the constructivism of Piaget, less attention has been given to its basis in the social constructivism of Vygotsky (Kayes, 2002). Piaget focused on the process of internal cognitive development in the individual, while the focus for Vygotsky was on the historical, cultural and social context of individuals in a relationship, emphasizing the "tools of culture" and mentoring by more knowledgeable community members. He is best known for his concept of the Zone of Proximal Development (ZPD)—a learning space that promotes the transition from a pedagogical stage, where something can be demonstrated with the assistance of a more knowledgeable other, to an expert stage of independent performance. The ZPD is based on his law of internalization where the child's novel capacities begin in the interpersonal realm and are gradually transferred into the intrapersonal realm (Vygotsky, 1978). What is internalized is "mediational means" or tools of culture, the most important of which is language.

The key technique for accomplishing this transition is called "scaffolding." In scaffolding the educator tailors the learning process to the individual needs and developmental level of the learner. Scaffolding provides the structure and support necessary to progressively build knowledge. The model of teaching around the cycle described above provides a framework for this scaffolding process. When an educator has a personal relationship with a learner, he or she can skillfully intervene to reinforce or alter a learner's pattern of interaction with the world (see Chapter 7 Update and Reflections).

Carl Jung (1875–1961)

Carl Jung was arguably the most radical scientific experiential learner; deriving most of his theory from deep engagement with his intense personal experiences, dreams, and unconscious symbols. This is particularly true of his concept of individuation and the course of development from specialization to integration, which he developed as a result of what has been called his own mid-life crisis (Staude, 1981). In 1913 Jung experienced a frightening confrontation with his unconscious—seeing visions and hearing voices. In 1914 he began a courageous self-experimentation using a technique he called active imagination to explore and dialogue with himself about the dreams, symbols, and associations that came to him. He recorded these over the course of 16 years in a series of notebooks that later became the Red Book or *Liber Novus* (Jung, 2009) as he called it. *Liber Novus* outlines his general theory of individuation based on his descriptions of his own process of individuation that ultimately integrated the two personalities that he was aware of since he was a child. Personality 1 was the school boy living in the conventional eighteenth-century world, which Jung called "the spirit of this time." Personality 2 pursued religious reflections and solitude in tune with nature and the cosmos, which he called "the spirit of the depths." Using the technique of active imagination, he established dialogues with fantasy figures from the collective unconscious, bringing them into consciousness to integrate with the spirit of the modern age. "If I speak in the spirit of this time I must say: no one and nothing can justify what I must proclaim to you. Justification is superfluous to me, since I have no choice, but I must. I have learned that in addition to the spirit of this time there is still another spirit at work, namely that which rules the depths of everything contemporary. The spirit of this time would like to hear of use and value. But the other spirit forces me nevertheless to speak, beyond justification, use and meaning. Filled with human pride and blinded by the presumptuous spirit of the times, I long sought to hold the other spirit away from me. But I did not consider that the spirit of the depths from time immemorial and for all the future possesses a greater power than the spirit of this time, who changes with the generations. The spirit of the depth has subjugated all pride and arrogance to the power of judgment. He took away my belief in science, he robbed me of the joy of explaining and ordering things, and let devotion to the ideals of this time die out in me. He forced me down to the last and simplest things" (Jung, 2009, pp. 119–120).

Jung's concept of individuation, the process of integrating opposites including the conscious with the unconscious, the dialectic psychological types of introversion and extraversion, thinking and feeling, etc., in order for a person to become whole, forms the basis of the experiential learning theory of development described in Chapters 6 and 8.

Carl Rogers (1902–1987)

Rogers' work has had three major influences on experiential learning theory. The first influence is his focus on experiencing as central to the fully functioning person and its importance for learning and change. This experiencing process is fluid and flexible based on the particular moment. It is highly differentiated with the locus of evaluation within the person. There is "a letting oneself down into the immediacy of what one is experiencing, endeavoring to sense and to clarify all its complex meanings . . . For there is involved in the present moment of experiencing the memory traces of all the relevant learnings from the past" (Rogers, 1964, p. 164).

The second influence is his identification of unconditional positive regard, respect, and psychological safety as essential conditions for a therapeutic or educational environment to promote learning and development. Under these conditions individuals develop a sense of self-worth: "One way of assisting the individual to move toward openness to experience is through a relationship in which he is prized as a separate person, in which the experiencing going on within him is empathically understood and valued and in which he is given the freedom to experience his own feelings and those of others without being threatened in doing so" (Rogers, 1964, p. 165).

The third influence is his theory of development toward self-actualization based on the individual's capacity for deep experiencing. In youth, individuals tend to introject the values of loved ones in order to gain their respect and approval. "He learns to have a basic distrust for his own experiencing as a guide to his behavior. He learns from others a large number of conceived values and adopts them as his own, even though they may be widely discrepant from what he is experiencing" (Rogers, 1964, p. 162). Development toward genuine experiencing occurs when, in the growth producing climate described above, "he can slowly begin to value the different aspects of himself. Most importantly, he can begin, with much difficulty at first, to sense and feel what is going on within him, what he is feeling, what he is experiencing, how he is reacting. He uses his experiencing as a direct referent to which he can turn in forming accurate conceptualizations and as a guide to his behavior" (Rogers, 1964, p. 163; see Chapter 6 Update and Reflections).

Paulo Freire (1921–1997)

Paulo Freire's great contribution to experiential learning theory is his theory of naming experience in a dialogue among equals; working with one another in a respectful and democratic way a to achieve a deeper understanding of their lived experiences in order to achieve praxis, making a difference in their world. He contrasted this educational approach to the "banking concept of education" where ideas are deposited in learners' heads.

Freire's work was inspirational for us in the creation of our theory of conversational learning in *Conversational Learning: An Experiential Approach to Knowledge Creation* (Baker, Jensen, and Kolb, 2002). We had a chance to work with him in 1994 in one of his last U.S. appearances before his death. He was the keynote speaker and workshop leader in *The International Experiential Learning Conference: A Global Conversation about Learning* jointly sponsored by The Council for Adult and Experiential Learning, The International Consortium for Experiential Learning, and The National Society for Experiential Education. Our CWRU Organizational Behavior Department designed a plan to conduct the Conference in terms of the principles of conversational learning and Freire's dialogue culture groups. The 1,500 participants were divided into diverse 10–12 person Exploration and Reflection groups that met regularly with a facilitator throughout the conference presentations and workshops. The aim was to counter-balance the "banking" format typical of most conventions and conferences with good conversation. In Freire's sessions, he modeled dialogue and conversation with other conference participants.

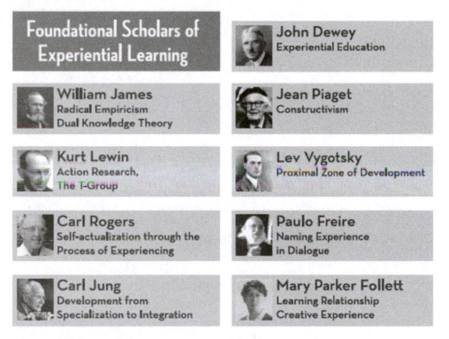

Figure 1.3   Foundational Scholars of Experiential Learning

The Process of Experiential Learning

We shall not cease from exploration
And the end of all our exploring
Will be to arrive where we started
And know the place for the first time.

—T.S. Eliot, Four Quartets*

Experiential learning theory offers a fundamentally different view of the learning process from that of the behavioral theories of learning based on an empirical epistemology or the more implicit theories of learning that underlie traditional educational methods, methods that for the most part are based on a rational, idealist epistemology. From this different perspective emerge some very different prescriptions for the conduct of education; the proper relationships among learning, work, and other life activities; and the creation of knowledge itself.

This perspective on learning is called "experiential" for two reasons. The first is to tie it clearly to its intellectual origins in the work of Dewey, Lewin, and Piaget. The second reason is to emphasize the central role that experience plays in the learning process. This differentiates experiential learning theory from rationalist and other cognitive theories of learning that tend to give primary emphasis to acquisition, manipulation, and recall of abstract symbols, and from behavioral learning theories that deny any role for consciousness and subjective experience in the learning process. It should be emphasized, however, that the aim of this work is not to pose experiential learning theory as a third alternative to behavioral and cognitive learning theories, but rather to suggest through experiential learning theory a holistic integrative perspective on learning that combines experience, perception, cognition, and behavior. This chapter will describe the

---

* From *Little Gidding* in FOUR QUARTETS, © 1943 by T.S. Eliot; renewed 1971 by Esme Valerie Eliot. Reprinted by permission of Harcourt Brace Jovanovich, Inc.

learning models of Lewin, Dewey, and Piaget and identify the common characteristics they share—characteristics that serve to define the nature of experiential learning.

Three Models of the Experiential Learning Process

The Lewinian Model of Action Research and Laboratory Training

In the techniques of action research and the laboratory method, learning, change, and growth are seen to be facilitated best by an integrated process that begins with here-and-now experience followed by collection of data and observations about that experience. The data are then analyzed and the conclusions of this analysis are fed back to the actors in the experience for their use in the modification of their behavior and choice of new experiences. Learning is thus conceived as a four-stage cycle, as shown in Figure 2.1. Immediate concrete experience is the basis for observation and reflection. These observations are assimilated into a "theory" from which new implications for action can be deduced. These implications or hypotheses then serve as guides in acting to create new experiences.

Two aspects of this learning model are particularly noteworthy. First is its emphasis on *here-and-now concrete experience* to validate and test abstract concepts. Immediate personal experience is the focal point for learning, giving life, texture, and subjective personal meaning to abstract concepts and at the same time providing a concrete, publicly shared reference point for testing the implications and validity of ideas created during the learning process. When human beings share an experience, they can share it fully, concretely, *and* abstractly.

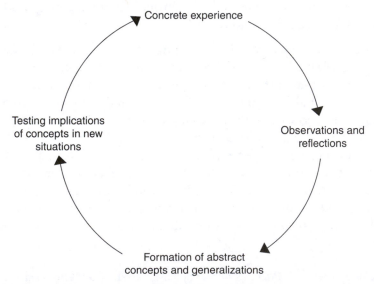

Figure 2.1   The Lewinian Experiential Learning Model

Second, action research and laboratory training are based on *feedback processes*. Lewin borrowed the concept of feedback from electrical engineering to describe a social learning and problem-solving process that generates valid information to assess deviations from desired goals. This information feedback provides the basis for a continuous process of goal-directed action and evaluation of the consequences of that action. Lewin and his followers believed that much individual and organizational ineffectiveness could be traced ultimately to a lack of adequate feedback processes. This ineffectiveness results from an imbalance between observation and action—either from a tendency for individuals and organizations to emphasize decision and action at the expense of information gathering, or from a tendency to become bogged down by data collection and analysis. The aim of the laboratory method and action research is to integrate these two perspectives into an effective, goal-directed learning process.

Dewey's Model of Learning

John Dewey's model of the learning process is remarkably similar to the Lewinian model, although he makes more explicit the developmental nature of learning implied in Lewin's conception of it as a feedback process by describing how learning transforms the impulses, feelings, and desires of concrete experience into higher-order purposeful action.

> The formation of purposes is, then, a rather complex intellectual operation. It involves: (1) observation of surrounding conditions; (2) knowledge of what has happened in similar situations in the past, a knowledge obtained partly by recollection and partly from the information, advice, and warning of those who have had a wider experience; and (3) judgment, which puts together what is observed and what is recalled to see what they signify. A purpose differs from an original impulse and desire through its translation into a plan and method of action based upon foresight of the consequences of action under given observed conditions in a certain way. . . . The crucial educational problem is that of procuring the postponement of immediate action upon desire until observation and judgment have intervened. . . . Mere foresight, even if it takes the form of accurate prediction, is not, of course, enough. The intellectual anticipation, the idea of consequences, must blend with desire and impulse to acquire moving force. It then gives direction to what otherwise is blind, while desire gives ideas impetus and momentum. [Dewey, 1938, p. 69]

Dewey's model of experiential learning is graphically portrayed in Figure 2.2. We note in his description of learning a similarity with Lewin, in the emphasis on learning as a dialectic process integrating experience and concepts, observations, and action. The impulse of experience gives ideas their moving force, and ideas give direction to impulse. Postponement of immediate action is essential for observation and judgment to intervene, and action is essential for achievement of purpose. It is through the integration of these opposing but symbiotically related processes that sophisticated, mature purpose develops from blind impulse.

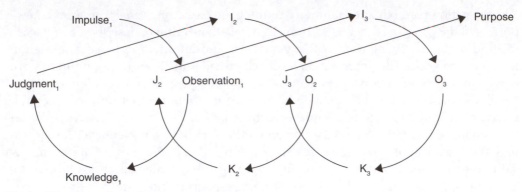

Figure 2.2 Dewey's Model of Experiential Learning

Piaget's Model of Learning and Cognitive Development

For Jean Piaget, the dimensions of experience and concept, reflection, and action form the basic continua for the development of adult thought. Development from infancy to adulthood moves from a concrete phenomenal view of the world to an abstract constructionist view, from an active egocentric view to a reflective internalized mode of knowing. Piaget also maintained that these have been the major directions of development in scientific knowledge (Piaget, 1970). The learning process whereby this development takes place is a cycle of interaction between the individual and the environment that is similar to the learning models of Dewey and Lewin. In Piaget's terms, the key to learning lies in the mutual interaction of the process of *accommodation* of concepts or schemas to experience in the world and the process of *assimilation* of events and experiences from the world into existing concepts and schemas. Learning or, in Piaget's term, intelligent adaptation results from a balanced tension between these two processes. When accommodation processes dominate assimilation, we have imitation—the molding of oneself to environmental contours or constraints. When assimilation predominates over accommodation, we have play—the imposition of one's concept and images without regard to environmental realities. The process of cognitive growth from concrete to abstract and from active to reflective is based on this continual transaction between assimilation and accommodation, occurring in successive stages, each of which incorporates what has gone before into a new, higher level of cognitive functioning.

Piaget's work has identified four major stages of cognitive growth that emerge from birth to about the age of 14–16. In the first stage (0–2 years), the child is predominantly concrete and active in his learning style. This stage is called the sensory-motor stage. Learning is predominantly enactive through feeling, touching, and handling. Representation is based on action—for example, "a hole is to dig." Perhaps the greatest accomplishment of this period is the development of goal-oriented behavior: "The sensory-motor period shows a remarkable evolution from nonintentional habits to experimental and exploratory activity which is obviously intentional or goal oriented" (Flavell, 1963, p. 107). Yet the child has few schemes or theories into which he can assimilate events, and as a result, his primary stance toward the world is accommodative. Environment plays a major role in shaping his ideas and intentions. Learning occurs primarily through the association between stimulus and response.

In the second stage of cognitive growth (2–6 years), the child retains his concrete orientation but begins to develop a reflective orientation as he begins to internalize actions, converting them to images. This is called the representational stage. Learning is now predominantly iconic in nature, through the manipulation of observations and images. The child is now freed somewhat from his immersion in immediate experience and, as a result, is free to play with and manipulate his images of the world. At this stage, the child's primary stance toward the world is divergent. He is captivated with his ability to collect images and to view the world from different perspectives. Consider Bruner's description of the child at this stage:

> What appears next in development is a great achievement. Images develop an autonomous status, they become great summarizers of action. By age three the child has become a paragon of sensory distractibility. He is victim of the laws of vividness, and his action pattern is a series of encounters with this bright thing which is then replaced by that chromatically splendid one, which in turn gives way to the next noisy one. And so it goes. Visual memory at this stage seems to be highly concrete and specific. What is intriguing about this period is that the child is a creature of the moment; the image of the moment is sufficient and it is controlled by a single feature of the situation. [Bruner, 1966b, p. 13]

In the third stage of cognitive growth (7–11 years), the intensive development of abstract symbolic powers begins. The first symbolic developmental stage Piaget calls the stage of concrete operations. Learning in this stage is governed by the logic of classes and relations. The child in this stage further increases his independence from his immediate experiential world through the development of inductive powers:

> The structures of concrete operations are, to use a homely analogy, rather like parking lots whose individual parking spaces are now occupied and now empty; the spaces themselves endure, however, and leave their owner to look beyond the cars actually present toward potential, future occupants of the vacant and to-be-vacant spaces. [Flavell, 1963, p. 203]

Thus, in contrast to the child in the sensory-motor stage whose learning style was dominated by accommodative processes, the child at the stage of concrete operations is more assimilative in his learning style. He relies on concepts and theories to select and give shape to his experiences.

Piaget's final stage of cognitive development comes with the onset of adolescence (12–15 years). In this stage, the adolescent moves from symbolic processes based on concrete operations to the symbolic processes of representational logic, the stage of formal operations. He now returns to a more active orientation, but it is an active orientation that is now modified by the development of the reflective and abstract power that preceded it. The symbolic powers he now possesses enable him to engage in hypothetico-deductive reasoning. He develops the possible implications of his theories and proceeds to experimentally test which of these are true. Thus his basic learning style is convergent, in contrast to the divergent orientation of the child in the representational stage:

> We see, then, that formal thought is for Piaget not so much this or that specific behavior as it is a generalized orientation, sometimes explicit and sometimes implicit, towards problem solving; an orientation towards organizing data (combinatorial analysis), towards isolation and control of variables, towards the hypothetical, and towards logical justification and proof. [Flavell, 1963, p. 211]

This brief outline of Piaget's cognitive development theory identifies those basic developmental processes that shape the basic learning process of adults (see Figure 2.3).

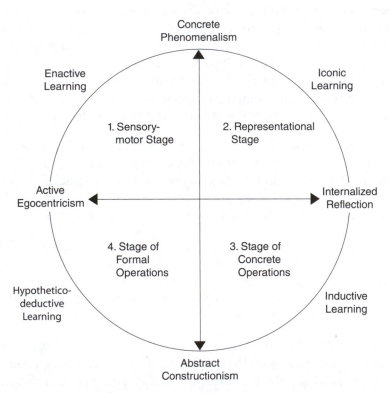

Figure 2.3   Piaget's Model of Learning and Cognitive Development

Characteristics of Experiential Learning

There is a great deal of similarity among the models of the learning process discussed above.[1] Taken together, they form a unique perspective on learning and development, a perspective that can be characterized by the following propositions, which are shared by the three major traditions of experiential learning.

Learning Is Best Conceived as a Process, Not in Terms of Outcomes

The emphasis on the process of learning as opposed to the behavioral outcomes distinguishes experiential learning from the idealist approaches of traditional education and from the behavioral theories of learning created by Watson, Hull, Skinner, and others. The theory of experiential learning rests on a different philosophical and epistemological base from behaviorist theories of learning and idealist educational approaches. Modern versions of these latter approaches are based on the empiricist philosophies of Locke and others. This epistemology is based on the idea that there are elements of consciousness—mental atoms, or, in Locke's term, "simple ideas"—that always remain the same. The various combinations and associations of these consistent elements form our varying patterns of thought. It is the notion of constant, fixed elements of thought that has had such a profound effect on prevailing approaches to learning and education, resulting in a tendency to define learning in terms of its outcomes, whether these be knowledge in an accumulated storehouse of facts or habits representing behavioral responses to specific stimulus conditions. If ideas are seen to be fixed and immutable, then it seems possible to measure how much someone has learned by the amount of these fixed ideas the person has accumulated.

Experiential learning theory, however, proceeds from a different set of assumptions. Ideas are not fixed and immutable elements of thought but are formed and re-formed through experience. In all three of the learning models just reviewed, learning is described as a process whereby concepts are derived from and continuously modified by experience. No two thoughts are ever the same, since experience always intervenes. Piaget (1970), for example, considers the creation of new knowledge to be the central problem of genetic epistemology, since each act of understanding is the result of a process of continuous construction and invention through the interaction processes of assimilation and accommodation (see Chapter 5, p. 153). Learning is an emergent process whose outcomes represent only historical record, not knowledge of the future.

When viewed from the perspective of experiential learning, the tendency to define learning in terms of outcomes can become a definition of nonlearning, in the process sense that the failure to modify ideas and habits as a result of experience is maladaptive. The clearest example of this irony lies in the behaviorist axiom that the strength of a habit

---

1. There are also points of disagreement, which will be explored more fully in the next chapter.

can be measured by its resistance to extinction. That is, the more I have "learned" a given habit, the longer I will persist in behaving that way when it is no longer rewarded. Similarly, there are those who feel that the orientations that conceive of learning in terms of outcomes as opposed to a process of adaptation have had a negative effect on the educational system. Jerome Bruner, in his influential book, *Toward a Theory of Instruction*, makes the point that the purpose of education is to stimulate inquiry and skill in the process of knowledge getting, not to memorize a body of knowledge: "Knowing is a process, not a product" (1966, p. 72). Paulo Freire calls the orientation that conceives of education as the transmission of fixed content the "banking" concept of education:

> Education thus becomes an act of depositing, in which the students are the depositories and the teacher is the depositor. Instead of communicating, the teacher issues communiques and makes deposits which the students patiently receive, memorize, and repeat. This is the "banking" concept of education, in which the scope of action allowed to the students extends only as far as receiving, filing, and storing the deposits. They do, it is true, have the opportunity to become collectors or cataloguers of the things they store. But in the last analysis, it is men themselves who are filed away through the lack of creativity, transformation, and knowledge in this (at best) misguided system. For apart from inquiry, apart from the praxis, men cannot be truly human. Knowledge emerges only through invention and reinvention, through the restless, impatient, continuing, hopeful inquiry men pursue in the world, with the world, and with each other. [Friere, 1974, p. 58]

Learning Is a Continuous Process Grounded in Experience

Knowledge is continuously derived from and tested out in the experiences of the learner. William James (1890), in his studies on the nature of human consciousness, marveled at the fact that consciousness is continuous. How is it, he asked, that I awake in the morning with the same consciousness, the same thoughts, feelings, memories, and sense of who I am that I went to sleep with the night before? Similarly for Dewey, continuity of experience was a powerful truth of human existence, central to the theory of learning:

> . . . the principle of continuity of experience means that every experience both takes up something from those which have gone before and modifies in some way the quality of those which come after. . . . As an individual passes from one situation to another, his world, his environment, expands or contracts. He does not find himself living in another world but in a different part or aspect of one and the same world. What he has learned in the way of knowledge and skill in one situation becomes an instrument of understanding and dealing effectively with the situations which follow. The process goes on as long as life and learning continue. [Dewey, 1938, pp. 35, 44]

Although we are all aware of the sense of continuity in consciousness and experience to which James and Dewey refer, and take comfort from the predictability and security it provides, there is on occasion in the penumbra of that awareness an element of doubt and uncertainty. How do I reconcile my own sense of continuity and predictability with what at times appears to be a chaotic and unpredictable world around me? I move through my daily round of tasks and meetings with a fair sense of what the issues are, of what others are saying and thinking, and with ideas about what actions to take. Yet I am occasionally upended by unforeseen circumstances, miscommunications, and dreadful miscalculations. It is in this interplay between expectation and experience that learning occurs. In Hegel's phrase, "Any experience that does not violate expectation is not worthy of the name experience." And yet somehow, the rents that these violations cause in the fabric of my experience are magically repaired, and I face the next day a bit changed but still the same person.

That this is a *learning* process is perhaps better illustrated by the nonlearning postures that can result from the interplay between expectation and experience. To focus so sharply on continuity and certainty that one is blinded to the shadowy penumbra of doubt and uncertainty is to risk dogmatism and rigidity, the inability to learn from new experiences. Or conversely, to have continuity continuously shaken by the vicissitudes of new experience is to be left paralyzed by insecurity, incapable of effective action. From the perspective of epistemological philosophy, Pepper (1942) shows that both these postures—dogmatism and absolute skepticism—are inadequate foundations for the creation of valid knowledge systems. He proposes instead that an attitude of provisionalism, or what he calls partial skepticism, be the guide for inquiry and learning (see Chapter 5, pp. 162–163).

The fact that learning is a continuous process grounded in experience has important educational implications. Put simply, it implies that all learning is relearning. How easy and tempting it is in designing a course to think of the learner's mind as being as blank as the paper on which we scratch our outline. Yet this is not the case. Everyone enters every learning situation with more or less articulate ideas about the topic at hand. We are all psychologists, historians, and atomic physicists. It is just that some of our theories are more crude and incorrect than others. But to focus solely on the refinement and validity of these theories misses the point. The important point is that the people we teach have held these beliefs whatever their quality and that until now they have used them whenever the situation called for them to be atomic physicists, historians, or whatever.

Thus, one's job as an educator is not only to implant new ideas but also to dispose of or modify old ones. In many cases, resistance to new ideas stems from their conflict with old beliefs that are inconsistent with them. If the education process begins by bringing out the learner's beliefs and theories, examining and testing them, and then integrating the new, more refined ideas into the person's belief systems, the learning process will be facilitated. Piaget (see Elkind, 1970, Chapter 3) has identified two mechanisms by which new ideas are adopted by an individual—integration and substitution. Ideas that evolve through integration tend to become highly stable parts of the person's conception of the world. On the other hand, when the content of a concept changes by means of substitution, there is always the possibility of a reversion to the earlier level of conceptualization and understanding, or to a dual theory of the world where espoused theories learned through substitution are incongruent with theories-in-use that are more integrated with the person's total conceptual and attitudinal view of the world. It is this latter outcome that stimulated Argyris and Schon's inquiry into the effectiveness of professional education:

> We thought the trouble people have in learning new theories may stem not so much from the inherent difficulty of the new theories as from the existing theories people have that already determine practices. We call their operational theories of action *theories-in-use* to distinguish them from the espoused theories that are used to describe and justify behavior. We wondered whether the difficulty in learning new theories of action is related to a disposition to protect the old theory-in-use. [Argyris and Schon, 1974, p. viii]

The Process of Learning Requires the Resolution of Conflicts between Dialectically Opposed Modes of Adaptation to the World

Each of the three models of experiential learning describes conflicts between opposing ways of dealing with the world, suggesting that learning results from resolution of these conflicts. The Lewinian model emphasizes two such dialectics—the conflict between concrete experience and abstract concepts and the conflict between observation and action.[2] For Dewey, the major dialectic is between the impulse that gives ideas their "moving force" and reason that gives desire its direction. In Piaget's framework, the twin processes of accommodation of ideas to the external world and assimilation of experience into existing conceptual structures are the moving forces of cognitive development. In Paulo Freire's work, the dialectic nature of learning and adaptation is encompassed in his concept of *praxis*, which he defines as "reflection and action upon the world in order

---

2. The concept of dialectic relationship is used advisedly in this work. The long history and changing usages of this term, and particularly the emotional and ideological connotations attending its usage in some contexts, may cause some confusion for the reader. However, no other term expresses as well the relationship between learning orientations described here—that of mutually opposed and conflicting processes the results of each of which cannot be explained by the other, but whose merger through confrontation of the conflict between them results in a higher order process that transcends and encompasses them both. This definition comes closest to Hegel's use of the term but does not imply total acceptance of the Hegelian epistemology (compare Chapter 5, p. 155).

to transform it" (1974, p. 36). Central to the concept of praxis is the process of "naming the world," which is both active—in the sense that naming something transforms it—and reflective—in that our choice of words gives meaning to the world around us. This process of naming the world is accomplished through dialogue among equals, a joint process of inquiry and learning that Freire sets against the banking concept of education described earlier:

> As we attempt to analyze dialogue as a human phenomenon, we discover something which is the essence of dialogue itself: the word. But the word is more than just an instrument which makes dialogue possible; accordingly, we must seek its constitutive elements. Within the word we find two dimensions, reflection and action, in such radical interaction that if one is sacrificed—even in part—the other immediately suffers. There is no true word that is not at the same time a praxis. Thus, to speak a true word is to transform the world.
>
> An unauthentic word, one which is unable to transform reality, results when dichotomy is imposed upon its constitutive elements. When a word is deprived of its dimension of action, reflection automatically suffers as well; and the word is changed into idle chatter, into verbalism, into an alienated and alienating "blah." It becomes an empty word, one which cannot denounce the world, for denunciation is impossible without a commitment to transform, and there is no transformation without action.
>
> On the other hand, if action is emphasized exclusively, to the detriment of reflection, the word is converted into activism. The latter—action for action's sake—negates the true praxis and makes dialogue impossible. Either dichotomy, by creating unauthentic forms of existence, creates also unauthentic forms of thought, which reinforce the original dichotomy.
>
> Human existence cannot be silent, nor can it be nourished by false words, but only by true words, with which men transform the world. To exist, humanly, is to name the world, to change it. Once named, the world in its turn reappears to the namers as a problem and requires of them a new naming. Men are not built in silence, but in word, in work, in action-reflection.
>
> But while to say the true word—which is work, which is praxis—is to transform the world, saying that word is not the privilege of some few men, but the right of every man. Consequently, no one can say a true word alone—nor can he say it for another, in a prescriptive act which robs others of their words. [Freire, 1974, pp. 75, 76]

All the models above suggest the idea that learning is by its very nature a tension- and conflict-filled process. New knowledge, skills, or attitudes are achieved through confrontation among four modes of experiential learning. Learners, if they are to be effective, need four different kinds of abilities—*concrete experience* abilities (CE), *reflective observation* abilities (RO), *abstract conceptualization* abilities (AC), and *active experimentation* (AE) abilities. That is, they must be able to involve themselves fully, openly, and without bias in new experiences (CE). They must be able to reflect on and observe their experiences from many perspectives (RO). They must be able to create concepts that integrate their observations into logically sound theories (AC), and they must be able to use these theories to make decisions and solve problems (AE). Yet this ideal is difficult to achieve. How can one act and reflect at the same time? How can one be concrete and immediate and still be theoretical? Learning requires abilities that are polar opposites, and the learner, as a result, must continually choose which set of learning abilities he or she will bring to bear in any specific learning situation. More specifically, there are two primary dimensions to the learning process. The first dimension represents the concrete experiencing of events at one end and abstract conceptualization at the other. The other dimension has active experimentation at one extreme and reflective observation at the other. Thus, in the process of learning, one moves in varying degrees from actor to observer, and from specific involvement to general analytic detachment.

In addition, the *way* in which the conflicts among the dialectically opposed modes of adaptation get resolved determines the level of learning that results. If conflicts are resolved by suppression of one mode and/or dominance by another, learning tends to be specialized around the dominant mode and limited in areas controlled by the dominated mode. For example, in Piaget's model, imitation is the result when accommodation processes dominate, and play results when assimilation dominates. Or for Freire, dominance of the active mode results in "activism," and dominance of the reflective mode results in "verbalism."

However, when we consider the higher forms of adaptation—the process of creativity and personal development—conflict among adaptive modes needs to be confronted and integrated into a creative synthesis. Nearly every account of the creative process, from Wallas's (1926) four-stage model of incorporation, incubation, insight, and verification, has recognized the dialectic conflicts involved in creativity. Bruner (1966a), in his essay on the conditions of creativity, emphasizes the dialectic tension between abstract detachment and concrete involvement. For him, the creative act is a product of detachment and commitment, of passion and decorum, and of a freedom to be dominated by the object of one's inquiry. At the highest stages of development, the adaptive commitment to learning and creativity produces a strong need for integration of the four adaptive modes. Development in one mode precipitates development in the others. Increases in symbolic complexity, for example, refine and sharpen both perceptual and behavioral possibilities. Thus, complexity and the integration of dialectic conflicts among the adaptive modes are the hallmarks of true creativity and growth.

Learning Is an Holistic Process of Adaptation to the World

Experiential learning is not a molecular educational concept but rather is a molar concept describing the central process of human adaptation to the social and physical environment. It is a holistic concept, much akin to the Jungian theory of psychological types (Jung, 1923), in that it seeks to describe the emergence of basic life orientations as a function of dialectic tensions between basic modes of relating to the world. To learn is not the special province of a single specialized realm of human functioning such as cognition or perception. It involves the integrated functioning of the total organism—thinking, feeling, perceiving, and behaving.

This concept of holistic adaptation is somewhat out of step with current research trends in the behavioral sciences. Since the early years of this century and the decline of what Gordon Allport called the "simple and sovereign" theories of human behavior, the trend in the behavioral sciences has been away from theories such as those of Freud and his followers that proposed to explain the totality of human functioning by focusing on the interrelatedness among human processes such as thought, emotion, perception, and so on. Research has instead tended to specialize in more detailed exploration and description of particular processes and subprocesses of human adaptation—perception, person perception, attribution, achievement motivation, cognition, memory—the list could go on and on. The fruit of this labor has been bountiful. Because of this intensive specialized research, we now know a vast amount about human behavior, so much that any attempt to integrate and do justice to all this diverse knowledge seems impossible. Any holistic theory proposed today could not be simple and would certainly not be sovereign. Yet if we are to understand human behavior, particularly in any practical way, we must in some way put together all the pieces that have been so carefully analyzed. In addition to knowing how we think and how we feel, we must also know when behavior is governed by thought and when by feeling. In addition to addressing the nature of specialized human functions, experiential learning theory is also concerned with how these functions are integrated by the person into a holistic adaptive posture toward the world.

Learning is *the* major process of human adaptation. This concept of learning is considerably broader than that commonly associated with the school classroom. It occurs in all human settings, from schools to the workplace, from the research laboratory to the management board room, in personal relationships and the aisles of the local grocery. It encompasses all life stages, from childhood to adolescence, to middle and old age. Therefore it encompasses other, more limited adaptive concepts such as creativity, problem solving, decision making, and attitude change that focus heavily on one or another of the basic aspects of adaptation. Thus, creativity research has tended to focus on the divergent (concrete and reflective) factors in adaptation such as tolerance for ambiguity, metaphorical thinking, and flexibility, whereas research on decision making has emphasized more convergent (abstract and active) adaptive factors such as the rational evaluation of solution alternatives.

The cyclic description of the experiential learning process is mirrored in many of the specialized models of the adaptive process. The common theme in all these models is that all forms of human adaptation approximate scientific inquiry, a point of view articulated most thoroughly by the late George Kelly (1955). Dewey, Lewin, and Piaget in one way or another seem to take the scientific method as their model for the learning process; or to put it another way, they see in the scientific method the highest philosophical and technological refinement of the basic processes of human adaptation. The scientific method, thus, provides a means for describing the holistic integration of all human functions.

Figure 2.4 shows the experiential learning cycle in the center circle and a model of the scientific inquiry process in the outer circle (Kolb, 1978), with models of the problem-

Figure 2.4   Similarities Among Conceptions of Basic Adaptive Processes: Inquiry/Research, Creativity, Decision Making, Problem Solving, Learning

solving process (Pounds, 1965), the decision-making process (Simon, 1947), and the creative process (Wallas, 1926) in between. Although the models all use different terms, there is a remarkable similarity in concept among them. This similarity suggests that there may be great payoff in the integration of findings from these specialized areas into a single general adaptive model such as that proposed by experiential learning theory. Bruner's work on a theory of instruction (1966b) shows one example of this potential payoff. His integration of research on cognitive processes, problem solving, and learning theory provided a rich new perspective for the conduct of education.

When learning is conceived as a holistic adaptive process, it provides conceptual bridges across life situations such as school and work, portraying learning as a continuous, lifelong process. Similarly, this perspective highlights the similarities among adaptive/learning activities that are commonly called by specialized names—learning, creativity, problem solving, decision making, and scientific research. Finally, learning conceived holistically includes adaptive activities that vary in their extension through time and space. Typically, an immediate reaction to a limited situation or problem is not thought of as learning but as *performance*. Similarly at the other extreme, we do not commonly think of long-term adaptations to one's total life situation as learning but as *development*. Yet performance, learning, and development, when viewed from the perspectives of experiential learning theory, form a continuum of adaptive postures to the environment, varying only in their degree of extension in time and space. Performance is limited to short-term adaptations to immediate circumstance, learning encompasses somewhat longer-term mastery of generic classes of situations, and development encompasses lifelong adaptations to one's total life situation (compare Chapter 6).

Learning Involves Transactions between the Person and the Environment

So stated, this proposition must seem obvious. Yet strangely enough, its implications seem to have been widely ignored in research on learning and practice in education, replaced instead by a person-centered psychological view of learning. The casual observer of the traditional educational process would undoubtedly conclude that learning was primarily a personal, internal process requiring only the limited environment of books, teacher, and classroom. Indeed, the wider "real-world" environment at times seems to be actively rejected by educational systems at all levels.

There is an analogous situation in psychological research on learning and development. In theory, stimulus-response theories of learning describe relationships between environmental stimuli and responses of the organism. But in practice, most of this research involves treating the environmental stimuli as independent variables manipulated artificially by the experimenter to determine their effect on dependent response characteristics. This approach has had two outcomes. The first is a tendency to perceive the person-environment relationship as one-way, placing great emphasis on how environment shapes behavior with little regard for how behavior shapes the environment. Second, the models of learning are essentially decontextualized and lacking in what Egon Brunswick (1943) called ecological validity. In the emphasis on scientific control of environmental conditions, laboratory situations were created that bore little resemblance to the environment of real life, resulting in empirically validated models of learning that accurately described behavior in these artificial settings but could not easily be generalized to subjects in their natural environment. It is not surprising to me that the foremost proponent of this theory of learning would be fascinated by the creation of Utopian societies such as Walden II (Skinner, 1948); for the only way to apply the results of these studies is to make the world a laboratory, subject to "experimenter" control (compare Elms, 1981).

Similar criticisms have been made of developmental psychology. Piaget's work, for example, has been criticized for its failure to take account of environmental and cultural circumstances (Cole, 1971). Speaking of developmental psychology in general, Bronfenbrenner states, "Much of developmental psychology as it now exists is *the science of the strange behavior of children in strange situations with strange adults for the briefest possible periods of time*" (1977, p. 19).

In experiential learning theory, the transactional relationship between the person and the environment is symbolized in the dual meanings of the term *experience*—one subjective and personal, referring to the person's internal state, as in "the experience of joy and happiness," and the other objective and environmental, as in, "He has 20 years of experience on this job." These two forms of experience interpenetrate and interrelate in very complex ways, as, for example, in the old saw, "He doesn't have 20 years of experience, but one year repeated 20 times." Dewey describes the matter this way:

> Experience does not go on simply inside a person. It does go on there, for it influences the formation of attitudes of desire and purpose. But this is not the whole of the story. Every genuine experience has an active side which changes in some degree the objective conditions under which experiences are had. The difference between civilization and savagery, to take an example on a large scale, is found in the degree in which previous experiences have changed the objective conditions under which subsequent experiences take place. The existence of roads, of means of rapid movement and transportation, tools, implements, furniture, electric light and power, are illustrations. Destroy the external conditions of present civilized experience, and for a time our experience would relapse into that of barbaric peoples. . . .

> The word "interaction" assigns equal rights to both factors in experience—objective and internal conditions. Any normal experience is an interplay of these two sets of conditions. Taken together . . . they form what we call a situation.

The statement that individuals live in a world means, in the concrete, that they live in a series of situations. And when it is said that they live in these situations, the meaning of the word "in" is different from its meaning when it is said that pennies are "in" a pocket or paint is "in" a can. It means, once more, that inter-action is going on between an individual and objects and other persons. The conceptions of situation and of interaction are inseparable from each other. An experience is always what it is because of a transaction taking place between an individual and what, at the time, constitutes his environment, whether the lat-ter consists of persons with whom he is talking about some topic or event, the subject talked about being also a part of the situation; the book he is reading (in which his environing conditions at the time may be England or ancient Greece or an imaginary region); or the materials of an experiment he is performing. The environment, in other words, is whatever conditions interact with personal needs, desires, purposes, and capacities to create the experience which is had. Even when a person builds a castle in the air he is interacting with the objects which he constructs in fancy. [Dewey, 1938, pp. 39, 42–43]

Although Dewey refers to the relationship between the objective and subjective condi-tions of experience as an "interaction," he is struggling in the last portion of the quote above to convey the special, complex nature of the relationship. The word *transac-tion* is more appropriate than *interaction* to describe the relationship between the per-son and the environment in experiential learning theory, because the connotation of interaction is somehow too mechanical, involving unchanging separate entities that become intertwined but retain their separate identities. This is why Dewey attempts to give special meaning to the word *in*. The concept of transaction implies a more fluid, interpenetrating relationship between objective conditions and subjective experience, such that once they become related, both are essentially changed.

Lewin recognized this complexity, even though he chose to sidestep it in his famous theoretical formulation, $B = f(P, E)$, indicating that behavior is a function of the person and the environment without any specification as to the specific mathematical nature of that function. The position taken in this work is similar to that of Bandura (1978)—namely, that personal characteristics, environmental influences, and behavior all operate in reciprocal determination, each factor influencing the others in an interlocking fashion. The concept of reciprocally determined transactions between person and learning envi-ronment is central to the laboratory-training method of experiential learning. Learning in T-groups is seen to result not simply from responding to a fixed environment but from the active creation by the learners of situations that meet their learning objectives:

The essence of this learning experience is a transactional process in which the members negotiate as each attempts to influence or control the stream of events and to satisfy his personal needs. Individuals learn to the extent that they expose their needs, values, and behavior patterns so that perceptions and reactions can be exchanged. Behavior thus becomes the currency for transaction. The amount each invests helps to determine the return. [Bradford, 1964, p. 192]

Learning in this sense is an active, self-directed process that can be applied not only in the group setting but in everyday life.

Learning Is the Process of Creating Knowledge

To understand learning, we must understand the nature and forms of human knowledge and the processes whereby this knowledge is created. It has already been emphasized that this process of creation occurs at all levels of sophistication, from the most advanced forms of scientific research to the child's discovery that a rubber ball bounces. Knowledge is the result of the transaction between social knowledge and personal knowledge. The former, as Dewey noted, is the civilized objective accumulation of previous human cultural experience, whereas the latter is the accumulation of the individual person's subjective life experiences. Knowledge results from the transaction between these objective and subjective experiences in a process called learning. Hence, to understand knowledge, we must understand the psychology of the learning process, and to understand learning, we must understand epistemology—the origins, nature, methods, and limits of knowledge. Piaget makes the following comments on these last points:

> Psychology thus occupies a key position, and its implications become increasingly clear. The very simple reason for this is that if the sciences of nature explain the human species, humans in turn explain the sciences of nature, and it is up to psychology to show us how. Psychology, in fact, represents the junction of two opposite directions of scientific thought that are dialectically complementary. It follows that the system of sciences cannot be arranged in a linear order, as many people beginning with Auguste Comte have attempted to arrange them. The form that characterizes the system of sciences is that of a circle, or more precisely that of a spiral as it becomes ever larger. In fact, objects are known only through the subject, while the subject can know himself or herself only by acting on objects materially and mentally. Indeed, if objects are innumerable and science indefinitely diverse, all knowledge of the subject brings us back to psychology, the science of the subject and the subject's actions.
>
> . . . it is impossible to dissociate psychology from epistemology . . . how is knowledge acquired, how does it increase, and how does it become organized or reorganized? . . . The answers we find, and from which we can only choose by more or less refining them, are necessarily of the following three types: Either knowledge comes exclusively from the object, or it is constructed by the subject alone, or it results from multiple interactions between the subject and the object—but what interactions and in what form? Indeed, we see at once that these are epistemological solutions stemming from empiricism, apriorism, or diverse interactionism. . . . [Piaget, 1978, p. 651]

It is surprising that few learning and cognitive researchers other than Piaget have recognized the intimate relationship between learning and knowledge and hence recognized the need for epistemological as well as psychological inquiry into these related processes. In my own research and practice with experiential learning, I have been impressed with the very practical ramifications of the epistemological perspective. In teaching, for example, I have found it essential to take into account the nature of the subject matter in deciding how to help students learn the material at hand. Trying to develop skills in empathic listening is a different educational task, requiring a different teaching approach from that of teaching fundamentals of statistics. Similarly, in consulting work with organizations, I have often seen barriers to communication and problem solving that at root are epistemologically based—that is, based on conflicting assumptions about the nature of knowledge and truth.

The theory of experiential learning provides a perspective from which to approach these practical problems, suggesting a typology of different knowledge systems that results from the way the dialectic conflicts between adaptive modes of concrete experience and abstract conceptualization and the modes of active experimentation and reflective observation are characteristically resolved in different fields of inquiry (compare Chapter 5). This approach draws on the work of Stephen Pepper (1942, 1966), who proposes a system for describing the different viable forms of social knowledge. This system is based on what Pepper calls world hypotheses. World hypotheses correspond to metaphysical systems that define assumptions and rules for the development of refined knowledge from common sense. Pepper maintains that all knowledge systems are refinements of common sense based on different assumptions about the nature of knowledge and truth. In this process of refinement he sees a basic dilemma. Although common sense is always applicable as a means of explaining an experience, it tends to be imprecise. Refined knowledge, on the other hand, is precise but limited in its application or generalizability because it is based on assumptions or world hypotheses. Thus, common sense requires the criticism of refined knowledge, and refined knowledge requires the security of common sense, suggesting that all social knowledge requires an attitude of partial skepticism in its interpretation.

Summary: A Definition of Learning

Even though definitions have a way of making things seem more certain than they are, it may be useful to summarize this chapter on the characteristics of the experiential learning process by offering a working definition of learning.[3] *Learning is the process whereby knowledge is created through the transformation of experience.* This definition emphasizes several critical aspects of the learning process as viewed from the experiential perspective. First is the emphasis on the process of adaptation and learning as opposed to content

---

3. From this point on, I will drop the modifier "experiential" in referring to the learning process described in this chapter. When other theories of learning are discussed, they will be identified as such.

or outcomes. Second is that knowledge is a transformation process, being continuously created and recreated, not an independent entity to be acquired or transmitted. Third, learning transforms experience in both its objective and subjective forms. Finally, to understand learning, we must understand the nature of knowledge, and vice versa.

Update and Reflections
The Learning Cycle and the Learning Spiral

> *The people who 'learn by experience' often make great messes of their lives, that is, if they apply what they have learned from a past incident to the present, deciding from certain appearances that the circumstances are the same, forgetting that no two situations can ever be the same. . . . All that I am, all that life has made me, every past experience that I have had—woven into the tissue of my life—I must give to the new experience. That past experience has indeed not been useless, but its use is not in guiding present conduct by past situations. We must put everything we can into each fresh experience, but we shall not get the same things out which we put in if it is a fruitful experience, if it is part of our progressing life . . . We integrate our experience, and then the richer human being that we are goes into the new experience; again we give ourself and always by giving rise above the old self.*
>
> —Mary Parker Follett, 1924, pp. 136–137

Chapter 2 defines the experiential learning cycle particularly as represented in the theories of Lewin and Dewey. It further suggests that Piaget's more linear model of development is consistent with the learning cycle adding his two dialectical dimensions of concrete phenomenalism/abstract constructionism and active ego-centrism/internalized reflection.

The learning cycle and the concept of learning style are the most widely known and used concepts in experiential learning theory; although there is considerable confusion and misunderstanding of the concepts often resulting from being taken out of the context of the wider experiential learning theory framework. This update will address these issues with regard to the learning cycle (the Chapter 4 update will do so for the concept of learning style).

Understanding the Learning Cycle

In its most current statement (Kolb and Kolb, 2013) experiential learning theory is described as a dynamic view of learning based on a learning cycle driven by the resolution of the dual dialectics of action/reflection and experience/abstraction. Learning is defined as "the process whereby knowledge is created through the transformation of experience" (Chapter 2, p. 49). Knowledge results from the combination of grasping and transforming experience. Grasping experience refers to the process of taking in information, and transforming experience is how individuals interpret and act on that information. The experiential learning theory learning model portrays two dialectically related modes of grasping experience—Concrete Experience (CE) and Abstract Conceptualization (AC)— and two dialectically related modes of transforming experience—Reflective Observation (RO) and Active Experimentation (AE). Learning arises from the resolution of creative tension among these four learning modes. This process is portrayed as an idealized learning cycle or spiral where the learner "touches all the bases"—experiencing (CE), reflecting (RO), thinking (AC), and acting (AE)—in a recursive process that is sensitive to the learning situation and what is being learned. Immediate or concrete experiences are the basis for observations and reflections. These reflections are assimilated and distilled into abstract concepts from which new implications for action can be drawn. These implications can be actively tested and serve as guides in creating new experiences (see Figure 2.5).

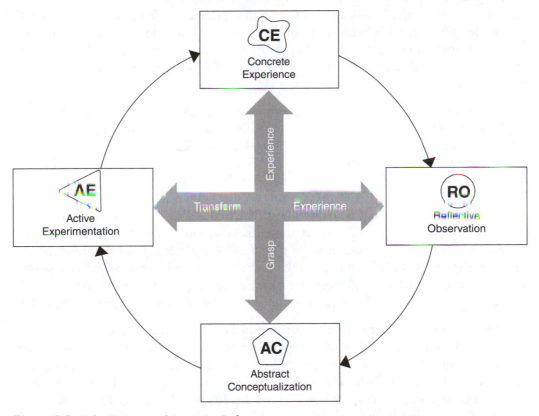

Figure 2.5   The Experiential Learning Cycle

This cycle of learning has been widely used and adapted in the design and conduct of countless educational programs. A Google image search of "learning cycle" produces a seemingly endless array of reproductions and variations of the cycle from around the world.

While I have been personally gratified by the scholarship and pragmatic utility generated by the concept, others have been alarmed and concerned by its apparent simplicity and failure to "problematize" experience. Reijo Miettinen asks, "Why is this conception so popular within adult education? . . . Perhaps the idea of experiential learning forms an attractive package for adult educators. It combines spontaneity, feeling, and deep individual insights with the possibility of rational thought and reflection. It maintains the humanistic belief in every individual's capacity to grow and learn, so important for the concept of lifelong learning. It comprises a positive ideology that is evidently important for adult education. However, I fear that the price of this package for adult education and research is high . . . the belief in an individual's capabilities and his individual experience leads us away from the analysis of cultural and social conditions of learning that are essential to any serious enterprise of fostering change and learning in real life." (2000, pp. 70–71). In an editorial in the *Adult Education Quarterly*, the editors echo this concern about the "unquestioned notion of experience in the pragmatic tradition": "Kolb's learning cycle has become as ubiquitous as Maslow's hierarchical triangle. This is not just unfortunate, but limiting, because it restricts the way we see and understand experience which thus limits the way we can learn in-from-to experience" (Wilson and Hayes, 2002, p. 174).

In a way I also, on occasion, have been disturbed by oversimplified interpretations and applications of the learning cycle. Many times this seems to be because the cycle has been taken out of the wider context of experiential learning theory, and/or I have failed to explain my perspective adequately. The *Adult Education Quarterly* editors should not be worried, for among the thousands of scholarly articles published about experiential learning theory, I have found over 50 that have examined and critiqued experiential learning theory from their perspective as well as others. The views expressed represent a wide range of opinion and theoretical orientations, sometimes contradicting each other. Collectively they open a valuable conversation about the future of experiential learning research and practice. *Experiential Learning* was not the first word on the subject (as we have seen in Chapter 1 and its update), and it certainly was not intended to be the last. With the help of the thoughtful critiques I will address some of these views from my perspective today.

The learning cycle describes an individual model of learning that ignores the historical, cultural, and social context of learning. Some critics (Hopkins, 1993; Seaman, 2008; Reynolds, 1997, 1998; Michelson, 1997, 1998, 1999; Fenwick, 2000, 2003) along with Miettinen and the journal editors have found the learning cycle and experiential learning theory in general to be too psychological and individualistic. Reynolds, for example, says experiential learning theory "is highly individualizing, and its psychological perspective, whether orthodox or humanist, ignores or downgrades the social context . . . being psychological in conception it takes little or no account of the meaning of difference in terms of social or political process" (1997, p. 128).

Michelson poses her critique from a broader historical perspective suggesting:

> "that mainstream theories of experiential learning . . . rest on an interiorized subjectivity that emerged only with the Enlightenment, when inner consciousness came to be seen as a 'space' to be explored, a realm separate from and discontinuous with any external reality . . . (and) reproduce the Enlightenment relationship between psychic and cognitive interiority and political and economic agency. Just as in the writings of Locke, the autonomy of privatized inner experience is what grounds our rights and liberties under the social contract: according to David Kolb, the fact that we are 'still learning from our experience' means that 'we are free' and able to 'chart the course of our own destiny' (Kolb, 1984, p. 109). Indeed, the conjoining of privatized experience with the claims to political agency is made explicit in the quotation by John Dewey with which Kolb (1984, p. 1) begins Experiential Learning: 'The modern discovery of inner experience, of a realm of purely personal events that are always at the individual's command and that are his [sic] exclusively . . . is also a great and liberating discovery. It implies a new worth and sense of dignity in human individuality'" (1999, p. 144).

Agreeing with Dewey, my aim for experiential learning theory was to create a model for explaining how individuals learn and to empower learners to trust their own experience and gain mastery over their own learning. My psychological training as a personality theorist has made me a great advocate of individuality. Each of us is deeply unique, and we have an imperative to embrace and express that uniqueness, for the good of ourselves and for the world. Martha Graham said it well, "There is a vitality, a life force, an energy, a quickening, that is translated through you into action, and because there is only one of you in all time, this expression is unique, and if you block it, it will never exist through any other medium and will be lost." Individuality is different than individualism, which is egocentric. In individualism, "the individual is not viewed as an integral part of his or her social world; the feeling of belonging to a group is not seen as giving life purpose and direction. Rather society is viewed as either corrupting or civilizing our basically asocial nature" (Guisinger and Blatt, 1994, p. 105).

Individuality and relatedness in experiential learning theory are poles of a fundamental dialectic of development, ". . . the capacities to form a mutual relationship with another, to participate in society, and to be dedicated to one's own self-interest and expression emerge out of the integration and consolidation of individuality and relatedness in the development of a self-identity . . ." (Guisinger and Blatt, 1994, pp. 108–109). Similarly, Susanne Cook-Greuter (1999) and David Bakan (1966) argue that there is a human need to fulfill the double goals of autonomy (differentiation, independence, mastery) and homonomy (integration, participation, belonging).

It is true that *Experiential Learning* is not a discourse on social and political factors that influence what people learn and believe in the tradition of critical theory. This was not my purpose, though I believe that experiential learning theory is not incompatible with these approaches. Both views together enhance our full understanding of experiential learning. Among the experiential learning theory foundational scholars, Dewey and Follett were leaders in the Progressive movement, and Freire's life was one of struggle for social justice in his country. Vygotsky's work is foundational for activity theory and social constructivism. From their contributions, experiential learning theory has much to offer critical cultural theory in pedagogy, feminist theory, post-structural scholarship, social constructionism, post-colonial, and indigenous culture studies.

The learning cycle is constructivist and cognitivist. These terms have been used to characterize the learning cycle as portraying learning in a way that separates the individual from the environment. Fenwick defines constructivism as a process where "the learner reflects on lived experience and then interprets and generalizes this experience to form mental structures. These structures are knowledge, stored in memory as concepts that can be represented, expressed, and transferred to new situations (2000, p. 248). . . . In the constructivist view, the learner is still viewed as fundamentally autonomous from his or her surroundings. The learner moves through context, is in it and affected by it, but the learner's meanings still exist in the learner's head and move with the learner from one context to the next. Knowledge is thus a substance, a third thing created from the learner's interaction with other actors and objects and bounded in the learner's head. Social relations of power exercised through language or cultural practices are not theorized as part of knowledge construction" (2000, p. 250).

Michelson seems to ignore the holistic characteristic of experiential learning theory (Chapter 2, pp. 43–45) when she argues that the constructivism of the learning cycle portrays learning as occuring in the mind alone, ". . . the mind accesses information about the world and uses that information to produce learning. The body functions essentially as sensate medium and testing instrument, while the emotions and the spirit do not participate at all" (1997, p. 48).

Constructivism, of course, originated in the work of Piaget and Vygotsky whose ideas play a big role in experiential learning theory. However, I modified the constructivist view in significant ways (see Chapter 3, p. 66; Chapter 6, pp. 201–205). Holman, Pavlica, and Thorpe use the somewhat pejorative term "cognitivist" preferred by critical theorists and social constructionists to at first acknowledge these modifications and then discount them, "KELT is rarely linked to, and often considered fundamentally different from cognitive learning schools. Indeed Kolb himself has sought to distance his theory from a strict Paigetiatian cognitivism by stressing its roots in pragmaticism and social action theories. . . . However, while KELT may have its roots in Dewey and Lewin, Kolb's reworking of these and other theorists upon whom he draws embeds his work in a number of cognitivist assumptions which relate to the nature of self and thought . . . to produce a work that is fundametally cognitivist" (1997, p. 136). The "cognitivist assumptions" they cite include the person is independent of the social/historical/cultural context, representational thinking and mental process can be studied in isolation.

What I think the critics from this perspective have missed in their reading of *Experiential Learning* is the posited transactional relationship of the individual and the social environment. The Gestalt foundational scholars, Kurt Lewin and Mary Parker Follett, William James (radical empiricism), and John Dewey (depiction of the difference between interaction and transaction), all portray an embedded and integrated view of the individual and the world that stands in contrast to Piaget's description of an individual developmental process that is universal across contexts (see Chapter 6, pp. 201–205). In the section describing learning as a transaction between the person and environment in Chapter 2 (pp. 45–48), I summarize the issue: "The word *transaction* is more appropriate than *interaction* to describe the relationship between the person and the environment in experiential learning theory because the connotation of *interaction* is somehow too mechanical, involving unchanging separate identities that become intertwined but retain their separate identities . . . The concept of transaction implies a more fluid interpenetrating relationship between objective conditions and subjective experience, such that once they become related, both are essentially changed." (See "The Learning Spiral" section below.) Mary Parker Follett describes this process which she calls "circular response" in human relationships: "Through circular response we are creating each other all the time . . . Accurately speaking the matter cannot be expressed by the phrase used above, I-plus-you meeting you-plus-me. It is I plus the-interweaving-between-you-and-me meeting you plus the-interweaving-between-you-and-me, etc., etc. 'I' can never influence 'you' because you have already influenced me; that is, in the very process of meeting, by the very process of meeting, we both become something different" (1924, pp. 62–63).

The Experiential Learning Cycle is an oversimplified view of learning describing a mechanical step-by-step process that distorts both learning and experience. Seaman, who calls for an end to the "Learning Cycles Era," suggests that "the definition of experiential learning as an orderly series of steps is either false . . . or represents only a narrow type of experiential learning. . . . The intent of this article is not to suggest that the routine patterns used in different experiential practices . . . should be abandoned. This approach has unquestionably served many practitioners throughout the years. Rather, this article has argued against the claim that experiential learning can be fundamentally understood as *equivalent* to these patterns" (2008, p. 15). Others have also viewed the distinct sequential stages of the learning cycle as an oversimplified description of learning (DiCiantis and Kirton, 1996; Holman, 1997; Smith, 2010; Jarvis, 1987, 1995).

As I described in the introduction, I, too, initially used the learning cycle in a simplistic way as a pragmatic tool to organize learning events. It was only after I saw the resulting rich experience and learning that was created for learners that I began to search for a theoretical explanation of the learning process in the work of the experiential learning theory foundational scholars. The concept of learning style was created later, based on the emerging theory of experiential learning. Our observations of different styles of learning were in fact different ways of engaging the learning cycle (Kolb and Kolb, 2013a). The insight that led me to think that the cycle of learning from experience was more complex was the identification of the two dialectically related dimensions of grasping experience via concrete experience and abstract conceptualization and transforming experience via active experimentation and reflective observation. I first noticed the dimensions in the theories of Lewin, Dewey, Piaget, and Freire and developed them further with the aid of Jung's introversion/extraversion transformation dialectic and with James' apprehension/comprehension grasping dialectic. (For my explanations of these dialectic dimensions and their relationship to the learning process, see Chapter 2, pp. 40–42; Chapter 3, pp. 65–86; Chapter 5, pp. 159–163; Chapter 6, pp. 199, 210–215; and Chapter 8, pp. 328–333.)

Introduction of the dialectic dimensions confuses structure and process. However, for Hopkins, an avid phenomenologist, the introduction of the dialectic structural analysis to the stage model doesn't work: "Kolb's theory as a formalistic reification of experiential process cannot withstand phenomenological reflection . . ." (1993, p. 54) He argues with Nelson and Grinder (1985) that my combination of structure and process doesn't work because it fails to "untangle" the relation between the two. Miettinen agrees that the stage model is not helped by the introduction of the dialectic dimensions: "The phases remain separate. . . . Kolb does not present any concept that would connect the phases to each other. . . . Kolb continuously speaks about 'dialectic tension' between experiential and conceptual. However, he resolves the tension simply by taking both as a separate phase to his model. There is surely no dialectics in this. Dialectic logic would show how these two are indispensable related to each other and are determined through other" (2000, p. 61).

For me, these dialectic opposites opened a space for experiencing that embraced the multidimensional aspects of experience and all modes of the learning cycle as described in James' radical empiricism and in phenomenology (Introduction, pp. xxii–xxiii). Experiencing, reflecting, thinking, and acting are not separate independent entities but inextricably related to one another in their dialectic opposition. They are mutually determined and in dynamic flux. The dialectic dimensions also formed the basis of the concept of learning style; a habit of learning that is formed when one or more of the learning modes is preferred over others to shape experience, resulting in a constriction and limiting of the experiencing space around the mode(s). The ranking format of the Learning Style Inventory was chosen precisely to describe the interdependent holistic relationship among the modes (generating considerable controversy about the resulting ipsativity of the data, to be discussed later in the Chapter 4 update). Miettinen has it backwards when he says, "The separateness of the phases and corresponding modes of learning are also based on the fact that the model is constructed to substantiate the validity of the learning style inventory. The construction of distinct styles makes it necessary to postulate distinct modes of adaptation. In this way the technological starting point partly dictates the mode and content of the 'theoretical' model" (2000, p. 61).

The conflicts between opposing dialectics help explain the dynamic nature of experience (Bassechess, 1984, 2005): as in Piaget's ongoing to-and-fro between assimilating experiences into existing concepts and accommodation of concepts to new experiences, or in Dewey's recursive uniting of desire and idea to form purpose. There may be pragmatic utility in organizing education around an idealized cycle that begins with concrete experience, is followed by reflection alone or with others, introducing concepts and theory to organize and conclude the meaning of the experience, and then concludes with action to test the conclusions in new experience. However, as learners, our experiences are seldom so orderly. In one moment we may be lost in thought only to be jolted to awareness of a dramatic event, sparking immediate action or cautious observation depending on our habit of learning. Our learning style may dictate where we begin a process of learning and/or the context may shape it. Learning usually does not happen in one big cycle but in numerous small cycles or partial cycles. Thinking and reflection can continue for some time before acting and experiencing. Experiencing and reflecting can also continue through much iteration before concluding in action.

The primary importance of reflection for learning and development is not emphasized. A number of important experiential learning theorists such as David Boud (Boud, Keogh, and Walker, 1985; Boud and Miller, 1996), Jack Mezirow (1990, 1996), Stephen Brookfield (1987, 1995), and Donald Schon (1983) place reflection as the primary source of the transformation that leads to learning and development. Unlike these advocates of reflective practice, reflection in experiential learning theory is not the sole determinant of learning and development but is one facet of a holistic process of learning from experience that includes experiencing, reflecting, thinking, and acting. As we have seen, the shock of direct concrete experience may be necessary to initiate it. Reflection in isolation can become retroflection, a turning in on itself that isolates the learners in their own self-confirming world unable to reach conclusions or test them in action. When reflection is structured in a critical theory framework, Kegan (1994) and Kayes (2002) have argued that it can have dysfunctional effects. "Critical approaches may help individuals gain insight into their social context, but this often leaves the individual stranded in a complex world without the appropriate tools to reorder this complexity. The newly 'emancipated' may experience more repression that ever as they become stripped of their own capacity to respond to new, more challenging demands that come with emancipation" (Kayes, 2002, p. 142).

Mary Parker Follett (1924) stresses the intimate relationship between experience, action, and reflection. "We often hear people talk of the interpretation of experience as if we first had an experience and then interpreted it, but there is a closer and different connection between these two; my behavior in that experience is as much a part of my interpretation as my reflection upon it afterwards; my intellectual, post-facto, reflective interpretation is only part of the story." Reflection also requires cognitive complexity and the capacity for critical thinking, the abstract conceptualization phase of the learning cycle. Deep reflection requires a rich and integrated cognitive structure to be able to adopt different perspectives and analytical strategies.

In experiential learning theory reflection is defined as the internal transformation of experience. This broad definition includes several more specific reflective processes that vary by learning style and developmental level. The three reflective learning styles in the KLSI 4.0 (Kolb and Kolb, 2011, 2013) define a continuum of reflection. The Imagining style is focused on iconic transformation of images that are still somewhat immersed in the concrete experiences of sensation and affect. At the other extreme is the Analyzing style, where reflection is more systematic manipulation of abstract symbols fully independent of experience and context. In between, the Reflecting style explores deeper meanings to integrate image and symbol.

The three stages of development in the experiential learning theory developmental frame work—acquisition, specialization, and integration each are characterized by different reflective processes. These processes have been articulated most clearly by Humphrey (2009) as reflection, reframing and reform.

- **Reflection.** Reflection at this elementary level constitutes spontaneous reflective observation of direct experiences. In Zull's depiction of experiential learning and the brain, direct sensory experiences are connected to memories, images and emotions in the temporal integrative cortex.

- **Reframing.** Dewey distinguished what he called casual spontaneous reflection at the first level from a more intense reflective process he called critical reflection (1933, p. 14). Critical reflection entails an examination and critique of reflective observations from specialized theories and analytic frameworks. The framework is used to examine assumption and reframe issues, adopting alternative perspectives that produce a deeper understanding. Critical reflection is often associated with critical theory (Brookfield, 1995, 2009) and post-structural deconstruction (Fook, 2002), frameworks for unmasking power manipulations and hidden forms of social control. However, other disciplined systems of inquiry, for example, aesthetics (Dewey, 1934; Rasanen, 1997), can also offer possibilities for reframing that produce creative new perspectives.

- **Reform.** Reflection at the integrative level, often referred to by Freire and others as praxis, integrates critical reflection with the full learning cycle producing a process whereby action is reformed by reflection and reflection is reformed and informed by action and its consequences in experience.

Is "Pure experience" impossible or necessary for learning? Another critique of the learning cycle is that there is no such thing as concrete experience independent from abstract theories and symbols (e.g., Holman, 1997; Miettinen, 2000; Seaman, 2008; Michelson, 1996; Fenwick, 2000, 2003). Indeed, it is axiomatic among contemporary cognitive theorists that all perception is influenced by cognitive schema. It is also true that the dialectic dimension of Concrete Experience/Abstract Conceptualization recognizes that experience and concept are usually related. James himself saw pure experience as the extreme pole of the dialectic, saying, "only new-born babes, or men in semi-coma from sleep, drugs, illnesses, or blows may be assumed to have an experience pure in the literal sense of a *that* which is not yet any definite *what*. . . . Its purity is only a relative term, meaning the proportional amount of un-verbalized sensation which it still embodies" (1912, 2010, p. 94).

Taylor and Wozniak in *Pure Experience* suggest that the idea of pure experience is foreign to Western thought: "The fact was, nothing in their history had prepared Western philosophers and psychologists for radical empiricism. As the reactions to his writings showed, it is exceptionally difficult to suspend our logical categories and see the immediate moment shorn of our labels of it. . . . Yet we have in James radical empiricism a position that goes right to the heart of the Western viewpoint, exposing its limits (Taylor and Wozniak, 1996, p. xxxi).

James' radical empiricism helps us to understand that all modes of the learning cycle are experiences—"If we take conceptual manifolds, or memories, or fancies, they also are in their first intention mere bits of pure experience" (1904, p. 483). "Pure" Concrete Experience is but one special form of experience—moment-to-moment, here-and-now consciousness: "the immediate flux of life which furnishes the material to our later reflection with its conceptual categories." Dewey call this "immediate empiricism" and agreed with James, radical empiricism that, "It is in the concrete thing *as experienced* that all the grounds and clues to its own intellectual and logical rectification are contained" (1905, p. 397).

As we saw in the Introduction Dewey saw that much experience was conservative, habitual "empirical experience" and required being "stuck" or a "shock" to provoke critical reflection and learning. In this he presaged contemporary research on automaticity, suggesting that conscious acts of self-regulation are rare and as much as 95 percent of behavior occurs automatically without them (Baumeister et al., 1998; Baumeister and Sommer, 1997; Bargh, J. A., and Chartrand, 1999). This insight is of profound importance for experiential learning. While many theorists described above, along with Dewey, have stressed that critical reflection is of primary importance for learning from experience, we see here that a concrete "pure" experience that violates the expectations of previous convictions and habits of thought is necessary to activate such reflection in the first place. This suggests that experience shorn of habit and cultural interpretation is necessary for learning anything new. Seaman goes further, ". . . evidence suggests that conscious reflection does not play a basic role in experiential learning as is widely believed: research in social practice" traditions show how people learn *in* experience not *from* or *after* it. . . . These findings . . . make the sentiment 'experience alone is not the key to learning' (Boud et al., 1985, p. 7) simply seem strange, if not misguided (2008, p. 11). While some learning probably occurs from empirical experience, it is probably the kind that reinforces previous conclusions or refines thought or behavior in small ways. For bigger changes such as overcoming addiction, we see that a "shock" that disrupts life is necessary.

There are, however, other ways beside "shock and awe" to strip a momentary concrete experience from its judgmental habitual biases. There are two deliberate learning practices for deep experiencing: focusing, derived from Carl Rogers' client-centered therapy, and mindfulness, derived from Eastern concepts of metaphysics and psychology.

Focusing

Rogers' nondirective therapy method brings awareness and trust of one's inner experience through the creation of a psychologically safe environment of unconditional positive regard. "As the client senses and realizes that he is prized as a person, he can slowly begin to value the different aspects of himself. Most importantly, he can begin with much difficulty at first, to sense and to feel what is going on within him, what he is feeling, what he is experiencing, how he is reacting. He uses his experiencing as a direct referent to which he can turn in forming accurate conceptualizations and as a guide to his behavior" (Rogers, 1964, p. 163). When Eugene Gendlin (1961, 1962) studied this kind of experiencing among clients of Rogerian and other forms of psychotherapy he discovered that assessments of a client's experiencing ability in the first two therapy sessions predicted success or failure of the therapy. Experiencing ability was more important than anything the therapist did in predicting outcomes. Gendlin calls this "focusing," an embodied way of experiencing that is beneath thought, language, and emotion. When this bodily sense comes to awareness, there is a physical change in the body, a felt shift that then can be analyzed and conceptualized. In *Focusing* (1978) he developed a six-step technique to help individuals learn how to engage in this kind of direct body experiencing.

Mindfulness

Taylor and Wozniak (1996) note that James' radical empiricism, while foreign to Western thinking, was highly compatible with Eastern metaphysics and psychology; giving the example of the Theraveda Buddhist image of moment consciousness as a string of pearls. The great Japanese Zen philosopher Kitaro Nishida (1911, 1990), who sought to integrate Eastern and Western thought, embraced James' radical empiricism, making pure experience the center of his life's work. While for James pure experience was a philosophical concept rarely experienced fully, for Nishida it was an experience to be lived fully and cultivated as a path to realization of an authentic, integrated humanity: "To experience means to know facts just as they are; to know in accordance with fact by completely relinquishing one's own fabrications. What we usually refer to as experience is adulterated with some sort of thought, so by pure I am referring to the state of experience just as it is, without the least addition of deliberative discrimination. The moment of seeing a color or hearing a sound, for example, is prior not only to the thought that the color or sound is the activity of an external object or that one is sensing it, but also to the judgment of what the color or sound might be. In this regard, pure experience is identical with direct experience. When one directly experiences one's own state of consciousness, there is not yet a subject or an object, and knowing and its object are completely united. This is the most refined type of experience" (1990, p. 3).

The practice of mindfulness aims to overcome automaticity and to reach direct, pure experience through mindful awareness and attention. A number of Western approaches to mindfulness have been developed in recent years. According to Kabat-Zinn, who created a medical program called mindfulness-based stress reduction, present moment experience is clouded by judgment and evaluation stemming from our needs and biases. It is "severely edited" by the habitual and unexamined activity of thoughts and emotions (2003, p. 148). We have lenses that we "slip unconsciously between observer and observed that filter and color, bend and shape our view" (1994, p. 54). Brown and Ryan (2003) quote William James who stated, "Compared to what we ought to be, we are only half awake." They go on to say, "Mindfulness captures a quality of consciousness that is characterized by clarity and vividness of current experience and functioning that stands in contrast to the mindless less 'awake' states of habitual or automatic functioning that may be chronic for many individuals" (2003, p. 823). In their definition, the mindful state involves flexible but stable awareness and attention, clear awareness, nonconceptual and nondiscriminatory perception, an empirically-oriented stance towards reality, and present-oriented consciousness.

The Learning Spiral

The learning cycle, of course, is not a circle but a spiral where, as T.S. Eliot reminds us, we return again to the experience and know it anew in a continuous recursive spiral of learning. It is this spiral of learning that embeds us in a co-evolution of mutually transforming transactions between ourselves and the world around us. The process is similar to Giddens' theory of structuration (1984, 1991), which describes a dialectic between social structure and human agency bringing a new emphasis on human agency to sociological theory. Giddens describes *The Constitution of Society* as an extended reflection on a quotation by Marx, "Men make history but not in circumstances of their own choosing" (1984, p. xxi). We are shaped and transformed by the physical, social, and historical forces in the world and at the same time have the capacity through our learning and actions to transform the world in an ongoing spiral of learning.

Learning and Life

The experiential learning spiral represents the highest culmination of a learning process that can be traced to the organization of life itself; one that even can be seen in nonliving physical systems. In his classic compilation of the ubiquitous presence of the spiral form in plants and animals of all kinds, Sir Theodore Cook (1914) argues that the spiral is a key to understanding the process of life and the living creations of the human mind. In his concluding chapter, he writes, "Throughout our investigations this idea of energy and growth under resistance seems consistently to be connected with the spiral, and we have found that idea recognized in the use of the spiral as a conventional decoration not only by the philosophers of ancient China but even by peoples as old as the Aurignacian civilization of 20,000 years ago. (408) . . . One of the chief beauties of the spiral as an imaginative conception is that it is always growing, yet never covering the same ground, so that it is not merely an explanation of the past, but is also a prophesy of the future; and while it defines and illuminates what has already happened, it is also leading constantly to new discoveries" (423). What a wonderful description of the learning process!

Humberto Maturana (1970) discovered the learning spiral in his search for the answer to his question "What is the organization of the living?" What is the pattern of organization that characterizes all living systems and distinguishes them from nonliving physical systems? His answer was that the organization of the nervous system of all living things was basically circular, that living systems are "organized in a closed circular process that allows for evolutionary change in a way the circularity is maintained but not for the loss of the circularity itself." So, a spiral. He called this process *autopoiesis*, which means "self-making," emphasizing the self-referential and self-organizing nature of the network of production processes that produce and transform one another in a continual process of self-making. The closure of the system creates boundaries that allow the system autonomy to shape its relationship with the world. Varela says, "Closure means that you actually shape what counts as information in the coupling you have with the world. Information is brought forth by the actual activity of the organism or a cognitive system embedded in the world" (Davis, 1995, pp. 28–29).

With his colleague Francisco Varela, Maturana proceeded to develop the systems theory of cognition arguing that cognition, the process of knowing, was identical with *autopoiesis*, the process of life (Maturana and Varela, 1980, 1987). Their definition of cognition, however, was more akin to the holistic concept of experiential learning than the popular definition of cognition as thinking. "The new concept of cognition, the process of knowing, is thus much broader than the concept of thinking. It involves perception, emotion, and action—the entire process of life. In the human realm cognition also includes language, conceptual thinking and all the other attributes of human consciousness. The general concept, however, does not necessarily involve thinking" (Capra, 1996, p. 175). In fact, Maturana and Varela argue that this new cognition is present in all living organisms, even those without brains or nervous systems.

Ryan and Deci further suggest that autopoiesis is the foundation of the autonomous self: "Thus, we attempt to place the idea of self back into biological perspective by acknowledging the continuity of our active phenomenal core with the coordinated and active nature of other entities with who we share the condition of life. We suggest that the phenomenal self has its roots in the very process from which organization unfolds. Although most animals lack awareness of individuality as such, they manifest an active organization of behavior. It is this organizational tendency that in evolutionary perspective represents the deep structure on which the sense of self and autonomy in humans is built" (2004, p. 471).

The way in which the *autopoietic* cognition is a learning process is further elaborated in the concept of structural coupling. Structural coupling defines the way a system interacts with its environment, recurrently renewing and recreating itself. The environment does not specify or direct structural changes in the organism because the system is self-referential and self-maintaining, but it triggers them. These structural changes produce changes in the future behavior of the system and its environment. Structural coupling describes the continuing path of the organism's structural changes over time and thus describes the course of the organism's learning and development. Figure 2.6 illustrates this *autopoietic* process in the life spiral of a shell. The spiral records the life history of the shell's path of growth around its self-referential spine. I have been inspired by these lowly mollusks and the beautiful result of their life and learning they leave behind.

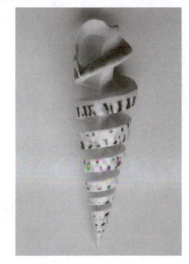

The order-creating and self-maintaining characteristics of life can also be seen in nonliving physical systems. The Belgian physicist and chemist Ira Prigogene won the Nobel Prize in Chemistry for his discovery of dissipative structures in physical systems. Dissipative structures arise in physical systems that are far from equilibrium

Figure 2.6   The Life Spiral of a Shell

introducing unique higher order structures, creating "order out of chaos" to quote the title of his famous book. His research caused a revision in the then-prevailing view based on the second law of thermodynamics that the universe was "winding down" and moving toward an ever increasing entropy. Dissipative structures are created in this disorder and maintain and increase their order and complexity at the expense of the disorder around them just as living systems do. Prigogene believed that the discovery of these parallels between living and nonliving systems could help overcome the separation of man from nature that was fostered by Newtonian physics.

Recently Davis and Sumara (1997) and Fenwick (2000, 2003) have introduced these ideas in what Fenwick calls the "co-emergence/enactivist perspective" on experiential learning. She describes this approach as one that explores how cognition and environment become simultaneously enacted through experiential learning. Davis and Sumara offer the example of Gadamer's concept of conversation (1965; Baker, Jensen, and Kolb, 2002) that suggests conversations are not predetermined as in a monologue but arise in the process of conversing. "Given its unspecifiable path, Gadamer suggests that it is more appropriate to think of the participants as *being led* by the conversation than as leading it. The conversation is something more than the actions of autonomous agents—in a sense it has us; we do not have it." Applied to education, they suggest that "the boundaries that currently define schools and universities be blurred so the relations between that which we call 'teaching' and that which we call 'learning' might be better understood as mutually specifying, co-emergent, pervasive and evolving practices that are at the core of our culture's efforts at self-organization and self-renewal" (1997, p. 110).

3

Structural Foundations of the Learning Process

Our intellectual process consists . . . in a rhythm of direct understanding—technically called apprehension—with indirect mediated understanding technically called comprehension.

—John Dewey, How We Think*

A term may be viewed in two ways, either as a class of objects . . . or as a set of attributes or characteristics which determine the objects. The first phase or aspect is called the denotation or extension of the term, while the second is called the connotation or intension. Thus the extension of the term "philosopher" is "Socrates," "Plato," "Thalus" and the like; its intension is "lover of wisdom," "intelligent" and so on. . . . Why a term is applied to a set of objects is indicated by its intension; the set of objects to which it is applicable constitutes its extension.

—Morris Cohen and Ernest Nagel
    Introduction to Logic and Scientific Method

The models of learning that were described in the last chapter provided tantalizing suggestions as to the nature of the learning process, but they also raise many important questions. How, for example, does one move through stages of the learning cycles described? Is this process identical for everyone? What determines how the dialectic conflicts between adaptive modes get resolved? With what consequences for learning and development? To answer these and other questions requires a more detailed examination and systematic formulation of the experiential learning process.

---

* John Dewey, *How We Think*, Lexington, MA: D.C. Heath Co., 1910. Reprinted with the permission of the Center for Dewey Studies, Southern Illinois University at Carbondale.

The approach taken in this chapter will be essentially structural. That is, the aim here is to identify the essential and enduring aspects of the learning process that determine its functioning, separating them from secondary, accidental aspects. In this sense, the structuralist approach seeks to draw the blueprints of how the "learning machine" functions ideally, not to document its actual functioning under varying conditions of circumstance, mood, culture, and the like. To achieve an adequate structural analysis of the learning process, we need to determine (1) its *holistic structure*, defining the interdependence of the internal components of the learning model without reliance on forces outside the model; (2) its *transformation process*, specifying the way in which structural components transact to maintain and elaborate themselves; and (3) its *process of self-regulation*, describing how the structural system maintains its identity and integrity (compare Piaget, 1968, p. 5).

In a sense, this analysis is already under way, for we have seen in the last chapter how the more phenomenological, descriptive models of learning described by Lewin and Dewey are enriched and corroborated by Piaget's structural dimensions of cognitive development—phenomenalism/constructivism and egocentricism/reflectivism. However, the model proposed in this chapter will deviate in some respects from Piaget's formulation. For Piaget, these two dimensions represent a developmental continuum, in which phenomenalism and egocentricism are lower forms of knowing than are constructivism and reflection. I will propose here that the poles of these two dimensions are equipotent modes of knowing that through dialectic transformations result in learning. This learning proceeds along a third, developmental dimension that represents not the dominance of one learning mode over another but the integration of the four adaptive modes.[1] We will have occasion to examine the details of the points of disagreement between my perspective and that of Piaget in the course of a more complete elaboration of the structure of experiential learning.

Process and Structure in Experiential Learning

As has been suggested, the process of experiential learning can be described as a four-stage cycle involving four adaptive learning modes—concrete experience, reflective observation, abstract conceptualization, and active experimentation. In this model, concrete experience/abstract conceptualization and active experimentation/reflective observation are two distinct dimensions, each representing two dialectically opposed adaptive orientations. The structural bases of the learning process lie in the transactions among these four adaptive modes and the way in which the adaptive dialectics get resolved. To

---

1. Those readers who are familiar with Piaget will already have noted this deviation from his linear idea of development in my description of the relationship between experiential learning and his model of development in Chapter 2. There I suggest an integrative developmental scheme by proposing that the stage of formal operations represents a return at a higher developmental level to the active orientation characteristic of stage 1.

■——

begin with, notice that the abstract/concrete dialectic is one of *prehension*, representing two different and opposed processes of grasping or taking hold of experience in the world—either through reliance on conceptual interpretation and symbolic representation, a process I will call *comprehension*, or through reliance on the tangible, felt qualities of immediate experience, what I will call *apprehension*. The active/reflective dialectic, on the other hand, is one of *transformation*, representing two opposed ways of transforming that grasp or "figurative representation" of experience—either through internal reflection, a process I will call *intention*, or active external manipulation of the external world, here called *extension*. These two dimensions of learning—*prehension* and *transformation*—correspond directly to Piaget's figurative and operative aspects of thought:[2]

> I shall begin by making a distinction between two aspects of thinking that are different, although complementary. One is the figurative aspect, and the other I call the operative aspect. The figurative aspect is an imitation of states taken as momentary and static. In the cognitive area the figurative functions are, above all, perception, imitation, and mental imagery, which is in fact interiorized imitation.
>
> The operative aspect of thought deals not with states but with transformations from one state to another. For instance, it includes actions themselves, which transform objects or states, and it also includes the intellectual operations, which are essentially systems of transformation. [Piaget, 1970, p. 14]

In the figurative aspects, perception and imitation correspond roughly to the apprehension process, and mental imagery corresponds to the comprehension process. For the operative aspect, there is a rough correspondence between action and the process of extension and between intellectual operations and the intention process.

With this brief overview of our structural perspective, we are now in a position to give more substance to the definition of learning proposed in the last chapter—namely, that learning is the process whereby knowledge is created through the transformation of experience. Knowledge results from the combination of grasping experience and transforming it (see Figure 3.1). And since there are two dialectically opposed forms of prehension and, similarly, two opposed ways of transforming that prehension, the result is four different elementary forms of knowledge. Experience grasped through apprehension and transformed through intention results in what will be called *divergent*

---

2. The concepts of prehension and transformation or figurative and operative aspects of thought have parallels in the computer modeling literature. For example, in Forrester's system-dynamics approach to model building, he distinguishes between rates and levels, specifying that in any model, rates can only directly influence levels and vice versa (Forrester, 1971). A level (e.g., population size at any given time) corresponds to the prehension or figurative aspect, and a rate (e.g., percent increase in a given time period) corresponds to the transformation or operative aspect.

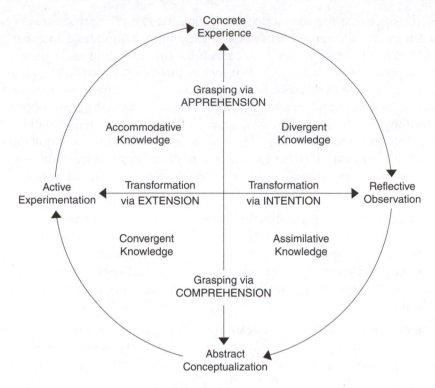

Figure 3.1 Structural Dimensions Underlying the Process of Experiential Learning and the Resulting Basic Knowledge Forms

knowledge. Experience grasped through comprehension and transformed through intention results in *assimilative* knowledge. When experience is grasped through comprehension and transformed through extension, the result is *convergent* knowledge. And finally, when experience is grasped by apprehension and transformed by extension, *accommodative* knowledge is the result. These elementary forms of knowledge, as will be shown in later chapters, become the building blocks for developmentally higher levels of knowing.

The central idea here is that learning, and therefore knowing, requires both a grasp or figurative representation of experience and some transformation of that representation. Either the figurative grasp or operative transformation alone is not sufficient. The simple perception of experience is not sufficient for learning; something must be done with it. Similarly, transformation alone cannot represent learning, for there must be something to be transformed, some state or experience that is being acted upon. This view is largely consistent with that of Piaget, although his work has tended to highlight the role of transformation processes over the prehension process, whereas I will seek in this exposition to give both aspects equal status (compare Piaget, 1970, pp. 14–15).

In what follows, we will examine evidence for the prehension and transformation dimensions of learning from three different perspectives—philosophy, psychology, and physiology. From these three fields there emerges a consistent picture of the structure and functioning of these two basic dimensions of the learning process.

The Prehension Dimension-Apprehension Versus Comprehension

That there are two distinct modes of grasping experience may not be readily apparent, but it is a fact that can be easily demonstrated with but a little effort. Pause in your reading for a moment and become aware of your surroundings. What you see, hear, and feel around you are those sensations, colors, textures, and sounds that are so basic and reliable that we call them reality. The continuous feel of your chair as it firmly supports your body, the smooth texture of the book and its pages, the muted mixture of sounds surrounding you—all these things and many others you know instantaneously without need for rational inquiry or analytical confirmation. They are simply there, grasped through a mode of knowing here called apprehension. Yet to describe these perceptions faithfully in words, as I have attempted here, is somewhat difficult. It is almost as though the words are vessels dipped in the sea of sensations we experience as reality, vessels that hold and give form to those sensations contained, while sensations left behind fade from awareness. The concept "chair," for example, probably describes where you are sitting (those of you in bed, standing in bookstore stalls, and so on notwithstanding). It is a convenient way to summarize a whole series of sensations you are having right now, although it tends to actively discourage attention to parts of that experience other than those associated with "chairness." The concept also ignores particular aspects of your chair that may be important to you, such as hardness or squeakiness.

In this sense, concepts and the associated mode of knowing called comprehension seem secondary and somewhat arbitrary ways of knowing. Through comprehension we introduce order into what would otherwise be a seamless, unpredictable flow of apprehended sensations, but at the price of shaping (distorting) and forever changing that flow. Yet knowing through comprehension has other qualities that have made it primary in human society—namely, that comprehensions of experience can be communicated and thereby transcend time and space. If you put down this book, get up from the chair, and leave the room, your apprehensions of that situation will vanish without trace (substituted for, of course, by new apprehensions of the hallway or whatever new immediate situation you are in). Your comprehension of that situation, however, will allow you to create for yourself and communicate to others a model of that situation that could last forever. Further, to the extent that the model was accurately constructed from your apprehensions, it allows you to predict and recreate those apprehensions. You can, for example, find again the comfortable chair you were sitting in, although if you did not attend to and comprehend the light source, you might not remember where the blue ceramic table lamp is. For these tremendous powers of communication, prediction, and control that symbolic comprehension brings, the loss of the nuance and security of raw apprehended experience seems a small price to pay. Yet, as Goethe notes in *Faust*, it is a price—"Gray are all theories, / And green alone Life's golden tree."

The relation between apprehension and comprehension has been an enduring philosophical concern. The philosophical distinction between these forms of knowing is perhaps best described by William James, whose *knowledge of acquaintance* and *knowledge-about* correspond to apprehension and comprehension respectively. The following quotation describes James' view of these two kinds of knowledge:

> *There are two kinds of knowledge* broadly and practically distinguishable: We may call them respectively *knowledge of acquaintance* and *knowledge-about*. Most languages express the distinction; thus, γνῶναι εἰδέναι; noscere, scire; kennen, wissen; connâitre, savoir. I am acquainted with many people and things, which I know very little about, except their presence in the places where I have met them. I know the color blue when I see it, and the flavor of a pear when I taste it; I know an inch when I move my finger through it; a second of time, when I feel it pass; an effort of attention when I make it; a difference between two things when I notice it; but *about* the inner nature of these facts or what makes them what they are, I can say nothing at all. I cannot impart acquaintance with them to anyone who has not already made it himself. I cannot *describe* them, make a blind man guess what blue is like, define to a child a syllogism, or tell a philosopher in just what respect distance is just what it is, and differs from other forms of relation. At most, I can say to my friends, Go to certain places and act in certain ways, and these objects will probably come. All the elementary natures of the world, its highest genera, the simple qualities of matter and mind, together with the kinds of relation that subsist between them, must either not be known at all, or known in this dumb way of acquaintance without *knowledge-about*. In minds able to speak at all there is, it is true, some knowledge about everything. Things can at least be classed, and the times of their appearance told. But in general, the less we analyze a thing, and the fewer of its relations we perceive, the less we know about it and the more our familiarity with it is of the acquaintance-type. . . . We can relapse at will into a mere condition of acquaintance with an object by scattering our attention and staring at it in a vacuous trance-like way. We can ascend to knowledge *about* it by rallying our wits and proceeding to notice and analyze and think. What we are only acquainted with is only present to our minds; we *have* it, or the idea of it. But when we know about it, we do more than merely have it; we seem, as we think over its relations, to subject it to a sort of *treatment* and to *operate* upon it with our thought. The words *feeling* and *thought* give voice to the antithesis. Through feelings we become acquainted with things, but only by our thoughts do we know about them. Feelings are the germ and starting point of cognition, thoughts the developed tree. . . . The men-

tal states usually distinguished as feelings are the *emotions*, and the *sensations* we get from skin, muscle, viscus, eye, ear, nose, and palate. The "thoughts," as recognized in popular parlance, are the *conceptions* and *judgments*. [James, 1890, Vol. I, pp. 221–22]

Similar distinctions are made by Bertrand Russell (1912), Herbert Feigl (1958), and G.E. Moore, who describes two forms of actualized knowledge that parallel the apprehension and comprehension processes of grasping experience—apprehension (in direct and indirect forms) and knowledge proper (Klemke, 1969). Perkins distinguishes knowledge gained from physical concept formation and theory construction (comprehension) from what he calls "internal whatlike understanding" (apprehension), a process he defines as "that understanding of an experience that consists in knowing what an experience is like; and we know what an experience is like by virtue of having that experience" (1971, pp. 3–4). Whitehead distinguishes between two kinds of perception: perception by causal efficacy, in which one sees objects in terms of what can be done with them (comprehension), and perception by presentational immediacy, where one sees patches of color and hears patterns of sound (apprehension). Magrite seems to be expressing the dual knowledge idea in *Les Idées Claires* (see Figure 3.2). Similarly, Pepper (1966, p. 68) distinguishes between conceptual knowledge and felt qualities.

Pepper and Feigl use the distinction between these two forms of grasping experience to propose a solution to a perennial question of philosophy—the mind-body problem. Feigl suggests that there are dual languages referring to the two forms of knowing: phenomenal language, referring to felt qualities of experience (apprehension), and physical language, referring to descriptive symbols (comprehension). Basing their ideas on research in neurophysiology, Pepper and Feigl maintained that the physical and phenomenal languages refer to the same thing—namely, the object of acquaintance directly referred to in phenomenal language. Feigl puts his mind-body identity thesis this way:

> The identity thesis which I wish to clarify and defend asserts that the states of direct experience which conscious human beings "live through," and those which we confidently ascribe to some of the higher animals, are identical with certain (presumably configurational) aspects of the neural processes in those organisms. To put the same idea in the terminology explained previously, we may say what is *had-in-experience*, and (in the case of human beings) *knowable by acquaintance*, is identical with the object of *knowledge by description* provided first by molar behavior theory and this in turn is identical with what the science of neurophysiology *describes* (or, rather, will describe when sufficient progress has been achieved) as processes of the central nervous system, perhaps especially in the cerebral cortex. In its basic core this is a double knowledge theory. [Feigl, 1958, p. 446]

Since Feigl published that paragraph in 1958, research in neurophysiology has advanced greatly, providing enticing new evidence for the "double knowledge" theory. Recent

Figure 3.2 René Magritte, *Les Idées Claires (Clear Ideas)*

research on the specialized functions of the left and right hemispheres of the neocortex has the most relevance for the distinction between apprehension and comprehension as dialectically opposed modes for grasping reality. The origins of this work stem from the research and clinical observation of Roger Sperry and his colleagues in the early 1960s (Sperry, Gazzaniga, and Bogen, 1969). They studied the behavior of so-called split-brain patients who, in order to relieve the frequency and severity of epileptic seizures, had undergone surgical division of the *corpus callosum*, a complex bundle of neural fibers connecting the left and right hemispheres of the neocortex. These patients as a result possessed two relatively normal hemispheres whose functions could be separately identified. The resulting studies produced results that are at odds with conventional and ancient wisdom about brain function. Until that time, it had been assumed that it was the left hemisphere that was responsible for all cognitive functioning worthy of the name—consciousness, verbal reasoning, analytic ability, and so on. The right hemisphere was thought to be something of a cerebral spare tire, a nonconscious automaton whose function was only to transmit information to the executive left hemisphere. Sperry showed that this was not the case. In fact, the right hemisphere was superior to the left in its functioning on some tasks, such as the visual construction required in drawing.

It is worth describing some of these split-brain studies to illustrate how dramatic the results were. Since the left hemisphere controls vision in the right visual field and the right hand, while the right hemisphere controls the left visual field and the left hand (see Figure 3.3), it was possible to do experiments that gave information on problems to only

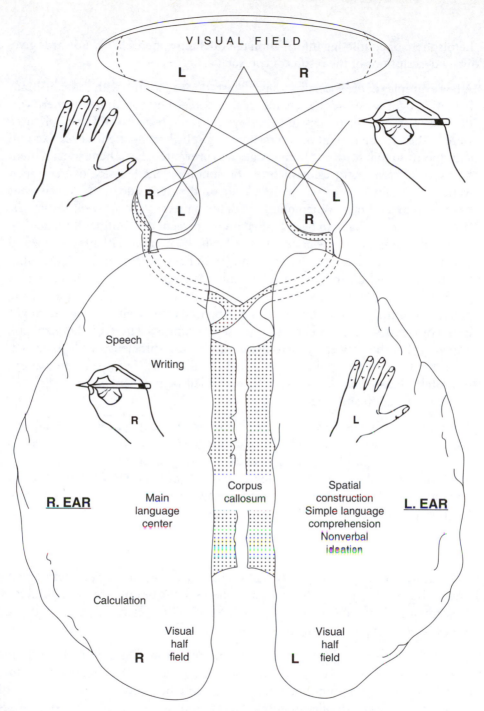

Figure 3.3 A Schematic Representation of the Functions of the Two Hemispheres of the Neocortex. The Right and Left Visual Fields Are Projected, Respectively, onto the Left and Right Occipital Lobes. Control of the Right and Left Sides of the Body Is Similarly Crossed, as is, Mainly, Hearing.

one hemisphere or conflicting information to both hemispheres. Betty Edwards gives the following descriptions of the results of two such experiments:

> A few examples of the specially designed tests devised for use with the split-brain patients might illustrate the separate reality perceived by each hemisphere and the special modes of processing employed. In one test two different pictures were flashed for an instant on a screen, with a split-brain patient's eyes fixed on a midpoint so that scanning both images was prevented. Each hemisphere, then, received *different* pictures. A picture of a spoon on the left side of the screen went to the right brain; a picture of a knife on the right side of the screen went to the verbal left brain. When questioned, the patients gave *different* responses. If asked to *name* what had been flashed on the screen, the confidently articulate left hemisphere caused the patient to say, "knife." Then the patient was asked to reach behind a curtain with his left hand (right hemisphere) and pick out what had been flashed on the screen. The patient then picked out a spoon from a group of objects that included a spoon and a knife. If the experimenter asked the patient to identify what he held in his hand behind the curtain, the patient might look confused for a moment and then say, "a knife." The right hemisphere, knowing that the answer was wrong but not having sufficient words to correct the articulate left hemisphere, continued the dialogue by causing the patient to mutely shake his head. At that, the verbal left hemisphere wondered aloud, "Why am I shaking my head?"
>
> In another test that demonstrated the right brain to be better at spatial problems, a male patient was given several wooden shapes to arrange to match a certain design. His attempts with his right hand (left hemisphere) failed again and again. His right hemisphere kept trying to help. The right hand would knock the left hand away; and finally, the man had to sit on his left hand to keep it away from the puzzle. When the scientists finally suggested that he use both hands, the spatially "smart" left hand had to shove the spatially "dumb" right hand away to keep it from interfering. [Edwards, 1979, pp. 30–31]

Further research with split-brain patients and later with normal subjects reinforced and elaborated the conclusion that the two hemispheres of the brain were specialized for two different modes of consciousness—the two different modes of knowing about the world that we are calling apprehension and comprehension.

Edwards (1979) has summarized the results of these studies in Figure 3.4. Left-mode functioning corresponds to the comprehension process. It is abstract, symbolic, analytical, and verbal. It functions in a linear sequential manner much like a digital computer. The right-mode function, corresponding to the apprehension process, is concrete, holistic, and spatial. Its functioning is analogic and synthetic, drawing together likenesses among things to recognize patterns. These different orientations to

L— MODE	R—MODE
Verbal: Using words to name, describe, define.	**Nonverbal:** Awareness of things, but minimal connection with words.
Analytic: Figuring things out step-by-step and part-by-part.	**Synthetic:** Putting things together to form wholes.
Symbolic: Using a symbol to *stand for* something. For example, the drawn form  ◑ stands for *eye*, the sign + stands for the process of addition.	**Concrete:** Relating to things as they are, at the present moment.
Abstract: Taking out a small bit of information and using it to represent the whole thing.	**Analogic:** Seeing likenesses between things; understanding metaphoric relationships.
Temporal: Keeping track of time, sequencing one thing after another: Doing first things first, second things second, etc.	**Nontemporal:** Without a sense of time.
Rational: Drawing conclusions based on *reason* and *facts*.	**Nonrational:** Not requiring a basis of reason or facts; willingness to suspend judgment.
Digital: Using numbers as in counting.	**Spatial:** Seeing where things are in relation to other things, and how parts go together to form a whole.
Logical: Drawing conclusions based on logic: one thing following another in logical order—for example, a mathematical theorem or a well-stated agrument.	**Intuitive:** Making leaps of insight, often based on incomplete patterns, hunches, feelings or visual images.
Linear: Thinking in terms of linked ideas, one thought directly following another, often leading to a convergent conclusion.	**Holistic:** Seeing whole things all at once; perceiving the overall patterns and structures, often leading to divergent conclusions.

Figure 3.4   A Comparison of Left-Mode and Right-Mode Characteristics
Source: Betty Edwards, *Drawing on the Right Side of the Brain* (Los Angeles: J. P. Tarcher, 1979)

prehension of the world are apparent in many human activities. In music, for instance, the left hemisphere governs the ability to read music, but it is the right hemisphere with its holistic pattern recognition sense that controls the ability to recognize, appreciate, and remember melodies. The left hemisphere is specialized for understanding language communication, but it is the right hemisphere that is most adept at nonverbal understanding, such as recognizing facial expressions (Benton, 1980), emotion, and so on. It is not the assumed anatomical location of the functions identified by this research that is primary, for this is currently highly speculative, but their description and recognition as representative of the dual-knowledge epistemology of experiential learning.

The hemisphere-dominance research provides compelling evidence for the theory that there are two distinct, coequal, and dialectically opposed ways of understanding the world. There is similar psychological evidence as well. In a recent *American Psychologist* article entitled, "Feeling and Thinking: Preferences Need No Inferences," Robert Zajonc (1980) summarizes evidence from the early studies of Wilhelm Wundt to his own present-day research indicating that feeling and thinking are separate processes. He further argues that affective responses are primary. Contrary to the accepted psychological doctrine that affective attributes are the result of cognitive analysis, Zajonc shows that in some cases, affective judgment occurs before cognitive analysis. These findings suggest a basis for that mysterious process we call intuition—namely, that intuitive behavior is guided by affective judgment (the apprehension process) rather than cognitive judgment. For example, in one of his experimental studies, he showed that subjects were able to distinguish between old and new stimuli flashed for very short periods of time on the basis of affective judgment (like/dislike) before they were able to directly identify the stimuli as old and new. Zajonc suggests that cognitive judgments are based on *discriminando*, the specific, analyzable, component features of a stimulus, whereas affective judgments are based on *preferenda*, which are more configural, vague, and global aspects of the stimulus.

> . . . the separation being considered here is between an affective and a cognitive system—a separation that distinguishes between *discriminanda* and preferenda and that takes us back to Wundt and Bartlett, who speculated that the overall impression or attitude has an existence of its own, independent of the components that contributed to its emergence. The question that cannot be answered with the data thus far collected is whether the affect-content separation is simply a matter of separate storage . . . or whether there isn't some separation already at the point of registration and encoding. The rapid processing times of affect suggest a more complete separation of the two processes at several junctures.

One is necessarily reminded in this context of the dual coding hypothesis proposed by Paivio (1975) for the processing of pictures and words. Paivio (1978a) suggested a number of differences between the processing of these types of content, for example, that representations of pictures emerge as perceptual isomorphs or analogs (imagens), whereas parallel units in the verbal system are linguistic components (logogens). He also proposed that pictorial information is organized in a synchronous and spatially parallel manner, whereas verbal information is discrete and sequential. Finally, he suggested that the processing of pictures is more likely to be the business of the right-brain hemisphere, whereas the processing of words is the business of the left. [Zajonc, 1980, p. 168]

The view that concrete apprehension processes are coequal with comprehension processes represents a dramatic change from that of the 1940's. Early research on brain damage viewed concreteness as a deficit, an indicator of brain damage (Goldstein and Scheerer, 1941). Piaget's work represents an intermediate position, considering concrete apprehension processes to be a sign of the young brain and immature thought. Now the theory of dual prehension processes has gained great credibility, based particularly on the hemisphere specialization research. It has been the basis for sharp critiques of the domination of comprehensive left-mode thinking throughout our society, particularly in education (Bogen, 1975). The process of apprehension as a mode of grasping experience and understanding the world is gaining scientific respectability, confirming the long-standing artistic recognition of these powers:

> *Lovers and madmen have such seething brains*
> *Such shaping fantasies, that apprehend*
> *More than cool reason ever comprehends.*
> *The lunatic, the lover and the poet*
> *Are of imagination all compact. . . .*

—William Shakespeare
   A Midsummer Night's Dream[3]

The Transformation Dimension-Intention and Extension

Although they are logical terms, and have thus been applied primarily to the symbolic processes of comprehension, I have chosen the terms *intention*[4] and *extension* to represent the basic transformation processes of learning as they apply to both the apprehensive and comprehensive modes of grasping experience. The dialectic nature of these dual transformation processes and their synergetic role in the creation of meaning has long been an accepted foundation of logical inquiry and the study of signs and symbols, the field of semiotics. The two major branches of semiotics—syntactics and semantics—correspond respectively to the study of the intentional formal characteristics of symbols and the extensional denotation of signs and symbols—that is, the objects in the world that signs and symbols refer to. The computer scientist Douglas Hofstadter describes

---

3. Shakespeare seemed fascinated with the distinction between apprehension and comprehension as two ways of knowing. Use of these terms is sprinkled appropriately throughout his works, including the humorous misuse of the distinction when the constable in *Much Ado About Nothing* reports, "Our watch, sir, have indeed comprehended two aspicious persons."

4. The spelling is changed here from the logical term intension to include the broader psychological as well as logical meanings of intention (e.g., intent, purpose, meaning).

the difference between these two processes and the central role that intention plays in thinking:

> Not all descriptions of a person need be attached to some central symbol for that person, which stores the person's name. Descriptions can be manufactured and manipulated in themselves. We can invent nonexistent people by making descriptions of them; we can merge two descriptions when we find they represent a single entity; we can split one description into two when we find it represents two things, not one—and so on. The "calculus of descriptions" is at the heart of thinking. It is said to be *intensional* and not *extensional*, which means that descriptions can "float" without being anchored down to specific, known objects. The intensionality of thought is connected to its flexibility, it gives us the ability to imagine hypothetical worlds, to amalgamate different descriptions or chop one description into separate pieces, and so on. . . . Fantasy and fact intermingle very closely in our minds, and this is because thinking involves the manufacture and manipulation of complex descriptions, which need in no way be tied down to real events or things. [Hofstadter, 1979, pp. 338–39]

What I propose here is that the transformation processes of intention and extension can be applied to our concrete apprehensions of the world as well as to our symbolic comprehensions. We learn the meaning of our concrete immediate experiences by internally reflecting on their presymbolic impact on our feelings, and/or by acting on our apprehended experience and thus extending it. Take, for example, the rose lying on my desk. I transform my apprehension of the rose intentionally by deploying my attention to its different aspects, noting the delicate pink color that is not solid but alternates subtly from white to a deeper rose. I sense its delicate fragrance and experience a blossoming of brief reminiscences. Here I cannot resist the impulse to transform the experience extensionally, to pick up the rose and hold it to my nose. In so doing, I prick my finger on the thorny stem and extend my apprehension of this rose still further. Now this new extended apprehension further stimulates my internal reflections and feelings. . . .

Learning, the creation of knowledge and meaning, occurs through the active extension and grounding of ideas *and* experiences in the external world and through internal reflection about the attributes of these experiences and ideas. As Yeats put it, "The human soul is always moving outward into the external world and inward into itself, and this movement is double because the human soul would not be conscious were it not suspended between contraries. The greater the contrast, the more intense the consciousness."

As previously indicated, the conception that extension and intention are the basic transformation processes in learning is largely consistent with Piaget's emphasis on the operative aspects of thought, which he divides into behavioral actions (extension) that transform objects or states, and intellectual operations (intention) that are internalized actions or systems of transformation (see Piaget, 1971, p. 67). It should be noted that Piaget seems to associate extensional transformation (individual actions) primarily with concrete apprehensions of the world, whereas intentional transformation (reflective abstraction) is reserved for logical and mathematical knowledge. This is perhaps a function of his focus on child development, where we see as the child matures that reflection and abstraction together do replace overt action and concrete apprehension. In addition, Piaget's tendency to view transformation by reflective abstraction as superior to overt action transformation also reflects this developmental focus. It will be argued here, however, that although the figurative and operative aspects develop together in childhood, in the mature adult the two dimensions are independent, producing four equipotent combinations of prehension and transformation (see Chapter 6, pp. 199–205).

In this sense, the transformation dimension is perhaps best described by the concepts of introversion (intention) and extraversion (extension), the primary concepts in the theory of types developed by Carl Jung:

> . . . one could describe the introverted standpoint as one that under all circumstances sets the self and the subjective psychological process above the object and the objective process, or at any rate holds its ground against the object. This attitude, therefore, gives the subject a higher value than the object. As a result, the object always possesses a lower value; it has secondary importance; occasionally it even represents merely an outward objective token of a subjective content, the embodiment of an idea in other words, in which, however, the idea is the essential factor; or it is the object of a feeling, where, however, the feeling experience is the chief thing, and not the object in its own individuality. The extroverted standpoint, on the contrary, sets the subject below the object, whereby the object receives the predominant value. The subject always has secondary importance; the subjective process appears at times merely as a disturbing or superfluous accessory to objective events. It is plain that the psychology resulting from these antagonistic standpoints must be distinguished as two totally different orientations. The one sees everything from the angle of his conception, the other from the viewpoint of the objective occurrence.
>
> These opposite attitudes are merely opposite mechanisms—a diastolic going out and seizing of the object, and a systolic concentration and release of energy from the object seized. Every human being possesses both mechanisms as an expression of his natural life-rhythm. . . . [Jung, 1923, pp. 12–13]

In this original conception, Jung laid great emphasis on the epistimological aspects of introversion and extraversion. He saw in the distinction the psychological underpinning of the philosophical debate between *nominalism*, the view that universals and ideas exist in name only, and *realism*, the doctrine that universals have a real objective existence. For Jung, truth lay neither in the nominalist or realist positions but in the dynamic integration of the introverted and extraverted attitudes:

> Every logico-intellectual formulation, however embracing it may be, divests the objective impression of its living and immediate quality. It must do this in order to reach any formulation whatsoever. But, in so doing, just that is lost which to the extraverted attitude seems absolutely essential, namely, the relationship to the real object. No possibility exists, therefore, that we shall find upon the line of either attitude any satisfactory and reconciling formula. And yet man cannot remain in this division—even if his mind could—for this discussion is not merely a matter of remote philosophy; it is the daily repeated problem of the relations of man to himself and to the world. And, because this at bottom is the problem at issue, the division cannot be resolved by a discussion of nominalist and realist arguments. For its solution a third, intermediate standpoint is needed. To the "*esse in intellectu*" tangible reality is lacking; to the "esse in re" the mind.
>
> Idea and thing come together, however, in the psyche of man, which holds the balance between them. What would the idea amount to if the psyche did not provide its living value? What would the objective thing be worth if the psyche withheld from it the determining force of the sense impression? What indeed is reality if it is not a reality in ourselves, an "esse in anima?" Living reality is the exclusive product neither of the actual, objective behavior of things, nor of the formulated idea; rather does it come through the gathering up of both in the living psychological process, through the "esse in anima." Only through the specific vital activity of the psyche does the sense-perception attain that intensity, and the idea that effective force, which are the two indispensable constituents of living reality. [Jung, 1923, p. 68]

In proposing *esse in anima* as the dialectic integration of *esse in re* and *esse in intellectu*, Jung was at great pains to assert the reality of the internal world of ideas and fantasy, placing it in an equal or perhaps even superior status with the demonstrable reality of the external world. He saw, in his time, that both the church and modern science had fostered attitudes that denied the reality of the inner world in favor of objective, publicly confirmable external events and objects. For the basic dialectic of introversion and extraversion to work, however, internal experience could not merely be reflections of the external world. The assertion of the validity and independent status of internal experiences in the face of the powerful social forces denying them was to become a central mission of Jung's work, reflected in his later inquiries into mysticism, alchemy, and religion for the fundamental symbols or archetypes that constitute what he called the collective unconscious. Jung defined these archetypes as "active living dispositions, ideas in the Platonic sense, that preform and continually influence our thoughts, feelings, and actions" (Read et al. eds., 1961–1967, Vol. 8, p. 154). For Jung, the role of personal experience was to actualize the potential that existed in the archetypes born within each and every living individual, inherited in the same way that physical characteristics are. By thus developing and playing our archetypes in personal life experiences, one achieved individuation or self-actualization by realizing one's genetic potential. Personal development was not the result of accumulated life experiences that shaped the personality (the Freudian/behaviorist view), but rather resulted from the interaction of internal subjective archetypical potentials and external circumstance.

I have included original excerpts from Jung here because as successive generations of researchers have explored introversion and extraversion, a kind of conceptual "genetic drift" has taken place, such that Jung's original epistomological concerns and his conception of the dialectic relationship between introversion and extraversion has been lost. Psychometricians have consistently conceived of introversion/extraversion (I/E) as a single dimension in spite of Jung's clear conception of introversion and extraversion as independent entities in dialectic opposition (for example, Eaves and Eysenck, 1975). Most research studies have been unable to demonstrate a single I/E factor, and this has often been considered evidence for doubting the validity of the concept (Carrigan, 1960) rather than as a failure to properly operationalize it. What these studies do show is that at least two independent factors are required to account for the intercorrelations between I/E variables. One factor, emphasizing the strengths of introversion skills, seems to coincide with the common European view of the dimension, with its emphasis on impulsiveness and weak-superego controls in the extravert; the other, emphasizing the positive skills of the extravert, fits the American conception that views extraverts as sociable and comfortable in interpersonal relations. Although both these conceptions reflect meaningful aspects of introversion and extraversion, I prefer to think of them as secondary to the basic epistemological dynamics emphasized by Jung, at least for the present purposes of inquiry about learning.

Another facet of the psychological perspective on the processes of intention and extension is provided by a contemporary of Jung's, Hermann Rorschach. The creator of the famous ink-blot projective test developed a measure of subjects' responses to the test that he called *experience balance*. This measure is the ratio of responses to the test that are judged to be determined by the colors of the ink, divided into those responses that describe movement (for instance, two dancing women). Those persons labeled *extratensive* by Rorschach, with a ratio favoring color, are said to be outwardly oriented, by virtue of their responsiveness to objective reality—color stimuli present in the blots. The perception of movement, on the other hand, has no corresponding external reality, and thus requires an intervening subjective process. Consequently, *intratensive* subjects, with a preponderance of movement responses, are described as having a more active "inner life" and less concern with external, objective reality.

Although Rorschach (1951) denied any relation between his experience balance concept and Jung's extraversion-introversion, the two viewpoints seem to have much in common (compare Bash, 1955). Rorschach's distinction between objective and subjective orientation is the crux of Jung's theory, and descriptions of the two Rorschach "experience types" are remarkably like Jung's characterizations of the extravert and introvert. Moreover, evidence from several studies indicates that some of the empirical differences between extratensive and intratensive subjects correspond to hypothesized or observed differences between extraverts and introverts. Intratensives are more cognitively complex than extratensives (Bieri and Messerley, 1957); they are more imaginative, have more active fantasy lives, and are more capable of motor inhibition (Singer, Wilensky, and McCraven, 1956); they have few doubts "that the self is a reasonably stable basis from which experience may be interpreted" (Palmer, 1956, p. 209; compare Mann, 1956; Singer and Spohn, 1954).

The contemporary work of Jerome Kagan adds further insights into the dynamics of intention and extension. His research on cognitive processes in children has identified a dimension that he calls impulsivity-reflection. This dimension, which he defines as "the degree to which the subject reflects on the validity of his solution hypothesis" (Kagan and Kogan, 1970, p. 1309), is very similar to the European view of introversion in its tendency to emphasize the positive skills of introversion, impulse control, and reflection. Kagan has used several tests to assess this dimension, the most common of which is the Matching Familiar Figures Test. This test asks the child to select one figure from a group of six that is identical with a given standard. Impulsive children tend to make more errors and respond more quickly on this task than do reflective children. Kagan finds that reflection increases with age from 5 to 11 years; that people have fairly stable dispositions toward impulsivity or reflection over time—that is, they maintain their position on this dimension relative to their age mates; and that a given person's tendency to be reflective or impulsive generalizes across different kinds of tasks. Kagan also finds, however, that people modify their orientations as a function of environmental demands; that is, when they are encouraged to take their time and be sure of answers, reflection increases (Kagan and Kogan, 1970). His interpretation of these and other findings suggests that impulsive and reflective people have different underlying motivational dynamics:

> . . . the greater the fear of making a mistake, the more reflective and cautious the performance. Minimal anxiety over a potentially inaccurate answer is likely to be a primary determinant of an impulsive performance. Reflectives seem to be overly concerned with making a mistake and wish to avoid error at all costs. Impulsives seem minimally apprehensive about error and consequently respond quickly. It will be recalled that impulsive subjects did not scan all the alternatives before offering a solution hypothesis and reported words they did not hear in a serial recall procedures. [Kagan and Kogan, 1970, pp. 13–14]

Thus, those with an orientation toward extensional transformation are primarily concerned with maximizing success, with little concern about failure or error. Being oriented toward intentional transformation is associated with primary concern about avoiding failure and error and a willingness to sacrifice opportunities for successful performance in order to do so. The differences in these two definitions of successful performance are not only useful for understanding the behavior of children; they also shed light on basic conflicts between intentional and extensional orientations in the adult world. Many of the conflicts between science and government or between professionals and academics have their origin in these differences. The scientist, for example, seeks the best approximation of absolute truth and is socialized to avoid "irresponsible" errors, whereas the politician is perpetually faced with the imperative of action under uncertainty. Here, doing something takes priority over doing what is ideal.

As with the prehension modes of apprehension and comprehension, there is evidence, although more tentative, of physiological bases for the transformation modes of intention and extension. Whereas the control of prehension modes seems to reside primarily in the left and right hemispheres of the neocortex, Bogen (in press) has suggested that transformation processes may be reflected in a front-to-back placement in the brain: "If there is a manipulative (extension) vs. perceptual (intention) gradient in the brain, it is more likely from front to back than from left to right." Other evidence suggests that orientations toward intention and extension are associated with changes in the limbic system, driven primarily by the arousal of parasympathetic and sympathetic nervous systems. The sympathetic nervous system is considered to have a generally mobilizing function in preparation for action and coping with the external world, whereas the parasympathetic nervous system is thought to work toward the person's protection, conservation, and relaxation when dealing with the external world is not required. These two portions of the limbic systems are somewhat independent but frequently are in competition, so that a person's extensional or intentional orientation would be a function of the joint momentary activity of the two systems.

The effect of the activation or inhibition of these two systems on performance and learning is illustrated by Broverman et al.'s (1968) review of the effects of drug-induced arousal or inhibition of these two systems. From their literature review of the effects of drugs on performance, they concluded that those substances that increased the organism's level of activation (extensional orientation), either by stimulating the sympathetic nervous system or by depressing the functioning of the parasympathetic system, result in increased effectiveness in dealing with simple perceptual-motor tasks such as visual acuity or reading and writing speed, but result in poorer performance on more complex perceptual restructuring tasks that require inhibition of action and higher-order thought processes. Those substances that tended to increase the organism's level of inhibition (intentional orientation) by depressing sympathetic nervous system functioning or by stimulating parasympathetic functioning produce the reverse pattern—poorer performance on the simple tasks and improved performance on the complex tasks. This symmetrical but rather complex pattern of results is portrayed in Table 3.1.

Table 3.1 The Effects of Stimulation and Depression of Sympathetic and Parasympathetic Nervous Systems on Simple Perceptual-Motor and Perceptual-Restructuring Task Performances

	Increased Activation (extensional orientation)		Increased Inhibition (intentional orientation)	
	Sympathetic Stimulation	Para-sympathetic Depression	Sympathetic Depression	Para-sympathetic Stimulation
Simple perceptual-motor tasks	Improvement	Improvement	Impairment	Impairment
Perceptual-restructuring tasks	Impairment	Impairment	Improvement	Improvement

Source: Donald Broverman et al., "Roles of Activation and Inhibition in Sex Differences in Cognitive Abilities, *Psychological Review* 75 (1968), pp. 23–50.

Overall, the evidence suggests that it is not the sympathetic/and/parasympathetic nervous systems alone that determine the individual's orientation toward intentional or extensional transformation of experience, but that these systems are major forces in determining a holistic pattern of psychological and physiological processes governing the person's orientation toward action or reflection. Arthur Diekman has described these two orientations as an action mode and a receptive mode of consciousness. He describes the components of these two holistic orientations as follows:

> The action mode is a state organized to manipulate the environment. The striate muscle system and the sympathetic nervous system are the dominant physiological agencies. The EEG shows beta waves, and baseline muscle tension is increased. The principle psychological manifestations of this state are focal attention, object-based logic, heightened boundary perception, and the dominance of formal characteristics over the sensory; shapes and meanings have a preference over colors and textures. The action mode is a state of striving, oriented toward achieving personal goals that range from nutrition to defense to obtaining social rewards, plus a variety of symbolic and sensual pleasures, as well as the avoidance of a comparable variety of pain. . . .

> In contrast, the receptive mode is a state organized around intake of the environment rather than manipulation. The sensory-perceptual system is the dominant agency rather than the muscle system, and parasympathetic functions tend to be most prominent. The EEG tends toward alpha waves, and baseline muscle tension is decreased. Other attributes of the receptive mode are diffuse attending, paralogical thought processes, decreased boundary perception, and the dominance of the sensory over the formal. [Diekman, 1971, p. 481]

With Jung, Diekman argues that the action mode has come to dominate the reflection mode in human society. The obvious survival value of orienting toward and coping with the external environment tends to overshadow the values of perception and experiencing, in the receptive mode, an orientation that tends to be commonly associated with infancy, passivity, and regression. This domination is particularly prominent in Western technological societies, whereas Eastern cultures have tended to give more emphasis to the receptive mode and have developed reflective adaptive skills highly in such disciplines as yoga and Zen meditation. Certain forms of yoga can develop demonstrable voluntary control over parasympathetically controlled processes such as heartbeat and respiration rate. Currently, there is great interest in developing introverted reflective functioning by using yogic meditative activities and other Eastern disciplines, such as the martial arts, as well as such Western technological variations as biofeedback, to cope with the stress and tension created by the overemphasis on the extraverted action mode and its attendant arousal of the sympathetic nervous system (for example, Ornstein, 1972).

Summary

This chapter has reported a convergence of evidence from the fields of philosophy, psychology, and physiology describing two basic structural dimensions of the learning process. The first is a prehension dimension that includes two dialectically opposed modes of grasping experience, one via direct apprehension of immediate concrete experience, the other through indirect comprehension of symbolic representations of experience. The second is a transformation dimension, which includes two dialectically opposed modes of transforming experience, one via intentional reflection, the other via extensional action.

Previous thinking has tended to confuse the grasping and transformation dimensions by collapsing them into one dimension. Thus, Jung first saw extraversion as associated with the feeling orientation and introversion with the thinking orientation (Bash, 1955). Only later did his research separate these as independent dimensions. Similarly, Piaget sees the dimension of phenomenalism/constructivism and the operative dimension of egocentricism/reflection as correlated throughout the developmental process, although he does emphasize the differences between the figurative and operative aspects of thought in his structural analysis of cognitive development. Much of the literature on left/right brain functions has, in my own opinion, also confused the grasping dimension with the prehension dimension and as a result attributed to the left and right hemispheres psychological functions that are controlled elsewhere (see Ornstein, 1972; or Diekman, 1971, quoted above). The position taken here is that it is useful to keep these dimensions analytically separate even though in some circumstances they are empirically correlated (such as in successive stages of child development).

In addition, it is important to note that these two basic dimensions are not unitary continua; rather, each represents a dialectic opposition between two independent but mutually enhancing orientations. Apprehension and comprehension are each independent modes of grasping experience. Physiological evidence suggests separate locations of these functions in the right and left cerebral hemispheres and an integrative mechanism in the *corpus callosum*.

Similarly, intention and extension are independent modes of transforming experience and appear to be controlled in part by the separate and interrelated parasympathetic and sympathetic nervous systems. Finally, it is maintained that apprehension and comprehension as prehension processes, and intention and extension as transformation processes, are equipotent contributions to the learning process. This is in disagreement with Piaget's view that comprehension and intention are superior processes. This relationship between apprehension and comprehension and between intention and extension is captured (at an admittedly intuitive, apprehension level) by Escher's etching, *Day and Night* (Figure 3.5).

After the description of the basic underlying structures of the experiential learning process, it now remains for us to describe how these structures function in the learning process. In the next chapter, we will examine patterns and vicissitudes in the learning process and the concept of individual learning styles.

Figure 3.5   Escher, *Dag en nacht—Day and night—Tag und Nacht—Jour et nuit*

Update and Reflections

Experiential Learning and the Brain

Biology gives you a brain. Life gives you a mind.

—Jeffrey Eugenides, Middlesex

Since the 1980s, there is no area of research that has advanced more rapidly than research on the brain. At the time I was writing *Experiential Learning*, much excitement had been generated by the split-brain research that identified different functions for the left and right hemispheres of the brain. Research by Roger Sperry and others in the 1960s gained widespread publicity and popularization when Sperry was awarded the 1981 Nobel Prize in Physiology and Medicine. The studies demonstrated that the left and right hemispheres of the brain specialize in different tasks. I saw this as related to William James, two modes of knowing the world, apprehension in the right brain and comprehension in the left brain (Chapter 3, pp. 71–77). At that time, the field of cognitive neuroscience was beginning to thrive as methods for directly examining brain engagement in cognition such as the fMRI became available. The 1990s was designated the "decade of the brain" by President George W.H. Bush. Today research on brain processes and structure and their role in learning is expanding dramatically. In 2008 alone, more than 26,500 refereed articles were published in over 400 neuroscience journals. The Society for Neuroscience's first conference in 1979 had 1,300 attendees; by 2000, 24,000 people attended. Today the brain has entered popular culture everywhere, and disciplines from education to law to marketing to economics to ethics have developed specialties called neuroeducation, neurolaw, and so on (Rose and Abi-Rached, 2013).

Recent fMRI research has added substantially to our understanding of James' dual knowledge theory which formed the foundation for contemporary work on dual-processing (Evans, 2008), made popular by Kahneman's recent book *Thinking, Fast and Slow* (2011) describing apprehension as system 1 and comprehension as system 2. Boyatzis, Rochford, and Jacks (2014) in a recent review of the fMRI studies by their team and others give a detailed picture of two large brain networks involved in dual processing—the task positive network (TPN) and the default mode network (DMN). Consistent with James' theory, the task positive network and default mode network have a dialectic relationship. Neural activity in the task positive network inhibits activity in the default mode network and vice versa. The task positive network is important for problem solving, focusing attention, decision making, and control of action (system 2). The default mode network plays a central role in control of emotions, social cognition, ethical decision-making, creativity, and openness to new ideas (system 2).

Macro level interpretations of brain research have used three perspectives on the brain. The differentiation between the right and left hemispheres is a lateral one; the others being up/down (which describes the reptilian brain, the limbic system, and the neo-cortex), and front to back. A recent paper by Eagleton (2011) combined the lateral perspective and the up/down, limbic/cortical perspectives to map the learning cycle on the brain. The left limbic senses and experiences through inquiry (CE), the left cortical is for reflective observation and critical thinking (RO), the right cortical is for lateral thinking and abstract analysis (AC), and the right limbic is for taking action and solving problems (AE). James Zull's perspective is primarily front to back ". . . the most striking line of functional division in the cortex is the boundary between the somatosensory and the primary motor. It divides the cortex into a front half and a back half . . ." (2002, p. 175).

James Zull and the Link between the Learning Cycle and Brain Functioning

One of my greatest pleasures in my 40-year academic career at Case Western Reserve University is my friendship and collaboration with Jim Zull. When he founded the University Center for Innovation in Teaching and Education (UCITE) in 1994, I served on his advisory board, and he and I taught the doctoral course on Learning and Development in the Organization Behavior Department for many years. I treasure our many conversations on learning and education. His great passion for teaching and his equally great passion for biological research are united in his two great books *The Art of Changing the Brain* (2002) and *From Brain to Mind* (2011). His aim is to understand how Piaget's concept of constructivism in learning could be understood in neurological terms. His basic idea is that knowledge resides in networks of neurons in the neocortex constructed through learning from experience. In constructivist terms, learning is a process that builds on the foundation of each individual's neuronal structure, and thus every learner is unique and will interpret experience uniquely. Learning from experience results in modification, growth, and pruning of neurons, synapses, and neuronal networks; thus learning physically changes the brain, and educating is the art of changing the brain.

Zull sees a parallel between the learning cycle and the structure of the nervous system that creates the neuronal networks (see Figure 3.6). "Put into words, the figure illustrates that concrete experiences come through the sensory cortex, reflective observation involves the integrative cortex at the back, creating new abstract concepts occurs in the frontal integrative cortex, and active testing involves the motor brain. In other words, the learning cycle arises from the structure of the brain" (Zull, 2002, pp. 18–19; 2011.) While acknowledging the greater complexity of brain functioning, he proposes that these regions of the brain are heavily, but not exclusively, involved in the modes of the learning cycle. Their respective functions, *sensing (CE), remembering (RO), theorizing (AC), and acting (AE)*, he calls the four pillars of learning.

Zull describes a cognitive neuroscience experiment showing that monkeys can distinguish cats from dogs, and more importantly, in doing so, they followed the sequence of the learning cycle in the pillar brain regions as his theory predicted: "*sensory (perceiving*

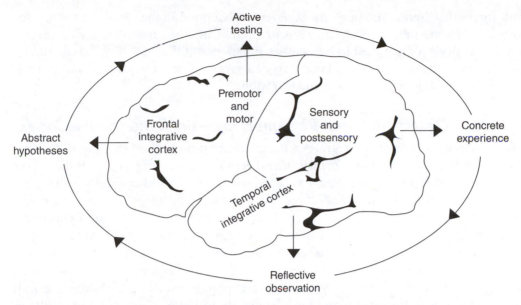

Figure 3.6   The Experiential Learning Cycle and Regions of the Cerebral Cortex
Source: Reprinted with permission of the author and publisher, Stylus Publishing (Zull, 2002).

major aspects of images of cats and dogs), *memory* (comparing the perceived image to remembered ones), *theorizing* (deciding the nature of perceived image as cat or dog), and testing the judgment by a specific *action* (pressing a red button if dog and a green button if cat)" (2012, p. 171).

Concrete Experience and Sensing—The Sensory Cortex

The sensory cortex receives information from the outside world through the senses. Zull describes how it operates: "During concrete experience, physical information from the world and from our bodies enters the brain through the sense organs . . . It is then sent in parallel to the emotion monitor (amygdala) and the specific parts of the cortex for each of the senses. If the amygdala recognizes the experience as dangerous, it will trigger an instinctive body action (fight or flight). . . . That is the extreme response. Normally, both the emotional and cognitive content of experience are sent to the cortex to be processed by the integrative cortex in the parietal and temporal lobes" (2002, p. 137). One implication of this parallel track is that attention can be diverted by unsafe and threatening conditions making it difficult to focus and take in the details of the experience fully. It also helps us understand James' concept of pure experience (Chapter 2 Update and Reflections) and why it is clouded by cultural interpretations and memories of previous experiences. The incoming direct experiencing through the senses is immediately identified and interpreted on one track or the other before it goes to the frontal cortex for thinking.

Zull argues that "sense-luscious" real experiences that flood all the senses are the best for learning. "We are more likely to trust sensory input from the experience itself. I suspect that this confidence and trust in our sensory experience of the 'real thing' has a calming effect on our amygdala. And a calmer amygdala means clearer thinking" (2002, p. 145). Teachers should do more showing and less telling.

Reflective Observation and Remembering—Back Integrative Cortex

The back integrative cortex integrates sensory information to create images and meaning. It is involved in memory formation and recall, enabling object recognition. It is also involved in language comprehension and spatial relationships. One of Zull's great contributions to the study of reflection is his emphasis on the importance of memory. At the first level of reflection described in the Chapter 2 Update and Reflections, experiences are integrated with memories to create meaning as in the simple case of naming a person. This is accomplished by integrating the sound of the name with the visual image. This memory of the person is extended by neuronal networks distributed throughout the cortex that are dynamically growing, connecting, and decaying with other memories of the person and our feelings about them. This plasticity results in the constant revision of memories over time. The most important part of forming the memory is its link with emotion. To endure, the memory must have neuronal pathways to emotion structures such as the amygdala, nucleus accumbens, and hypothalamus. Emotion creates attention, and if we are not paying attention to an experience, it will not be sensed. Rich experiences, such as those which change and surprise or use all the senses, are more memorable. We may not remember someone's name because we never formed the memory in the first place or because the neuronal connections for recall are weak.

Abstract Conceptualization and Theorizing—Front Integrative Cortex

The frontal integrative cortex uses short term memory to choose, plan, problem solve, and make decisions. It makes judgments and evaluations directing the rest of the brain and actions of the body. It does this through abstract conceptualization, manipulating concepts and images to go beyond present knowledge to invent and choose new actions.

This integration is a creative and active, rather than reflective, process. "This means that we can change our purpose at any time. We can change our reasons for thinking; the content of our thoughts. We can discard specific facts and ideas, and replace them with others. We can choose what we want to think about and what problems we want to work on, and play with them in our mind. We can identify the elements that make up our thoughts, and move them around in our mental pictures as we work toward a specific goal or purpose. We can discard things that do not serve our purpose and add things that do. All this freedom! All this choice! This is what makes creative integration creative" (Zull, 2011, p. 93).

The integrative front cortex uses working memory to organize a sequence of movements that will accomplish a goal. Working memory selects memories and facts from the back integrative cortex relevant to the planned action and organizes them into a sequence of actions that will solve the problem. This is accomplished by a unique network of neurons in the cortex that fires when stimulated but continues firing for a while after the stimulus ends, "remembering" the stimulus. But if another stimulus occurs, the firing is interrupted, making short-term memory unstable and limited in how much it can hold. So working memory literally requires work and paying attention to avoid being distracted.

These functions are most associated with intelligence, though Zull stresses that the frontal cortex is driven by emotion through the dopamine reward system of the nucleus accumbens. The emotional aspects of learning and problem solving are as important as the mechanistic ones. It is driven by our desires and needs. He particularly emphasizes the feeling of ownership as essential for voluntary purposeful action.

Active Experimentation and Acting—Motor Cortex

Another of Zull's insights about the learning cycle is the importance of action for learning. Action closes the learning cycle and reconnects the processing inside the brain with the world. It generates consequences there that create new experiences that begin the cycle anew. He calls this the "great transformation—*changing sensory experience into action experience*." This transformation happens in two ways, one directly from the sensory cortex to the motor cortex and the other around the learning cycle through the back (reflecting) and front (thinking) integrative cortex.

The direct route is illustrated by the simple reflex, stimulus and response with no intervening cognitive activity. More complex activities are exploration and mimicry. Exploration is the continuing interaction between sensing and acting as in the way the eyes continuously move to explore something. Mimicry is copying sensory information and repeating it in action as when a child repeats her mother's words to learn language. The neurons involved in mimicry are called mirror neurons. Mirror neurons match observations with actions and are located in Broca's area, which is responsible for language. Direct recursive cycling between experience and action can actually produce skill mastery with little cognitive help (see Figure 3.7). Hoover, Giambatista, and Belkin (2012) have called this cycle "vicarious observational experiential learning," suggesting that it lightens the cognitive demands of direct experiential learning and is therefore useful as a precursor to learning from direct experience, for example, observing a performance before doing it oneself.

The longer route around the learning cycle engages reflection and previous memories, coming to the motor cortex where coordinated voluntary muscle contractions that produce movement are triggered. These movements carry out plans and goals originating in the front integrative cortex including the actions of producing language through speech and writing.

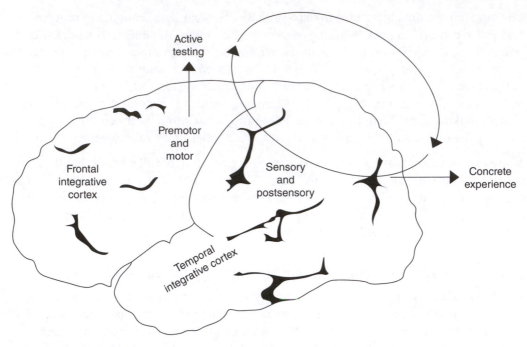

Figure 3.7   The Exploration/Mimicry Learning Cycle

Meta-cognition and the Anterior Cingulate

Zull ends his journey *From Brain to Mind* (2011) by introducing us to the anterior cingulate. This structure appears to be an evolutionarily new specialization of the neocortex containing spindle-shaped neurons that are connected to diverse parts of the brain and appear to serve an integrating function for the sensory and motor cortexes and emotional centers. It appears to be involved heavily in self-awareness and self-reflective thought, as well as emotional self-control and adaptive responses to changing conditions. This executive meta-cognitive function is central to self-regulation, deliberate learning, and learning how to learn. I will examine these processes in more detail in the Chapter 8 Update and Reflections.

The meta-cognitive abilities related to the self are essential for the function of episodic memory and what Tulving (1983, 2005) calls autonoetic (self-knowing) consciousness: "Only through the sophisticated representation of the self can an individual autonoetically recollect personal events from the past and mentally project one's existence into the subjective future. It is not known which regions of the frontal lobes are especially critical for self-awareness but the most anterior regions are good candidates" (Wheeler, Stuss, and Tulving, 1997, p. 333). Episodic memory, which includes some semantic memory, is different than semantic memory alone in that it recalls events in which the self participated in context and in time; while semantic memory registers, stores, and uses only decontextualized facts of the world, with no sense of when they were encountered.

Episodic memory is particularly important for experiential learning because it remembers by re-experiencing and mentally traveling back in time. "Its essence lies in the subjective feeling that, in the present experience, one is re-experiencing something that has happened before in one's life . . . the self doing the experiencing now is the same self that did it originally" (Wheeling, Stuss, and Tulving, 1997, p. 349). Recall of these personal episodes forms the basis for future plans and actions. William James says of this "remembering" that "remembrance is like a direct feeling: its object is suffused with a warmth and intimacy to which no object of mere conception ever attains" (1890, p. 239). Most education focuses on semantic memory and thus makes the personal application of such facts and ideas in context difficult. The episodic memory of a statistics class, for example, may be trying to stay awake by watching formulas written on the blackboard. Experiential education and situated learning (Lave and Wenger, 1991), on the other hand, would work on using the statistics on a personally relevant research project. This episodic memory carries with it ideas on how to apply the concepts in future research.

James Zull on Education

Zull's books are filled with implications and recommendations for educators and learners. Here are a few related to experiential learning.

- The opportunities for deep learning are enhanced with a balanced use of all four learning modes and their corresponding parts of the brain.

- The learning cycle's four modes give four times the chance to remember. It is metacognitive and produces episodic memory central to future deliberate transfer of learning.

- Emotion influences thinking more than thinking influences emotion. Positive emotions (joy) enhance learning.

- Physical changes occur in the brain when we learn. Begin with existing neuronal networks which are the physical form of prior knowledge and build on it.

- Learning how to learn should be a focus of education.

- It is better to start with concrete examples rather than abstract principles. Abstract principles are where we are, not where the learners are.

- Be careful to not overload the limited capacity of working memory. Shoving information in at one end only pushes out information at the other.

- Always provoke an active reaction from learners. A safe environment for failure can help in this.

My Brain Made Me Do It?

When I studied philosophy as an undergraduate, I was always amused when philosophers would accuse someone who was trying to resolve the problem of mind-body dualism of committing the homunculus fallacy, also known as the Cartesian Theatre. The homunculus was a tiny little person inside the head viewing incoming information from the senses, interpreting it, deciding what to do, and controlling action. The homunculus replaced Descartes' pineal gland as the seat of the soul and served as a proxy that the mind, with its subjective qualities and intentional states, is a solely physical concept. The juxtaposition of such silly ideas and mundane examples with deep philosophical issues made philosophy fun for me. So, I was surprised to find the term rehabilitated in neuroscience in the term "cortical homunculus" describing the very real anatomical divisions of the sensory and motor cortex (see Figure 3.8) that form the basis for the mimicry/exploration cycle of learning described above.

Indeed the physicalists appear to have won the day, and it is now generally agreed that the mind is a physical phenomenon—the mind is the brain. Even so, it is far from proven. A passionate advocate of the mind-is-brain idea, Daniel Dennett, who authored *Consciousness Explained* (1991), admits that he is only offering steps along the way to that goal. Stephen Jay Gould argues that reductionism in integrating the phenomena of mind and

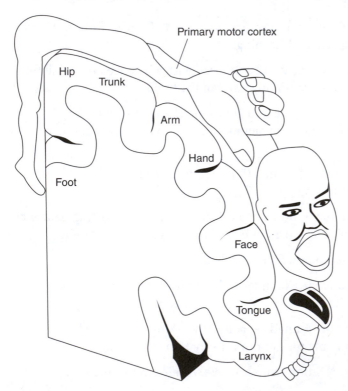

Figure 3.8   The Cortical Homunculus

brain must fail for two reasons, "First, *emergence*, or the entry of novel explanatory rules in complex systems, laws arising from nonlinear or nonadditive interactions among constituent parts that therefore, in principle, cannot be discovered from properties of parts considered separately. . . . Second, *contingency*, or the growing importance of 'unique' historical accidents that cannot, in principle, be predicted, but remain fully accessible to factual explanation after their occurrence" (2003, pp. 201–202). Carla Hannaford (1995) argues that learning is holistic, involving the whole body, "But we have missed a most fundamental and mysterious aspect of the mind: learning, thought, creativity and intelligence are not processes of the brain alone but of the whole body. Sensations, movements, emotions and brain integrative functions are grounded in the body. The human qualities we associate with the mind can never exist separate from the body" (1995, p. 11).

Jim Zull is with the "brain is mind" majority: "Ultimately even the spiritual is physical. . . . A physical brain means a physical mind; *meaning* itself is physical" (2000, pp. 5–6). My view is that brain and mind represent two realms of discourse, two different perspectives that are useful for different purposes and together can enhance both perspectives. Brain talk is about physiology, neurons, receptors, and neurotransmitters. Mind talk is about intentions, ideas, beliefs, emotions, and desires. Ironically, neuroscience has increased conversation about consciousness and mind, not eliminated it. I completely support the neuroscientists in their pursuit for a deeper and more complete understanding of the brain. Their passionate belief in the physical nature of the mind serves them well in their drive to achieve this goal. I feel confident that humanity can deal with whatever they discover. In the meantime, the humanities discourse of mind and spirit still survives and thrives while digesting their discoveries. We have seen how Jim Zull's humble presentation of the physical brain enlightens our understanding of how to learn and educate.

Would that always were the case. Disciplines have a way of privileging their discourse over others and extending it into areas where they have no expertise, while demeaning the expertise of other disciplines. And the "physics envy" of soft social scientists leads them to seek legitimacy with the neuro patina. Ordinary folks are impressed by the brain images and are led to believe that Post Traumatic Stress Disorder (PTSD) is a "real" disease just because it lights up the brain in a fMRI. Whether it does or not, PTSD is very real in the experience of those who must deal with it in their daily lives. Some, like Ryan and Deci, are concerned that popularization of neuroscience denies choice and free will. My brain made me do it. "The sense of self is just a post-behavioral 'spin,' whereas the brain, reified as if it were an intentional agent does the acting, deciding and gadget activating. Such interpretations, found pervasively in today's popular neuropsychology are fraught with philosophical confounds. First, the brain replaces the philosophical homunculus in this description. Second, the logic is that if the brain is involved, it is therefore the ultimate and most relevant cause. No matter that the brain may itself be stimulated into action by social events . . . mediated by psychological interpretations and construals or that awareness and active reflection can alter these construals" (2004, p. 465).

Viewed from the perspective of radical empiricism where everything begins and ends in experience, both discourses come together in lived experience. As humans, we live our daily lives with both discourses competing to interpret what we are experiencing. Dewey call lived experience "immediate empiricism" and agreed with James, radical empiricism that, "It is in the concrete thing *as experienced* that all the grounds and clues to its own intellectual and logical rectification are contained" (1905, p. 397). Francisco Varela, the creator of embodied experiential learning and autopoiesis agrees: "The only real way to do a science of mind is to accept the hard and solid fact that the realm of experience is ontologically irreducible. It is what it is. The realm of explanation is also irreducible—it is what it is. I cannot do away with explanations. The whole point here is to make these two things not just coexist as two separate drawers in the huge chest of drawers of the universe, but to actually affect each other. . . . I'm just a very hard-headed, very respectful observer of what's in front of me; and what's in front of me is both material causal explanations and my experience. Both!" (Davis, 1995, p. 31).

In lived experience we are most comfortable explaining our experience with the discourse of mind—perceptions, beliefs, thoughts, feelings, and intentions. However, the insights of neuroscience, when integrated with lived experience, can make a difference in our lives. Carol Dweck studied the "folk" psychology of school children, specifically their common sense understanding of the brain and intelligence. She discovered two different views which she called the fixed view, that people are born a certain way and intelligence is fixed, and a view that she called incremental, that people can change and become better learners. With her research team, she found that teaching neuroscience findings about the neuroplasticity of the brain improves their academic performance. Eight 25-minute classes for seventh graders focused on the message that "learning changes the brain by forming new connections and that students are in charge of this process" (Blackwell, Trzesniewski, and Dweck, 2007, p. 254), which led to increased classroom motivation and reversed a decline in grades experienced by the control group. Similarly, Good, Aronson, and Inzlicht (2003) found that a similar incremental learning intervention led to significant improvements in adolescents' achievement test scores and Aronson, Fried, and Good (2002) found that such teaching led to higher grades among college students. The lesson of neuroplasticity is that the mind can shape the brain as much as the brain shapes the mind.

4

Individuality in Learning and the Concept of Learning Styles

But the complicated external conditions under which we live, as well as the presumably even more complex conditions of our individual psychic disposition, seldom permit a completely undisturbed flow of our psychic activity. Outer circumstances and inner disposition frequently favor the one mechanism, and restrict or hinder the other; whereby a predominance of one mechanism naturally arises. If this condition becomes in any way chronic, a type is produced, namely an habitual attitude, in which the one mechanism permanently dominates; not, of course, that the other can ever be completely suppressed, inasmuch as it also is an integral factor in psychic activity. Hence, there can never occur a pure type in the sense that he is entirely possessed of the one mechanism with a complete atrophy of the other. A typical attitude always signifies the merely relative predominance of one mechanism.

—Carl Jung, Psychological Types

The structural model of the learning process described in the last chapter is a complex one, capable of producing a rich variety of learning processes that vary widely in subtlety and complexity. The model gives the basic prehension processes of apprehension and comprehension independent structural status. The same is true for the transformation processes of intention and extension. In addition, apprehension and comprehension as well as intention and extension are dialectically related to one another, such that their synthesis produces higher levels of learning. Thus, the learning process at any given moment in time may be governed by one or all of these processes interacting simultaneously. Over time, control of the learning process may shift from one of these structural bases for learning to another. Thus, the structural model of learning can be likened to a musical instrument and the process of learning to a musical score that depicts a succession and combination of notes played on the instrument over time. The melodies and themes of a single score form distinctive individual patterns that we will call learning styles.

The Scientific Study of Individuality

In this analogy, I am suggesting that the learning process is not identical for all human beings. Rather, it appears that the physiological structures that govern learning allow for the emergence of unique individual adaptive processes that tend to emphasize some adaptive orientations over others. When the matter is viewed from an evolutionary perspective, there appears to be good reason for this variability and individuality in human learning processes.

Human individuality does not just result from random deviations from a single normative blueprint; it is a positive, adaptive adjustment of the human species. If there are evolutionary pressures toward "the survival of the fittest" in the human species, these apply not to individuals but to the human community as a whole. Survival depends not on the evolution of a race of identical supermen but on the emergence of a cooperative human community that cherishes and utilizes individual uniqueness (compare Levy, 1980).

Attempts to understand the nature of human individuality and to describe the essential dimensions along which individuals vary began long before psychology was a recognized field of inquiry. For example, gnostic philosophers of the second century conceived of human variability as occurring along three dimensions: the *pneumatici* (thinking orientation), the *psychici* (feeling orientation), and the *hylici* (sensation orientation). In the eighteenth century, the poet and philosopher Fredrich Schiller divided people into "naive" and sentimental types, paralleling realist and idealist philosophical orientations. In the century that followed, Nietzsche developed the famous Apollonian and Dionysian typology. In 1923, Carl Jung combined these and other approaches to individuality into what must be considered one of the most important books on individual differences ever written, *Psychological Types*. Today, psychology abounds with every type of individual difference measures—in traits, values, motives, attitudes, cognitive styles, and so on (compare Tyler, 1978).

The scientific study of human individuality poses some fundamental dilemmas. The human sciences, unlike the physical sciences, place an equal emphasis on the discovery of general laws that apply to all human beings and on the understanding of the functioning of the individual case. In chemistry, for example, a researcher is apt to discard a sample of a given compound if it does not perform as the general laws of chemistry indicate it should. Impurities or contaminants in the sample are usually seen as irrelevant-error variance to be eliminated. In the human sciences, however, each sample is a human being whose uniqueness and individuality are highly prized, particularly by the person him- or herself. We are interested, therefore, not only in general laws of behavior, but in their specific relevance and application for each individual case. The basic dilemma for the scientific study of individual differences, therefore, is how to conceive of general laws or categories for describing human individuality that do justice to the full array of human uniqueness.

Theories describing psychological types or personality styles have been much criticized in this regard. Psychological categorizations of people such as those depicted by psychological "types" can too easily become stereotypes that tend to trivialize human complexity and thus end up denying human individuality rather than characterizing it. In addition, type theories often have a static and fixed connotation to their descriptions of individuals, lending a fatalistic view of human change and development. This view often gets translated into a self-fulfilling prophecy, as with the common educational strategy of "tracking" students on the basis of individual differences and thereby perhaps reinforcing those differences. Another problem with type theories is that they tend to become somewhat idealized. Descriptions tend to be cast in the form of "pure" types, with the caveat that no person actually represents a pure type. We are thus left with the problem of describing and attempting to research an ideal profile that does not exist empirically.

These problems with type theories seem to stem from the underlying epistemology on which they are based. Type theories, like many scientific theories, have tended to be based on the epistemological root metaphor of formism (see Chapter 5 for further elaboration of the role of root metaphors in epistemology). In the formist epistemology, forms or types are the ultimate reality, and individual particulars are simply imperfect representations of the universal form or type. Type theories thus easily fall into the problems identified above. An alternative epistemological root metaphor, one that we will use in our approach to understanding human individuality, is that of contextualism. In contextualism, the person is examined in the context of the emerging historical event, in the processes by which both the person and event are shaped. In the contextualist view, reality is constantly being created by the person's experience. As Dewey notes, "an individual is no longer just a particular, a part without meaning save in an inclusive whole, but is a subject, self, a distinctive centre of desire, thinking and aspiration" (1958, p. 216).

The implication of the contextualist world view for the study of human individuality is that psychological types or styles are not fixed *traits* but stable *states*. The stability and the endurance of these states in individuals comes not solely from fixed genetic qualities or characteristics of human beings; nor, for that matter, does it come solely from the stable, fixed demands of environmental circumstances. Rather, stable and enduring patterns of human individuality arise from consistent patterns of transaction between the individual and his or her environment. Leona Tyler calls these patterns of transaction *possibility-processing structures*.

We can use the general term *possibility-processing structures* to cover all of these concepts having to do with the ways in which the person controls the selection of perceptions, activities, and learning situations. Any individual can carry out, simultaneously or successively, only a small fraction of the acts for which his sense organs, nervous system, and muscles equip him. Only a small fraction of the energies constantly bombarding the individual can be responded to. If from moment to moment a person had to be aware of all of these stimulating energies, all of these possible responses, life would be unbearably complicated and confusing. The reason that one can proceed in most situations to act sensibly without having to make hundreds of conscious choices is that one develops organized ways of automatically processing most of the kinds of information encountered. In computer terms, one does what one is "programmed" to do. Much of the programming is the same for all or most of the human race; much is imposed by the structure of particular culture and subcultures. But in addition there are programs unique to individuals, and these are fundamental to psychological individuality (Tyler, 1978, pp. 106–107).

The concept of possibility-processing structure gives central importance to the role of individual choice in decision making. The way we process the possibilities of each new emerging event determines the range of choices and decisions we see. The choices and decisions we make, to some extent, determine the events we live through, and these events influence our future choices. Thus, people create themselves through their choice of the actual occasions they live through. In Tyler's words, to some degree we write our own "programs." Human individuality results from the pattern or "program" created by our choices and their consequences.

Learning Styles as Possibility-Processing Structures

The complex structure of learning allows for the emergence of individual, unique possibility-processing structures or styles of learning. Through their choices of experience, people program themselves to grasp reality through varying degrees of emphasis on apprehension or comprehension. Similarly, they program themselves to transform these prehensions via extension and/or intention. This self-programming conditioned by experience determines the extent to which the person emphasizes the four modes of the learning process: concrete experience, reflective observation, abstract conceptualization, and active experimentation (see Figures 4.1 and 4.2 for examples).

To illustrate the variety and complexity of the learning process, let us examine in some detail how these processes unfold in the specific situation of playing and learning the game of pool. Pool players, be they novice or expert, use a variety of learning strategies in the course of their play. In some of these strategies, we see very clearly the four basic elemental forms of learning: $A\Delta I$, apprehension transformed by intention; $A\Delta E$, apprehension transformed by extension; $C\Delta I$, comprehension transformed by intention; and $C\Delta E$, comprehension transformed by extension. In addition, we also see higher-order combinations of these basic elemental forms—for example, $A\Delta I\Delta C$, apprehension linked via intentional transformation with comprehension.

- $C\Delta E$—A very common learning strategy in playing pool is comprehension transformed by extension. Here the pool player uses an abstract model or theory about how the ball will travel when it is struck with the cue to predict a course for the cue ball such that it will strike the object ball into the pocket. The player may explicitly recall basic physics, that the angle of incidence equals the angle of reflection, and may actually measure out on the table the corresponding angles necessary. This strategy emphasizes the abstract conceptualization and active experimentation modes of the learning process.

- $A\Delta E$—Another common approach is apprehension transformed by extension. This learning strategy does not rely on a theoretical model about how the cue ball and object ball will travel, but rather focuses on the concrete position of the balls on the table. The player relies on a global intuitive feel of the situation. In this situation, the player often seems to be making minor adjustments before hitting the ball, with the criteria for these adjustments being not some theoretical calculation but the finding of a position that "feels right." Here, concrete experience and active experimentation are the dominant learning modes used.

- $A\Delta I$—Since pool is an active game, learning through intentional transformations is less obvious. Intentional transformation of apprehensions may take the form of watching one's opponent or partner as he or she shoots, or of reflecting on the course of one's own shots. Here, one learns in fairly concrete ways by modeling or picking up hints from someone else's approach to the game or trying to do again what one did on the last shot. This strategy relies on reflective observation and concrete experience.

- $C\Delta I$—Intentional transformation of comprehensions, on the other hand, is a kind of inductive model-building process relying on abstract conceptualization and reflective observation. For example, one might try to understand the consequences of applying "English" to the ball by compiling and organizing into laws one's observations of the various attempts by oneself and others.

All the learning strategies above taken separately have a certain incompleteness to them. Although one can analytically identify certain learning achievements in each of the four elementary learning modes just described, more powerful and adaptive forms of learning emerge when these strategies are used in combination. For example, if the theory of "English" that I develop through comprehension transformed by intension—$C\Delta I$—is combined with the empirical testing of hypotheses derived from that theory—$C\Delta E$—I have developed a way of checking the validity of my inductive process that uses three of the four modes of the learning process: reflective observation, abstract conceptualization and active experimentation ($I\Delta C\Delta E$). Similarly, if I combine these hypotheses about the effects of "English" ($C\Delta E$) with my concrete feel of the situation ($A\Delta E$), these abstract ideas about how to impart English to the ball will be translated into the appropriate motor and perceptual behavior: I will increase my confidence that my hypotheses about "English" have in fact been adequately tested; that is, I did actually hit the ball the way I had planned to ($C\Delta E\Delta A$). Thus, these pairwise combinations of elementary learning strategies that share a common prehension or transformation mode produce a somewhat higher level of learning beyond the elementary forms. This second-order learning includes not only some goal-directed behavior, such as deriving a hypothesis from a theory or garnering observations from a specific experience, but also some process for testing out how adequately that goal-directed activity has been carried out. This second-order feedback loop stimulates the development of the learning modality in common between the two elementary learning modes. Thus, in the example just cited, the linking of apprehension and comprehension through extension allows for increasing sophistication in extensional learning skills. When apprehension/extension ($A\Delta E$) is combined with apprehension/intention ($A\Delta I$), a similar result occurs. That is, when I relax and hit the ball ($A\Delta E$) and then watch carefully where it goes ($A\Delta I$), my awareness of the situation becomes more sophisticated and higher-level ($E\Delta A\Delta I$).

The combination of all four of the elementary learning forms produces the highest level of learning, emphasizing and developing all four modes of the learning process. Here, the specialized achievements of the four elementary learning strategies combine in a unified adaptive process. Here our pool player observes the events around him/her ($A\Delta I$), integrates these into theories ($I\Delta C$) from which he or she derives hypotheses, which are then tested out in action ($C\Delta E$), creating new events and experiences ($E\Delta A$). Any new observations are used to modify theories and adjust action, thereby creating an increasingly sophisticated adaptive process that is progressively attuned to the requirement of the game:

$$\begin{array}{ccc} & A & \\ \Delta & & \Delta \\ E & & I \\ \Delta & & \Delta \\ & C & \end{array}$$

If you were to analyze your own approach to learning the game of pool or to spend some time observing players at your local pool hall, I suspect you would find that very few people follow this highest level of learning much of the time. Some people just step up and hit the ball without bothering to look very carefully at where their shot went unless it went in the pocket. Others seem to go through a great deal of analysis and measurement but seem a bit hesitant on the execution. Thus there seem to be distinctive styles or strategies for learning and playing the game. Yet even when people have distinctive styles that rely heavily on one of the elementary learning strategies, there are occasions in their learning process when they rely on other of the elementary forms and combine these with their preferred orientation into the second and third orders of learning.

Individual styles of learning are complex and not easily reducible into simple typologies—a point to bear in mind as we attempt to describe general patterns of individuality in learning. Perhaps the greatest contribution of cognitive-style research has been the documentation of the diversity and complexity of cognitive processes and their manifestation in behavior. Three important dimensions of diversity have been identified:

- Within any single theoretical dimension of cognitive functioning, it is possible to identify consistent subtypes. For example, it appears that the dimension of cognitive complexity/simplicity can be further divided into at least three distinct subtypes: the tendency to judge events with few variables versus many; the tendency to make fine versus gross distinctions on a given dimension; and the tendency to prefer order and structure versus tolerance of ambiguity (Vannoy, 1965).

- Cognitive functioning will vary among people as a function of the area of content it is focused on, the so-called cognitive domain. Thus, a person may be concrete in his interaction with people and abstract in his work (Stabell, 1973), or children will analyze and classify persons differently from nations (Signell, 1966).

- Cultural experience plays a major role in the development and expression of cognitive functioning. Lessor (1976) has shown consistent differences in thinking style across different American ethnic groups; Witkin (1976) has shown differences in global and abstract functioning in different cultures; and Bruner et al. (1966) have shown differences in the rate and direction of cognitive development across cultures. Although the evidence is not conclusive, it would appear that these cultural differences in cognition, in Michael Cole's words, "reside more in the situations to which cognitive processes are applied than in the existence of a process in one cultural group and its absence in another" (1971, p. 233). Thus, Cole found that African Kpelle tribesmen were skillful at measuring rice but not at measuring distance. Similarly, Wober (1967) found that Nigerians function more analytically than Americans when measured by a test that emphasizes proprioceptive cues, whereas they were less skilled at visual analysis.

Our investigation of learning styles will begin with an examination of generalized differences in learning orientations based on the degree to which people emphasize the four modes of the learning process as measured by a self-report test called the Learning Style Inventory. From these investigations we will draw a clearer picture of the programs or patterns of behavior that characterize the four elementary forms of learning. With these patterns as a rough map of the terrain of individuality in learning, the next chapter will examine the relationships among these styles of learning and the structure of knowledge. Chapter 6 will consider the higher levels of learning and the relation between learning and development.

Assessing Individual Learning Styles: The Learning Style Inventory

To assess individual orientations toward learning, the Learning Style Inventory (LSI) was created. The development of this instrument was guided by four design objectives: First, the test should be constructed in such a way that people would respond to it in somewhat the same way as they would a learning situation; that is, it should require one to resolve the opposing tensions between abstract-concrete and active-reflective orientations. In technical testing terms, we were seeking a test that was both *normative,* allowing comparisons between individuals in their relative emphasis on a given learning mode such as abstract conceptualization, and *ipsative,* allowing comparisons within individuals on their relative emphasis on the four learning modes—for instance, whether they emphasized abstract conceptualization more than the other three learning modes in their individual approach to learning.

Second, a self-description format was chosen for the inventory, since the notion of possibility-processing structure relies heavily on conscious choice and decision. It was felt that self-image descriptions might be more powerful determinants of behavioral choices and decisions than would performance tests. Third, the inventory was constructed with the hope that it would prove to be valid—that the measures of learning styles would predict behavior in a way that was consistent with the theory of experiential learning. A final consideration was a practical one. The test should be brief and straightforward, so that in addition to research uses, it could be used as a means of discussing the learning process with those tested and giving them feedback on their own learning styles.

The final form of the test is a nine-item self-description questionnaire. Each item asks the respondent to rank-order four words in a way that best describes his or her learning style. One word in each item corresponds to one of the four learning modes—concrete experience (sample word, *feeling*), reflective observation (*watching*), abstract conceptualization (*thinking*), and active experimentation (*doing*). The LSI measures a person's relative emphasis on each of the four modes of the learning process—concrete experience (CE), reflective observation (RO), abstract conceptualization (AC), and active experimentation (AE)—plus two combination scores that indicate the extent to which the person emphasizes abstractness over concreteness (AC-CE) and the extent to which the person emphasizes action over reflection (AE-RO). The four basic learning modes are defined as follows:

- An orientation toward *concrete experience* focuses on being involved in experiences and dealing with immediate human situations in a personal way. It emphasizes feeling as opposed to thinking; a concern with the uniqueness and complexity of present reality as opposed to theories and generalizations; an intuitive, "artistic" approach as opposed to the systematic, scientific approach to problems. People with concrete-experience orientation enjoy and are good at relating to others. They are often good intuitive decision makers and function well in unstructured situations. The person with this orientation values relating to people and being involved in real situations, and has an open-minded approach to life.

- An orientation toward *reflective observation* focuses on understanding the meaning of ideas and situations by carefully observing and impartially describing them. It emphasizes understanding as opposed to practical application; a concern with what is true or how things happen as opposed to what will work; an emphasis on reflection as opposed to action. People with a reflective orientation enjoy intuiting the meaning of situations and ideas and are good at seeing their implications. They are good at looking at things from different perspectives and at appreciating different points of view. They like to rely on their own thoughts and feelings to form opinions. People with this orientation value patience, impartiality, and considered, thoughtful judgment.

- An orientation toward *abstract conceptualization* focuses on using logic, ideas, and concepts. It emphasizes thinking as opposed to feeling; a concern with building general theories as opposed to intuitively understanding unique, specific areas; a scientific as opposed to an artistic approach to problems. A person with an abstract-conceptual orientation enjoys and is good at systematic planning, manipulation of abstract symbols, and quantitative analysis. People with this orientation value precision, the rigor and discipline of analyzing ideas, and the aesthetic quality of a neat conceptual system.

- An orientation toward *active experimentation* focuses on actively influencing people and changing situations. It emphasizes practical applications as opposed to reflective understanding; a pragmatic concern with what works as opposed to what is absolute truth; an emphasis on doing as opposed to observing. People with an active-experimentation orientation enjoy and are good at getting things accomplished. They are willing to take some risk in order to achieve their objectives. They also value having an influence on the environment around them and like to see results.

Norms for scores on the LSI were developed from a sample of 1,933 men and women ranging in age from 18 to 60 and representing a wide variety of occupations. These norms, along with reliability and validity data for the LSI, are reported in detail

---

elsewhere (Kolb, 1976, 1981). The following sample LSI profiles are included along with the respondents' self-descriptions to illustrate the kind of self-assessment information generated by the inventory. The first profile is that of a 20-year-old female social worker currently completing a graduate degree in social work (see Figure 4.1). Her high scores on concrete experience and active experimentation are evident not only in the content of the following excerpts from her self-analysis but also in the way the analysis is written, with its strong feeling tone:

> The Learning Style exercise and assignment had a tremendous effect on me, forcing me to take stock of my standard learning and problem solving pattern. And, obviously, these patterns more or less represent my general life patterns and attitudes. In the past, I have noted my methods of handling specific problems, but the assignment really pulled it all together, which was more than a little terrifying. . . . [She describes her recent experience in choosing an apartment.]

> Those are the specifics. I can recall many other examples where my learning and problem solving style was exactly the same. In fact, I'm writing this paper right now, twenty minutes after class, as a direct result of my poor score on the paper just returned to me. If I sat and analyzed what it meant to receive a poor mark, I would become too upset. I had to do something about it, to fix it, so I immediately went home and sat down to write a good paper to prove I could do better.

> The general process is clear: When I first become emotionally concerned with a problem, the only way I can see to relieve the worry is to jump into action, "solving" the problem as quickly as possible. It's too hard, too hurting, to sit and think and analyze. When a problem touches me on a gut level, be it a love affair or a beautiful pair of shoes in a store window, I jump to concrete action; I accommodate.

> During the aforementioned apartment search, as during most of my escapades, a little voice in the back of my head knew what was going on and warned and cautioned me. Yet I proceeded just the same. It's as if my process is compulsive and inevitable; I feel it to be almost beyond any conscious control on my part.

> I realize that my problem solving process is not 100% destructive. My instincts are often very good, and I'm just as likely to make the right decision as not, based on my experience. In fact, this same compulsive need to act has led me into many beautiful and exciting adventures which I wouldn't have missed for the world. What frightens me is my apparent inability to try out other problem solving techniques.

> My accommodator style [see below, under "Characteristics of the Basic Learning Styles"] most concerns me in the context of professional situations. When

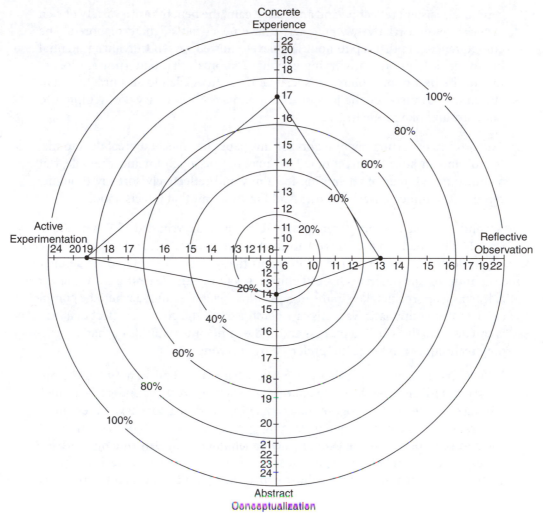

Figure 4.1 Example Learning-Style Profile—Female Social Worker

working with a client, I tend to promote and encourage action choices or solutions before we have fully analyzed the problem at hand; it breaks my heart to see a client suffer, so I want to relieve his or her pain with the same medicine I use on myself. I am always trying to slow down, to check and double check, to consider a wide range of options. But on the other hand, my action instincts have many times procured immediate vital services for a client, while my more reflective colleagues were still putzing around on paper.

I'm also concerned about the effect of this style on my life plans. I've jumped from major to major in college, and recently from career to career, without much careful, consistent reflection and analysis. Again, the benefits are a variety of rich experiences at a relatively young age; I have never felt stagnant or bored. The consequences are that, up to now, I've never allowed myself to realize potential in any field. I am presently trying very hard to break that pattern. I am focusing, to the best of my ability, on social work, both academic and practical. I'm attempting to discover the joys of thoroughness. It's not easy. I'm tempted to jump around like a little flea. . . .

The process of sorting my thoughts for this paper has meant a great deal to me. It took me an hour to sort it out. That may not be much for most people, but a concentrated hour of attempting to calmly and reflectively sort my thoughts represents a minor miracle for me! And I must admit that it feels good.

The second example is a very different one. It is from a 32-year-old M.B.A. student (see Figure 4.2). This man's high scores on abstract conceptualization and reflective observation are reflected in a self-interpretation report that is more formal and academic in its tone. In addition, he describes his difficulties in valuing and learning from the experiential learning approach taken in the organization behavior course where he completed the LSI. In a rather dramatic way, this case demonstrates the powerful effect that learning styles can have on the learning process and at the same time reminds us that experiential learning techniques per se are not preferred by everyone:

"They, assimilators [see below], are often frustrated and benefit little from unstructured 'discover' learning approaches such as exercises and simulations." Falling onto the extreme edge of the assimilator category, I, too, have experienced frustration with the experiential learning approach and much of the content of the course to date. This first conceptual paper will briefly describe my learning style, recount some of my experiences in the course, relate my feelings, present my intellectual reactions to those experiences and feelings, and outline my expected future course of action.

Since the learning process is a dynamic, circular one of building on past experience and learning, some description of my background is needed to understand my learning style preference. The Learning Styles Inventory very clearly identified my assimilator predisposition. Both concrete experience and active experimentation scores were inside the twentieth percentile circle. Reflective observation was in the middle range, while abstract conceptualization fell on the outer circle. This result corresponds well with my formal educational and professional experience. Typically, both mathematicians and economists are assimilators, drawing on theoretical models to describe reality. My degrees in these areas reflect my strength in and affinity for that style of learning. Kolb reports that members of the research and planning departments of organizations tend to be the most assimilative group. Prior to entering the M.B.A. program, I had spent

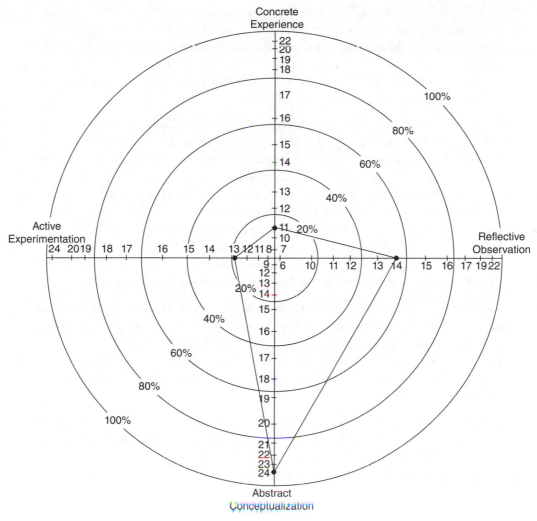

Figure 4.2   Example Learning-Style Profile—Male M.B.A. Student

two years in such a capacity, leaving _____ college as Associate Director of Institutional Research and Planning.

Entering the organizational behavior class, I anticipated difficulty, but did not anticipate the wholesale assault on my value system which I encountered. Detailing those incidents and my reactions comprises the body of this essay. Prior to describing concrete situations, I need to present my definition of concrete and active as they apply to learning. Basically, I propose to generalize from the physical definitions to include those activities of the mind which are active and concrete, rather than passive and imprecise. For example, much of the active part

---

of active listening is a mental, rather than a physical, activity. Similarly, for me, active participation in a novel, textbook, or journal article is more "active" than engaging in typical sporting activities. To view my learning as balanced, rather than ivory-towerish, one must surmount what economists term the "fallacy of misplaced concreteness." Cerebral as well as sensual participation in life can be concrete and active.

Experiences with classmates, instructors, and the texts have all contributed to my feelings of isolation, defensiveness, and frustration. During my group's first discussion session I expressed my distaste for experiential learning. I noted that it seemed to be the opposite of normal science or education, where the goal of furthering man's knowledge required building upon the work and achievements of others, rather than egocentrically assuming that individuals would be able to replicate past acts of genius. I was motivated to get my views on the table so that future discussion on my part would be understood in the proper light. Unwittingly, I was combatting what Argyris terms "double loop learning." I was immediately questioning the rules of the game by putting my views forward.

Reaction by some other members of the group was swift and harsh. Replies such as, "You can't learn anything from books," and "Books are irrelevant to business, you learn by doing," shocked me. Coming from an institution (_____ College) where life revolved almost entirely around intellectual activities, I was surprised to find that students at an apparently similar school possessed anti-intellectual attitudes.

Our group leader reported this discussion as, "One of our members said that he preferred passive learning, had gone to a school where experiential learning was used, and did not like it." The whole group's reaction was surprise. I felt embarrassed and misunderstood, wanted to defend my views and straighten out the group leader. Feelings of isolation and serious questioning of my reasons for being in business school followed that session.

During the second group session, a number of our group members discussed the Learning Styles Inventory. One member questioned the validity of the measurement and what it really measured. I presented my views on inductive versus deductive reasoning and the difficulty of constructing an index which is unidimensional. One group member remarked, "I never know what he's talking about," leading to snickers from the group. Score crushed ego and feelings a third time.

The physical placement of students on the Learning Styles Inventory grid in the lounge further confirmed my feelings of isolation. From my perspective, four students were extreme assimilators, eight others were assimilators near the center, ten were convergers, twelve were divergers, and twenty were accommodators. The four members of our group discussed the advantages and disadvantages of assimilation as a learning style, questioned the realism of our goals in management vis-à-vis our learning orientation, and related the LSI to our majors and computer programming. I felt a sense of community and cohesion forming in the group. In particular, a lawyer and I confirmed our commonality of vision.

This activity did result in constructive reflection on my part. It appears to me that people under stress or feeling isolated seek others with similar feelings for security. In addition, the experience spurred me to look in the reader for more information. The last article presented findings on the distribution of academics majors on the LSI grid which satisfied some of my curiousity about the applicability of the inventory. . . .

Evidence for the Structure of Learning

The structural model of learning developed in the preceding chapter postulates two fundamental dimensions of the learning process, each describing basic adaptive processes standing in dialectical opposition. The prehension dimension opposes the process of apprehension and an orientation toward concrete experience against the comprehension process and an orientation toward abstract conceptualization. The transformation dimension opposes the process of intention and reflective observation against the process of extension and active experimentation. We have emphasized that these dimensions are not unitary theoretically, such that a high score on one orientation would automatically imply a low score on its opposite, but rather that they are dialectically opposed, implying that a higher-order synthesis of opposing orientations makes highly developed strengths in opposing orientations possible. If this reasoning is applied to scores on the Learning Style Inventory, we would predict a moderate (but not perfect) negative relation between abstract conceptualization and concrete experience and a similar negative relation between active experimentation and reflective observation. Other correlations should be near zero. Intercorrelations of the scale scores for a sample of 807 people shows this to be the case (see Kolb, 1976, for details). CE and AC were negatively correlated ($-.57$, $p < .001$). RO and AE were negatively correlated ($-.50$, $p < .001$). Other correlations were low but significant because of the large sample size (CE) with RO = .13, RO with AC = $-.19$, AC with AE = $-.12$, and AE with CE = $-.02$). All but the last are significant ($p < .001$). As a result of the intercorrelations, we felt justified in creating two combination scores to measure the abstract/concrete dimension (AE-CE) and active/reflective dimension (AE-RO). With the abstract/concrete dimension, CE correlated $-.85$ and AC correlated .90. With the active/reflective dimension, AE correlated .85 and RO correlated $-.84$. Subsequent studies with more limited and specialized populations have shown patterns of correlation similar to those described above. One longitudinal study of changes in learning style during college examined the relationship between the Learning Style Inventory and commonly used instruments designed to measure cognitive development according to Piaget, Kohlberg, Loevinger, and Perry theoretical descriptions of growth. Analyses of the interrelationships of college student performance on these measures found that the concrete/abstract dimension correlated with these measures. The reflective/active dimension did not. For these college students, dimensions of learning and development designed to tap cognitive growth do not reflect movement on the reflective/active dimension. The latter dimension also does not correlate with age at entrance to college for younger or older students, which supports the idea that the two dimensions are independent (Mentkowski and Strait, 1983).

A more rigorous test of these hypothesized relationships requires controlling for the built-in negative correlations in the LSI caused by the forced-ranking procedure and validation of the scales against external criteria. It is possible to control for the "bias" introduced by the forced-choice format of the LSI by using data from a study by Certo and Lamb (1979), who generated 1,000 random responses to the LSI instrument and intercorrelated the resulting scale scores. The resulting correlations measure the magnitude of the inbuilt negative correlations in the LSI. If these correlations are used as the null hypothesis instead of the traditional zero point to test for significance of difference, the hypothesized negative relationships between AC and CE and between AE and RO can be tested with the forced-ranking effect partialed out. Thus, when Certo and Lamb's random correlations are compared to the empirical correlations obtained from 807 subjects using the formula provided by McNemar (1957, p. 148), both the AC/CE correlations and AE/RO correlations are significantly *more* negative than the random correlations (random AC/CE = $-.26$, empirical = $-.57$, p of difference < .001; random AE/RO = $-.35$, empirical = $-.50$, p of difference < .001).

External validation of these negative relationships comes from a recent study by Gypen (1980). He correlated ratings by professional social workers and engineers of the extent to which they were oriented toward each of the four learning modes in their current job with their LSI scores obtained four to six months earlier. Each mode was rated separately on a seven-point scale describing the learning mode in a way that attempted to minimize social-desirability bias. Table 4.1 shows the correlations between the subjects' LSI scores and self-ratings of their current job orientation. These results provide strong support for the negative relation between concrete experience and abstract conceptualization, and somewhat weaker support for the negative relation between active experimentation and reflective observation. The Gypen study and the "corrected" internal correlations among LSI scales both demonstrate empirical support for the bipolar nature of the experiential learning model that is independent of the forced-ranking method used in the LSI.

Although these data do not prove validity of the structural learning model, they do suggest an analytic heuristic for exploring with the LSI the characteristics of the four elemental forms of knowing proposed by the model (refer to Figure 3.1). If for purposes

Table 4.1 Pearson Correlation Coefficients between the Learning Style Inventory Scales and Ratings of Learning Orientations at Work ($N = 58$)

LSI Scales	Learning Orientation on Current Job			
	Concrete Experience	Reflective Observation	Abstract Conceptualization	Active Experimentation
Concrete Experience (CE)	.49 p < .001	−.17 n.s.	−.37 p < .0 1	.08 n.s.
Reflective Observation (RO)	.03 n.s.	.22 p < .05	.12 n.s.	−.34 p < .01
Abstract Conceptualization (AC)	−.30 p < .05	−.04 n.s.	.27 p < .05	−.09 n.s.
Active Experimentation (AE)	.01 n.s.	−.09 n.s.	−.06 n.s.	.37 p < .01
Abstract-Concrete (AC-CE)	−.42 p < .001	.06 n.s.	.36 p < .003	−.07 n.s.
Active-Reflective (AE-RO)	−.02 n.s.	−.18 p < .08	−.07 n.s.	.43 p < .001

of analysis we treat the abstract-concrete (AC-CE) and active-reflective (AE-RO) dimensions as negatively related in a unidimensional sense, it is possible to create a two-dimensional map of learning space that can be used to empirically characterize differences in the four elementary forms of knowing: convergence, divergence, assimilation, and accommodation. In so doing, I will save the third dimension for depicting in Chapter 6 the process of development and higher forms of knowing achieved through the dialectic synthesis of action/reflection and abstract/concrete orientations.

Since the AC and CE scales and AE and RO scales are not perfectly negatively correlated, two other types of LSI scores do in fact occur occasionally: those that are highest on AC and CE, and those that are highest on AE and RO. These so-called "mixed" types of people, on the basis of what fragmentary evidence we have, seem to be those who rely on the second- and third-order levels of learning. Thus, through integrative learning experiences, these people have developed styles that emphasize the dialectically opposed orientations. Some support for this argument comes from Rita Weathersby's study of adult learners at Goddard College (1977). The important point, however, is that the LSI measures differences only in the elementary knowledge orientations, since the forced-ranking format of the inventory precludes integrative responses.

Characteristics of the Basic Learning Styles

In using the analytic heuristic of a two-dimensional-learning-style map, it is proposed that a major source of pattern and coherence in individual styles of learning is the underlying structure of the learning process. Over time, individuals develop unique possibility-processing structures such that the dialectic tensions between the prehension and transformation dimensions are consistently resolved in a characteristic fashion. As a result of our hereditary equipment, our particular past life experience, and the demands of our present environment, most people develop learning styles that emphasize some learning abilities over others. Through socialization experiences in family, school, and work, we come to resolve the conflicts between being active and reflective and between being immediate and analytical in characteristic ways, thus lending to reliance on one of the four basic forms of knowing: *divergence*, achieved by reliance on apprehension transformed by intention; *assimilation*, achieved by comprehension transformed by intention; *convergence*, achieved through extensive transformation of comprehension; and *accommodation*, achieved through extensive transformation of apprehension.

Some people develop minds that excel at assimilating disparate facts into coherent theories, yet these same people are incapable of or uninterested in deducing hypotheses from the theory. Others are logical geniuses but find it impossible to involve and surrender themselves to an experience. And so on. A mathematician may come to place great emphasis on abstract concepts, whereas a poet may value concrete experience more highly. A manager may be primarily concerned with the active application of ideas, whereas a naturalist may develop his observational skills highly. Each of us in a unique way develops a learning style that has some weak and some strong points. Evidence for the existence of such consistent unique learning styles can be found in the research of Kagan and Witkin (Kagan and Kogan, 1970). They find, in support of Piaget, that there is a general tendency to become more analytic and reflective with age, *but* that individual rankings within the population tested remain highly stable from early years to adulthood. Similar results have been found for measures of introversion/extraversion. Several longitudinal studies have shown introversion/extraversion to be one of the most stable characteristics of personality from childhood to old age. Although there is a general tendency toward introversion in old age, studies show that people tend to retain their relative ranking throughout their life span (Rubin, 1981). Thus, they seem to develop consistent stable learning or cognitive styles relative to their age mates. The following is a description of the characteristics of the four basic learning styles based on both research and clinical observation of these patterns of LSI scores.

- The *convergent* learning style relies primarily on the dominant learning abilities of abstract conceptualization and active experimentation. The greatest strength of this approach lies in problem solving, decision making, and the practical application of ideas. We have called this learning style the *converger* because a person with this style seems to do best in situations like conventional intelligence tests, where there is a single correct answer or solution to a question or problem (Torrealba, 1972; Kolb, 1976). In this learning style, knowledge is organized in such a way that through hypothetical-deductive reasoning, it can be focused on specific problems. Liam Hudson's (1966) research on those with this style of learning (using other measures than the LSI) shows that convergent people are controlled in their expression of emotion. They prefer dealing with technical tasks and problems rather than social and interpersonal issues.

- The *divergent* learning style has the opposite learning strengths from convergence, emphasizing concrete experience and reflective observation. The greatest strength of this orientation lies in imaginative ability and awareness of meaning and values. The primary adaptive ability of divergence is to view concrete situations from many perspectives and to organize many relationships into a meaningful "gestalt." The emphasis in this orientation is on adaptation by observation rather than action. This style is called *diverger* because a person of this type performs better in situations that call for generation of alternative ideas and implications, such as a "brainstorming" idea session. Those oriented toward divergence are interested in people and tend to be imaginative and feeling-oriented.

- In *assimilation*, the dominant learning abilities are abstract conceptualization and reflective observation. The greatest strength of this orientation lies in inductive reasoning and the ability to create theoretical models, in assimilating disparate observations into an integrated explanation (Grochow, 1973). As in convergence, this orientation is less focused on people and more concerned with ideas and abstract concepts. Ideas, however, are judged less in this orientation by their practical value. Here, it is more important that the theory be logically sound and precise.

- The *accommodative* learning style has the opposite strengths from assimilation, emphasizing concrete experience and active experimentation. The greatest strength of this orientation lies in doing things, in carrying out plans and tasks and getting involved in new experiences. The adaptive emphasis of this orientation is on opportunity seeking, risk taking, and action. This style is called *accommodation* because it is best suited for those situations where one must adapt oneself to changing immediate circumstances. In situations where the theory or plans do not fit the facts, those with an accommodative style will most likely discard the plan or theory. (With the opposite learning style, assimilation, one would be more likely to disregard or reexamine the facts.) People with an accommodative orientation tend to solve problems in an intuitive trial-and-error manner (Grochow, 1973), relying heavily on other people for information rather than on their own analytic ability (Stabell, 1973). Those with accommodative learning styles are at ease with people but are sometimes seen as impatient and "pushy."

The patterns of behavior associated with these four learning styles are shown consistently at various levels of behavior, from personality type to specific task-oriented skills and behaviors. We will examine these patterns at five such levels: (1) Jungian personality type, (2) early educational specialization, (3) professional career, (4) current job, and (5) adaptive competencies.

Personality Type and Learning Style

We have already acknowledged and examined to some extent the indebtedness of experiential learning theory to Jung's theory of psychological types. Now we examine more specifically the relations between Jung's types and the four basic learning styles. In his theory of psychological types, Jung developed a holistic framework for describing differences in human adaptive processes. He began by distinguishing between those people who are oriented toward the external world and those oriented toward the internal world—the distinction between extravert and introvert examined in the last chapter. He then proceeded to identify four basic functions of human adaptation—two describing alternative ways of perceiving, sensation and intuition; and two that describe alternative ways of making judgments about the world, thinking and feeling. In his view, human individuality develops through transactions with the social environment that reward and develop one function over another. He saw that this specialized adaptation is in service of society's need for specialized skills to meet the differentiated, specialized role demands required for the survival of and development of culture. Jung saw a basic conflict between the specialized psychological orientations required for the development of society and the need for people to develop and express all the psychological functions for their own individual fulfillment. His concept of individuation describes the process whereby people achieve personal integrity through the development and reassertion of the nonexpressed and nondominant functions integrating them with their dominant specialized orientation into a fluid, holistic adaptive process. He describes the conflict between specialized types and individual development in this way:

> The natural, instinctive course, like everything in nature, follows the principle of least resistance. One man is rather more gifted here, another there; or, again, adaptation to the early environment of childhood may demand either relatively more restraint and reflection or relatively more sympathy and participation, according to the nature of the parents and other circumstances. Thereby a certain preferential attitude is automatically moulded, which results in different types. Insofar then as every man, as a relatively stable being, possesses all the basic psychological functions, it would be a psychological necessity with a view to perfect adaptation that he should also employ them in equal measure. For there must be a reason why there are different ways of psychological adaptation: Evidently one alone is not sufficient, since the object seems to be only partially comprehended when, for example, it is either merely thought or merely felt. Through a

one-sided (typical) attitude there remains a deficit in the resulting psychological adaptation, which accumulates during the course of life; from this deficiency a derangement of adaptation develops, which forces the subject towards a compensation. [Jung, 1923, p. 28]

Thus, his conception of types or styles is identical to that proposed here—a basic but incomplete form of adaptation with the potential for development via integration with other basic types into a fluid, holistic adaptive process.

Jung's typology of psychological types includes four such pairs of dialectically opposed adaptive orientations, describing individuals' (1) mode of relation to the world via introversion or extroversion, (2) mode of decision making via perception or judgment, (3) preferred way of perceiving via sensing or intuition, and (4) preferred way of judging via thinking or feeling. These opposing orientations are described in Table 4.2.

Table 4.2 Jung's Psychological Types

Mode of relation to the world	E EXTROVERT TYPE	I INTROVERT TYPE
	Oriented toward external world of other people and things	Oriented toward inner world of ideas and feelings
Mode of decision making	J JUDGING TYPE	P PERCEIVING TYPE
	Emphasis on order through reaching decision and resolving issues	Emphasis on gathering information and obtaining as much data as possible
Mode of perceiving	S SENSING TYPE	N INTUITION TYPE
	Emphasis on sense perception, on facts, details, and concrete events	Emphasis on possibilities, imagination, meaning, and seeing things as a whole
Mode of judging	T THINKING TYPE	F FEELING TYPE
	Emphasis on analysis, using logic and rationality	Emphasis on human values, establishing personal friendships, decisions made mainly on beliefs and likes

As was indicated in the preceding chapter, there is a correspondence between the Jungian concepts of introversion and the experiential learning mode of reflective observation via intentional transformation, and between extraversion and active experimentation via extension. In addition, concrete experience and the apprehension process are clearly associated with both the sensing approach to perception and the feeling approach to judging. Abstract conceptualization and the comprehension process, on the other hand, are related to the intuition approach to perceiving and the thinking approach to judging. Predictions about perception and judgment types are difficult to make, since this preference is a second-order one; for instance, if I prefer perception, I could perform it via sensing or intuition. Myers-Briggs states, "In practice the JP preference is a by-product of the choice as to which process, of the two liked best (*N* over *S* or *T* over *F*), shall govern one's life" (1962, p. 59).

The Myers-Briggs Type Indicator (MBTI) is a widely used psychological self-report instrument used to assess people's orientation toward the Jungian types (Myers, 1962). Correlations between individuals' scores on the MBTI and the LSI should give some empirical indication of validity of relationships between Jung's personality types and the learning styles proposed above. Some caution in using such data is appropriate, however. First, both the LSI and the MBTI instruments are based on self-analysis and report. Thus, we are testing whether those who take the two tests agree with our predictions of the similarity between Jung's concepts and those of experiential learning theory; we are not testing, except by inference, their actual behavior. Second, it is not clear how adequately the MBTI reflects Jung's theory. In particular, the items in the MBTI introversion/extraversion scale seem to be heavily weighted in favor of the American conception of the dimension mentioned earlier—extraversion as social and interpersonal ease, and introversion as shyness and social awkwardness.

Table 4.3 reports data from three studies by different investigators of three populations: Kent State undergraduates (Taylor, 1973), University of Wisconsin M.B.A.s (Wynne, 1975), and education administrators (McBer and Company, personal communication). The data in Table 4.3 tend to support our hypotheses, but not consistently in all groups: The strongest and most consistent relationships appear to be between concrete/abstract and feeling/thinking and between active/reflective and extravert/introvert.

In a more systematic study of 220 managers and M.B.A. students, Margerison and Lewis (1979) investigated the relations between LSI and MBTI scores using the technique of canonical correlation. They found a significant canonical correlation of .45 ($p < .01$) between the two sets of test scores. When the resulting pattern of psychological types is plotted on the two-dimensional LSI learning-space, relationships between the Jungian types and learning styles become clear and consistent with our predictions (see Figure 4.3). The sensing type is associated with the accommodative learning style, and the intuitive type falls in the assimilative quadrant; the feeling personality type is divergent in learning style, and thinking types are convergent.

Regarding introversion and extraversion, Margerison and Lewis conclude:

> It is clear that extroverts describe themselves as very active in learning situations. This is to be expected, in that extroverts use their energy to go out into their environment and enjoy contact with people and things. In contrast, introverts are far more reflective as would be expected. However, it is noticeable that both extroverts and introverts prefer involvement in learning situations which are neither excessively detached nor concrete. Clearly, while there is a fair degree of

Table 4.3 Correlations between Learning Style Inventory Scores and the Myers-Briggs Type Indicator

Group		Learning Style Inventory Scores						
		n	CE	RO	AC	AE	AC-CE	AE-RO
MYERS-BRIGGS TYPE INDICATOR[a]								
Extraversion/Introversion	Kent State undergrads	135	.06	.06	.03	-.18[c]	-.01	-.13
	U. of Wisc. M.B.A.s	74	.08	.34[d]	.03	-.27[c]	—	—
Sensation/Intuition	Undergrads	135	-.25[d]	-.07	.23[d]	-.20[c]	.29[d]	.09
	M.B.A.s	74	-.02	-.15	.19	-.12	—	—
Thinking/Feeling	Undergrads	135	.34[d]	-.02	-.25[d]	.05	-.35[d]	.04
	M.B.A.s	74	.08	-.17	.00	-.01	—	—
Judging/Perceiving	Undergrads	135	-.06	.11	-.11	-.13	-.02	-.16
	M.B.A.s	74	.01	-.12	.06	-.05	—	—
MYERS-BRIGGS TYPE INDICATOR[b]								
Extraversion	Education administr.	46	-.13	-.27	.28	—	.25	-.16
Introversion	Education administr.	46	.18	.36[c]	-.35[c]	—	-.20	-.33[c]
Sensation	Education administr.	46	—	.12	-.26	-.11	-.19	-.13
Intuition	Education administr.	46	—	—	.20	—	.14	—
Thinking	Education administr.	46	-.31[c]	—	.22	-.16	.30[c]	-.16
Feeling	Education administr.	46	.39[d]	—	-.34[c]	.12	-.42[d]	.11
Judging	Education administr.	46	-.22	—	—	—	.14	—
Perceiving	Education administr.	46	.19	—	—	—	—	—

[a] High scores on MBTI variables indicate that the mode listed second is dominant (e.g., a high score on thinking/feeling indicates the dominance of feeling orientation). Missing correlations are due to missing data.

[b] Scores on these MBTI variables are limited to the single modes and are not comparable to paired modes. Missing correlations are due to missing data.

[c] $p < .05$

[d] $p < .01$, 2-tailed test

Data sources: Kent State, Taylor, 1973; U. of Wisc. Wynne, 1976; education administrators, McBer and Company personal communication.

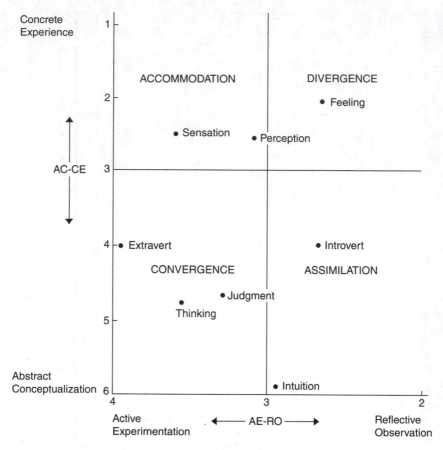

Figure 4.3   The Relations between Learning Styles and Jung's Psychological Types
Source: Adapted from C. J. Margerison and R. G. Lewis, *How Work Preferences Relate to Learning Styles* (Bedfordshire, England: Cranfield School of Management, 1979).

variance, the evidence from our sample illustrates that there is little difference between introverts and extroverts overall in this aspect. The real difference is in their emphasis on a preference for active as against reflective types of role. [Margerison and Lewis, 1979, p. 13]

They also find judgment related to the abstract-conceptualization mode and perception related to concrete experience, but unrelated to action or reflection.

Taken together, these studies suggest that the Jungian personality type associated with the accommodative learning style is extraverted sensing.[1] This personality type

---

1. The procedure for determining types and dominant and auxiliary processes is complicated (see Myers, 1962, pp. 51–62, and Appendix A1–A8). Basically, the choice of introversion or extraversion plus the choice of a single perceiving or judgment mode determines a dominant process.

as described by Myers is remarkably similar to our description of the accommodative learning orientation:

> This combination makes the adaptable realist, who good-naturedly accepts and uses the facts around him, whatever they are. He knows what they are, since he notices and remembers more than any other type. He knows what goes on, who wants what, who doesn't, and usually why. And he does not fight those facts. There is a sort of effortless economy in the way he goes at a situation, never uselessly bucking the line.
>
> Often he can get other people to adapt, too. Being a perceptive type, he looks for the satisfying solution, instead of trying to impose any "should" or "must" of his own, and people generally like him well enough to consider any compromise that he thinks "might work." He is unprejudiced, open-minded, and usually patient, easygoing and tolerant of everyone (including himself). He enjoys life. He doesn't get wrought up. Thus he may be very good at easing a tense situation and pulling conflicting factions together. . . .
>
> Being a realist, he gets far more from first-hand experience than from books, is more effective on the job than on written tests, and is doubly effective when he is on familiar ground. Seeing the value of new ideas, theories and possibilities may well come a bit hard, because intuition is his least developed process. [Myers, 1962, p. A5]

The divergent learning style is associated with the personality type having introversion and feeling as the dominant process. Here again, Myers's description of this type fits ours:

> An introverted feeling type has as much wealth of feeling as an extraverted feeling type, but uses it differently. He cares more deeply about fewer things. He has his warm side inside (like a fur-lined coat). It is quite as warm but not as obvious; it may hardly show till you get past his reserve. He has, too, a great faithfulness to duty and obligations. He chooses his final values without reference to the judgment of outsiders, and sticks to them with passionate conviction. He finds these inner loyalties and ideals hard to talk about, but they govern his life.
>
> His outer personality is mostly due to his auxiliary process, either S or N, and so is perceptive. He is tolerant, open-minded, understanding, flexible and adaptable (though when one of his inner loyalties is threatened, he will not give an inch). Except for his work's sake, he has little wish to impress or dominate. The contacts he prizes are with people who understand his values and the goals he is working toward.
>
> He is twice as good when working at a job he believes in, since his feeling for it puts added energy behind his efforts. He wants his work to contribute to

something that matters to him, perhaps to human understanding or happiness or health, or perhaps to the perfecting of some product or undertaking. He wants to have a purpose beyond his paycheck, no matter how big the check. He is a perfectionist wherever his feeling is engaged, and is usually happiest at some individual work involving personal values. With high ability, he may be good in literature, art, science, or psychology. [Myers, 1962, p. A4]

The assimilative learning style is characterized by the introverted intuitive type. Myers's description of this type is similar to the description of the assimilative conceptual orientation but suggests a slightly more practical orientation than we indicate:

The introverted intuitive is the outstanding innovator in the field of ideas, principles and systems of thought. He trusts his own intuitive insight as to the true relationships and meanings of things, regardless of established authority or popularly accepted beliefs. His faith in his inner vision of the possibilities is such that he can remove mountains—and often does. In the process he may drive others, or oppose them, as hard as his own inspirations drive him. Problems only stimulate him; the impossible takes a little longer, but not much.

His outer personality is judging, being mainly due to his auxiliary, either *T* or *F*. Thus he backs up his original insight with the determination, perseverance, and enduring purpose of a judging type. He wants his ideas worked out in practice, applied and accepted, and spends any time and effort necessary to that end. [Myers, 1962, p. A8]

The convergent learning style is characterized by the extraverted thinking type. Here, Myers's description is very consistent with the learning orientation of convergence:

The extraverted thinker uses his thinking to run as much of the world as may be his to run. He has great respect for impersonal truth, thought-out plans, and orderly efficiency. He is analytic, impersonal, objectively critical, and not likely to be convinced by anything but reasoning. He organizes facts, situations, and operations well in advance, and makes a systematic effort to reach his carefully planned objectives on schedule. He believes everybody's conduct should be governed by logic, and governs his own that way so far as he can.

He lives his life according to a definite set of rules that embody his basic judgments about the world. Any change in his ways requires a conscious change in the rules.

He enjoys being an executive, and puts a great deal of himself into such a job. He likes to decide what ought to be done and to give the requisite orders. He abhors confusion, inefficiency, halfway measures, and anything aimless and ineffective. He can be a crisp disciplinarian, and can fire a person who ought to be fired. [Myers, 1962, p. A1]

Educational Specialization

A major function of education is to shape students' attitudes and orientations toward learning—to instill positive attitudes toward learning and a thirst for knowledge, and to develop effective learning skills. Early educational experiences shape individual learning styles; we are taught how to learn. Although the early years of education are for the most part generalized, there is an increasing process of specialization that develops beginning in earnest in high school and, for those who continue to college, developing into greater depth in the undergraduate years. This is a specialization in particular realms of social knowledge; thus, we would expect to see relations between people's learning styles and the early training they received in an educational specialty or discipline.

These differences in learning styles can be illustrated graphically by the correspondence between people's LSI scores and their undergraduate majors. This is done by plotting the average LSI scores for managers in our sample who reported their undergraduate college major; only those majors with more than ten people responding are included (see Figure 4.4). When we examine these people who share a common professional commitment

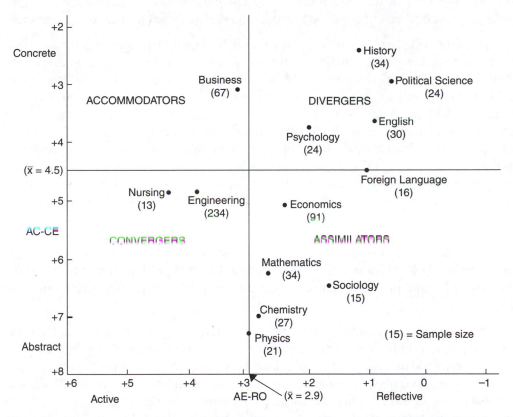

Figure 4.4 Average LSI Scores on Active Reflective (AE-RO) and Abstract/Concrete (AC-CE) by Undergraduate College Major

to management, we see that some of the differences in their learning orientations are explained by their early educational specializations in college. Undergraduate business majors tend to have accommodative learning styles; engineers on the average fall in the convergent quadrant; history, English, political science, and psychology majors all have divergent learning styles; mathematics, economics, sociology, and chemistry majors have assimilative learning styles; physics majors are very abstract, falling between the convergent and assimilative quadrants.

Some cautions are in order in interpreting these data. First, it should be remembered that all the people in the sample are managers or managers-to-be. In addition, most of them have completed or are in graduate school. These two facts should produce learning styles that are somewhat more active and abstract than those of the population at large (as indicated by total sample mean scores on AC-CE and AE-RO of +4.5 and +2.9, respectively). The interaction among career, high level of education, and undergraduate major may produce distinctive learning styles. For example, physicists who are not in industry may be somewhat more reflective than those in this sample. Second, undergraduate majors are described only in the most gross terms. There are many forms of engineering or psychology. A business major at one school can be quite different from one at another.

Liam Hudson's (1966) work on convergent and divergent learning styles predicts that people with undergraduate majors in the arts would be divergers and that those who major in the physical sciences would be convergers. Social-science majors should fall between these two groups. In order to test Hudson's predictions about the academic specialities of convergers and divergers, the data on undergraduate majors were grouped into three categories: the arts (English, foreign language, education/liberal arts, philosophy, history, and other miscellaneous majors such as music, not recorded in Figure 4.4, total $n = 137$); social science (psychology, sociology/anthropology, business, economics, political science, $n = 169$); and physical science (engineering, physics, chemistry, mathematics, and other sciences, such as geology, $n = 277$). The prediction was that the arts should be concrete and reflective and the physical sciences should be abstract and active, with the social sciences falling in between. The mean scores for these three groups of the six LSI scales are shown in Table 4.4. All these differences are highly significant and in the predicted direction, with the exception that the social sciences and physical sciences do not differ significantly on the active/reflective dimension.

Another pattern of significance in the data portrayed in Figure 4.4 is the fact that managers who majored in basic academic disciplines are far more reflective in their learning styles than are the managers who made early professional career commitments in either business or engineering. As we will discuss in greater depth later (see Chapter 7), the traditional nonprofessional collegiate learning environment is highly reflective and develops this orientation in its students. As a result, the transition from education to work involves for many a transition from a reflective learning orientation to an active one.

Table 4.4 Learning-Style Inventory Scores for People Whose Undergraduate College Majors Were in the Arts, Social Sciences, and Physical Sciences

	Concrete Experience (CE)		Reflective Observation (RO)		Abstract Conceptualization (AC)		Active Experimentation (AE)		Abstract/ Concrete (AC-CE)		Active/ Reflective (AE-RO)	
	X̄	SD	X̄	SD	X̄	SD	X̄	SD	X̄	SD	X̄	SD
A. Arts	15.41		14.20		16.69		15.11		+1.31		+0.96	
n = 137		3.26		3.35		3.68		3.37		6.18		5.95
B. Social Science	14.26		12.75		18.05		16.09		+3.86		+3.31	
n = 169		3.35		3.68		3.67		3.43		6.23		6.37
C. Physical Science	13.32		12.70		18.98		16.53		+5.64		+3.83	
n = 277		3.16		3.17		3.57		3.35		5.83		5.69

T-tests for significance between groups (1-tail, only probabilities < .10 are shown)

Arts vs. physical sciences, all differences are significant; p < .005.

Arts vs. social sciences, CE. p < .005; RO. p < .0005: AC, p < .005; AE, p < .01; AC-CE, p < .0005; AE-RO. p < .0005.

Physical sciences vs. social sciences, CE, p < .005; RO. n.s.; AC, p < .005; AE, p < .10; AC-CE, p < .005; AE-RO, n.s.

What these data show is that one's undergraduate education is a major factor in the development of his or her learning style. Whether this is because people are shaped by the fields they enter or because of the selection processes that put people into and out of disciplines is an open question at this point. Most probably, both factors are operating—people choose fields that are consistent with their learning styles and are further shaped to fit the learning norms of their field once they are in it. When there is a mismatch between the field's learning norms and the individual's learning style, people will either change or leave the field.

Professional Career

A third set of forces that shape learning style stems from professional career choice. One's professional career choice not only exposes one to a specialized learning environment; it also involves a commitment to a generic professional problem, such as social service, that requires a specialized adaptive orientation. In addition, one becomes a member of a reference group of peers who share a *professional mentality*, a common set of values and beliefs about how one should behave professionally. This professional orientation shapes learning style through habits acquired in professional training and through the more immediate normative pressures involved in being a competent professional (see Chapter 7, p. 261). In engineering, for example, this involves adapting a rigorous scientific and objective stance toward problems. In nursing, it may involve compassion and caring for the sick. In management, much of the professional orientation centers on decisiveness and a pragmatic orientation.

Learning Style Inventory scores have been collected for a number of different professional groups, allowing a comparison between them. The studies are not representative samples of the professions and hence cannot with certainty be said to describe each profession as a whole. They do, however, offer reasonable indications of the learning-style orientations that characterize the different professions. The results of these studies are shown in Figure 4.5. The first conclusion to be drawn from this figure is that the professions in general have an active, as opposed to a reflective, learning orientation. The social professions—education, nursing, social work, and agricultural extension—comprise people who are heavily or primarily accommodative in their learning style. Professions with a technical or scientific base—accounting, engineering, medicine, and, to a lesser degree, management—have people with primarily convergent learning styles. There is considerable variation around these professional averages, however. In medicine, for example, about half of practitioners and students are convergers (Plovnick, 1974; Wunderlich and Gjerde, 1978), but some medical specialties, such as occupational therapy, are accommodative in their orientation. In social work and nursing, practitioners are clearly concrete as opposed to abstract but fall heavily in the diverger as well as accommodator quadrant (Sims, 1980; Christensen and Bugg, 1979). As will be seen in the next section, some of this variation can be accounted for by the professional's specific job role.

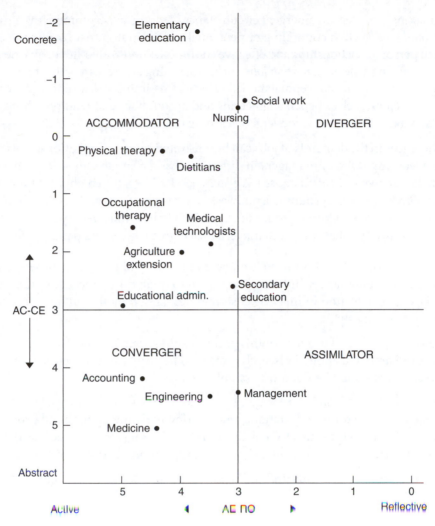

Figure 4.5   Learning-Style Scores for Various Professional Groups

Data Sources: Medicine: Practitioners, 46% of sample convergers, Wunderlich and Gjerde, 1978. Students, 56% of sample convergers, Plovnick, 1974. Nursing: 70% of sample diverger or accommodator, Christensen and Bugg, 1979. 62% of sample diverger or accommodator, Bennet, 1978. Social work and engineering, Sims, 1980. Agricultural extension, 44% accommodators, Pigg, 1978. Accounting, Clark et al., 1977. Management, educational administration, secondary education, elementary education, Kolb, 1976. Occupational therapy, physical therapy, dietitians, and medical technicians, Bennet, 1978.

Current Job Role

The fourth level of factors influencing learning style is the person's current job role. The task demands and pressures of a job tend to shape a person's adaptive orientation. *Executive jobs,* such as general management, that require a strong orientation to task accomplishment and decision making in uncertain emergent circumstances require an accommodative learning style. *Personal jobs*, such as counseling or personnel administrator, that require the establishment of personal relationships and effective communication with other people demand a divergent learning style. *Information jobs*, such as planning and research, that require data gathering and analysis and conceptual modeling have an assimilative learning-style requirement. *Technical jobs*, such as bench engineering and production, that require technical and problem-solving skills require a convergent learning orientation.

These differences in the demands of jobs can be illustrated by an examination of variations among the learning styles of managers in different jobs in a single industrial firm. (For a more detailed analysis of this data, see Weisner, 1971.) We studied about 20 managers from each of five functional groups in a midwestern division of a large American industrial corporation. The five functional groups are described below, followed by our hypothesis about the learning style that should characterize each group given the nature of the work.

1. *Marketing* ($n = 20$). This group is made up primarily of former salesmen. They have a nonquantitative, "intuitive" approach to their work. Because of their practical sales orientation in meeting customer demand, they should have accommodative learning styles.

2. *Research* ($n = 22$). The work of this group is split about 50/50 between pioneer research and applied research projects. The emphasis is on basic research. Researchers should be the most assimilative group.

3. *Personnel/Labor Relations* ($n = 20$). In this company, men from this department serve two primary functions, interpreting personnel policy and promoting interaction among groups to reduce conflict and disagreement. Because of their "people orientation," these men should be predominantly divergers.

4. *Engineering* ($n = 18$). This group is made up primarily of design engineers who are quite production-oriented. They should be the most convergent subgroup, although they should be less abstract than the research group. They represent a bridge between thought and action.

5. *Finance* ($n = 20$). This group has a strong computer, information-system bias. Finance men, given their orientation toward the mathematical task of information-system design, should be highly abstract. Their crucial role in organizational survival should produce an active orientation. Thus, finance-group members should have convergent learning styles.

Figure 4.6 shows the average scores on the active/reflective (AE-RO) and abstract/concrete (AC-CE) learning dimensions for the five functional groups. These results are consistent with the predictions above, with the exception of the finance group, whose scores are less active than predicted and thus fall between the assimilative and the

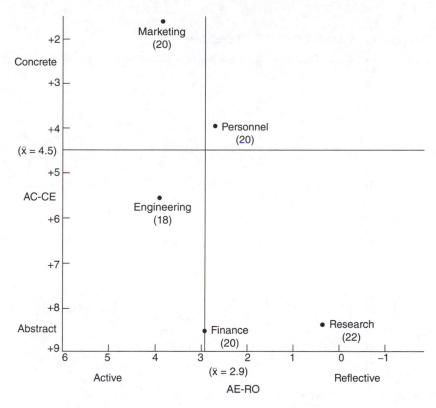

Figure 4.6 Average LSI Scores on Active/Reflective (AE-RO) and Abstract/Concrete (AC-CE) by Organizational Function

convergent quadrants. The LSI clearly differentiates the learning styles that characterize managers with different jobs in a single company.

Further evidence for the proposed relationship between job demands and learning style comes from the medical profession. Plovnick (1974, 1975) studied the relationship between learning style and the job specialty choices of senior medical students. He hypothesized that academic jobs stressing research and teaching would attract assimilators more than other learning-style types, and practice-oriented specialties requiring frequent patient interaction would attract the more active types. In addition, he expected that subspecialty practices (such as cardiology), having a more "scientific" orientation, would attract convergers more, whereas practices in family medicine or primary care involving more concern for the socioemotional aspects of patient care would attract accommodators more. Psychiatry was expected to attract divergers, because of its humanistic orientation and because of the more reserved, reflective nature of the

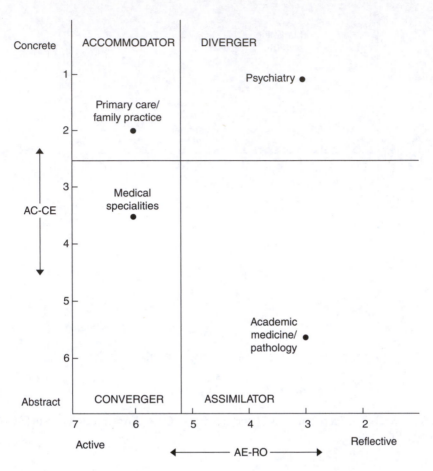

Figure 4.7 Relations between Learning Style and Senior Medical Student's Choice of Specialty
Source: Adapted from Mark Plovnick, "Primary Career Choices and Medical Student Learning Styles," *Journal of Medical Education, 50,* September 1975.

practitioner role in psychiatry. As can be seen in Figure 4.7, these predictions were borne out.[2]

Sims (1981), in his study of job role demands in the social-work and engineering professions, found that social-work administrators were primarily accommodative in their learning style, whereas those in direct service had divergent learning styles.

---

2. A follow-up study by Wunderlich and Gjerde (1978) failed to replicate these findings with active medical practitioners. This may be due to a difference in data analysis procedures between the two studies. Plovnick created types by dividing AE-RO and AC-CE scores at the sample median, whereas Wunderlich and Gjerde used the zero point on the scales to create types.

However, he found no differences among the three major job roles of professional engineers—bench engineer, technical manager, and general manager—even though he did identify significant differences in the actual learning style demands of these three job roles.

Adaptive Competencies

The fifth most specific and immediate level of forces that shapes learning style is the specific task or problem the person is currently working on. Each task we face requires a corresponding set of skills for effective performance. The effective matching of task demands and personal skills results in an *adaptive competence*. The concept of competence represents a new approach to the improvement of performance by matching persons with jobs. The previous approach, that of measurement and selection of personnel by generalized aptitudes has proved a dismal failure in spite of heroic efforts to make it succeed (see Tyler, 1978, Chapter 6 for a review). The basic problem of the aptitude-testing approach was that aptitudes were too generalized and thus did not relate to the specific tasks in a given job, producing low correlations between the aptitude measure and performance. In addition, the aptitude and task measures often were not commensurate; that is, they did not measure the person and the task demand in the same terms. The competency-assessment approach focuses on the person's repertoire of skills as they relate to the specific demands of a job.

We have conceived of the elementary learning styles as *generic adaptive competencies*; that is, as higher-level learning heuristics that facilitate the development of a generic class of more specific skills that are required for effective performance on different tasks (see Chapter 6, p. 216). To study the relations between learning styles as generic adaptive competencies and the specific competencies associated with each of the four styles, the self-rated competencies of professional engineers and social workers were correlated with LSI AC-CE and AE-RO scales. Although this self-rating methodology is of limited usefulness in assessing with great accuracy a person's level of competence in a given situation, it can be used to assess the patterns of interrelationship among competencies, which was the objective of this research study. The correlations between LSI scores and competence self-ratings were plotted on the two-dimensional learning space (see Figure 4.8). For example, the skill of "being personally involved" correlated −.25 with AC-CE and +.10 with AE-RO, placing it in the accommodative quadrant of the learning-style space. As a result of this study, the list of competencies was revised and expanded and a second study was conducted with a sample of social-work and engineering graduates (see Figure 4.9). These data were subjected to further factor analysis and refinement, resulting in what can be called a "competency circle" describing specific competencies arranged

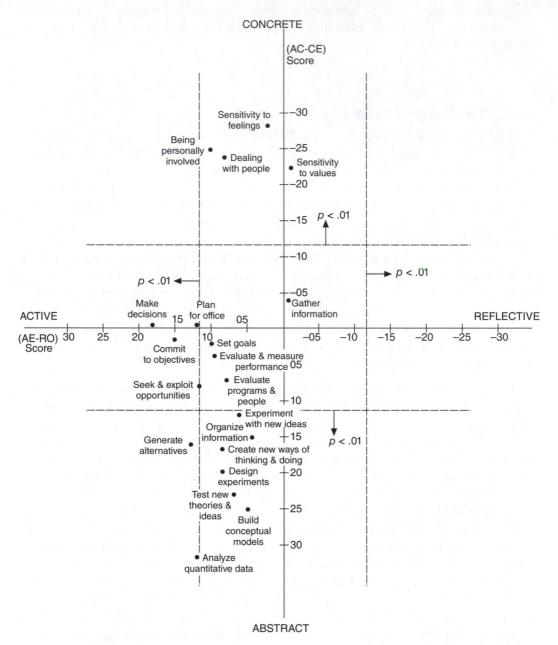

Figure 4.8 Correlations among Work Abilities and Learning Styles (Social-Work and Engineering Graduates; $N = 420$)

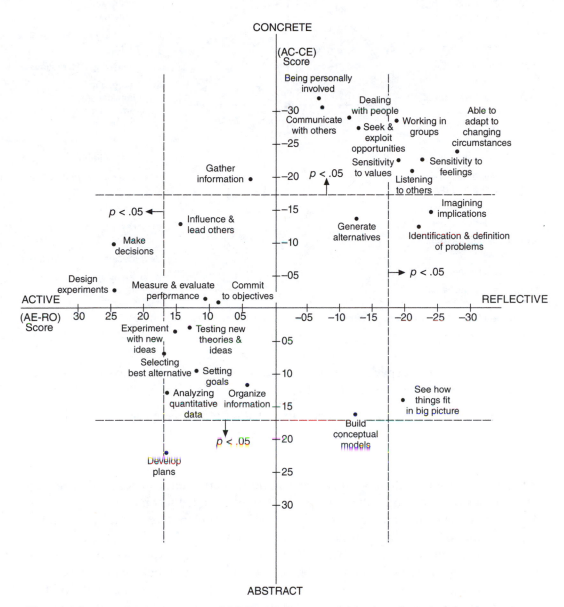

Figure 4.9 Correlations among Work Abilities and Learning Styles (Social-Work and Engineering Graduates; $N = 59$)

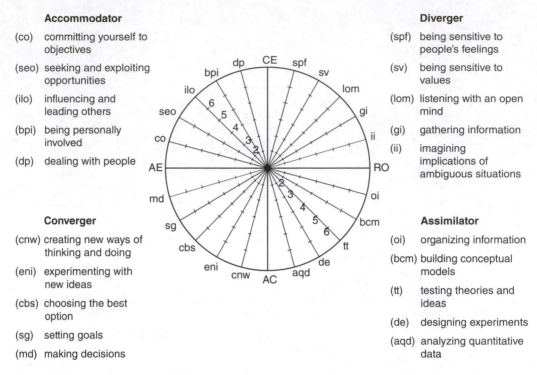

Accommodator

(co) committing yourself to objectives

(seo) seeking and exploiting opportunities

(ilo) influencing and leading others

(bpi) being personally involved

(dp) dealing with people

Diverger

(spf) being sensitive to people's feelings

(sv) being sensitive to values

(lom) listening with an open mind

(gi) gathering information

(ii) imagining implications of ambiguous situations

Converger

(cnw) creating new ways of thinking and doing

(eni) experimenting with new ideas

(cbs) choosing the best option

(sg) setting goals

(md) making decisions

Assimilator

(oi) organizing information

(bcm) building conceptual models

(tt) testing theories and ideas

(de) designing experiments

(aqd) analyzing quantitative data

Figure 4.10   The Competency Circle, Showing Adaptive Competencies as They Relate to Learning Styles

in a two-dimensional space by their association with the generic adaptive competence of learning style (see Figure 4.10).

The accommodative learning style encompasses a set of competencies that can best be termed *acting skills*: committing oneself to objectives, seeking and exploiting opportunities, influencing and leading others, being personally involved, and dealing with people. The divergent learning style is associated with *valuing skills*: being sensitive to people's feelings and to values, listening with an open mind, gathering information, and imagining implications of ambiguous situations. Assimilation is related to *thinking competencies*: organizing information, building conceptual models, testing theories and ideas, designing experiments, and analyzing quantitative data. The convergent learning style is associated with *decision skills*: creating new ways of thinking and doing, experimenting with new ideas, choosing the best solution to problems, setting goals, and making decisions. Since these adaptive competencies are defined as congruences between personal skills and task demands, it seems reasonable to conclude that tasks requiring given specific skills will to some degree influence the expression of the learning style associated with those skills.

Summary and Conclusion

This chapter has described individual differences in learning by introducing the concept of learning styles. Learning styles are conceived not as fixed personality traits but as possibility-processing structures resulting from unique individual programming of the basic but flexible structure of human learning. These possibility-processing structures are best thought of as adaptive states or orientations that achieve stability through consistent patterns of transaction with the world; for example, my active orientation helps me perform well in active tasks, and since I am rewarded for this performance, I choose more active tasks, which further improves my active skills, and so on.

We have examined five levels at which these transactions between people and the world around them shape the basic learning styles—accommodation, divergence, assimilation, and convergence. For example, my own learning style at this moment is shaped by my *personality disposition* toward introversion and feeling, my *undergraduate specializations* in psychology, philosophy, and religion, my *professional academic career* commitment, the *demands of my current job as a professor*, and the *specific task* I am working on now—writing this book. Thus, my learning style is clearly reflective and, at the moment, tipped toward assimilation, although other tasks in my professional role, such as teaching and counseling students, may shift me toward divergence. The forces that shape learning styles at these five levels are summarized in Figure 4.11. At one extreme there are those basic past experiences and habits of thought and action, our basic personality orientation and education, that exert a moderate but pervasive influence on our behavior in nearly all situations. At the other end of the continuum are those increasingly specific environmental demands stemming from our career choice, our current job, and the specific tasks that face us. These forces exert a somewhat stronger but more situation-specific influence on the learning style we adopt.

When learning style is viewed from the two-dimensional perspective proposed here, we can represent the current state of a person's learning style as a single point on the abstract/concrete and active/reflective learning space. The position of this point—for example, in the center of the grid or at one of the extreme corners—is determined by the summative influence of the forces described above. But this representation summarizes only qualitative differences in elementary learning orientations. To fully appreciate a person's approach to learning, we need to understand his or her position on a third dimension, that of development. An explanation of this dimension is yet to come, in Chapter 6. But before describing the experiential learning theory of development, we turn first (in Chapter 5) to an examination of the nature of knowledge and how it is created by learning from experience, since individual approaches to learning and development, as we have seen, are determined by one's transactions with the various systems of social knowledge.

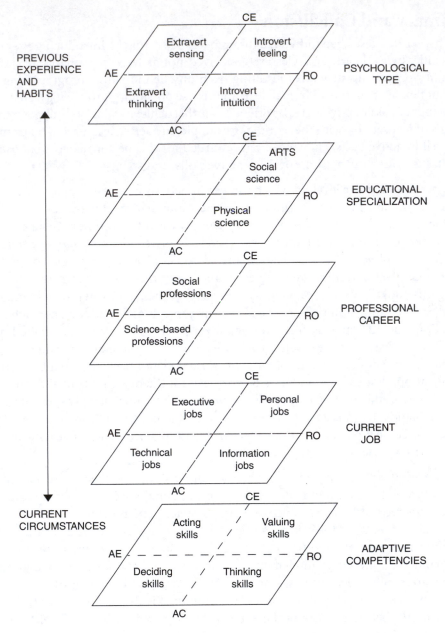

Figure 4.11   Forces that Shape Learning Styles

Update and Reflections
Individuality, the Self, and Learning Style

"For it happens to be an inborn and imperative need of all men to regard the self as a unit. However often and however grievously this illusion is shattered, it always mends again. The judge who sits over the murderer and looks into his face, and at one moment renders all the emotions and potentialities and possibilities of the murderer in his own soul and hears the murderer's voice as his own is at the next moment one and indivisible as the judge, and scuttles back into the shell of his cultivated self and does his duty and condemns the murderer to death. . . . In reality, however, every ego, so far from being a unity, is in the highest degree a manifold world, a constelled heaven, a chaos of forms, of states and stages, of inheritances and potentialities. It appears to be a necessity as imperative as eating and breathing for everyone to be forced to regard this chaos as unity and to speak of his ego as though it were a one-fold and clearly detached phenomenon. Even the best of us share the delusion."

—Herman Hesse Steppenwolf

"At each intersection of Indra's Net is a light-reflecting jewel and each jewel contains another net, ad infinitum. The jewel at each intersection exists only as a reflection of all the others and therefore has no self-nature. Yet it also exists as a separate entity to sustain the others. Each and all exist only in their mutuality."

—The metaphor of Indra's Net from the *Avatamsaka Sutra*

Many years ago Kluckholm and Murray described three different kinds of order in human behavior, "Every person is like every other person in some ways. Every person is like some other person in some ways. Every person is like no other person in some ways." (1948, p. 1). Individuality is a pivotal concept in experiential learning theory. Learning style is one aspect of individuality, one of an almost infinite number of ways that individuals differ. In experiential learning theory, learning style is not a fixed trait but a dynamic characteristic describing how the self processes experience. Every individual is a center of experiencing that is grasped and transformed to create a continuity of experience that among other things includes a unique sense of self.

Western and Eastern Views of the Self

In Western psychology there is a long standing controversy about whether there is a unitary self. Early research (Block, 1961) saw a unified consistent self as indicative of a strong ego, and lack of self consistency as a sign of neurosis. More contemporary research has been influenced by post-modern social constructionism and tends to show that complex self differentiation allows flexibility and is thus a healthy "buffer" to the complex demands of modern life (Linville, 1982, 1985, 1987). Akrivou (2009) used Linville's measure of self complexity and two measures of the higher stages of adult development (described in Chapter 6 Update and Reflections), namely self-ideal congruence and self-integrating process. She found that self-complexity was positively related to both of these measures of self integration; indicating that self-complexity was important for a person to achieve a higher order synthesis of identity, as manifested in the constructivist notion of self-integration described in experiential learning theory. Development from specialization to integration is the progressive and continuous acquisition of subtler distinctions among self categories and concepts and their ordering into hierarchical systems of meaning.

Lynch and Ryan (2014) studied self consistency and authenticity as predictors of well-being in three cultures, the United States, China, and Russia. Both were related to well-being in all three countries. Authenticity, defined as "being true to yourself" and being genuine and congruent with one's values and beliefs, was a more powerful predictor of well-being than consistency.

Recent research by Kahneman and Riis calls into question the methodology of this line of research. Their research on happiness and well-being of life found differences between measurements based on what they called the experiencing self and the remembered/thinking self. The work cited above as well as most psychological research on the self is based on a remembered, thinking self where research participants complete Likert scale ratings or other descriptions of how they see themselves. This abstract conception of self is contrasted with real time experience in the moment: "An individual's life could be described—at impractical length—as a string of moments. A common estimate is that each of these moments of psychological present may last up to 3 seconds, suggesting that people experience some 20,000 moments in a waking day, and upwards of 500 million moments in a 70-year life. Each moment can be given a rich multidimensional description. . . . What happens to these moments? The answer is straightforward: With very few exceptions, they simply disappear. The experiencing self that lives each of these moments barely has time to exist. . . . Unlike the experiencing self, the remembering self is relatively stable and permanent. It is a basic fact of the human condition that memories are what we get to keep from our experience, and the only perspective we can adopt as we think about our lives is that of the remembering self" (2005, pp. 285–286). The authors go on to say that these memories of experience are flawed by a number of cognitive illusions and are often wrong. For example, a study of vacations found substantial difference between recalled enjoyment and actual experienced enjoyment. It was recalled enjoyment that predicted desire to repeat the vacation. In another study, people predict that they are happier on their birthday, but actual experience of happiness is the same as other days.

Some Eastern conceptions of the self see it as an illusion spawned by the seeming continuity of discrete momentary experiences. We referred earlier, in the Chapter 2 Update and Reflections, to the Theraveda Buddhist image of moment consciousness as a string of pearls. In Western views, the string is seen as the continuous self, but not in Buddhism. As with the experiencing self described above, experience is described as a string of discontinuous experiential moments which are estimated to be much shorter than 3 seconds, around 1/500th to 1/75th of a second. In each of these moments of experience, there is *discernment*, recognition of an object which is accompanied by the dualistic awareness of a self attending to the object.

"Between moments of experience of self are gaps in which there is no sense of self or separateness from what is being experienced. . . . By this they meant a dharma which is not conditioned at all by previous patterns. It enters freely and brings with it a sense of freedom from habitual thought. . . . This unconditioned dharma is called *nirvana*, literally 'extinction.' This does not mean extinction of all experience, but only of the grasping onto the belief that one is a permanent self" (Hayward, 1998, p. 619).

Continuity of self or the 'stream of consciousness' is attributed to the coarseness of ordinary attention. With meditation practice it is possible to sharpen attention to become aware of the nirvana background. "Egolessness is not some state of mind to be attained as something foreign to one's present state, nor is it a 'higher state of being'. . . . It is a fundamental, ever-present aspect of one's ordinary being, which is covered up due to ignorance and bewilderment, believing in ego's continuity, and which can therefore be uncovered by knowledge and insight." (1998, p. 622) . . . "Egolessness is not a state in which there is no sense of self at all. Rather it is a state in which the self is perceived not as a solid permanent thing . . . but as a constant momentary flashing into existence out of a boundless background. Gradual identification with the background, rather than with the illusion of a permanent self, brings a sense of harmony, clarity, wisdom and energy to one's life" (1998, p. 625).

Experiential Learning and the Self

The self in experiential learning theory is dynamic and developmental, moving toward a coherent identity and integrity. The self is a dynamic continuous process of learning from experience that takes a unique developmental path for every individual, motivated by a holistic organismic drive for actualization. Carl Rogers describes his theoretical system this way: "It should be noted that this basic actualizing tendency is the only motive which is

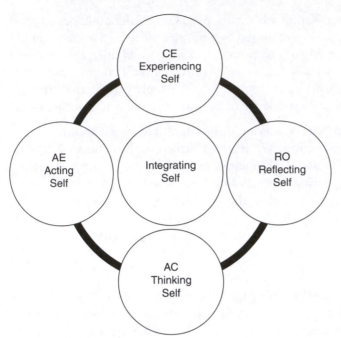

Figure 4.12 The Self in Experiential Learning Theory

postulated in this theoretical system . . . it is the organism as a whole, and only the organism as a whole, which exhibits this tendency. There are no homunculi, no other sources of energy or action in the system. The self, for example, is an important construct in our theory, but the self does not 'do' anything. It is only one expression of the general tendency of the organism to behave in those ways which maintain and enhance itself" (1959, p. 196).

Self individuality is created through the on–going spiraling of the learning cycle in transaction with the social and relational context. Each mode of the learning cycle forms a facet of the self moving toward integration (see Figure 4.12). Everyone develops a unique configuration of these selves through a process of accentuation (Chapter 7, pp. 242–244).

Kahneman's identification of the experiencing and the remembered/thinking self are consistent with the dual knowledge concept of experiential learning theory (Chapter 3, pp. 69–77). The experiencing self is based on direct, present-oriented, concrete experience composed of the discrete brief moments of experiences and the self-less spaces between: the nirvana background of Buddhist thought. I see a similarity between James' concept of pure experience and the nirvana background. The moments of direct self experiencing are somewhat influenced by personal history, culture, and context as Dewey emphasized (see Chapter 2 Update and Reflections). The thinking self is constructed through memories of concrete experiences that have been given meaning through cognitive interpretation. While the remembered self is inevitably a biased representation of the directly experienced self, it is nonetheless the basis on which we make most life choices and decisions. The remembered self is constructed from numerous cases of episodic memory (Chapter 3 Update and Reflections). Mindful cycling through the learning cycle may increase the congruence between the thinking and experiencing self.

A number of experiential learning scholars, including Jack Mezirow (1990), Stephen Brookfield (1987), and David Boud (Boud, Keogh, and Walker, 1985), see the reflecting self as the major pathway to self integration and transformation in the integrating self. Others emphasize self integration through the acting self. Richard Boyatzis' Intentional Change Theory (2008), Deci and Ryan's Self-Determination Theory (1995, 2004), and the Self-Authorship Theory of Kegan (1994) and Baxter-Magolda (2007, 2008) all focus on agentic self-actualization. For Rogers (1961, 1964) and Gendlin (1962, 1978), the path to integration lies in the experiencing self. And for Kohlberg (1981, 1984, 1987), it is the thinking self that guides development toward integration.

Thus the self in experiential learning theory is seen as an ongoing process of special-ized differentiation and integration through an executive meta-self; the consistency and unity of which varies across individuals and their life span. The meta-self is created in Mead's (1934) process of self generation as a response to a "generalized other" created in moments of experiencing with others in one's life. The integrating process itself is an internal conversation with the "I" speaking to the "Me." Power (2007), in a special issue of the *Journal of Clinical Psychology* on the multiplicity of self, quotes the Portuguese writer Fernando Pessoa: " My soul is a hidden orchestra; I know not what instruments, what fiddle strings and harps, drums and tambours I sound and clash inside myself. All I hear is the symphony" (2007, p. 187). He uses this example of the self as a symphony orchestra to describe this dynamic differentiation and integration, "when the different parts of the orchestra play in harmony with each other, then the overall experience is of an integrated whole. . . . Indeed, this same experience of integration can be apparent when one or more sections of the orchestra is silent or absent. Alternatively, there can be a discordant sense of disintegration if the different orchestral parts do not coordinate with each other, for example if each part were to play a different tune" (2007, p. 188)

Learning Style

I created the Learning Style Inventory to describe the unique ways that individual selves "process possibilities" (to use Tyler's term) (see Chapter 4, pp. 99–100) by spiraling through the learning cycle based on their preference for the four different learning modes—CE, RO, AC, and AE. It is therefore focused on that aspect of individuality related to how indi-viduals learn from experience. As a dynamic holistic concept of style, it describes human uniqueness by examining normative descriptions of personal style across individuals and an idiographic profiling within an individual of the different styles within the holistic model.

The original Learning Style Inventory (LSI 1) was created in 1969 as part of a MIT cur-riculum development project that resulted in the first management textbook based on experiential learning (Kolb, Rubin, and McIntyre, 1971). There have been six versions of the Learning Style Inventory published over the last 45 years. Through this time, attempts have been made to openly share information about the inventory, its scoring, and technical characteristics with other interested researchers. The results of their research have been instrumental in the continuous improvement of the inventory.

I coined the term *learning style* to describe these individual differences; differentiating them from the cognitive style research that was popular at the time. As described in Chapter 4 (Chapter 4, pp. 98–100), I sought to distinguish styles of learning from experience not as fixed traits, but as dynamic states arising in an on–going process of learning. For this reason, the format of the LSI is a forced choice format that asks individuals to rank their relative choice preferences among the four modes of the learning cycle. This is in contrast the more common normative or free choice format, such as the widely used Likert scale, that rates absolute preferences on independent dimensions.

The forced choice format of the LSI was dictated by the theory of experiential learning and by the primary purpose of the instrument. Experiential learning theory is a holistic, dynamic, and dialectic theory of learning. Because it is holistic, the four modes that comprise the experiential learning cycle—CE, RO, AC, and AE—are conceived as interdependent. Learning involves resolving the creative tension among these learning modes in response to the specific learning situation. Since the two learning dimensions—AC-CE and AE-RO—are related dialectically, the choice of one pole involves not choosing the opposite pole. Therefore, because experiential learning theory postulates that learning in life situations requires the resolution of conflicts among interdependent learning modes, to be ecologically valid the learning style assessment process should require a similar process of conflict resolution in the choice of one's preferred learning approach. The LSI is not a criterion-referenced test and is not intended for use to predict behavior for purposes of selection, placement, job assignment, or selective treatment. This includes not using the instrument to assign learners to different educational treatments, a process sometimes referred to as "tracking." Such categorizations based on a single test score amount to stereo-typing that runs counter to the philosophy of experiential learning that emphasizes individual uniqueness. "When it is used in the simple, straightforward, and open way intended, the LSI usually provides a valuable self-examination and discussion that recognizes the uniqueness, complexity, and variability in individual approaches to learning. The danger lies in the reification of learning styles into fixed traits, such that learning styles become stereotypes used to pigeonhole individuals and their behavior" (Kolb, 1981a, pp. 290–291).

The most relevant information for the learner is about intra-individual differences, his or her relative preference for the four learning modes, not inter-individual comparisons. Ranking relative preferences among the four modes in a forced choice format is the most direct way to provide this information. While individuals who take the inventory sometimes report difficulty in making these ranking choices; nonetheless, they report that the feedback they get from the LSI gives them more insight than has been the case when we use a normative Likert rating scale version. This is because the social desirability response bias in the rating scales fails to define a clear learning style; that is, they say they prefer all learning modes. This is supported by Harland's (2002) finding that feedback from a forced choice test format was perceived as more accurate, valuable, and useful than feedback from a normative version.

The adoption of the forced choice method for the LSI has at times placed it in the center of an ongoing debate in the research literature about the merits of forced choice instruments and other issues. For a detailed analysis of these issues, see the *Kolb Learning Style Inventory Guidebook* (Kolb and Kolb, 2013a).

The Kolb Learning Style Inventory 4.0

The research reported in this chapter (Chapter 4 on individuality in learning) is based on the first version of the Kolb Learning Style Inventory (KLSI) (Kolb, LSI 1971, pp. 1976a and b). The latest version, the Kolb Learning Style Inventory 4.0 (KLSI 4.0) (Kolb and Kolb, 2011), is the first major revision of the KLSI since 1999 and the third since the original Learning Style Inventory (LSI) was published in 1971. It is based on many years of research involving scholars around the world and data from many thousands of respondents. The KLSI 4.0 maintains the high scale reliability of the KLSI 3.1 while offering higher internal validity. Scores on the KLSI 4.0 are highly correlated with scores on the previous KLSI 3.1, thus maintaining the external validity that the instrument has shown over the years. Validity research on the KLSI since the publication of *Experiential Learning* is also reviewed in the *Kolb Learning Style Inventory 4 Guidebook*.

Data from empirical and clinical studies over the years have shown that these original four learning style types—Accommodating, Assimilating, Converging, and Diverging—can be refined further into a nine-style typology that better defines the unique patterns of individual learning styles and reduces the confusions introduced by borderline cases in the old four-style typology (Eickmann, Kolb, and Kolb, 2004; Kolb and Kolb, 2005a&b; Boyatzis and Mainemelis, 2000). With feedback from users, we first began noticing a fifth "balancing" style describing users who scored at the center of the Learning Style grid. Later we discovered that individuals who scored near the grid boundary lines also had distinctive styles. For example, an "Experiencing" style was identified between the Accommodating and Diverging styles. Four of these style types emphasize one of the four learning modes—Experiencing (CE), Reflecting (RO), Thinking (AC), and Acting (AE) (Abbey, Hunt, and Weiser, 1985; Hunt, 1987). Four others represent style types that emphasize two learning modes, one from the grasping dimension and one from the transforming dimension of the experiential learning theory model—Imagining (CE and RO), Analyzing (AC and RO), Deciding (AC and AE), and Initiating (CE and AE). The final style type balances all four modes of the learning cycle—Balancing (CE, RO, AC, and AE) (Mainemelis, Boyatzis, and Kolb, 2002).

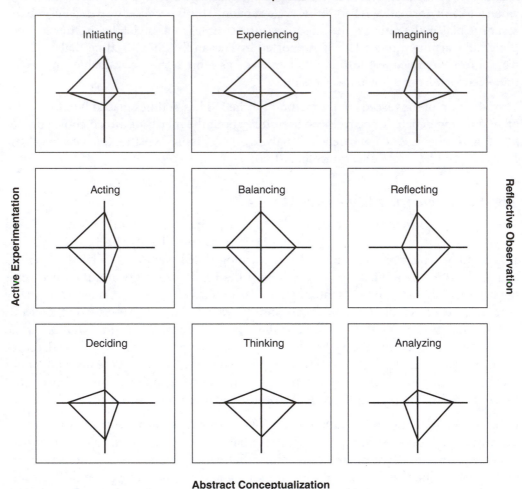

Figure 4.13   The Nine Learning Styles in the KLSI 4.0

The new KLSI 4.0 introduces these nine style types by moving from a 4-pixel to 9-pixel resolution of learning style types as described below. The learning style types can be systematically arranged on a two-dimensional learning space defined by Abstract Conceptualization-Concrete Experience and Active Experimentation-Reflective Observation. This space, including a description of the distinguishing kite shape of each style, is depicted in Figure 4.13.

The Initiating Style   The Initiating style is characterized by the ability to initiate action in order to deal with experiences and situations. It involves active experimentation (AE) and concrete experience (CE).

The Experiencing Style   The Experiencing style is characterized by the ability to find meaning from deep involvement in experience. It draws on concrete experience (CE) while balancing active experimentation (AE) and reflective observation (RO).

The Imagining Style   The Imagining style is characterized by the ability to imagine possibilities by observing and reflecting on experiences. It combines the learning steps of concrete experience (CE) and reflective observation (RO).

The Reflecting Style   The Reflecting style is characterized by the ability to connect experience and ideas through sustained reflection. It draws on reflective observation (RO) while balancing concrete experience (CE) and abstract conceptualization (AC).

The Analyzing Style   The Analyzing style is characterized by the ability to integrate and systematize ideas through reflection. It combines reflective observation (RO) and abstract conceptualization (AC).

The Thinking Style   The Thinking style is characterized by the capacity for disciplined involvement in abstract and logical reasoning. It draws on abstract conceptualization (AC) while balancing active experimentation (AE) and reflective observation (RO).

The Deciding Style   The Deciding style is characterized by the ability to use theories and models to decide on problem solutions and courses of action. It combines abstract conceptualization (AC) and active experimentation (AE).

The Acting Style   The Acting style is characterized by a strong motivation for goal directed action that integrates people and tasks. It draws on active experimentation (AE) while balancing concrete experience (CE) and abstract conceptualization (AC).

The Balancing Style   The Balancing style is characterized by the ability to adapt: weighing the pros and cons of acting versus reflecting and experiencing versus thinking. It balances concrete experience, abstract conceptualization, active experimentation, and reflective observation.

These nine KLSI 4.0 learning styles further define the experiential learning cycle by emphasizing four dialectic tensions in the learning process. In addition to the primary dialectics of Abstract Conceptualization/Concrete Experience and Active Experimentation/Reflective Observation, the combination dialectics of Assimilation/Accommodation and Converging/Diverging are also represented in an eight stage learning cycle with Balancing in the center. The formulas for calculating the continuous scores on these combination dialectics are reported in the *Kolb Learning Style Inventory 4 Guidebook* (Kolb and Kolb, 2013a).

Thus, the Initiating style has a strong preference for active learning in context (Accommodation), while the Analyzing style has a strong preference for reflective conceptual learning (Assimilation). The concepts of assimilation and accommodation are central to Piaget's (1952) definition of intelligence as the balance of adapting concepts to fit the external world (accommodation) and the process of fitting observations of the external world into existing concepts (assimilation). This measure was used in the validation of the Learning Flexibility Index (Sharma and Kolb, 2010; see Chapter 6) and has been used by other researchers in previous studies (Wierstra and de Jong, 2002; Allinson and Hayes, 1996).

The Imagining style has a strong preference for opening alternatives and perspectives on experience (Diverging), while the Deciding style has a strong preference for closing on the single best option for action (Converging). The concepts of converging and diverging originated in Guilford's (1988) structure of intellect model as the central dialectic of the creative process. This dialectic concept has been used in research on experiential learning theory by Gemmell (2012) and Kolb (1983).

Some studies have used continuous balance scores for ACCE and AERO to assess balanced learning style scores (Mainemelis, Boyatzis, and Kolb, 2002; Sharma and Kolb, 2010). These variables compute the absolute values of the ACCE and AERO scores adjusted to center on the fiftieth percentile of the normative comparison group. Figure 4.14 depicts this expanded learning cycle and illustrates how an individual's particular style represents his or her preferred space in the cycle.

Learning Flexibility

Another important aspect of learning style is learning flexibility, the extent to which an individual adapts his or her learning style to the demands of the learning situation. As we have seen above, learning style is not a fixed personality trait but more like a habit of learning shaped by experience and choices. It can be an automatic, unconscious mode of adapting, or it can be consciously modified and changed. The stability of learning style arises from consistent patterns of transaction between individuals and learning situations in their life. This process is called accentuation—the way we learn about a new situation determines the range of choices and decisions we see, the choices and decisions we make influence the next situation we live through, and this situation further influences future choices. Learning styles are thus specialized modes of adaptation that are reinforced by the continuing choice of situations where a style is successful.

Since a specialized learning style represents an individual preference for only one or two of the four modes of the learning cycle, its effectiveness is limited to those learning situations that require these strengths. Learning flexibility indicates the development of a more holistic and sophisticated learning process. The learning style types described above portray how one prefers to learn in general. Many individuals feel that their learning style

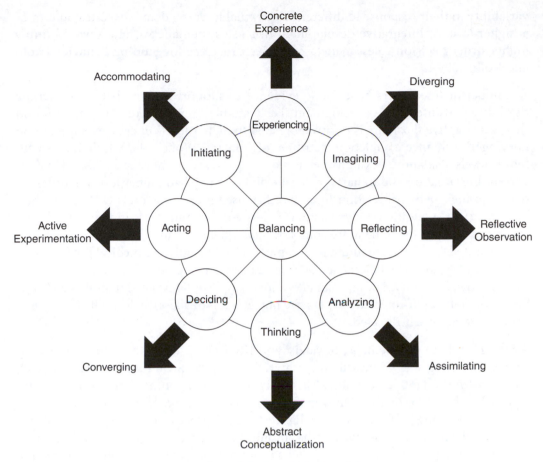

Figure 4.14   The Nine Learning Styles and the Four Dialectics of the Learning Cycle

type accurately describes how they learn most of the time. They are consistent in their approach to learning. Others, however, report that they tend to change their learning approach depending on what they are learning or the situation they are in. They may say, for example, that they use one style in the classroom and another at home with their friends and family. These are flexible learners.

The KLSI 4.0 also includes an assessment of learning flexibility by integrating the Adaptive Style Inventory (ASI) into the instrument. Chapter 8 describes the creation of the ASI, which was designed to assess individuals' level of integrative complexity as they progressed from the specialized to integrated stage of the experiential learning theory developmental model (see Figure 6.3). The instrument assessed adaptive flexibility by measuring how individuals change their learning style in response to different situational demands. It was based on the theory that if people show systematic variability in their response to different contextual learning demands, one could infer a higher level of integrative development because systematic variation would imply higher order decision rules or meta-cognitive processes for guiding behavior (Kolb and Kolb, 2009).

A number of researchers have found evidence to support the link between learning flexibility and integrative development. Early studies (reported in Chapter 8) found that ASI adaptive flexibility is positively related to higher levels of ego development on Loevinger's sentence completion instrument (Kolb and Wolfe, 1981). Individuals with higher levels of adaptive flexibility perceived themselves to be more self-directed in their current life situation and to have greater flexibility. They had higher levels of differentiation in their personal relationships, and they used more constructs to describe their life structure. In addition, they experienced less conflict and stress in their life despite experiencing their life to be more complex. Subsequent research on learning flexibility has replicated some of these findings. Perlmutter (1990) studied 51 medical professionals and found significant relationships between Loevinger's ego development instrument and adaptive flexibility. Thompson (1999), in a sample of 50 professionals from various fields, found that self-directed learners had higher levels of adaptive flexibility than learners who were not self-directed.

Another study by Mainemelis, Boyatzis, and Kolb (2002) examined the relationship between learning style as measured by the Kolb Learning Style Inventory (Kolb, 1999, 2005) and ASI adaptive flexibility. The study tested the hypothesis that learners with equal preferences for dialectically opposed learning modes would be better able to integrate their learning preferences into a flexible learning process. The study proposed that a balanced learning style (as given by the absolute value for the dialectics of experiencing/conceptualizing and acting/reflecting adjusted for population mean) would be related to learning flexibility. In other words, the more an individual is balanced on the conceptualizing/experiencing and acting/reflecting dialectics, the more he or she will exhibit learning flexibility. This was supported for the dialectic of conceptualizing/experiencing. No significant result was found for the dialectic of acting/reflecting. However, the study also found an equally strong relationship between learning flexibility and a preference for concreteness over abstraction, the KLSI AC-CE score.

Akrivou (2008) found a relationship between learning flexibility and integrative development as measured by her Integrative Development Scale (IDS). She created this scale by identifying items that describe the integrative stage of adult development as defined in the works of Loevinger (1966, 1976, 1998), Rogers (1961), Perry (1970), Kegan (1982, 1994), and Kolb (1984, 1988, 1991). In her comprehensive review of ASI research, Bell (2005) reported other construct validity evidence but suggested a need for revision of the original instrument and the creation of new measures of adaptive flexibility.

Sharma and Kolb (2010) modified the ASI to fit the format of the KLSI and created a Learning Flexibility Index (LFI) based on the Kendall's W statistic. They showed construct validity for the LFI measure by testing six hypotheses about the place of the LFI in a nomological net. The LFI was negatively related to age and educational level. Women and those in concrete professions tended to be more flexible. Individuals with an assimilating learning style tended to be less flexible. The LFI was positively related to Akrivou's Integrative Development Scale, replicating her earlier findings. Individuals who are men, older, highly educated, and specialists in abstract, paradigmatic fields were more assimilative in learning style and had less learning flexibility. The results suggest that it is the orientation toward abstraction and reflection characteristic of the assimilative learning style that leads to inflexibility. Since it is the assimilative style that is the most favored and most developed in formal education systems, one might ask if this abstract approach is producing the unintended negative consequence of learning inflexibility. Emphasis on conceptual learning at the expense of contextual learning may lead to dogmatic adherence to ideas without testing them in experience, what Whitehead called "the fallacy of misplaced concreteness." Contextual learning approaches like experiential learning (Kolb, 1984) and situated learning (Lave and Wenger, 1991) may help education to nurture integrated learners who are as sensitive to context as they are to abstract concepts. A related issue concerns the priority placed on specialized over integrative learning in education. Specialization in subject matter and the learning style most suited to learning it may well produce higher levels of specialized mastery. Mainemelis et al. (2002) found that specialized learning styles led to greater development of learning skills related to the specialization than did balanced learning styles.

A study by Moon (2008) using the new KLSI 4.0 Learning Flexibility Index examined sales performance in financial services, finding that learning flexibility influenced sales success as measured by monthly volume of sales. Gemmell (2012) studied 172 technology entrepreneurs who were founders/CEOs of their current company. He examined the relationship between their KLSI and LFI 4.0 scores and their company's innovation and performance. Results shown in Figure 4.15 display a positive relationship between Active Experimentation (AE-RO) and experimentation, which in turn influenced innovation and performance. Entrepreneurs with high learning flexibility were more likely to take longer to make key strategic decisions; however, in the process of doing so, they were more innovative. "Technology entrepreneurs who are flexible learners—in spite of the enormous environmental pressures—appear to achieve greater innovation by taking slightly longer to consider more alternatives, to reflect upon those alternatives and to ultimately converge to a solution and take action" (2012, p. 90).

Learning flexibility indicates the development of a more holistic and sophisticated learning process. Following Jung's theory that adult development moves from a specialized

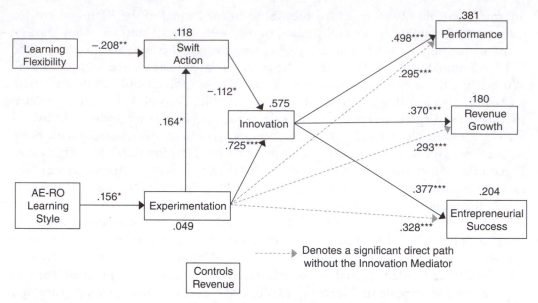

Figure 4.15 The Influence of Entrepreneur's Learning Style and Learning Flexibility on Their Company's Innovation and Performance (Gemmell 2012)

way of adapting toward a holistic integrated way, development in learning flexibility is seen as a move from specialization to integration. Integrated learning is a process involving a creative tension among the four learning modes that is responsive to contextual demands. Learning flexibility is the ability to use each of the four learning modes to move freely around the learning cycle and to modify one's approach to learning based on the learning situation. Experiencing, reflecting, thinking, and acting each provide valuable perspectives on the learning task in a way that deepens and enriches knowledge.

This can be seen as traveling through each of the regions of the learning space in the process of learning. The flexibility to move from one learning mode to another in the learning cycle is important for effective learning. Learning flexibility can help us move in and out of the learning space regions, capitalizing on the strengths of each learning style. Learning flexibility broadens the learning comfort zone and allows us to operate comfortably and effectively in more regions of the learning space, promoting deep learning and development. In addition to providing a measure of how flexible one is in their approach to learning, the KLSI 4.0 also provides an indication of which learning space they move to in different learning contexts—their back–up learning styles. Figure 4.16 shows the backup styles of Initiating and Balancing for an Experiencing type with a low flexibility score and the backup styles of Experiencing, Imagining, Balancing, Reflecting,

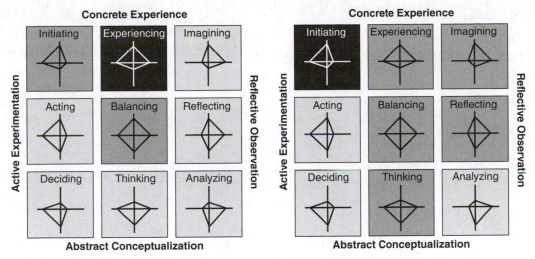

Figure 4.16　Backup Styles for a Low and High Learning Flexibility Learner

and Thinking for an Initiating learning style with a high flexibility score. High flexibility individuals tend to show more backup styles and hence a greater ability to move around the learning cycle.

5

The Structure of Knowledge

Experience is not a veil that shuts off man from nature, it is a means of penetrating continually further into the heart of nature.

—John Dewey

No account of human learning could be considered complete without an examination of culturally accumulated knowledge, its nature and organization, and the processes whereby individual learners contribute to and partake of that knowledge. Individual learning styles are shaped by the structure of social knowledge and through individual creative acts; knowledge is formed by individuals. To understand learning fully, we must understand the nature and forms of human knowledge and the processes whereby this knowledge is created and recreated. Piaget, in the conclusion to his 1970 book, *Genetic Epistemology*, describes three approaches to learning and knowledge creation and their relation to learning from experience:

> These few examples may clarify why I consider the main problem of genetic epistemology to be the explanation of the construction of novelties in the development of knowledge. From the empiricist point of view, a "discovery" is new for the person who makes it, but what is discovered was already in existence in external reality and there is therefore no construction of new realities. The nativist or apriorist maintains that the forms of knowledge are predetermined inside the subject and thus again, strictly speaking, there can be no novelty. By contrast, for the genetic epistemologist, knowledge results from continuous construction, since in each act of understanding, some degree of invention is involved; in development, the passage from one stage to the next is always characterized by the formation of new structures which did not exist before, either in the external world or in the subject's mind. [Piaget, 1970a, p. 77]

The empiricist, apriorist (rationalist), and genetic-epistemology (interactionist) perspectives on the acquisition of knowledge have defined epistemological debates in Western philosophy since the classical Greek philosophers. In the seventeenth century came the first challenge to the dogma of religious and political authority. The unitary worldview of medieval scholasticism that had dominated the Christian world up until that time gave way to the development of rational and later, empirical concepts that made possible control and mastery of the material world. In the seventeenth century, knowledge was thought to be accessible to the mind alone through rational analysis and introspection. The rationalist philosophers—most notably Descartes, Spinoza, and Libnetz—posed the thesis that truth was to be discovered by use of the tools of logic and reason. Ideas were real and *a priori* to the empirical world. Since experiences were merely reflections of ideal forms, it was the ideal forms in the mind that gave meaning to experiences in the world. As Descartes put it:

> [God] laid down these laws in nature just as a king lays down laws in his kingdom. There is no single one that we cannot understand if our minds turn to consider it. They are all inborn in our minds just as a king would imprint his laws on the hearts of his subjects if he had enough power to do so. [Cited in Frankfurt, 1977, p. 36]

The eighteenth century gave rise to the antithesis of rationalism—empiricism. According to the empiricist philosophers—Locke, Hobbes, and others—knowledge was to be found in the accumulated associations of our sense impressions of the world around us. The mind was a *tabula rasa*, recording these accumulated sense impressions but making no contribution of its own save its capacity to recognize "substance." Truth was to be found in careful observation of the world, a notion that gave rise to a burgeoning of scientific investigation in the eighteenth century.

The nineteenth century saw a synthesis of the rationalist and empiricist positions in the critical idealism of Kant, the first of the interactionist epistemologists. For Kant, the mind possessed *a priori* equipment that enabled it to interpret experience—specifically, equipment to locate forms in time and space and equipment to understand order and uniformity. Thus, the laws of geometry and logic were considered to be beyond experience and essential for interpreting it. Truth in critical idealism was the product of the interaction between the mind's forms and the material facts of sense experience.

Apprehension vs. Comprehension— A Dual-Knowledge Theory

This brief overview of the history of epistemological philosophy is perhaps sufficient to frame the contribution of experiential learning theory to the question of how knowledge is acquired. A moment's reflection on the experiential learning cycle (see Figure 3.1) will suffice to illustrate the limitations of either the rationalist or the empiricist philosophies alone as an epistemological foundation for experiential learning. As we have seen in Chapter 3, experiential learning is based on a dual-knowledge theory: the empiricists' concrete experience, grasping reality by the process of direct apprehension, and the rationalists' abstract conceptualization, grasping reality via the mediating process of abstract conceptualization. We are thus left with Piaget in the interactionist position.

The interactionist epistemology of experiential learning theory, however, is different in some significant ways from the Piagetian interactionism of genetic epistemology. As has been suggested, Piaget's interactionism is decidedly rationalist in spirit. Consider, for example, his explanation of how it is that mathematical formulations have consistently anticipated subsequent empirical findings:

> This harmony between mathematics and physical reality cannot in positivist fashion be written off as simply the correspondence of a language with the object it designates. . . . Rather it is a correspondence of human operations with those of object operators, a harmony, then, between this particular operator—the human being as body and mind—and the innumerable operators in nature—physical objects at their several levels. Here we have remarkable proof of that preestablished harmony among windowless monads of which Liebnitz dreamt. . . the most beautiful example of biological adaptation that we know of. [Piaget, 1970a, pp. 40–41]

Substitute the processes of "biological adaptation" for "imprinting of his laws on our hearts," and the "human operations" of the mind according to Piaget are nearly identical with the "inborn laws" of Descartes in the quote just cited. For both men, the powers of the mind are directly connected with the structure of reality. This rationalist orientation is reflected in the predominant position of action in Piaget's theory about how knowledge is created. For him, sensations and perceptions are only the starting point of knowing; it is the organization and transformation of these sensations through action, most particularly internalized actions or thoughts, that creates knowledge. Knowledge then, for Piaget, is the progressive internalization of the action transformations through which we construct reality—a decidedly rationalist interactionism in which sensation (or knowing by apprehension) is secondary.

The interactionism of experiential learning theory places knowing by apprehension on an equal footing with knowing by comprehension, resulting in a stronger interactionist position, really a transactionalism, in which knowledge emerges from the dialectic relationship between the two forms of knowing.[1] This dialectic relationship is not the Kantian dialectic, in which thesis and antithesis stand only in logical contradiction, but the Hegelian dialectic, in which contradictions and conflicts are borne out of both logic and emotion in a thesis and antithesis of mutually antagonistic convictions.

---

1. We focus in this chapter on the prehension dimension of apprehension and comprehension rather than the transformation dimension of intention and extension, because the prehension dimension describes the current state of our knowledge of the world—the content of knowledge, if you will— whereas the transformation dimension describes the rates or processes by which that knowledge is changed. Although both content and process are legitimate aspects of structure, it is the content of knowledge and its form that have been the primary concern of epistemology, Piaget's emphasis on behavioral transformation notwithstanding. This is in a sense a convenience of exposition, since enduring effects of transformation processes will be represented in the content of knowledge just as the rate of water flowing into a tub is reflected in the level of water in the tub.

To better understand the nature of this dialectic, let us examine the nature of the two knowing processes whose opposition fuels it. To begin with, knowing by apprehension is here-and-now. It exists only in a continuously unfolding present movement of apparently limitless depth wherein events are related via synchronicity—that is, a patterned inter-relationship in the moment (compare Jung, 1960). It is thus timeless—at once instantaneous and eternal, the dynamic form of perceiving that Werner calls physiognomic (see Chapter 6, p. 204). Comprehension, on the other hand, is by its very nature a record of the past that seeks to define the future; the concept of linear time is perhaps its most fundamental foundation, underlying all concept of causality. As Hume pointed out, the mind cannot learn causal connections between events by experience alone (apprehension). All we learn through apprehension is that event B follows event A. There is nothing in the sense impression to indicate that A causes B. This judgment of causality is based on inferences from our comprehension of A and B.

The interplay between these two forms of knowing in the creation of knowledge is illustrated in what has been a difficult circular-argument problem in physics—the fact that speed is defined by using time and time is measured by speed. In classical mechanics, speed and time are coequal, since speed is defined as the relation between traveled space and duration. In relativistic mechanics, however, speed is more elementary, since it has a maximum velocity (the speed of light). This formulation led Einstein to ask Piaget, when they met in 1928, to investigate from the psychological viewpoint questions as to whether there was a sense of speed that was independent of time and that was more fundamental (acquired earlier). What Piaget and his associates found (Piaget, 1971) was that speed is the more basic notion, based on perception (apprehension), whereas time is a more inferential, complex construct (based on comprehension). Their experiments involved asking children to describe a moving object that passed behind nine vertical bars. Seventy to 80 percent of the subjects reported movement acceleration when the object passed behind the bars. Piaget's conclusion was that following the moving object with one's eyes was handicapped in the barred sections by momentary fixations on the bars, causing an impression of greater speed in the moving object. The apprehension of speed thus seems to be based on the muscular effort expended in attending to a moving object. The comprehension of time, however, occurs later developmentally and is much more complex. The apparent circularity of space/time equations in physics therefore appears to be psychologically rooted in the dialectic relationships of knowing speed by apprehension and time by comprehension.

A second difference between knowing by apprehension and knowing by comprehension is that apprehension is a registrative process transformed intentionally and extensionally by appreciation, whereas comprehension is an interpretive process transformed intentionally and extensionally by criticism. Michael Polanyi describes this difference in his comparison of articulate form (comprehension-based knowledge) and tacit knowledge (based on apprehension):

Where there is criticism, what is being criticized is, every time, *the assertion of an articulate form*. . . . The process of logical inference is the strictest form of human thought, and it can be subjected to severe criticism by going over it stepwise any number of times. Factual assertations and denotations can also be examined critically, although their testing cannot be formalized to the same extent.

In this sense just specified, tacit knowing cannot be critical . . . systematic forms of criticism can be applied only to articulate forms which you can try out afresh again and again. We should not apply, therefore, the terms *critical* or *uncritical* to any process of tacit thought *by itself* any more than we would speak of the critical or uncritical performance of a high jump or a dance. Tacit acts are judged by other standards and are to be regarded accordingly as *a-critical*. [Polanyi, 1958, p. 264]

The enduring nature of the articulate forms of comprehensive knowledge makes it possible to analyze, criticize, and rearrange these forms in different times and contexts. It is through such critical activity that the network of comprehensive knowledge is refined, elaborated on, and integrated. Any attempt to be critical of knowledge gained through apprehension, however, only destroys that knowledge. Criticism requires a reflective, analytic, objective posture that distances one from here-and-now experience; the here-and-now experience in fact becomes criticizing, replacing the previous immediate apprehension. Since I am an avid golfer, this fact has been illustrated in my experience many times. In approaching a green to putt the ball, I note the distance of the ball from the hole, the slope of the green, the length and bend of the grass, how wet or dry it is, and other relevant factors. I attempt to attend to these factors without analyzing them, for when my mind is dominated by an analytic formula for hitting the ball (for instance, hit it harder because it's wet), the putt invariably goes awry. What seems to work better is an appreciation of the total situation (the situation being defined by my previous comprehension of relevant aspects to attend to) in which I, the putter, ball, green, and hole are experienced holistically (no pun intended, compare Polanyi, 1966, pp. 18–19).

Much can be said about the process and method of criticism; indeed, most scholarly method is based on it. The process of appreciation is less recognized and understood. Thus, it is worth describing in some detail the character of appreciation. First, appreciation is intimately associated with perceptual attention processes. Appreciation is largely the process of attending to and being interested in aspects of one's experience. We notice only those aspects of reality that interest us and thereby "capture our attention." Interest is the basic fact of mental life and the most elementary act of valuing. It is the selector of our experience. Appreciation involves attending to and being interested in our apprehensions of the world around us. Such attention deepens and extends the apprehended experience. Vickers, along with Zajonc (see Chapter 3), suggests that such appreciative apprehensions precede judgments of fact; in other words, that preferences preceded inferences:

> For even that basic discriminatory judgment "this" is a "that" is no mere finding of *fact,* it is a decision to assimilate some object of attention, carved out of the tissue of all that is available to some category to which we have learned, rightly or wrongly, that it is convenient to assimilate such things. [Vickers, 1968, pp. 139–140]

A second characteristic of appreciation, already alluded to, is that it is a process of valuing. Appreciation of an apprehended moment is a judgment of both value and fact:

> Appreciative behavior involves making judgments of value no less than judgments of reality. . . . Interests and standards . . . are systematically organized, a value system, distinguishable from the reality system yet inseparable from it. For facts are relevant only by reference to some judgment of value and judgments of value are meaningful only in regard to some configuration of fact. Hence the need for a word to embrace the two, for which I propose the word appreciation, a word not yet appropriated by science which in its ordinary use (as in "appreciation of a situation") implies a combined judgment of value and fact. [Vickers, 1968, pp. 164–198]

Appreciation of apprehended reality is the source of values. Most mature value judgments are combinations of value and fact. Yet it is the affective core of values that fuel them, giving values the power to select and direct behavior.

Finally, appreciation is a process of affirmation. Unlike criticism, which is based on skepticism and doubt (compare Polanyi, 1958, pp. 269ff.), appreciation is based on belief, trust, and conviction. To appreciate apprehended reality is to embrace it. And from this affirmative embrace flows a deeper fullness and richness of experience. This act of affirmation forms the foundation from which critical comprehension can develop. In Polanyi's words:

> We must now recognize belief once more as the source of all knowledge. Tacit assent and intellectual passions, the sharing of an idiom and of a cultural heritage, affiliation to a like-minded community; such are the impulses which shape our vision of the nature of things on which we rely for our mastery of things. No intelligence, however critical or original, can operate outside such a fiduciary framework. [Polanyi, 1958, p. 266]

Appreciative apprehension and critical comprehension are thus fundamentally different processes of knowing. Appreciation of immediate experience is an act of attention, valuing, and affirmation, whereas critical comprehension of symbols is based on objectivity (which involves *a priori* control of attention, as in double-blind controlled experiments), dispassionate analysis, and skepticism. As we will see, knowledge and truth result not from the preeminence of one of these knowing modes over the other but from the intense coequal confrontation of both modes.

A third difference between knowing by apprehension and by comprehension is perhaps the most critical for our understanding of the nature of knowledge in its relationship to learning from experience. Apprehension of experience is a personal subjective process that cannot be known by others except by the communication to them of the comprehensions that we use to describe our immediate experience. Comprehension, on the other hand, is an objective social process, a tool of culture, as Engels would call it. From this it follows that there are two kinds of knowledge: *personal knowledge,* the combination of my direct apprehensions of experience and the socially acquired comprehensions I use to explain this experience and guide my actions; and *social knowledge,* the independent, socially, and culturally transmitted network of words, symbols, and images that is based solely on comprehension. The latter, as Dewey noted, is the civilized objective accumulation of the individual person's subjective life experience.

It is commonly assumed that what we are calling social knowledge stands alone from the personal experience of the user. When we think of knowledge, we think of books, computer programs, diagrams, and the like, organized into a coherent system or library. Social knowledge, however, cannot exist independently of the knower but must be continuously recreated in the knower's personal experience, whether that experience be through concrete interaction with the physical and social world or through the media of symbols and language. With symbols and words in particular, we are often led into the illusion that knowledge exists independently in the written work or mathematical notation. But to understand these words and symbols requires a knower who understands and employs a transformational process in order to yield personal knowledge and meaning. If, for example, I read that a "black hole" in astronomy is like a gigantic spiral of water draining from a bathtub, I can create for myself some knowledge of what a black hole is like (such as the force of gravity drawing things into it) based on my concrete experiences in the bath. This, however, is quite a different knowledge of black holes from that of the scientists who understand the special theory of relativity, the idea that gravity curves space, and so on. Personal knowledge is thus the result of the transaction between the form or structure of its external representational and transformational grammar (social knowledge, such as the bathtub image or the formal theory of relativity) and the internal representational and transformation processes that the person has developed in his or her personal knowledge system.

The Dialectics of Apprehension and Comprehension

> *Thoughts without content are empty*
> *Intuitions without concepts are blind.*
>
> —Immanuel Kant

The dynamic relation between apprehension and comprehension lies at the core of knowledge creation. The mind, to use Sir Charles Sharrington's famous phrase, is "an enchanted loom where millions of flashing shuttles weave a dissolving pattern, always a meaningful pattern though never an abiding one. . . ." Normal human consciousness is a combination of two modes of grasping experiences, forming a continuous experiential fabric, the warp of which represents apprehended experiences woven tightly by the weft of comprehended representations. Just as the patterns in a fabric are governed by the interrelations among warp and weft, so too, personal knowledge is shaped by the inter-relations between apprehension and comprehension. The essence of the interrelationship is expressed in Kant's analysis of their interdependence: Apprehensions are the source of validation for comprehensions ("thoughts without content are empty"), and comprehensions are the source of guidance in the selection of apprehensions ("intuitions without concepts are blind").

Immediate apprehended experience is the ultimate source of the validity of comprehensions in both fact and value. The factual basis of a comprehension is ultimately judged in terms of its connection with sense experience. Its value is similarly judged ultimately by its immediate affective utility. Albert Einstein describes the relation between apprehension and comprehension thus:

> For me it is not dubious that our thinking goes on for the most part without use of signs (words) and beyond that to a considerable degree unconsciously. For how otherwise should it happen that sometimes we "wonder" quite spontaneously about some experience? This "wondering" seems to occur when an experience comes into conflict with a world of concepts which is already sufficiently fixed in us. Whenever such a conflict is experienced hard and intensively, it reacts back upon our thought world in a decisive way. The development of this thought world is in a certain sense a continuous flight from "wonder." . . .

> I see on the one side the totality of sense experiences and, on the other, the totality of the concepts and propositions which are laid down in books. The relations between the concepts and propositions among themselves and each other are of a logical nature, and the business of logical thinking is strictly limited to the achievement of the connection between concepts and propositions among each other according to firmly laid down rules which are the concern of logic. The concepts and propositions get "meaning," viz. "content," only through their connection with sense-experiences. The connection of the latter with the former is purely intuitive, not itself of a logical nature. The degree of certainty with which this relation, viz. intuitive connection, can be undertaken, and nothing else differentiates empty phantasy from scientific "truth." [Schilpp, 1949]

More directly, the physicist David Bohm says, "All knowledge is a structure of abstractions, the ultimate test of the validity of which is, however, in the process of coming into contact with the world that takes place in immediate perception" (1965, p. 220).

Comprehensions, on the other hand, guide our choices of experiences and direct our attention to those aspects of apprehended experience to be considered relevant. Comprehension is more than a secondary process of representing selected aspects of apprehended reality. The process of critical comprehension is capable of selecting and reshaping apprehended experience in ways that are more powerful and profound. The power of comprehension has led to the discovery of ever-new ways of seeing the world, the very connection between mind and physical reality that Piaget noted earlier (compare Dewey, 1958, pp. 67–68). Dewey describes the powers of comprehension over the immediacy of apprehension in his reference to William James:

> Genuine science is impossible as long as the object esteemed for its own intrinsic qualities is taken as the object of knowledge. Its completeness, its immanent meaning, defeats its use as indicating and implying.

> Said William James, "Many were the ideal prototypes of rational order: teleological and esthetic ties between things . . . as well as logical and mathematical relations. The most promising of these things at first were of course the richer ones, the more sentimental ones. The baldest and least promising were mathematical ones; but the history of the latter's application is a history of steadily advancing successes, while that of the sentimentally richer ones is one of relative sterility and failure. Take those aspects of phenomena which interest you as a human being most . . . and barren are all your results. Call the things of nature as much as you like by sentimental moral and esthetic names, no natural consequences follow from the naming. . . . But when you give the things mathematical and mechanical names and call them so many solids in just such positions, describing just such paths with just such velocities, all is changed. . . . Your "things" realize the consequences of the names by which you classed them."

> A fair interpretation of these pregnant sentences is that as long as objects are viewed telically, as long as the objects of the truest knowledge, the most real forms of being, are thought of as ends, science does not advance. Objects are possessed and appreciated, but they are not *known*. To know means that men have become willing to turn away from precious possessions; willing to let drop what they own, however precious, in behalf of a grasp of objects which they do not as yet own. Multiplied and secure ends depend upon letting go existent ends, reducing them to indicative and implying means. [John Dewey quoting William James, 1958, pp. 130–131]

Dialectics, Doubt, and Certainty

The relationship between apprehension and comprehension is dialectic in the Hegelian sense that although the results of either process cannot be entirely explained in terms of the other, these opposite processes merge toward a higher truth that encompasses and transcends them. The process whereby this synthesis is achieved, however, is somewhat mysterious; that is, it cannot be explained by logical comprehension alone. Thus the development of knowledge, our sense of progress in the refinement of ideas about ourselves and the world around us, proceeds by a dynamic that in prospect is filled with surprising, unanticipated experiences and insights, and in retrospect makes our earlier earnest convictions about the nature of reality seem simplistic and dogmatic. As learners, engaged in this process of knowledge creation, we are alternatively enticed into a dogmatic embrace of our current convictions and threatened with utter skepticism as what we thought were adamantine crystals of truth dissolve like fine sand between our grasping fingers. The posture of partial skepticism, of what Perry (1970) calls commitment within relativism, that is needed to openly confront the conflict inherent in the dialectic process is difficult to maintain. The greatest challenge to the development of knowledge is the comfort of dogmatism—the security provided by unquestioned confidence in a statement of truth, or in a method for achieving truth—or even the shadow dogmatism of utter skepticism (for to be utterly skeptical is to dogmatically affirm that nothing can be known).

Our primitive ancestors leaned toward a dogmatic affirmation of apprehension and a tenacious reliance on immediate sensation and feelings, a concrete approach to knowledge that was manifest in the formulation of animistic world views and a "science of the concrete" (Levi-Strauss, 1969). In Plato's *Phaedrus,* the ancients' mistrust of comprehension is nicely portrayed in the mythical conversation between the Egyptian god Thoth, who invented writing, and Thamus, a god-king who chastises Thoth for his invention:

> This discovery of yours will create forgetfulness in the learners' souls because they will not use their memories; they will trust to the external written characters and not remember of themselves. The specific which you have discovered is an aid not to memory, but to reminiscence; and you give your disciples not truth, but only the semblance of truth; they will be hearers of many things and will have learned nothing; they will appear to be omniscient and will generally know nothing; they will be tiresome company, having the show of wisdom without its reality. [From Sagan, 1977, pp. 222–223]

The modern tendency, however, is to embrace the comprehension pole of the knowledge dialectic and to view with suspicion the intuitions of subjective experience. The clearest and most extreme intellectual expressions of modern reliance on comprehension are manifest in the domination of American psychology by behaviorist theories and methodologies and in the epistemological philosophy that spawned behaviorism—logical positivism. In a zeal born out of the upending of the tidy system of classical physics before the discoveries of modern twentieth-century physics, positivism sought to affirm that all knowledge must ultimately be based on empirical or logical data. In this way, the most dogmatic of the positivists denied the existence of subjective experiences (apprehensions) except insofar as these were verifiable by a community of observers following logical and scientific conventions (comprehensions).

In response to the positivists' dogmatic embrace of comprehension, Polanyi proposes an equally dogmatic embrace of apprehension to confront the modern supremacy of analytic powers:

> As I surveyed the operations of the tacit coefficient in the act of knowing, I pointed out how everywhere the mind follows its own self-set standards, and I gave my tacit or explicit endorsement to this manner of establishing truth. Such an endorsement is an action of the same kind as that which it accredits and is to be classed therefore as a *consciously a-critical statement*.

> This invitation to dogmatism may appear shocking; yet it is but the corollary to the greatly increased critical powers of man. These have enhanced our mind with a capacity for self-transcendence of which we can never divest ourselves. We have plucked from the Tree a second apple which has forever emperiled our knowledge of Good and Evil, and we must learn to know these qualities henceforth in the blinding light of our new analytical powers. Humanity has been deprived a second time of its innocence, and driven out of another garden which was, at any rate, a Fool's Paradise. Innocently, we had trusted that we could be relieved of all personal responsibility for our beliefs by objective criteria of validity—and our own critical powers have shattered this hope. Struck by our sudden nakedness, we may try to brazen it out by flaunting it in a profession of nihilism. But modern man's immorality is unstable. Presently his moral passions reassert themselves in objectivist disguise and the scientistic Minotaur *is born*. [Polanyi, 1958, p. 268]

We are thus led to the conclusion that the proper attitude for the creation of knowledge is neither a dogmatism of apprehension or comprehension nor an utter skepticism, but an attitude of partial skepticism in which the knowledge of comprehension is held provisionally to be tested against apprehensions, and vice versa. The critical difference between personal and social knowledge is the presence of apprehension as a way of knowing in personal knowledge. It should be clear that the apprehensional portion of personal knowledge is all that prevents us from losing our identity as unique human beings, to be swallowed up in the command feedback loops of the increasingly computerized social-knowledge system. Because we can still learn from our *own experience*, because we can subject the abstract symbols of the social-knowledge system to the rigors of our own inquiry about these symbols and our personal experience with them, we are free. This process of choosing to believe is what we feel when we know that we are free to chart the course of our own destiny.

The Structure of Social Knowledge: World Hypotheses

Since all social knowledge is learned, it is reasonable to suspect that there is some isomorphism between the structure of social knowledge and the structure of the learning process. Thus it seems likely that some systems of knowledge will rely heavily on comprehension and others will rely on apprehension; some will be oriented to extension and practical application and others will be oriented toward intention and basic understanding. The philosopher Stephen Pepper, in his seminal work, *World Hypotheses,* proposes just such a framework for describing the structure of knowledge based on the fundamental metaphysical assumptions or "root metaphors" of systems for developing refined knowledge from common sense:

> This tension between common sense and expert knowledge, between cognitive security without responsibility and cognitive responsibility without full security, is the interior dynamics of the knowledge situation. The indefiniteness of much detail in common sense, its contradictions, its lack of established grounds, drive thought to seek definiteness, consistency, and reasons. Thought finds these in the criticized and refined knowledge of mathematics, science, and philosophy, only to discover that these tend to thin out into arbitrary definitions, pointer readings, and tentative hypotheses. Astounded at the thinness and hollowness of these culminating achievements of conscientiously responsible cognition, thought seeks matter for its definitions, significance for its pointer readings, and support for its wobbling hypotheses. Responsible cognition finds itself insecure as a result of the very earnestness of its virtues. But where shall it turn? It does, in fact, turn back to common sense, that indefinite and irresponsible source which it so lately scorned. But it does so, generally, with a bad grace. After filling its empty definitions and pointer readings and hypotheses with meaning out of the rich confusion of common sense, it generally turns its head away, shuts its eyes to what it has been doing, and affirms dogmatically the self-evidence and certainty of the common-sense significance it has drawn into its concepts. Then it pretends to be securely based on self-evident principles or indubitable facts. If our recent criticism of dogmatism is correct, however, this security in self-evidence and indubitability has proved questionable. And critical knowledge hangs over a vacuum unless it acknowledges openly the actual, though strange, source of its significance and security in the uncriticized material of common sense. Thus the circle is completed. Common sense continually demands the responsible criticism of refined knowledge, and refined knowledge sooner or later requires the security of common-sense support. [Pepper, 1942, pp. 44–46]*

---

* Reprinted from *World Hypotheses* by Stephen C. Pepper by permission of the University of California Press, Berkeley, California.

Root metaphors are drawn from experiences of common sense and are used by philosophers to interpret the world. Each of the major philosophies has cognitively refined one of these root metaphors into a set of categories that hang together and claim validity by all evidence of every kind. From the seven or eight such clues or root metaphors in the epistemological literature, Pepper argues that there are only four that are relatively adequate in precision (how accurately they fit the facts) and scope (the extent to which all known facts are covered) and can thus claim the status of a world hypothesis.

The first of these, Pepper calls *formism* (also known as realism), whose root metaphor is the observed similarity between objects and events. The second is *mechanism* (also called naturalism or materialism), whose root metaphor is the machine. The third is *contextualism* (better known as pragmatism), with the root metaphor of the changing historical event. The final relatively adequate world hypothesis is *organicism* (absolute idealism), whose root metaphor is achievement of harmonious unity. None of these world hypotheses is reflected in pure form in the work of any single philosopher, since most philosophers tend to be somewhat eclectic in their use of world hypotheses. For purposes of understanding, however, we can say that formism originated in the classical works of Socrates, Plato, and Aristotle, and mechanism in the works of Democritus, Lucretius, and Galileo. Contextualism is more modern, originating in the works of Dewey, James, Peirce, and Mead, as is organicism, developed primarily in the work of Hegel and Royce.

The isormorphism between Pepper's system of world hypotheses and the structure of the learning process becomes apparent in his analysis of the interrelationships among the four world hypotheses. Formism and mechanism, the two world hypotheses underlying modern science, are primarily analytic in nature, wherein elements and factors are the basic facts from which any synthesis is a derivative. Contextualism and organicism, on the other hand, are synthetic, wherein the basic facts are contexts and complexes such that analysis of components is a derivative of the synthetic whole. Within both the analytic and synthetic world hypotheses there is a further polarity between dispersive and integrative strategies of inquiry. Formism and contextualism are both dispersive in their plan, explaining facts one by one without systematic relationship to one another. Indeed, both formism and contextualism see the world as indeterminate and unpredictable. Organicism and mechanism are integrative in their plan, believing in an integrated world order where indeterminance is simply a reflection of inadequate knowledge. Because they seek integrative determinant explanations, the strength of the integrative world hypotheses (organicism and mechanism) is precision and predictability; their weakness is lack of scope, their inability to achieve an integrated explanation of all things. The dispersive world hypotheses, on the other hand, are weak in precision, offering several possible interpretations for many events, but strong in scope, since their explanatory range is not restricted by any integrative principle.

Figure 5.1 shows Pepper's system of world hypotheses overlaid on the structural dimensions of the learning process. The analytic world views emphasize knowing by

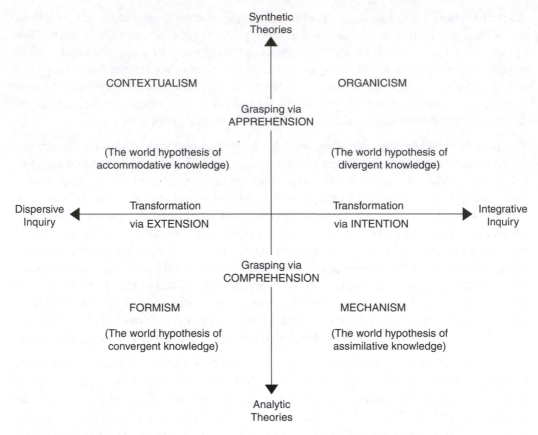

Figure 5.1 Pepper's System of World Hypotheses and the Structure of Learning

comprehension, and the synthetic world views give primary emphasis to knowing by apprehension. The dispersive philosophies emphasize transformation by extension, the discovery and explanation of laws and events in the external world; the integrative philosophies emphasize transformation by intention, the search for underlying principles and integrated meaning.

Formism and Mechanism—The Analytic World Hypotheses Based on Comprehension

Inquiry in modern science rests primarily on the metaphysical foundations of formism and mechanism. The modern version of formism, realism, incorporates many of the characteristics of mechanism, such as an emphasis on space/time location, so that the two root metaphors are often indistinguishable. E. A. Burtt describes this interrelationship between the two analytic world hypotheses by illustrating how both are central to the concept of law:

> In its very essence this concept [law] preserves something vital in the formistic conception of "form" as well as something vital in the mechanistic conception of "regular interrelationship" among the parts of a machine. And I can think of no statement of either formism or mechanism as a metaphysical view, calculated to appear at all persuasive to any modern mind, which has not somewhere drawn upon those features of modern science which synthesize earlier formism and mechanism in precisely this fashion. [Burtt, 1943, p. 600]

There is, however, an important sense in which the two analytic world hypotheses support different modes of inquiry based on the dispersive nature of formism and the integrative nature of mechanism. Mechanism as an integrative strategy is better suited as a foundation for basic research in the physical sciences and mathematics, whereas formism's dispersive plan is more attuned to inquiry in the applied sciences and the science-based professions, where the dictates of practical circumstance often take precedence over the achievement of integrative frameworks. Even though the dispersive nature of formism creates constant difficulties of precision because of the many interpretations to which a single fact is amenable, from a practical standpoint this variety offers flexibility in problem solving.

Formism's root metaphor of similarity is based on the commonsense perception of similar things. It is reliance on this root metaphor that allows the creation of systems of classifications based on similarity, such as the periodic table of elements or biological phyla. It is also the basis by which the validity of models, maps, and mathematical relationships is judged—that is, by similarity of these symbolic comprehensions to the reality being studied. Thus, the formist theory of truth is correspondence; the truth of a description lies in its degree of correspondence to the object of reference.

The modern formist inquiry strategy, sometimes called scientific empiricism, places great emphasis on the judgments of concrete existence through reports of sense experience controlled by the conventions of logic and scientific method. In this sense, even logical positivism, which adamantly denies any metaphysical foundation, is based on formism, since *similar* judgments by scientists of their sense experience are the basis for confidence in positivistic statements. Knowledge in modern formist inquiry is created when the community of scientists is able to agree on the reliable and accurate location of phenomena in time and space—to answer the inquiry questions, "When?" and "Where?" Singer (1959) traces the Platonic origins of such space/time individuation and compares this empirical approach to the rationalist Leibnitzian approach:

> As for the tradition, it goes back at least as far as to Plato, who in his Timaeus makes space the "pure matter" that individuates general qualities (i.e., takes care of the distinction between *this* thing and *that other* precisely like thing). And from Plato's time down, it would be possible to trace an imposing history of space-time individuation. As for practical sanctions, our courts of justice recognize the

all-important difference between the evidence established by "identification by minute description" and the evidence established by "individuation by space-time coordinates." The former, Leibnitzian, method of identification is exactly the one underlying our present method of "police identification." With sufficient refinement of detail, Bertillon measurements may be made to constitute an indefinitely minute description of the *kind* of man a certain individual is. But suppose the accused "identified" with the culprit to the limit of available description; how long would he remain in the dock could he establish an "alibi"? In insisting that the same individual cannot be in two places at the same time, in admitting that two individuals, however like, can be, the law throws the whole weight of its authority on the side of Kant and against Leibnitz. [Singer, 1959, p. 43]

The basic units of knowledge in formism are empirical uniformities and natural laws. The emphasis is on the analysis, measurement, and categorization of observable experience and the establishment of empirical uniformities defining relationships between observed categories—that is, natural laws—with a minimum of reliance on inferred structures or processes that are not directly accessible to public experience.

Mechanism as a world hypothesis is less trusting of the appearances of sense experience and relies more on rationalist principles to analytically separate appearances from reality. The root metaphor of mechanism is the machine, and knowledge in mechanism is refined by analyzing the world as if it were a machine. Central to this analysis is the distinction between primary and secondary qualities. Primary qualities are those features and characteristics that are essential to describing the functioning of the machine. The traditional primary qualities have been size, shape, motion, solidity, mass, and number. In the case of a lever, for example, the primary qualities would be the length of the lever, the location of the fulcrum, and the weights applied at either end. Secondary qualities would be all other characteristics of the lever, such as its color and the material the weights are made of, that are not essential to explaining its functioning. As Democritus, one of the classical founders of mechanism, put it, "By convention colored, by convention sweet, by convention bitter; in reality only atoms and the void." There are six steps or categories in mechanistic analysis:

1. Specification of the field of location in time and space. (In mechanism, everything that exists exists somewhere, unlike classical formism, where form exists independently of particulars in time and space.)

2. Identification of primary qualities.

3. Description of laws governing primary qualities.

4. Description of secondary qualities.

5. Principles for connecting secondary qualities and primary qualities.

6. Laws for regularities among secondary qualities.

The theory of truth in mechanism is somewhat problematic, since, as Pepper points out, primary qualities can be known only by inference from secondary qualities; in other words, they are comprehensions:

> . . . all immediate evidence seems to be of the nature of secondary qualities (all ultimate primary qualities such as the properties of electrons and the cosmic field being far from the range of immediate perceptions); moreover, this evidence seems to be correlated with the activities of organisms, specifically with each individual organism that is said to be immediately aware of evidence. All immediate evidence is, therefore, private to each individual organism. It follows that knowledge of the external world must be symbolic and inferential. . . . So that in a mature mechanism, the primary qualities and all the primary categories are not evidence but inference, or if you will, speculation. [Pepper, 1942, pp. 221 and 224]

The proper theory of truth for mechanism thus lies in the correlation of primary qualities with secondary qualities in what Pepper calls the causal adjustment theory of truth: Does knowledge of the machine in question allow the person to make causal adjustments with predictable consequences for secondary qualities?

The basic units of knowledge in mechanism are the primary qualities or structures that make up the world. Structuralism is thus a modern variant of mechanism. Model building is a typical inquiry method of mechanism that seeks to answer the basic inquiry question, "What is real? What are the basic structures of reality?"—as, for example, in the discovery of the structure of the DNA molecule.

We must stand in awe of the achievements of modern science and thereby give great credibility to the scientific inquiry methods based on formism and mechanism. These represent the highest refinement of human powers of comprehension. Yet ironically, the greatest achievement of scientific inquiry may be the discovery of its own limitations. The history of science is marked by the successive overthrow of widely accepted views of the nature of reality in favor of new, more all-encompassing but more question-provoking views. Today there is little dogma in enlightened scientific inquiry, for the assumptions on which scientific systems of comprehension are based have been challenged by scientific discoveries at the forefront of knowledge. The invention and later validation of non-Euclidian geometry in Einstein's theory of space and time brought down the principles of nineteenth-century science and the "self-evident" Kantian *a priori* forms on which they were based. A number of subsequent discoveries brought into question the very notion of permanent external objects independent of the observer. Whether light is a wave or particle depends on how it is measured. The so-called "bootstrap" theory of the nucleus suggests that subatomic particles inside the nucleus of the atom have no self-sufficient existence, since their properties are determined by their neighbors, and vice versa. Thus, particles in the nucleus gain existence only when they are knocked out of the nucleus by a scientist. The well-known Heisenberg principle of indeterminacy showed that one cannot measure both the location and the momentum of a particle with certainty. In Heisenberg's words, "What we observe is not nature itself, but nature exposed to our methods of questioning."

There are corresponding limitations and indeterminacies in formal systems of logic. In 1931, Kurt Gödel showed that no consistent formal system sufficiently rich to contain elementary arithmetic can by its own principles of reasoning demonstrate its own consistency, a theorem that defined the limits of comprehension as a way of knowing. From Gödel's theorem we are led to the conclusion that to judge the logical consistency of any complex formal system, we must go outside it. Commenting on this indeterminate characteristic of formal systems, a characteristic that he calls tacit meaning, Polanyi says:

> Thus to speak a language is to commit ourselves to the double indeterminacy due to our reliance both on its formalism and on our own continued reconsideration of this formalism in its bearing on our experience. For just as, owing to the ultimately tacit character of all our knowledge, we remain ever unable to say all that we know, so also in view of the tacit character of meaning, we can never quite know what is implied in what we say. [Polanyi, 1958, p. 95]

Contextualism and Organicism—The Synthetic World Hypotheses Based on Apprehension

The recently recognized limitations of comprehension-based knowledge structures have undoubtedly given sustenance to the development of the synthetic world hypotheses based on apprehension. John Dewey, in *Experience and Nature,* argued that the earlier dogmatic intellectualism of science created an unnatural separation of primary experience from nature in which nature became indifferent and dead and human beings were alienated from their own subjective experience, their hopes and dreams, fears and sorrows:

> The assumption of intellectualism goes contrary to the facts of what is primarily experienced. For things are objects to be treated, used, acted upon and with, enjoyed and endured, even more than things to be known. They are things *had* before they are things cognized. . . . When intellectual experience and its material are taken to be primary, the *cord* that binds experience and nature is cut. [Dewey, 1958, pp. 21 and 23]

The systems of social knowledge based on the synthetic world hypotheses operate under something of a handicap, since they must express understandings stemming from apprehension in the social language of comprehension. When the linear, digital descriptions of language and mathematics are used to describe the holistic, analogic context of apprehended experience, the result often seems exceedingly complex and abstract. Yet organicism and contextualism have proven themselves strong in the field of human values and practical affairs—areas where the analytic world theories are weak. Pepper states, for example:

> It may be pointed out that the mechanistic root metaphor springs out of the commonsense field of uncriticized physical fact, so that there would be no analogical stretch, so to speak, in the mechanistic interpretations of this field, while the stretch might be considerable in the mechanistic interpretation of the commonsense field of value; and somewhat the same, in the reverse order, with respect to organistic interpretations. Moreover, mechanism has for several generations been particularly congenial to scientists and organicism to artists and to persons of religious bent. Also, the internal difficulties which appear from a critical study of the mechanistic theory seem to be particularly acute in the neighborhood of values, and counterwise the internal difficulties of organicism seem to be particularly acute in the neighborhood of physical fact. [Pepper, 1942, p. 110]

Like mechanism and formism, the synthetic world theories contextualism and organicism tend to combine and:

> . . . are so nearly allied that they may almost be called the same theory, the one with a dispersive, the other with an integrative plan. Pragmatism has often been called an absolute idealism without an absolute; and, as a first approximate description, this is acceptable. So a little more emphasis on integration, as Dewey for instance shows in his *Art as Experience,* produces a contextualistic-organistic eclecticism; as likewise a little less emphasis on final integration in organicism, as *is* characteristic of Royce. Royce even called himself somewhere a pragmatic idealist. [Pepper, 1942, p. 147]

The contextualist approach, however, has a certain affinity to the world of practical affairs in business, politics, and the social professions, whereas the organistic approach, with its emphasis on absolute values and ideals, is more attuned to the humanities, arts, and social sciences.

The root metaphor of organicism is what Burtt calls harmonious unity. The metaphor stems from the biological organism growing to its fulfillment. The central concern of organismic worldviews is growth and development, with a focus on the processes whereby the ideal is realized from the actual. These processes are most often conceived as some process of differentiation and higher-order integration. This process is teleological toward the absolute, not evolutionary as in the biological principles of natural selection, which are closer to contextualism's open-ended developmental processes. The organismic view of development is the basis of modern humanistic developmental psychology—most notably, Abraham Maslow's theory of self-actualization—and in somewhat more dispersive, contextual, evolutionary forms, organicism is the basis for research in cognitive and adult development. Much historical analysis is loosely based on the organistic world hypothesis, although Hegel's teleological progression to the Absolute is widely questioned. To modern organicists, Hegel's view of development was a dogmatic and unnecessarily narrow progression from maximum fragmentation to his ultimate integration via the dialectic process:

> Hegel was right, say these later organicists, in the inevitability of the trend of cognition toward a final organization in which all contradictions vanish. He was right in his observation that the nexes of fragments lead out toward other fragments which develop contradictions and demand coherent resolution. He was right in his idea that these nexes have a particular attraction for those relevant traits which are peculiarly recalcitrant to harmonization with the facts already gathered. It was the aberrations in the orbit of Uranus, those recalcitrant data which refused to harmonize with the Newtonian laws, that particularly attracted the attention of astronomers and led to the discovery of Neptune. In all these things Hegel was right. But he was wrong and invited undeserved ridicule for the organistic program by his fantastic, arbitrary, and rigid picture of the path of progress. [Pepper, 1942, pp. 294–295]

The theory of truth in organicism is coherence and is derived from the endpoint of development, the Absolute—an organic whole that includes everything in a totally determinant order. Thus, the truth of a proposition is the degree to which it is inclusive, determinant, and organized in an organic whole where every element relates to every other in an interdependent system. There is a certain similarity in this description of organismic truth to the primary quality structures of mechanism, but in mechanism, the emphasis is on structures, whereas in organicism, it is on the processes by which progress is made to the determinant orderliness of the whole.

The basic inquiry question of organicism is one of ultimate values—why things are as they are. Whereas mechanism relies on symbols and the denotative functions of language, there is a tendency in organicism to rely on images and the connotative aspects of language to describe the apprehensions (appearances) from which reality emerges. DeWitt identifies five characteristics of organic concepts: They are holistic, visually apprehended, organized aesthetically and neatly, and functionally based:

> In sum [these characteristics] emphasize the relation of organic concepts to ordinary experience; that is, experience in a universe where straight parallel lines meet at infinity, where the sun visibly rises and sets, where the earth is flat (at least its curvature is of no practical importance), where cause and effect have a direct sequential relationship, where action does not take place without an immediate objective as the motive of the action, where objects are visibly finite. This is the universe which accounts for almost all our everyday experiences but

represents a very limited range of experience—involving, if you will, the statistical fallacy that frequency of occurrence is an index of importance. [DeWitt, 1957, p. 182]

The final world hypothesis is contextualism. Although Pepper treats each of the four systems evenhandedly in his 1942 book, later, in *Concept and Quality* (1966), he embraces a modified version of contextualism (he calls his new world hypothesis "selectivism") as the most adequate of the existing world hypotheses. The advantage of contextualism (selectivism) over the other three world hypotheses is that it integrates fact and value in an open-minded and open-eyed way—a way that is emergent and slightly optimistic, with no dogma of method or tool save a commitment to humanity. The root metaphor of contextualism is the historical event—not the past historical event, but the immediate event, alive in the present—actions in their context evolving and creating the future. Contextualism as a synthetic world hypothesis is concerned with the concrete event as experienced in all its complexity. The one constant in contextualism is change. Reality is constantly being created and re-created. Thus, the permanent forms of formism or structures of mechanism cannot exist in the contextualist worldview. Whitehead (1933, p. 255) puts it this way: "Thus the future of the universe, though conditioned by the immanence of its past, awaits for its complete determination the spontaneity of the novel individual occasions as in their season they come into being."

Inquiry in contextualism is focused on the quality and texture of the immediate event as experienced; hence its association with phenomenology. Lewin's (1951) conception of the person's life space as a field of forces in which behavior is determined by ahistorical causation (only forces existing in the moment, such as a memory, determine behavior) is a primary example of contextually based theory. In this theory of truth, the contextualist works from the present event outward in what is called the operational theory of truth. The basic inquiry question is how to act or think. Actions are true if they are workable; that is, if they lead to desired end states in experience. Hypotheses are true when they give insight into—are verified by—the quality and texture of the event to which they refer. Hypotheses thus achieve qualitative confirmation by the experiences to which they refer. In pure contextualism, however, the truth of a hypothesis gives no insight into the qualities of nature; for nature is constantly emerging and changing. A hypothesis is only a tool for controlling nature. "It does not mirror nature in the way supposed by the correspondence theory, nor is it a genuine partial integration of nature in the way supposed by the coherence theory of organicism" (Pepper, 1942, p. 275).

Summary

Table 5.1 summarizes the characteristics of the four world hypotheses—contextualism, organicism, formism, and mechanism—relating them to the fields of inquiry in which they seem to flourish best: respectively, the social professions, the humanities and social

Table 5.1 A Typology of Knowledge Structures (World Hypotheses) and Their Respective Fields of Inquiry

World hypothesis	Contextualism	Formism	Mechanism	Organicism
Root metaphor	Changing historical event	Similarity	The machine	Harmonious unity
Inquiry strategy	Discrete synthesis	Discrete analysis	Integrative analysis	Integrative synthesis
Modern philosophical forms	Pragmatism, phenomenology	Realism, scientific empiricism (positivism)	Materialism, naturalism, structuralism	Idealism, absolute idealism
Theory of truth	Operationalism—workability, verification, qualitative confirmation	Correspondence	Causal adjustment—correlation of structure with secondary qualities	Coherence—inclusiveness, determinacy, organicity
Basic inquiry question	How	When, where	What	Why
Basic units of knowledge	Events	Natural laws; empirical uniformities	Structures: the locations and laws governing primary qualities	Processes
Dominant method of portraying knowledge	Actions	Things	Symbols	Images
Field of inquiry where it dominates	Social professions	Science-based professions	Natural science and mathematics	Humanities and social sciences

science, the science-based professions, and natural science and mathematics. The significance of Pepper's metaphysical analysis lies in the identification of the basic inquiry structures for refining knowledge. These are derived from simple metaphors of common sense, which lay bare the root assumptions on which knowledge in each system is based. His typology introduces some order to the tangled, fast-growing thicket of social knowledge. The system is perhaps best treated in the framework of contextualism—as a set of hypotheses to be verified, as useful tools for examining knowledge structures in specific contexts. It is to just such an analysis that we now turn.

Social Knowledge as Living Systems of Inquiry— The Relation between the Structure of Knowledge and Fields of Inquiry and Endeavor

Knowledge does not exist solely in books, mathematical formulas, or philosophical systems; it requires active learners to interact with, interpret, and elaborate these symbols. The complete structure of social knowledge must therefore include living systems of inquiry, learning subcultures sharing similar norms and values about how to create valid social knowledge. Academic disciplines, professions, and occupations are homogeneous cultures that differ on nearly every dimension associated with the term. There are different languages (or at least dialects). There are strong boundaries defining membership and corresponding initiation rites. There are different norms and values, particularly about the nature of truth and how it is to be sought. There are different patterns of power and authority and differing criteria for attaining status. There are differing standards of intimacy and modes for its expression. Cultural variation is expressed in style of dress (lab coats and uniforms, business suits, beards and blue jeans), furnishings (wooden or steel desks, interior decoration, functional rigor, or "creative disorder"), architecture, and use of space and time. Most important, these patterns of variation are not random but have a meaning and integrity for the members. There is in each discipline or profession a sense of historical continuity and, in most cases, historical mission.

If the central mission of the university is learning in the broadest sense, encompassing the student in the introductory lecture course and the advanced researcher in the laboratory, library, or studio, then it seems reasonable to hypothesize that different styles of learning, thinking, and knowledge creation are the focal points for cultural variation among disciplines. Different styles of learning manifest themselves in variations among the primary tasks, technologies, and products of disciplines—criteria for academic excellence and productivity, teaching methods, research methods, methods for recording and portraying knowledge—and in other patterns of cultural variation—differences in faculty and student demographics, personality and aptitudes, values and group norms. For example, Anthony Biglan (1973b) has found significant variations in departmental concerns and organization. In the soft areas (social professions and humanities/social science), there is less faculty interaction than in the hard areas (science-based professions and natural science/mathematics); and in the hard areas, this interaction is strongly associated with research productivity. Hard-area scholars produce fewer manuscripts but more journal articles. The emphasis in soft areas is on teaching, and in hard areas on research. Applied areas (social and science-based professions) show more faculty social connectedness than do basic areas (humanities/social science, natural science/mathematics). Their research goals are influenced more by others, including outside agencies, although they are less interested in research than are their basic area colleagues. They publish more technical reports than their basic area colleagues, whose interest in research is not reflected in the time they spend on it.

In reviewing other research on differences among academic disciplines, one is struck by the fact that relatively little comparative research has been done on academic disciplines and departments. The reason for this lies in the same difficulties that characterize all cross-cultural research—the problem of access and the problem of perspective. The relatively closed nature of academic subcultures makes access to data difficult, and it is equally difficult to choose an unbiased perspective for interpreting data. To analyze one system of inquiry according to the ground rules of another is to invite misunderstanding and conflict and further restrict access to data.

To study disciplines from the perspective of learning offers some promise for overcoming these difficulties, particularly if learning is defined not in the narrow psychological sense of modification of behavior but in the broader sense of acquisition of knowledge. The access problem is eased, because every discipline has a prime commitment to learning and inquiry and has developed a learning style that is at least moderately effective. Viewing the acquisition of knowledge in academic disciplines from the perspective of the learning process promises a dual reward—a more refined epistemology that defines the varieties of truth and their interrelationships, and a greater psychological understanding of how people acquire knowledge in its different forms. Twenty years ago, Carl Bereiter and Mervin Freedman envisioned these rewards:

> There is every reason to *suppose* that studies applying tests of these sorts to students in different fields could rapidly get beyond the point of demonstrating the obvious. We should, for instance, be able to find out empirically whether the biological taxonomist has special aptitudes similar to his logical counterpart in the field of linguistics. And there are many comparisons whose outcomes it would be hard to foresee. In what fields do the various memory abilities flourish? Is adaptive flexibility more common in some fields than in others? Because, on the psychological end, these ability measures are tied to theories of the structure or functioning of higher mental processes, and because, on the philosophical end, the academic disciplines are tied to theories of logic and cognition, empirical data linking the two should be in little danger of remaining for long in the limbo where so many correlational data stay. [Bereiter and Freedman, 1962, pp. 567–568]

It is surprising that with the significant exception of Piaget's pioneering work on genetic epistemology, few have sought to reap these rewards.

The research that has been done has instead focused primarily on what, from the perspective above, are the peripheral norms of academic disciplines rather than the pivotal norms governing learning and inquiry. Thus, studies have examined political/social attitudes and values (Bereiter and Freedman, 1962), personality patterns (Roe, 1956), aspirations and goals (Davis, 1965), sex distribution and other demographic variables (Feldman, 1974), and social interaction (Biglan, 1973b; Hall, 1969). The bias of these studies is no doubt a reflection of the fact that psychological research has until quite recently been predominantly concerned with the social/emotional aspects of human behavior and development. Concern with cognitive/intellectual factors has been neatly wrapped into concepts of general intelligence. Thus, most early studies of intellectual differences among disciplines were interested only in which discipline has the smarter students (for example, Wolfe, 1954; Terman and Oden, 1947).

The hypothesis to be explored in this section is that since learning, broadly conceived as adaptation, is the central mission of every discipline and profession, the cultural variations among fields of inquiry and endeavor will be organized in a way that is congruent with the structure of the learning process and the structure of knowledge. When one examines academic disciplines in the four major groupings we have identified—the social professions, the science-based professions, humanities/social science, and natural science/mathematics—it becomes apparent that what constitutes valid knowledge in these four groupings differs widely. This is easily observed in differences in how knowledge is reported (for instance, numerical or logical symbols, words or images), in inquiry method (such as case studies, experiments, logical analysis), and in criteria for evaluation (say, practical vs. statistical significance). Figure 5.2 illustrates the specific relationship predicted among fields of inquiry, the structure of knowledge, and the structure of the learning process. We have in the preceding section elaborated on the relation between knowledge structures and the learning process and have seen in this analysis suggestions concerning the relation of knowledge and learning to living systems of inquiry. Synthetic knowledge structures learned via apprehension are associated with qualitative, humanistic fields, whereas analytic knowledge structures learned via comprehension are related to the quantitative scientific fields, dispersive knowledge structures learned via extension are related to the professions and applied sciences, and integrative knowledge structures learned via intention are related to the basic academic disciplines.

The Structure of Academic Fields

The first suggestion that experiential learning theory might provide a useful framework for describing variations in the inquiry norms of academic disciplines came in Chapter 4, when we examined the undergraduate majors of practicing managers and graduate students in management (see Figure 4.4). Although these people shared a common occupation,

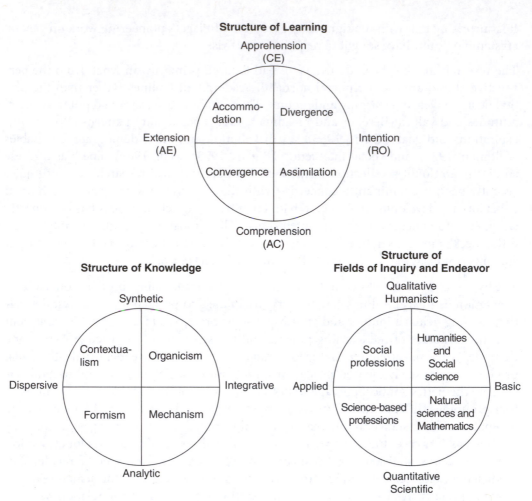

Figure 5.2 Relationships Among the Structure of the Learning Process, the Structure of Knowledge, and Fields of Inquiry and Endeavor

variations in their learning styles were strongly associated with their undergraduate educational experience. There was a good fit with the predictions outlined in Figure 5.2, showing a relation between the structure of learning as measured by individual learning style and one's chosen field of specialization in college. Undergraduate business majors tended to have accommodative learning styles; engineers, on the average, fell in the convergent quadrant; history, English, political science, and psychology majors all had divergent learning styles; mathematics and chemistry majors had assimilative learning styles, as did economics and sociology majors; and physics majors were very abstract, falling between the convergent and assimilative quadrants. These data suggested that undergraduate education was a major factor in shaping individual learning style, either by the process of selection into a discipline or socialization while learning in that discipline, or, as is most likely the case, both.

We now examine how others perceive the differences between academic disciplines and whether these perceptions are congruent with the structure of knowledge and learning. Anthony Biglan (1973a) used a method well suited to answer these questions in his studies of faculty members at the University of Illinois and a small western college. Using the technique of multidimensional scaling, he analyzed the underlying structures of scholars' judgments about the similarities of subject matter in different academic disciplines. The procedure required faculty members to group subject areas on the basis of similarity without any labeling of the groupings. Through a kind of factor analysis, the similarity groupings are then mapped onto an n-dimensional space where n is determined by goodness of fit and interpretability of the dimensions. The two dimensions accounting for the most variance in the University of Illinois data were interpreted by Biglan to be hard-soft and pure-applied. When academic areas at Illinois are mapped on this two-dimensional space (Figure 5.3), we see a great similarity between the pattern of Biglan's data and the structure of knowledge and learning described in Figure 5.2. Business (assumed equivalent to accounting and finance) is accommodative in learning style and contextualist in knowledge structure. Engineering fits with convergent learning and formist knowledge. Physics, mathematics, and chemistry are related to assimilative learning and mechanistic knowledge, and the humanistic fields—history, political science, English, and psychology—fall in the divergent, organistic quadrant. Foreign languages, economics, and sociology were divergent in Biglan's study rather than assimilative as in Figure 4.4. Biglan also reported that the pattern of academic-area relationships in the small-college data was very similar to that in the Illinois data.

These two studies suggest that the two basic dimensions of experiential learning theory, abstract/concrete and active/reflective, are major dimensions of differentiation among academic disciplines. A more extensive database is needed, however. The learning-style data came from a single occupation, and in the case of some academic areas, sample sizes were small. Biglan's study, on the other hand, was limited to two universities, and differences here could be attributed to the specific characteristics of these academic departments.

In search of a more extensive and representative sample, data collected in the Carnegie Commission on Higher Education's 1969 study of representative American colleges and universities were examined. These data consisted of 32,963 questionnaires from graduate students in 158 institutions and 60,028 questionnaires from faculty in 303 institutions. Using tabulations of these data reported in Feldman (1974), *ad hoc* indices were created of the abstract/concrete and active/reflective dimensions for the 45 academic fields identified in the study. The abstract/concrete index was based on graduate student responses to two questions asking how important an undergraduate background in mathematics or humanities was for their fields. The mathematics and humanities questions were highly

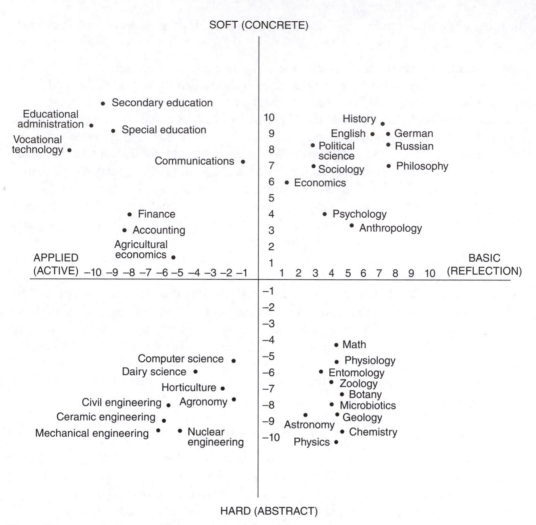

Figure 5.3 Similarities Among 36 Academic Specialties at the University of Illinois

Source: Adapted from A. Biglan, "The Characteristics of Subject Matter in Different Academic Areas," *Journal of Applied Psychology,* 57 (1973).

negatively correlated (−.78). The index was computed using the percentage of graduate-student respondents who strongly agreed that either humanities or mathematics was very important:

$$\frac{\% \text{ Math important} + (100 - \% \text{ Humanities important})}{2}$$

Thus, high index scores indicated a field where a mathematics background was important and humanities was not important.

The active/reflective index used faculty data on the percentage of faculty in a given field who were engaged in paid consultation to business, government, and so on. This seemed to be the best indicator on the questionnaire of the active, applied orientation of the field. As Feldman observed, "Consulting may be looked upon not only as a source of added income but also as an indirect measure of the 'power' of a discipline; that is, as a chance to exert the influence and knowledge of a discipline outside the academic setting" (1974, p. 52). The groupings of academic fields based on these indices are shown in Figure 5.4.

The indices produce a pattern of relationships among academic fields that is highly consistent with Biglan's study and the managerial learning-style data. The results suggest that the widely shared view that cultural variation in academic fields is predominantly unidimensional, dividing the academic community into two camps—the scientific and the artistic (for example, Snow, 1963; Hudson, 1966)—is usefully enriched by the addition of a second dimension of action/reflection or applied/basic. When academic fields are mapped on this two-dimensional space, a fourfold typology of disciplines emerges. In the abstract/reflective quadrant, the *natural sciences and mathematics* are clustered; the abstract/active quadrant includes the *science-based professions,* most notably the engineering fields; the concrete/active quadrant encompasses what might be called the *social professions,* such as education, social work, and law; the concrete/reflective quadrant includes the *humanities and social sciences.*

Some fields seem to include within their boundaries considerable variation on these two dimensions of experiential learning theory. Several of the professions (particularly management, medicine, and architecture) are themselves multidisciplinary, encompassing specialties that emphasize different learning styles. Medicine requires both a concern for human service and scientific knowledge. Architecture has requirements for artistic and engineering excellence. Management involves integration of both quantitative and qualitative analysis in active decision making. Several of the social sciences, particularly psychology, sociology, and economics, can vary greatly in their basic inquiry paradigm. Clinical psychology emphasizes divergent learning skills, experimental psychology emphasizes convergent skills, and industrial and educational psychology emphasize practical, accommodative skills. Sociology can be highly abstract and theoretical (as in Parsonian structural functionalism) or concrete and active (as in phenomenology or ethnomethodology). Some economics departments may be very convergent, emphasizing the use of econometric models in public policy, and others are divergent, emphasizing economic history and philosophy. Indeed, every field will show variation on these dimensions within a given department, between departments, from undergraduate to graduate levels, and so on. The purpose of this analysis is not to "pigeonhole" fields but to identify a common structural model for learning, knowledge, and field of inquiry that is useful for describing variations in the learning/inquiry process in any specific educational or work setting.

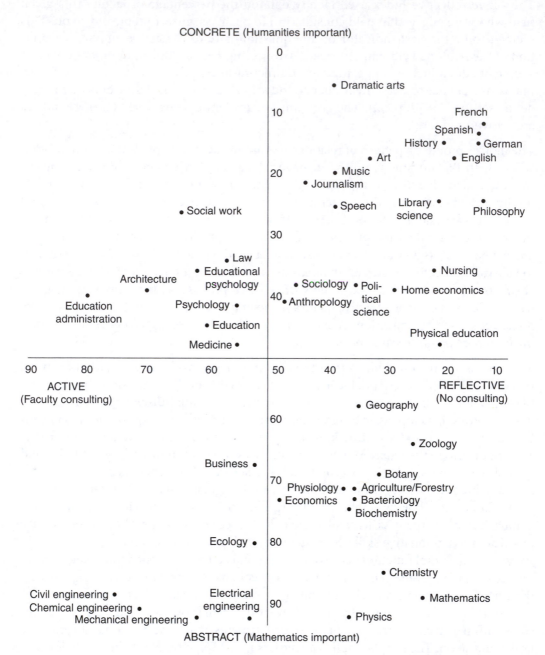

Figure 5.4   Concrete/Abstract and Active/Reflective Orientations of Academic Fields Derived from the Carnegie Commission Study of American Colleges and Universities

The Structure of Careers and Career Development

Since learning is a lifelong process and knowledge is created at work as well as at the university, there is reason to suspect a similar isomorphism between knowledge/learning structures and the structure of career paths. The data presented in Chapter 4, showing the relationships with learning style of professional careers (Figure 4.5) and jobs (Figures 4.6 and 4.7), support this contention. More systematic relationships, however, can be seen in the occupational classification scheme developed by Anne Roe. In her book, *The Psychology of Occupations,* she develops a two-dimensional scheme that defines eight general categories of occupations with six developmental levels in each category. The eight occupational categories and paths of career development are these:

1. Service (from chambermaid to therapist)

2. Business contact (from peddler to promoter)

3. Organization (from messenger to president)

4. Technology (from laborer to inventor)

5. Outdoor (from laborer to specialist)

6. Science (from helper to scientist)

7. General culture (from clerk to scholar)

8. Arts and entertainment (from stagehand to artist)

Reviewing studies of the characteristics of persons in these fields, she states:

> Groups are so arranged that, with one exception, contiguous ones are more closely related than noncontiguous ones. Each of groups IV, V, and VI is related to the other two to about the same degree. Group V placed between IV and VI, observing the close relationship between these two. The groups are arranged in this way because IV is also related to III and VI to VII, whereas V is less closely related to any of the others. The arrangement should be thought of as circular, that is, Group VIII is related to Group I as well as to Group VII. [Roe, 1956, pp. 144–145]

In her later work she suggests that in the circle arrangement, Groups I, II, III, VII, and VIII are classified as people-oriented career areas, whereas Groups IV, V, and VI are non-people-oriented, and thus "an ordered, counterclockwise arrangement of these groups is not untenable" (1957, p. 217). These remarks serve to orient her career classifications on the two-dimensional framework of experiential learning theory.[2] Figure 5.5 shows the correspondence between Roe's circle of careers and the structures of learning, knowledge, and fields of inquiry postulated by experiential learning theory. (Categories IV and

---

2. Other schemes show a similar isomorphism, such as that of Holland (Osipow, 1973, p. 60); compare Samuelson (1982) for the suggested link between experiential learning and Roe's work.

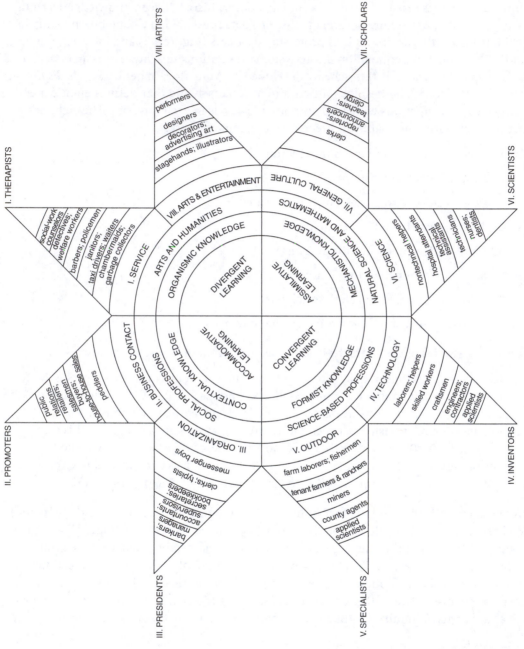

Figure 5.5 The Structure of Careers Shown in Relationship to the Structure of Learning Knowledge and Fields of Inquiry

V are reversed here, since I share Roe's concern about the misplacement of the outdoor category, and in experiential learning theory terms, category IV (technology) should be more abstract.)

In addition, Figure 5.5 represents the developmental levels within each career path as six-level pyramids rising from each category. These levels, according to Roe, are defined by increasing levels of responsibility, capacity, and skill.[3] In this framework, higher-level jobs require greater integrative complexity and adaptive flexibility (see Chapter 8) in order to deal with the greater extension of their responsibilities in time and space. Jacques has suggested that this extension can be measured with great reliability in jobs by what he calls the time span of discretion. As he defines it:

> The higher a person goes in an executive system, the longer is the time frame-work within which he or she works. . . . A job's size can be directly and simply measured by completion times targeted for the longest tasks that are required to be carried out in that role, namely the time span of discretion. [Jacques, 1979, pp. 126–127]

Thus, the highest-level jobs in the eight career paths, such as scientist, inventor, and artist, have time spans of discretion that transcend even lifetimes, whereas jobs at the lower levels are increasingly constrained in their time (and space) limits.

Figure 5.5 may serve as a focal point for a review of the very lengthy progress of argument in this chapter. It shows the relationships among the structure of learning, the structure of social knowledge, and living systems of inquiry (academic fields) and endeavor (careers). It has been argued here that the isomorphism among these structures is rooted in the structure of learning and, in particular, in the integration of the apprehensive and comprehensive way of knowing the world. Social knowledge is a cultural tool that comes alive only in the personal knowledge of the user. In the unique individuality of apprehended experience lies the creative force for expanding, shaping, and validating social knowledge. This social knowledge, in turn, is invaluable in guiding people in their choices of experiences in a field of personal life space and physical reality that is expanding continuously, often by the proactive human tendency to choose experiences that explore and expand these boundaries. We have seen that the success of this learning venture is highly dependent on the proper attitude—an attitude of partial skepticism requiring that each act of knowing be steadily steered between the Scylla of appreciative apprehension and the Charybdis of critical comprehension. The course thus steered is the path to development.

---

3. In experiential learning theory terms, these levels can be seen as stages of development toward integrative complexity. Referring to the cone model of development to be described in Chapter 6 (Figure 6.3), the reader can imagine viewing the cone from the bottom with the facing slopes of the cone peeled back to display the six levels of development described in each of the eight pyramids. These six levels roughly correspond to the six levels of consciousness described in Chapter 6 (Figure 6.2).

Update and Reflections

It is sometimes said that a man's philosophy is a matter of temperament and there is something in this. A preference for certain similes could be called a matter of temperament and it underlies far more disagreements than you might think . . .
One keeps forgetting to go right down to the foundations.
One doesn't put the question marks deep enough down.

—Ludwig Wittgenstein *Culture and Value*

We don't see things as they are, we see them as we are.

—Anias Nin

In Chapter 5, The Structure of Knowledge, I described William James' dual knowledge theory that poses a dialectic relationship between appreciative apprehension and critical comprehension. The opposing realms of direct experience and abstract thought make knowledge not a static thing but a dynamic process of *knowing* where abstract social knowledge is continually created and re-created in the personal knowledge of individuals. The apparent certainty of the written word is continually judged and evaluated throughout history by the experience of those who read it.

The experiential learning theory definition of learning as the creation of knowledge through the transformation of experience implies an isomorphism between the learning process, the nature of the knowledge created through it, and the learning spaces such as academic disciplines and occupations where knowledge is created (see Figure 5.2). The relationships between learning styles and educational specialization, professional careers, jobs, and adaptive competencies described in Figure 4.11 provide one example of this isomorphism. Chapter 5 further explores these relationships through the work of Stephen Pepper and Michael Polanyi.

The Spiral of Knowledge Creation

Another parallel is the spiral of learning from experience and the spiral of knowledge creation. Like the way the experiential learning cycle becomes a spiral through successive iterations of experiencing, reflecting, thinking, and acting to create new experiences for another cycling through the learning process, knowledge creation also is a spiraling process between subjective personal knowledge and objective social knowledge. Social knowledge, the explicit abstract concepts and processes that Vygotsky called the "tools" of culture, is created from the personal knowledge of individuals and returns to transform the subjective personal knowledge experience of those persons and others, leading to the further creation and modification of social knowledge, and so on.

The experiential learning theory knowledge creation process is influenced by Polanyi's concepts of tacit and explicit knowledge paralleling the experiential learning theory concepts of personal and social knowledge (see pp. 157, 158, and 163). He believed that the tacit knowledge that underlies explicit knowledge is more fundamental; the base on which all knowledge resides. We know more than we can tell and, because of this, language and data alone cannot make knowledge explicit. Every human creation began with the appreciative apprehension of a concrete experience much of which lay in a tacit dimension beyond explicit naming and communication. The experience was shaped, named, and renamed forming an "idea" that was shared with others to become social knowledge that continued to be refined in their personal knowledge.

This spiraling process of personal and social knowledge in the process of knowledge creation is illustrated in one of the first experiential learning theory knowledge creation studies. Carlsson, Keane, and Martin used the experiential learning theory learning cycle framework to analyze the bi-weekly reports of research and development project teams in a large consumer products corporation. Successful project teams had work process norms that supported a recursive cycling through the experiential learning cycle. Projects that deviated from this work process by skipping stages or being stuck in a stage "indicated problems deserving of management attention" (Carlsson et al., 1976, p. 38).

In the mid-nineties Nonaka and Takeuchi (1995) introduced a similar spiral of knowledge creation using Polanyi's tacit/explicit dimension of knowing to create a four-phase model of knowledge creation in Japanese companies that describes four modes of knowledge conversion. The first phase, *Socialization*, is tacit to tacit knowledge conversion through sharing concrete experiences. *Externalization* is the second phase converting tacit knowledge into explicit knowledge through dialogue and reflection that articulates one's tacit knowledge into words and images while eliciting the same process from others. This is followed by *Combination*, explicit to explicit knowledge conversion to systematize and apply explicit knowledge and information for organizational transfer. The fourth phase is *Internalization* where explicit knowledge is converted back into individual tacit knowledge by direct experiences that actualize and apply explicit knowledge through learning by doing. The model describes a continuous learning spiral that requires an organizational learning process that initiates and sustains it.

The model was later updated (Nonaka, Toyama, and Konno, 2000) to include Kitaro Nishida's concept of *ba* (Nonaka and Konno, 1998) or learning space as it is called in experiential learning theory (see Chapter 7 Update and Reflections). Arguing that knowledge needs a place to be created, shared, and used, they see *ba* as the time and space necessary for individuals to meet and interact for knowledge creation. They describe four types of these learning spaces that correspond to the four modes of the knowledge creation cycle respectively: *Originating ba,* an experiential place where individuals share and empathize with others; *Dialoguing ba,* where individuals share mental models to articulate tacit knowledge into concepts; *Systematizing ba,* where explicit knowledge is translated into written form for communication to larger groups; *Exercising ba,* where explicit knowledge is translated into action renewing the tacit component of knowledge in individuals.

Personal Characteristics and Ways of Knowing

The origin of explicit knowledge in tacit knowledge is similar to Stephen Pepper's idea that refined ways of knowing are ultimately grounded in common sense. "And critical knowledge hangs over a vacuum unless it acknowledges openly the actual, though strange source of its significance and security in the uncriticized material of common sense. Thus the circle is completed. Common sense continually demands the responsible criticism of refined knowledge, and refined knowledge sooner or later requires the security of common sense support" (Pepper, 1942, p. 46). Pepper identifies four independent metaphysical worldviews based on common sense root metaphors that are equally adequate in their ability to provide credible explanations of facts and events. Formism is analytic and dispersive and is based on the root metaphor of similarity, while mechanism is analytic and integrative and is based on the root metaphor of the machine. Contextualism is synthetic and dispersive and is based on the root metaphor of the historical event, while organicism is synthetic and integrative and is based on the root metaphor of the developing living organism (see pp. 164–175).

Pepper's framework for describing philosophical systems has continued to be the source of many investigations since the publication of *Experiential Learning.* This work supports the idea that the philosophical preferences and inquiry preference of Pepper's four metaphysical worldviews are deeply rooted in the tacit, personal knowledge of the individual. Of particular interest to the examination of the role of personal knowledge in knowledge creation are those studies which have created and validated measures of a person's adherence to the four worldviews of formism, mechanism, contextualism, and organicism (Germer, Efran, and Overton, 1982; Johnson, Germer, Efran, and Overton, 1988; Harris, Fontana, and Dowds, 1977; Super and Harkness, 2003). The study by Super and Harkness, who developed the Child Behavior Questionnaire (CBQ) based on Pepper's four worldviews, supports the isomorphic relationship between the world hypotheses and the structure of learning shown in Figure 5.1 (p. 166). They found large negative correlations between the diagonal opposites formism and organicism (–.51) and mechanism and contextualism (–.58) with small to insignificant correlations between adjoining styles in Figure 5.1. Johnson et al. (1988) also found support for the isomorphism with a significant negative correlation between the LSI abstract/concrete (AC-CE) scale and organicism/

mechanism on the OMPI accounted for largely by a strong correlation between concrete experience (CE) and organicism.

Other research with the measures has found relationships with the worldviews and personality characteristics. Germer et al. (1982) developed the Organicism/Mechanism Paradigm Inventory (OMPI) to assess individual relative preferences for two of Pepper's worldviews: organicism and mechanism. The OMPI is a forced choice inventory that asks individuals to choose their preference for the mechanistic or organic alternative on items that cover philosophical issues such as ontology, epistemology, image of man, analysis and causality, change, dynamics, and methodology, and practical concerns of ordinary people such as marital relationships, parenting, occupational, legal, and other interpersonal relationships. It is not clear why the OMPI creators chose these two worldviews to oppose each other since the primary oppositions as described above seem to be formism vs. organicism or mechanism vs. contextualism. Also, Pepper's linear arrangement of the four by their relative distance from each other is formism-mechanism-contextualism-organicism. Pepper states, for example, "Formism and Organicism are especially hostile to each other" (1942, p. 147). That being said, the OMPI does seem to contrast the analytic (abstract) worldview with the synthetic (concrete) view since neighboring formism/mechanism and organicism/mechanism "seem to shade into one another" (1942, p. 147). Johnson et al. (1988) found that both formism and mechanism in the World Hypothesis Scale (WHS) (Harris, Fontana, and Dowds, 1977) correlate with OMPI mechanism, and organicism and contextualism from the WHS correlate with OMPI organicism.

Johnson et al. (1988), in a validation study of the OMPI, found that the two worldviews are associated with different personality characteristics. Organicists, who view reality in terms of changing, holistic patterns, are imaginative, aesthetic, complex, and changeable. They tend to be fluid, changing and creative, non-conforming, participative, and imaginative in their cognitive style and interpersonally active, autonomous, and individualistic. Mechanists, who see reality in terms of stable, isolated elements, are down-to-earth, inartistic, simple, and predictable. They tend to be orderly, conventional, conforming, objective, and realistic in cognitive style, and interpersonally passive, dependent, and reactive. They conclude, "In short, individuals' personalities mirror their overall philosophical views" (1988, p. 833).

Also found were relationships between worldviews and theoretical orientations and practices. They studied four groups of scientists—sociobiologists, behaviorists, personality theorists, and human developmentalists—finding that their philosophical preferences on the OMPI were related to their theoretical predilections based on analysis of written statements of theoretical preference, journal publications, and symposia presentations. For example, they found that dialectically oriented human developmentalists endorsed an organismic worldview, whereas behaviorists espoused a mechanistic philosophical worldview on the OMPI.

Johnson, Howey, Reedy, Gibble, and Ortiz (1989) studied four different occupational groups. In a group of hospitality educators, organismic scorers on the OMPI had an orientation that values theory above facts, choice over impersonal causality, and nonreductionism over physicalism. The reverse was true of mechanistic educators. A group of Head Start employees and day care workers who were organismically inclined tended to value a holistic over a problem-solving approach to teaching. A group of psychology faculty and graduate student psychologists with artistic vocational interests scored high on organicism. In the fourth group organismically oriented psychotherapists showed more positive attitudes toward using music in psychotherapy.

Harris et al. (1977) developed the World Hypothesis Scale (WHS) to measure Pepper's four worldviews. They found that pairs of friends sharing compatible world hypotheses experienced greater satisfaction in their relationships. Incompatible friends stated that they had less in common and would be less likely to remain friends and would not like to work together on an academic project. Similarly, patients who participated in psychotherapies based on world hypotheses compatible with their own perceived the therapies more positively.

Knowledge Structures and Disciplinary Learning Spaces

In addition to the structural correspondence between the structure of learning and the structure of knowledge just described, Table 5.1 proposes that this structural similarity also extends into academic disciplines, professions, and other fields of endeavor. These define the learning spaces or *ba* where learning and knowledge creation are nurtured and facilitated with each field accomplishing this task in its own unique culture. In *Academic Tribes and Territories* Tony Becher (1989) used the structure of knowledge framework in Chapter 5 to explore in depth the differences among these cultures through a study of research norms and practices in 12 contrasting disciplinary fields: biology, chemistry, economics, engineering, geography, history, law, mathematics, modern languages, pharmacy, physics, and sociology. Becher argues that, "Knowledge is the prime commodity of academic life, and it is the nature of knowledge itself which gives shape to, even if it does not entirely determine, the working patterns of academic communities" (1990, p. 337). He described the traditions, taboos, territories, and tacit ways of knowing in four groupings of fields corresponding to the typology of fields of inquiry and endeavor in Figure 5.1. The *pure sciences,* where knowledge is atomistic, cumulative, and concerned with universals, had cultures described as competitive, gregarious, politically organized, and task-oriented with high publication rates. The *humanities,* where knowledge is reiterative, holistic and organic, and concerned with particulars and interpretation, had cultures that were individualistic, pluralistic, loosely structured, and person-oriented with low publication rates. Technologies, where knowledge is purposive, pragmatic, and concerned with mastery of the physical world through production of products and techniques, had cultures described as entrepreneurial, cosmopolitan, role-oriented, and regulated by professional values, where patents were substitutable for publications. The *applied social sciences,* where knowledge is functional, utilitarian, and concerned with enhancing professional practice through protocols and procedures, had cultures that were outward-looking, power-oriented, uncertain in status, and dominated by intellectual fashion with consulting taking precedence over publication (Becher, 1994).

In a subsequent analysis Becher extended his analysis to examine disciplinary subcultures, the sub-disciplines or specialties within disciplines. In many cases these sub-disciplines fragment the unity of a discipline and are countercultural to the dominant norms of the discipline: ". . . there is an anarchic tendency for some sub-units, even in the heartlands of their discipline, to appear more closely related to counterparts in the heartlands of other disciplines than to sub-units in their own" (1990, p. 336). These specialties can also facilitate communication and interaction with other disciplines that share their inquiry norms, and can be the breeding ground for new ideas and approaches. There have been numerous studies of learning style differences within disciplinary sub-specialties that support Becher's analysis. For example, Plovnick (1975, 1980) studied learning style differences in senior medical students finding that family medicine and primary care were specialties chosen by accommodative and divergent medical students, internal medicine was chosen more often by convergers, and academic medicine and pathology tended to be chosen by assimilative students. Similarly, Loo (2002a, 2002b) found learning style differences among business students majoring in accounting, finance, and marketing.

Ludwig Huber (1990), while agreeing with Becher that the structure of knowledge influences the structure of disciplines, argues that the cultures of disciplines are embedded more deeply in social structure and are associated with traits such as political affiliations, social class, and private life preferences that cannot be solely attributed to epistemological differences through a process of social reproduction based on Bourdieu's concept of *habitus.*

Bourdieu defines *habitus* as, "systems of durable, transposable dispositions, structured structures predisposed to function as structuring structures, that is, as principles which generate and organize practices and representations that can be objectively adapted to their outcomes without presupposing a conscious aiming at ends or an express mastery of the operations necessary in order to attain them" (1990, p. 53). The practices emerging from *habitus* are both durable "structured structures," rules of the game, and generative structuring structures, strategies of the game, that allow for creativity and innovation within the structure. *Habitus*-shaped practices operate for the most part at practical and tacit levels with little conscious intention and reflection. Gerholm, for example, argues that acquiring tacit knowledge is critical for success in academia and disciplines such as the arts, though there are few possibilities to acquire it in graduate education. Thus, success in these fields favors those with *habitus*-acquired cultural capital, "a stock of knowledge, a frame of reference and a capacity to make the proper judgments which are called 'taste' " (1990, p. 269).

The concept of *habitus,* though more encompassing in a scope that includes lifestyle, values, and dispositions, is similar to the experiential learning theory concept of learning style. "*Habitus* gives practices a particular manner or style. The disposition of *habitus* identifies certain individuals as risk takers, others as cautious, some as bold, others as timid, some as balanced, others as awkward. Individuals do not simply conform to the external constraints and opportunities given them. They adapt, seize the moment, or miss the chance in characteristic manners" (Swartz, 2002, p. 63S).

Habitus practices and the academic fields where they are enacted are part of a deeper spiral of learning and knowledge creation that extends beyond individuals into the social structure. "Born into certain fields and then initiated into others, and finding themselves in certain positions, people somehow grasp how the game works, learn by doing and incorporate the generating schemes very much as a child learns its mother tongue and patterns of social behavior, i.e., a practical competence (*le sens pratique,* a feel for the game) without knowing the rules or consciously complying with them. Thus, a correspondence—not determination—is at work between the *field* (the structures in which the history of a society has become institutionalized) and the *habitus* (the actors' dispositions in which the same history has been incorporated): they produce and structure one another and are reproduced and structured by one another" (Huber, 1990, p. 248).

The Knowledge Structures of *Experiential Learning*

Experiential Learning itself provides an interesting case study of the use of Pepper's knowledge structures as defined in *World Hypotheses.* First, a reflection on my own tacit to explicit spiral of knowledge creation. I first read *World Hypotheses* as an undergraduate at Knox College and was immediately drawn to its holistic worldview framework that defined the limited viewpoint of different knowledge structures and disciplines. I read the book in a seminar called "Personal Reconstruction" given by Bernard Loomer, who was a process theologian and a visiting scholar from his position as Dean of the University of Chicago Divinity School. He decried dogma and stressed the limitations of human understanding of the mysteries of the world. A particularly impactful assignment for me was a paper to be titled "My Elephant." Using the famous tale of the blind man and the elephant as an analogy of our limited view of the world, he asked us to describe the elephant as we experienced and thought about it. In writing the paper I was acutely aware of the socializing tugs and pulls in the fields I loved—philosophy, religion, theatre, and psychology. In my primary major, psychology, I was also caught up in the internal battles between behaviorism and personality theory. What to this day still remains largely tacit for me is an understanding of my attraction to holistic models and my lingering suspicion about the certainty with which the specialized perspectives in them advocate their perspectives. My hunch is that it is rooted in my blue-collar upbringing in a small Midwestern farm town where humility was a valued virtue and the few professionals in town were seen as prestigious but cosmopolitan outsiders. While *World Hypotheses* did not resolve these issues it gave me a perspective on them.

So some 25 years later when I had found another holistic worldview in experiential learning, I was delighted to discover that book again. The way his structural analysis of knowledge mapped so perfectly onto the structure of learning in experiential learning theory gave me confidence that I was onto something important. It also gave me a holistic perspective on how to approach my research. Pepper argues that his world theories should be kept pure and consistent in their internal structural corroboration, but used eclectically in their application in practice. "Hence the insistence upon the exclusion of eclecticism within the world theories, and at the same time the recommendation to make reasonable use of it in estimating the results of world theories" (1942, p. 341). "Since these four world theories were regarded by us as having about the same degree of adequacy, no one of them can be the judge of the others. Our general stand, therefore, is for *rational clarity in theory and reasonable eclecticism in practice*. . . . In practice, therefore, we shall want to be not rational but reasonable, and to seek, on the matter in question, the judgment supplied from each of these relatively adequate world theories" (1942, p. 330). "None of these theories of truth gives way to the others. Nevertheless, this survey gives a more balanced and informed conception of the subject than could be got in any other manner" (1942, p. 347).

In any event, I did not begin *Experiential Learning* with an explicit plan to use "reasonable eclecticism" in my reliance on the worldviews of formism, mechanism, contextualism, and organicism, but it gradually became explicit in the process of writing that I was doing just that. Writing Chapters 1 and 2 I was not aware of explicitly following a contextualist approach though it is how they appear in retrospect. In Chapter 3 I did explicitly recognize that I was taking a mechanistic approach with my structural analysis of the foundations of the learning process followed by the structure of knowledge in Chapter 5. Chapter 4 contrasted the typical formist roots of individual type theories with my contextual approach to learning style. Chapter 7 was less explicitly constructed with a combination of formism and mechanism known more commonly as logical empiricism. Being about development, Chapters 6 and 8 were inevitably based on the organismic or idealist worldview.

Reading critical reviewers of this book, I fear that I may have confused readers by approaching the topic with Pepper's "post-rational eclecticism." Miettinen (2000) is particularly upset by my eclectic use of multiple root metaphors and holistic approach. "Kolb says that he. . . [wants] to suggest through experiential learning theory a holistic integrative perspective on learning. . . . The method and procedure can be called eclectic. Kolb unites terms and concepts, extracting them from their historical context and purposes and puts them to serve the motives of his own presentation. As a result theoreticians with quite different backgrounds, motives and incompatible conceptions can be used as founders and 'supporters' of experiential learning. . . . One cannot help concluding that Kolb's motive is not critical evaluation or interdisciplinarity but an attempt to construct an 'attractive' collection of ideas that can be advocated as a solution to the social problems of our time and to substantiate the usefulness of his learning style inventory" (2000, p. 56). Miettinen then, mistakenly, argues that my eclectic approach is contrary to Pepper's approach citing a passage which argues that an eclectic method that takes the best of the world hypotheses is not appropriate for the creation of an adequate world hypothesis. Pepper was referring there to the creation of an adequate world hypothesis that could compete with his four adequate hypotheses, not to the application of world hypotheses where he advocates a "reasonable eclecticism" in practice (see the Pepper quote above).

Others more pointedly suggest that I have botched or ignored their particular epistemological preference and adopted another that is particularly distasteful to them. Richard Hopkins, an avid phenomenologist, in "David Kolb's Learning Machine" writes, "And it is curious that in a book that couples experience with learning, and that draws on a variety of philosophical perspectives, there should be so little reference to the major world philosophy of experience" (1993, p. 53). He argues that the book "ultimately breaks down under the weight of its structuralist reductions." (1993, p. 46). He cites a paragraph at the beginning of Chapter 3 that begins, "The approach. . . will essentially be structural," as evidence for his argument that the book is based on a structuralist, mechanistic approach. In the omission he leaves out the words "in this chapter" (see Chapter 3, pp. 65–66) and ignores the first sentence of the next paragraph, ". . . we have seen in the last chapter how the more phenomenological, descriptive models of learning described by Lewin and Dewey are enriched and corroborated by Piaget's structural dimensions of cognitive development—phenomenalism/constructivism and egocentrism/relativism."

Similarly, Garner (2000) argues that my work is based on a formist epistemology citing a paragraph in Chapter 4 where I suggest the problem with type theories is their formist epistemological base. He discounts a sentence later in the paragraph that states, "An alternative epistemological root metaphor, one that we will use in our approach to understanding human individuality is that of contextualism." As an avowed Jungian organicist (or idealist as he calls it), Garner says that Jung's typologies, "are the main foundations for the development of his learning styles" (2000, p. 341), which is not the case. He states, "Kolb is arguing that his work falls within a contextualist position and, at the same time believes he is able to connect his work directly with Jung's idealist position. To bring together these two contradictory epistemologies is highly problematic and connections between the two must be viewed exceptionally cautiously" (2000, p. 343).

What I take from the above examples are the perils of trans-disciplinary, integrative scholarship that falls outside of established institutional and disciplinary boundaries. As others have noted, work that falls between disciplines is likely to be acceptable to neither. D. Christopher Kayes in his review and critique of experiential learning theory critics examined their argument against the multi-paradigm approach of experiential learning theory. "Because ELT lacks strong institutional standing, the argument goes, it lacks the institutional clout necessary to contribute to codified knowledge, and thus, ELT remains impotent in furthering any one profession" (2002, pp. 141–142). His reply emphasizes the value of the multi-disciplinary approach. "Criticisms that ELT lacks sufficient institutional standing to influence academic advancement may suffer from a kind of professional myopia that constrains learning research to a highly consensual body of knowledge. . . . If the study of management learning seeks to increase learning in the academy, then it might use experiential learning theory as a guide. If the best learning systems engender diversity, then the best approach is to broaden, not narrow the field of inclusion. . . . An alternative approach comes from Geertz's (1983) idea of 'blurred genres' in which scholars enlist multiple disciplines. . . . ELT—with its humanist ideology, pragmatic aims, scientific justification and interdisciplinary roots—provides a lucid example of such blurring" (2002, p. 142).

Such is the deep and passionate adherence, which I have described above, to our epistemological worldview that we are particularly alert, and sometimes "hostile," to use Pepper's term, to perceived challenges from other worldviews. While Pepper maintains that his four-world hypotheses are independent and of about equal adequacy, capable of presenting credible interpretation of any facts and events, dialogue among adherents to the different worldviews can be difficult. Because they are based on different root metaphors, they ask different questions and have different criteria for successful answers. Yet I still persist in my holistic multi-disciplinary view. The scholarly conversations generated, including the misunderstandings, are enlightening to us all. I find some company with Pepper, who responding to critics of *World Hypotheses* replied, ". . . whether the root metaphor theory was not a world theory itself or one of the already described world theories pretending to be neutral, it is almost a sufficient reply to record that the root metaphor theory has been accused by various persons of being every one of these world theories. . ." (1942, pp. 347–348).

6

The Experiential Learning Theory of Development

The course of nature is to divide what is united and to unite what is divided.

—Goethe

There is a quality of learning that cannot be ignored. It is assertive, forward-moving, and proactive. Learning is driven by curiosity about the here-and-now and anticipation of the future. It was John Dewey who saw that the experiential learning cycle was not a circle but a spiral, filling each episode of experience with the potential for movement, from blind impulse to a life of choice and purpose (see Chapter 2, "Dewey's Model of Learning"). He compared this progression in learning from experience to the advance of an army:

> Each resting place in experience is an undergoing in which is absorbed and taken home the consequences of prior doing, and unless the doing is that of utter caprice or sheer routine, each doing carries in itself meaning that has been extracted and conserved. As with the advance of an army, all gains from what has been already effected are periodically consolidated, and always with a view to what is to be done next. If we move too rapidly, we get away from the base of supplies—of accrued meanings—and the experience is flustered, thin, and confused. If we dawdle too long after having extracted a net value, experience perishes of inanition. [Dewey, 1934, p. 56]

Learning is thus the process whereby development occurs. This view of the relation between learning and development differs from some traditional conceptions that suggest that the two processes are relatively independent. This latter perspective, which is shared by the intelligence-testing movement and classical Piagetians, suggests that learning is a subordinate process not actively involved in development: To learn, one uses the achievements of development, but this learning does not modify the course of development. In intelligence testing, for example, development is seen as a prerequisite for learning—it is necessary for a child's mental functions to mature before more complex subject matter can be taught. Similarly, for Piaget, development forms the superstructure within which learning occurs. His research has been guided by the implicit assumption that the sequence of cognitive-developmental stages evolves from an internal momentum and logic, with little influence from environmental circumstance. Recent research by those who might be called neo-Piagetians (such as Bruner et al., 1966) have called this assumption into question by showing in cross-culture studies that the child's level of cognitive development at a given age is strongly influenced by access to Western-type schooling.

Learning and Development as Transactions between Person and Environment

Without denying the reality of biological maturation and developmental achievements (that is, enduring cognitive structures that organize thought and action), the experiential learning theory of development focuses on the transaction between internal characteristics and external circumstances, between personal knowledge and social knowledge. It is the process of learning from experience that shapes and actualizes developmental potentialities. This learning is a social process; and thus, the course of individual development is shaped by the cultural system of social knowledge.

This position has been best articulated by the Soviet cognitive theorist, L. S. Vygotsky. He used the concept of the zone of proximal development to explain how learning shapes the course of development. The zone of proximal development is defined as "the distance between the actual developmental level as determined by independent problem solving and the level of potential development as determined through problem solving under adult guidance or in collaboration with more capable peers" (Cole et al., 1978, p. 86). The zone of proximal development is where learning occurs. Through experiences of imitation and communication with others and interaction with the physical environment, internal developmental potentialities are enacted and practiced until they are internalized as an independent development achievement. Thus, learning becomes the vehicle for human development via interactions between individuals with their biologic potentialities and the society with its symbols, tools, and other cultural artifacts. Human beings create culture with all its artificial stimuli to further their own development. Vygotsky's ideas about how the tools of culture shape development were greatly influenced by Friedrich Engels, who saw culturally created tools as the specific symbol of man's transformation of nature—that is, production. As Vygotsky himself put it:

> The keystone of our method . . . follows directly from the contrast Engels drew between naturalistic and dialectical approaches to the understanding of human history. Naturalism in historical analysis, according to Engels, manifests itself in

the assumption that only nature affects human beings and only natural conditions determine historical development. The dialectical approach, while admitting the influence of nature on men, asserts that man in turn affects nature and creates, through his changes in nature, new natural conditions for his existence. . . .

All stimulus response methods share the inadequacy that Engels ascribes to the naturalistic approach to history. Both see the relation between human behavior and history as unidirectionally reactive. My collaborators and I, however, believe that human behavior comes to have that "transforming reaction on nature" which Engels attributed to tools. [Cole et al., 1978, pp. 60–61]

It is this proactive adaptation that is the distinctive characteristic of human learning, a proactive adaptation that is made possible by the use of auxiliary cultural stimuli, social knowledge, to actively transform personal knowledge. For example, the symbolic tools acquired through the internalization of language allow us to anticipate, plan for, and practice reactions to upcoming situations in our life. As the tools of culture change, so too will the course of human development be altered (as with the widespread use of home computers; compare Papaert, 1980). In this sense, the laws and limitations of human development can never be known, since human nature is constantly emerging in the transaction between individuals and their culture.

The process of learning that actualizes development requires a confrontation and resolution of the dialectic conflicts inherent in experiential learning. The process is one that Paulo Freire describes as praxis—using dialogue to stimulate reflection and action on the world in order to transform it. Denis Goulet, in the introduction to Freire's *Education for Critical Consciousness*, describes it this way:

Paulo Freire's central message is that one can know only to the extent that one "problematizes" the natural, cultural and historical reality in which s/he is immersed . . . to "problematize" in his sense is to associate an entire populace to the task of codifying total reality into symbols which can generate critical consciousness and empower them to alter their relations with nature and social forces. This reflective group exercise . . . thrusts all participants into dialogue with others whose historical "vocation" is to become transforming agents of their social reality. Only thus do people become subjects, instead of objects, of their own history. [Freire, 1973, p. ix]

Differentiation and Integration in Development

From the dialectics of learning comes a human developmental progression marked by increasing differentiation and hierarchic integration of functioning. The concepts of differentiation and hierarchic integration are fundamental to virtually all theories of cognitive development and adult development. This principle of psychological development was borrowed from biological observations of evolution and development that show increasing physical differentiation and integration as one moves up the phylogenetic scale, particularly in the evolution of the nervous system.

Differentiation has two aspects, an increasing complexity of units and a decreasing interdependence of parts. The course of learning and development is to refine, discriminate, and elaborate the categories of experience and the variety of behavior while at the same time increasing the independence of functioning among these separate parts. An example of differentiation can be seen in the development of the infant's emotional life. In an early observational study of young children, Katherine Bridges (1932) described the increasing differentiation of the growing infant's emotions from undifferentiated excitement to the basic distinction between distress and delight, to a refined spectrum of emotions encompassing fear, disgust, anxiety, jealousy, joy, parental affection, and so on (see Figure 6.1).

Hierarchic integration is the organism's organizing response to the complexity and diffusion caused by increasing differentiation. Hierarchic integration is multilevel. At the first level are simple fixed rules for organizing differentiated dimensions of experience in an absolutistic way. For example, experience may be classified as either good or bad. At a somewhat higher level, alternative interpretive rules emerge, allowing for alternative interpretations of situations. The absolutistic right-wrong view of the world becomes somewhat more flexible by the use of simple contingency thinking; for instance, in situation A, this rule is true, but in situation B, another rule holds. At a still higher level, more complex rules than simple contingency thinking are developed for determining the perspective taken on experience. These rules are more "internalized," free from fixed application based on past experience or the external stimulus. The highest level of integration

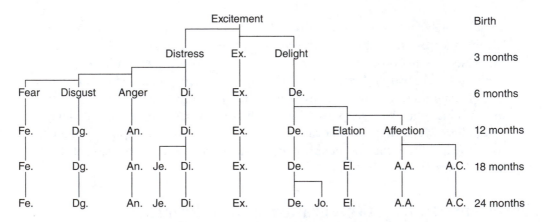

Key: A.A. = Affection for Adults; A.C. = Affection for Children; An. = Anger; De. = Delight; Dg. = Disgust; Di. = Distress; El. = Elation; Ex. = Excitement; Fe. = Fear; Je. = Jealousy; Jo. = Joy

Figure 6.1   Differentiation of Infant's Emotional Life

Source: Katherine Bridges, "Emotional Development in Early Infancy," *Child Development,* 3 (1932).

adds still another system of rules that forms a structure for generating very complex relationships. This highest level allows great flexibility in the integration and organization of experience, making it possible to cope with change and environmental uncertainty by developing complex alternative constructions of reality. These four levels of hierarchic integration, as they are described by Schroder, Driver, and Streufert (1967), are shown graphically in Figure 6.2.

Through hierarchic integration, the individual maintains integrity and wholeness through the creation of superordinate schema, including concepts, sentiments, acts, and observations. These schema organize and control the deployment of subordinate, differentiated concepts, sentiments, acts, and observations. In the example above of differentiation of the infant's emotional life, the growing child develops progressively higher-order sentiments to control the application of these refined emotions to different settings and persons, introducing continuity and meaning to his or her experience. The unity and consistency of experience that at birth was the benefit of an undifferentiated view of the world must increasingly be purchased by integrative organizational efforts. Yet the dividends of these developmental processes are great—an increasingly conscious awareness and sophisticated control of ourselves in the world around us. In Lewin's conception, integration was presumed to lag behind differentiation, producing cyclic patterns of development alternating between stages dominated by the diffusion of differentiation and stages dominated by the unity of hierarchic integration—a description not unlike Dewey's advancing-army metaphor quoted earlier.

Unilinear vs. Multilinear Development

The experiential learning theory of development differs significantly from most Piaget-inspired theories of adult development in its emphasis on development as a multilinear process. The Piagetian theories of cognitive and adult development portray the course of development as unilinear, as some form of movement toward increasing differentiation and hierarchic integration of the structures that govern behavior. This is true of Piaget's theory of cognitive development (Flavell, 1963), Loevinger's theory of ego development (1976), Kohlberg's theory of moral development (1969), Perry's theory of moral and intellectual development (1970), the conceptual systems approach of Harvey, Hunt, and Schroeder (1961) and its derivatives by Hunt in education (1974), by Schroder et al. in information processing (1967), and by Harvey in personality theory (1966). Although experiential learning theory recognizes the overall linear trend in development from a state of globality and lack of differentiation to a state of increasing differentiation, articulation, and hierarchic integration, it takes issue with the exclusive linearity of the Piagetian approach in three respects.

First, it recognizes individual differences in the developmental process. In Piagetian schemes, individuality is manifest only in differential progression along the single yardstick of development—progression toward the internalized logic of scientific rationality.

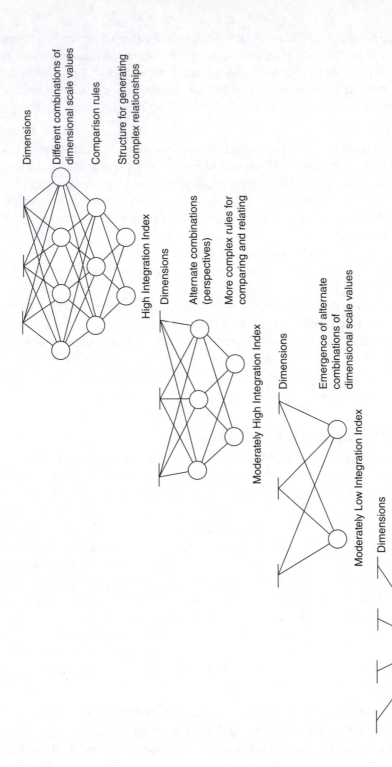

Figure 6.2 Levels of Hierarchic Integration

Source: H. M. Schroder, M. J. Driver, and S. Streufert, *Human Information Processing* (New York: Holt, Rinehart & Winston, 1967).

Individuals are different only insofar as they are at different stages of development. In experiential learning theory, however, individuality is manifest not only in the stage of development but also in the course of development—in the particular learning style the person develops. In this respect, the theory follows the Gestalt development approach of Heinz Werner:

> The orthogenetic law, by its very nature, is an expression of unilinearity of development. But, as is true of the other polarities discussed here, the ideal unilinear sequence signified by the universal developmental law does not conflict with the multiplicity of actual developmental forms . . . coexistence of unilinearity and multiplicity of individual developments must be recognized for psychological just as it is for biological evolution. In regard to human behavior in particular, this polarity opens the way for a developmental study of behavior not only in terms of universal sequence, but also in terms of individual variations, that is, in terms of growth viewed as a branching-out process of specialization. . . . [Werner, 1948, p. 137]

A second difference arises from the transactional perspective of experiential learning that conceptualizes development as the product of personal knowledge and social knowledge. Since a person's state of development is the product of the transaction between personal experience and the particular system of social knowledge interacted with, it is unreasonable to conceive of this state as solely a characteristic of the person, the view held by Piaget.[1] The developmental structures observed in human thought are just as likely to be characteristics of the social knowledge system; thus the findings that children with Western schooling display Piaget's developmental progressions more consistently than those whose schooling is embedded in other cultural knowledge systems (Bruner et al., 1966). This is an important proposition, for it argues that the paths of development can be as varied as the many systems of social knowledge. David Feldman has developed the ramifications of this view most thoroughly, suggesting a continuum of developmental regions ranging from the *universals* of intellect studied by Piaget (such as object permanence) through cognitive skills that are specific to a given *culture*, to a *discipline-based* knowledge system, and finally to *idiosyncratic* and *unique* capabilities that are developed by individuals through interactions with specialized or unique environments. Some of these unique accomplishments are judged to be creative, Feldman argues, and are fed back into the system of social knowledge, perhaps ultimately achieving disciplinary, cultural, or even universal status.

Emphasis on the specialized paths of development leads to the third difference with Piagetian theories. For Piaget, all development is *cognitive* development. Experiential learning

---

1. "We have seen that there exist structures that belong only to the subject, that they are built, and that this is a step-by-step process. We must therefore conclude that there exist stages of development" (Piaget, 1970a, p. 710).

theory describes four development dimensions—affective complexity, perceptual complexity, symbolic complexity, and behavioral complexity—all interrelated in the holistic adaptive process of learning. The recognition of separate developmental paths helps to explain certain developmental phenomena that are anomalous in the Piagetian scheme. Werner gives one such example, the case of physiognomic perception. This affective mode of perceiving, in which perception and feeling are fused (for example, a gloomy landscape), is characteristic of young children but also seems to be highly developed in the adult artist:

> To illustrate, "physiognomic" perception appears to be a developmentally early form of viewing the world, based on the relative lack of distinction between properties of persons and properties of inanimate things. But the fact that in our culture physiognomic perception, developmentally, is superseded by logical, realistic, and technical conceptualization poses some paradoxical problems, such as, What genetic standing has adult aesthetic experience? Is it to be considered a "primitive" experience left behind in a continuous process of advancing logification, and allowed to emerge only in sporadic hours of regressive relaxation? Such an inference seems unsound; it probably errs in conceiving human growth in terms of a simple developmental series rather than as a diversity of individual formations, all conforming to the abstract and general developmental conceptualization. Though physiognomic experience is a primordial manner of perceiving, it grows, in certain individuals such as artists, to a level not below but on a par with that of "geometric-technical" perception and logical discourse. [Werner, 1948, p. 138]

Similar questions can be raised about the highly developed intuitive and behavioral skill of the executive (Mintzberg, 1973), which resembles in structure the child's trial-and-error enactive learning process.

Another example is what Turner (1973) calls recentered thinking, in which the relationship of social knowledge to the specific knowing individual must be established in order for people to particularize general cognitive principles. This particularization requires the synthesis of affective and cognitive components. Although Piaget's developmental theory specifies how concepts gain independence from concrete experience, it does not specify the processes by which concepts are revisited with personal experience. In Piaget's terms, assimilation ultimately takes priority over accommodation in his theory of development.

The final point of difference lies in the practical implications of the issues above. As was indicated in the first chapter, Piagetian theories have had a profound influence on American education, primarily through Jerome Bruner's introduction of Piaget's work at the prestigious Woods Hole conference on education in 1958. This conference, which framed our nation's educational response to the Sputnik challenge, found in Piaget's developmental theory the ideal framework for emphasizing and rationalizing the technoscientific dominance of education. In the race to regain the lead over the Soviets in technological supremacy, the educational system embraced scientific thinking as *the* way of knowing. Nurtured by federal largesse, educational institutions were transformed into technological institutions where scientific inquiry prospered and other approaches to knowing—the affective expression of the arts, the metaphysical reflection of philosophy and religion, and the integrative ideals of liberal education—all atrophied. Without in any way denigrating the intrinsic value or achievements of scientific inquiry, the multilinear developmental perspective of experiential learning suggests that science and technology alone are not enough. It rejects the view that other forms of inquiry must be subjected to science; that what ought to be is discovered in empirical investigation of what is; that the role of the humanities is to help us understand and cope with technological change rather than shape its directions. The true path toward individual and cultural development is to be found in equal inquiry among affective, symbolic, perceptual, and behavioral knowledge systems. Its intelligent direction requires integrated judgments about the future of humanity born from conflict and dialogue among these perspectives (compare Chapter 8, pp. 327–333).

The Experiential Learning Theory of Development

The way learning shapes the course of development can be described by the level of integrative complexity in the four learning modes—affective complexity in concrete experience results in higher-order sentiments, perceptual complexity in reflective observation results in higher-order observations, symbolic complexity in abstract conceptualization results in higher-order concepts, and behavioral complexity in active experimentation results in higher-order actions. Figure 6.3 illustrates this experiential learning model of development. The four dimensions of growth are depicted in the shape of a cone, the base of which represents the lower stages of development and the apex of which represents the peak of development—representing the fact that the four dimensions become more highly integrated at higher stages of development. Development on each dimension proceeds from a state of embeddedness, defensiveness, dependence, and reaction to a state of self-actualization, independence, proaction, and self-direction. This process is marked by increasing complexity and relativism in dealing with the world and one's experience and by higher-level integrations of the dialectic conflicts among the four primary learning modes. In the early stages of development, progress along one of these four dimensions can occur with relative independence from the others. The child and young adult, for example, can develop highly sophisticated symbolic proficiencies and remain naive emotionally. At the highest stages of development, however, the adaptive commitment to learning and creativity produces a strong need for integration of the four adaptive modes. Development in one mode precipitates development in the others. Increases in symbolic complexity, for example, refine and sharpen both perceptual and behavioral possibilities. Thus, complexity and the integration of dialectic conflicts among the adaptive modes are the hallmarks of true creativity and growth.

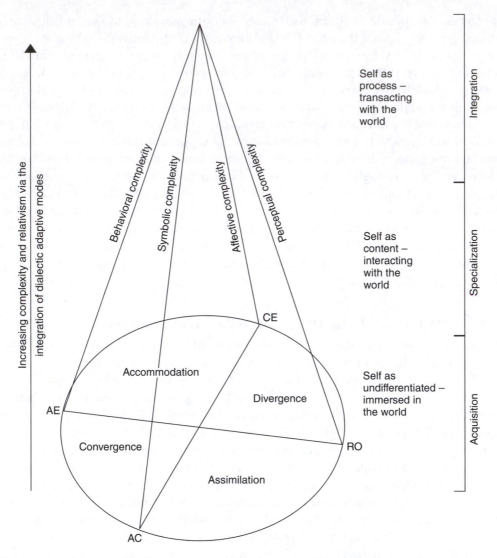

Figure 6.3 The Experiential Learning Theory of Growth and Development

The human developmental process is divided into three broad development stages of maturation: acquisition, specialization, and integration. By maturational stages we refer to the rough chronological ordering of ages at which developmental achievements become possible in the general conditions of contemporary Western culture. Actual developmental progress will vary depending on the individual and his or her particular cultural experience. Even though the stages of the developmental growth process are depicted in the form of a simple three-layer cone, the actual process of growth in any single life history probably proceeds through successive oscillations from one stage to another. Thus, a person may move from stage 2 to stage 3 in several separate subphases of integrative advances, followed by consolidation or regression into specialization.

Stage One: Acquisition

This stage extends from birth to adolescence and marks the acquisition of basic learning abilities and cognitive structures. This, the most intensively studied period of human development, is described by Piaget as having four major substages (Chapter 2, pp. 34–36). The first stage, from birth until about 2 years, is called the sensorimotor stage, because learning is primarily *enactive*; that is, knowledge is externalized in actions and the feel of the environment. Thus, accommodative learning, apprehension transformed by extension, is the dominant mode of adaptation. The second stage, from 2 to 6 years, is called the *iconic* stage, because at this point, internalized images begin to have independent status from the objects they represent. It is at this stage that early forms of divergent learning, apprehension transformed by intention, are acquired. The third stage, from 7 to 11 years, marks the beginning of symbolic development in what Piaget calls the stage of concrete operations. Here the child begins development of the logic of classes and relations and inductive powers—in other words, assimilative learning via the transformation of comprehension by intention. The final stage of development in Piaget's scheme occurs in adolescence (12 to 15 years). Here, symbolic powers achieve total independence from concrete reality in the development of representational logic and the process of hypothetical deductive reasoning. These powers enable the child to imagine or hypothesize implications of purely symbolic systems and test them out in reality—convergent learning via transformation of comprehensions by extension. Development in the acquisition phase is marked by the gradual emergence of internalized structures that allow the child to gain a sense of self that is separate and distinct from the surrounding environment. This increasing freedom from undifferentiated immersion in the world begins with basic discrimination between internal and external stimuli and ends with that delineation of the boundaries of selfhood that Erikson (1959) has called the identity crisis.

Stage Two: Specialization

This stage extends through formal education and/or career training and the early experiences of adulthood in work and personal life. People shaped by cultural, educational, and organizational socialization forces develop increased competence in a specialized mode of adaptation that enables them to master the particular life tasks they encounter in their chosen career (in the broadest sense of the word) paths. Although children in their early experiences in family and school may already have begun to develop specialized preferences and abilities in their learning orientations (see Hudson, 1966), in secondary school and beyond they begin to make choices that will significantly shape the course of their development. The choice of college versus trade apprenticeship, the choice of academic specialization, and even such cultural factors as the choice of where to live begin to selectively determine the socialization experiences people will have and thereby influence and shape their mode of adaptation to the world. The choices a person makes in this process tend to have an accentuating, self-fulfilling quality that promotes specialization.

In the experiential learning theory of adult development, stability and change in life paths are seen as resulting from the interaction between internal personality dynamics and external social forces in a manner much like that described by Super et al. (1963). The most powerful developmental dynamic that emerges from this interaction is the tendency for there to be a closer and closer match between self characteristics and environmental demands. This match comes about in two ways: (1) Environments tend to change personal characteristics to fit them (socialization), and (2) people tend to select themselves into environments that are consistent with their personal characteristics. Thus, development in general tends to follow a path toward accentuation of personal characteristics and skills (Feldman and Newcomb, 1969; Kolb and Goldman, 1973), in that development is a product of the interaction between choices and socialization experiences that match these choice dispositions such that resulting experiences further reinforce the same choice disposition for later experience. This process is inherent in the concept of learning styles as possibility-processing structures that govern transactions with the environment and thereby define and stabilize individuality.

Thus, in the specialization stage of development, the person achieves a sense of individuality through the acquisition of a specialized adaptive competence in dealing with the demands of a chosen "career." One's sense of self-worth is based on the rewards and recognition received for doing "work" well. The self in this stage is defined primarily in terms of *content*—things I can do, experiences I have had, goods and qualities I possess. The primary mode of relating to the world is *interaction*—I act on the world (build the bridge, raise the family) and the world acts on me (pays me money, fills me with bits of knowledge), but neither is fundamentally changed by the other. Paulo Freire describes this stage-2 sense of self and the "banking" concept of education that serves to reinforce it:

> Implicit in the banking concept is the assumption of a dichotomy between man and the world: Man is merely in the world, not with the world or with others; man is spectator, not re-creator. In this view, man is not a conscious being; he is rather the possessor of a consciousness; an empty "mind" passively open to the reception of deposits of reality from the world outside. . . . This view makes no distinction between being accessible to consciousness and entering consciousness. The distinction, however, is essential: The objects which surround me are simply accessible to my consciousness not located within it.

> It follows logically from the banking notion of consciousness that the educator's role is to regulate the way the world "enters into" the students. His task is to

organize a process which already occurs spontaneously, to "fill" the students by making deposits of information which he considers to constitute true knowledge. And since men "receive" the world as passive entities, education should make them more passive still, and adapt them to the world. The educated man is the adapted man, because he is better "fit" for the world. [Freire, 1974, p. 62]

Stage Three: Integration

The specialized developmental accomplishments of stage 2 bring social security and achievement, often paid for by the subjugation of personal fulfillment needs. The restrictive effects that society's socializing institutions have on personal fulfillment have been a continuing theme of Western thought, particularly since the Enlightenment. Freud and his followers in psychoanalysis developed the socioemotional dimensions of this conflict between individual and society—libidinous instincts clashing with repressive social demands. In modern organization theory, this conflict has been most clearly articulated by Argyris (1962). Yet it is Carl Jung's formulation of this conflict and the dimensions of its resolution in his theory of psychological types that is most relevant here. The Jungian theory of types, like the experiential learning model, is based on a dialectic model of adaptation to the world. Fulfillment, or individuation, as Jung calls it, is accomplished by higher-level integration and expression of nondominant modes of dealing with the world. This drive for fulfillment, however, is thwarted by the needs of civilization for specialized role performance.

The needs of Western specialized society have long stood in conflict with individuals in their drive for integrative development. In 1826, the German poet and historian, Friedrich Schiller, wrote:

> When the commonwealth makes the office or function the measure of the man; when of its citizens it does homage only to the memory in one, to a tabulating intelligence in another, and to a mechanical capacity in a third; when here, regardless of character, it urges only towards knowledge while there it encourages a spirit of order and law-abiding behavior with the profoundest intellectual obscurantism—when, at the same time, it wishes these single accomplishments of the subject to be carried to just as great an intensity as it absolves him of extensity—is it to be wondered at that the remaining faculties of the mind are neglected, in order to bestow every care upon the special one which it honors and rewards? [Schiller, 1826, p. 23]

Commenting on this passage by Schiller, Jung says:

> The favoritism of the superior function is just as serviceable to society as it is prejudicial to the individuality. This prejudicial effect has reached such a pitch that the great organizations of our present day civilization actually strive for the

complete disintegration of the individual, since their very existence depends upon a mechanical application of the preferred individual functions of men. It is not man that counts but his one differentiated function. Man no longer appears as man in collective civilization; he is merely represented by a function— nay, further, he is even exclusively identified with this function and denied any responsible membership to the level of a mere function, because this it is what represents a collective value and alone affords a possibility of livelihood. But as Schiller clearly discerns, differentiation of function could have come about in no other way: "There was no other means to develop man's manifold capacities than to set them one against the other. This antagonism of human qualities is the great instrument of culture; it is only the instrument, however, for so long as it endures man is only upon the way to culture." [Jung, 1973, p. 94]

The transition from stage 2 to stage 3 of development is marked by the individual's personal, existential confrontation of this conflict. The personal experience of the conflict between social demands and personal fulfillment needs and the corresponding recognition of self-as-object precipitates the individual's transition into the integrative stage of development. The experience can develop as a gradual process of awakening that parallels specialized development in stage 2, or it can occur dramatically as a result of a life crisis such as divorce or losing one's job. Some may never have this experience, so immersed are they in the societal reward system for performing their differentiated specialized function.

With this new awareness, the person experiences a shift in the frame of reference used to experience life, evaluate activities, and make choices. The nature of this shift depends upon the specifics of the person's dominant and nonexpressed adaptive modes. For the reflective person, the awakening of the active mode brings a new sense of risk to life. Rather than being influenced, one now sees opportunities to influence. The challenge becomes to shape one's own experience rather than observing and accepting experiences as they happen. For the person who has specialized in the active mode, the emergence of the reflective side broadens the range of choice and deepens the ability to sense implications of actions. For the specialist in the concrete mode, the abstract perspective gives new continuity and direction to experience. The abstract specialist with a new sense of immediate experience finds new life and meaning in abstract constructions of reality. The net effect of these shifts in perspective is an increasing experience of self as *process*. A learning process that has previously been blocked by the repression of the nonspecialized adaptive modes is now experienced deeply to be the essence of self.

Consciousness, Learning, and Development

In the experiential learning model of development, there are three distinct levels of adaptation, representing successively higher-order forms of learning. These forms of learning are governed by three qualitatively different forms of consciousness. We will refer to these three levels of adaptation as performance, learning, and development.

In the acquisition phase of development, adaptation takes the form of performance governed by a simple registrative consciousness. In the specialization phase of development, adaptation occurs via a learning process governed by a consciousness that is increasingly interpretative. The integrative phase of development marks the achievement of a holistic developmental adaptive process governed by a consciousness that is integrative in its structure. Thus, each developmental stage of maturation is characterized by acquisition of a higher-level structure of consciousness than the stage preceding it, although earlier levels of consciousness remain; that is, adults can display all three levels of consciousness: registrative, interpretative, and integrative. These consciousness structures govern the process of learning from experience through the selection and definition of that experience.

How Learning Shapes Consciousness

To understand the role of consciousness in learning and development requires further examination of the structural learning model proposed earlier. Previous chapters have described four elementary forms of learning—accommodation, assimilation, convergence, and divergence—and alluded to higher-order forms of learning that emerge from combinations of these elementary forms. In the developmental terms of differentiation and integration, the elementary learning processes are the primary means for differentiation of experience; the higher-order combinations of the elementary forms represent the integrative thrust of the learning process. The conscious focus of experience that is selected and shaped by one's actual developmental level is refined and differentiated in the zone of proximal development by grasping and transforming it.

To illustrate, take the example of my recent trip to the auto museum. Preoccupied as I was with explaining how learning from experience is developmental, I found myself during the visit focusing on how I was developing my concept of automobile. First, I walked around and found many forms and variations of cars to refine and elaborate the concept; here I was learning via convergence, differentiating my concept through extension. Later I began learning about automobiles via assimilation, intensively transforming the concept to search for its precise meaning and critical attributes: How is an auto different from a bicycle? Must an automobile have an engine? In both cases, I was differentiating my conscious experience of the automobile concept.

Integrative learning occurs when two or more elementary forms of learning combine to produce a higher-order integration of the elementary differentiations around their common learning mode(s). In the automobile example, if I use the assimilative and convergent forms of learning together, I search the museum for cars without engines and find none, although I do find a tricycle-like contraption with a small motor. The result is an incremental increase in the symbolic integrative complexity of my concept of automobile. Not only do I have a more extensive population of cars in my concept (acquired via convergence) and a more refined elaboration of the essential and nonessential attributes of the concept (acquired via assimilation), but in their combination, my comprehension of automobiles is increased. In determining that automobiles have some form of self-propulsion as an essential attribute and that "looking like a bicycle" is a nonessential attribute, my automobile concept has become more complex and integrated—an increase in actual developmental level. As such, it now asserts a greater measure of control over the choice and definition of my future focal experiences; for example, I now begin to see motorcycles as a special subcategory of automobiles.

In serving as the integrative link between dialectically opposed learning orientations, the common learning mode of any pair of elementary learning forms becomes more hierarchically integrated, thereby giving that common learning orientation a greater measure of organization and control over the person's experience. This process is depicted in Figure 6.4 using the automobile example. Here, in the classic confrontation of the dialectic between intention and extension of a concept, we find a unique resolution via the refinement of the concept to encompass greater differentiation via hierarchic integration—that is, an increase in *symbolic* integrative complexity.

Similar increases in hierarchic integration of the common learning mode occur with other pairs of elementary learning forms. When convergence and accommodation combine, the result is an increase in *behavioral* integrative complexity via the resolution of the dialectic between comprehension and apprehension. In the pool-playing example cited in Chapter 4, convergent problem solving suggesting that the angle of incidence equals the angle of reflection, combined with the accommodative feel of the table, the cue stick, and the position of the balls produces refined behavioral skills in controlling the course of the cue ball. This refinement results from the comprehension of the basic laws of physics and the apprehension of the internal body cues and external physical circumstances integrated through extension—behavioral acts that operationalize the abstract concept in the concrete physical setting. The behavioral acts are guided and refined by a negative feedback loop between the goal defined by comprehension and the actual circumstance experience by apprehension; I keep practicing until I can hit the ball to the position I predict.

When the elementary learning forms of accommodation and divergence combine, the result is an increase in *affective* integrative complexity via the resolution of the dialectic between intention and extension. The artist stands before the canvas, brush in hand, experiencing a flow of images and feelings (divergence). The stroke of color applied (accommodation) externalizes the internal flow of experience, creating a frozen record of a dynamic process. The extent to which the stroke is successful in capturing that internal process is measured by its ability to recreate the internal gestalt of the moment of its birth, thus allowing the wholeness of that re-created experience to carry forward into the

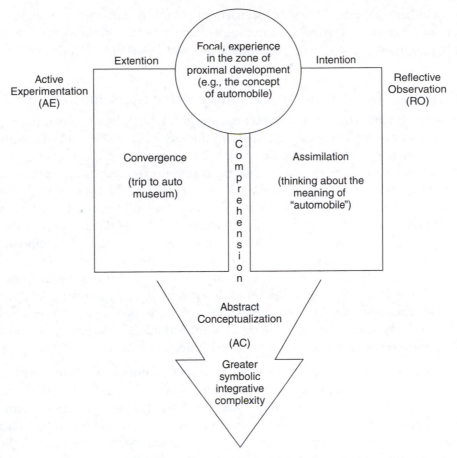

Figure 6.4 Convergence and Assimilation Combine to Produce Increased Symbolic Complexity

second stroke . . . and the third. It is from this cycle of action and reaction that sentiments are crystalized and refined, sentiments whose level of development is measured by their ability to sustain and carry forward experience (Gendlin, 1964).

The combination of the divergent and assimilative learning forms produces increases in *perceptual* integrative complexity via the resolution of the dialectic between apprehension and comprehension. The inductive model building of assimilation in combination with the apprehended observations of divergence produces more integratively complex categories of perception. Detective stories offer numerous examples of the synthesis of these two elementary learning forms, wherein the investigator is simultaneously inducing scenarios of how the crime was committed from the clues gathered and creating new clues and observations by juxtaposing scenarios with actual events. The creative synthesis of the comprehended scenario and apprehended events is illustrated by the fact that these new observations are not only about what happened but also about what did not happen but should have happened if a given scenario or alibi were correct. Thus, higher-order perceptual observations are not carbon copies of reality but integrations of what "is" and what "ought to be."

Registrative, Interpretative, and Integrative Consciousness

To illustrate further the levels of consciousness in learning, let us return to my automobile museum trip. The focal experience in this case was my concept of automobile. In my learning from that experience using the elementary convergent form of learning, my comprehension of the automobile concept was extended by my examination of the array of cars in the local auto museum. In this process, the concept of automobile was elaborated via a consciousness that was basically registrative. Each car I examined was "filed away" as another instance of an automobile. The focal experience "concept of automobile" did not change but was elaborated through grasping it via comprehension and transforming it via extension. When this convergent learning process was combined with assimilation (thinking about the meaning and critical attributes of the concept of automobile), my consciousness took on an interpretive quality that began to alter the focal experience itself; that is, the combination of these two learning forms produced an increase in the symbolic complexity of my concept "automobile," which in turn modified the focal experience to include bicycle-like self-propelled vehicles.

This second-level interpretative consciousness has two important characteristics that are lacking in the first-level registrative consciousness associated with the elementary learning forms. First, the combination of the two elementary learning modes creates an evaluative process that selectively interprets the focal experience. This is accomplished in the dialectic resolution of opposing learning modes (intention and extension, in the auto example). Second, this interpretation of the focal experience alters it selectively, redefining it and carrying it forward in terms of the hierarchically integrated learning mode. The combination of assimilative and convergent learning about the concept automobile refined the concept and enhanced the abstract/symbolic focus of the experience.

Thus the (second) interpretative level of consciousness associated with pairwise combinations of the elementary learning forms serves to define and shape the flow of experience, channeling it into more highly integrated forms of affective, perceptual, symbolic, and behavioral complexity. This level of consciousness gives direction and structure to the unfocused elaboration of registrative consciousness. But how then is the direction of the interpretative level of consciousness determined? How does one choose what experience to attend to and how to define it, either affectively, perceptually, symbolically, or behaviorally? In the absence of third-order integrative consciousness, the process is the one of random accentuation described in the specialization phase of development. An experience is chosen (concept of automobile) that "pulls for" a particular orientation (comprehension), and the refinement of the orientation (via increases in symbolic complexity) further increases the "pull" for that orientation, creating a positive feedback loop that serves to channel experience more and more in that direction.

Integrative consciousness introduces purpose and focus to this random process via integration of the opposition between the grasping dialectic of apprehension and comprehension and the transformation dialectic of intention and extension. This "centering" of experience, although not easily achieved, serves to answer the more strategic questions of life, such as, why think about automobiles anyway? And why focus on the concept of automobile as opposed to the apprehension and aesthetic appreciation of particular cars? In this particular case, I choose automobiles more or less randomly to illustrate a point about the learning process. I choose to focus on the "concept" of automobile because the example of the dialectic between intention and extension is clearest for abstract concepts (see Chapter 3, pp. 77–78). As I now try to push the example to explain integrative consciousness, I experience a kind of "stuckness." The example seems academic, trivial, and unrelated to me personally; I am lacking any apprehension about the focal experience, "concept of automobile." In searching for this personal relevance, I recall thinking, at the museum, that I would like to own a classic car, and further, that I often pause in airports to admire and get literature about those classic-car kits one builds on a Volkswagen chassis. On impulse, I have even bought a set of mechanic's tools with this idea vaguely in mind. By my bringing these accommodative learning experiences to bear on my conscious focal experience, its nature changes to include apprehensions of my personal feelings and desires about cars. The focal experience changes from *concept* of car to include specific cars and my relation to them, including the attractive fantasy of building one from a classic-car kit. Suddenly I begin to experience questions, and a fourth perspective on the experiences emerges—divergence, the transformation of these apprehensions by intention. How much of my self-image, money, and time do I really want to invest in a car? There is something vaguely decadent and ostentatious about fancy cars. And come to think of it, the whole concept of a self-propelled vehicle makes little sense in my life, where most things are close by and I need the exercise.

Even though this example may be a bit strained, it serves to illustrate the nature of integrative consciousness. To interpretative consciousness, integrative consciousness adds a holistic perspective. Interpretative consciousness is primarily analytic; experiences can be treated singly and in isolation. Integrative consciousness is primarily synthetic, placing isolated experiences in a context that serves to redefine them by the resulting figure-ground contrasts. Another feature of integrative consciousness is its scope. Its concern is more strategic than tactical, and as a result, issues in integrative consciousness are defined broadly in time and space. Finally, integrative consciousness creates integrity by centering and carrying forward the flow of experience. This centering of experience is created by a continuous learning process fueled by successive resolutions of the dialectic between apprehension and comprehension and intention and extension.

Adaptation, Consciousness, and Development

With this example as a starting point, let us now turn to a more systematic formulation of the interrelationships among the stages of developmental maturation, the levels of adaptation, and the structure of consciousness as summarized in Table 6.1. It was Kurt Lewin who first articulated how consciousness increases in time/space extension with developmental maturation:

> The three-month-old child living in a crib knows few geographical areas around him, and the areas of possible activities are comparatively few. The child of one year is familiar with a much wider geographical area and a wider field of activities. He is likely to know a number of rooms in the house, the garden, and certain streets. . . .
>
> During development, both the space of free movement and the life space usually increase. The area of activity accessible to the growing child is extended because his own ability increases, and it is probable that social restrictions are removed more rapidly than they are erected as age increases, at least beyond the infant period. . . . The widening of the scope of the life space occurs sometimes gradually, sometimes in rather abrupt steps. The latter is characteristic for so-called crises in development. This process continues well into adulthood.
>
> A similar extension of the life space during development occurs in what may be called the "psychological time dimension." During development, the scope of the psychological time dimension of the life space increases from hours to days, months, and years. In other words, the young child lives in the immediate present; with increasing age, an increasingly more distant psychological past and future affect present behavior. [Lewin, 1951, pp. 103–104]

As the extension of consciousness increases, the same behavioral action is imbued with broader significance, representing an adaptation that takes account of factors beyond the immediate time and space situation. The infant will instinctively grasp the shiny toy before it; the young child may hesitate before picking up her brother's toy gun, knowing it will make him angry; an adult may ponder the purchase of that same toy gun, considering the moral implications of letting her child play with guns. Thus, what is considered the correct or appropriate response will vary depending on the conscious perspective used to judge it. When we judge performance, our concern is usually limited to relatively current and immediate circumstances. When we judge learning, the time frame is extended to evaluate successful adaptation in the future, and the situational circumstance is enlarged to include generically similar situations. When we evaluate development, the adaptive achievement is presumed to apply in all life situations throughout one's lifetime; and if the achievement is recorded as a cultural "tool," the developmental scope may extend even beyond one's lifetime.

Table 6.1 Experiential Learning Theory of Development: Levels of Adaptation and the Structure of Consciousness

	Acquisition	Specialization	Integration
Developmental stage of maturation	Acquisition	Specialization	Integration
Level of adaptation	Performance	Learning	Development
Structure of consciousness:	Registrative	Interpretative	Integrative
Extension in time	seconds / minutes / hours	days / weeks / months	years / decades / lifetimes
Extension in life space	responses / acts / tasks	projects / jobs / occupations	careers / lives / generations
Feedback structure	Goal-directed first-order feedback to achieve goals	Learning how to learn; second-order feedback to change goals and strategies	Consciousness/Integrity; third-order feedback to link goals to life purpose
Hierarchic integration of learning modes	Many differentiated structures with low integration between them	Fewer but larger specialized structures; high integration within structures; low integration between structures	Development of complementary specialized structures; high integration between structures
Concrete experience—affective complexity via apprehension	Direct sensing and feeling · Continuity of sensation and feeling—emergence of enduring sentiments	Self-aware system of sentiments and values · Differentiating self's and others' sentiments and values	Relativistic appreciation of value systems · Value commitment within relativism
Reflective observation—Perceptual complexity via intention	Attention · Watching—development of continuous images	Reflection; giving observations personal meaning · Creating alternative meaning and observation schemes	Relativistic appreciation of different meaning schemes and points of view · Intuition; choosing meaningful perspectives
Abstract conceptualization—Symbolic complexity via comprehension	Recognizing; enactive thought · Object constancy; "iconic" thought	Concrete symbolic operations · Formal hypothetico-deductive reasoning	Attaching concrete meanings to symbol systems · Finding and solving meaningful problems
Active experimentation—Behavioral complexity via extension	Responding to circumstance · Doing; short range intentional acts toward goals	Achieving; development of clear goals and longer-range · Risk taking; making goal and strategy tradeoffs	Experimental hypothesis testing; change goals and strategies based on results · Responsible action; accepting unknown emergent reality

Along with this relatively continuous expansion of the scope of consciousness, there are also discontinuous qualitative shifts in the organization of consciousness as growth occurs. These shifts represent the hierarchic addition of more complex information-processing structures, giving consciousness an interpretative and integrative capability to supplement the simple registrative consciousness of infancy. William Torbert, in his seminal book, *Learning from Experience: Toward Consciousness*, has described the hierarchic structure of consciousness as a three-tiered system of higher-order feedback loops. As in our approach, he uses this three-level structure of consciousness to solve problems that arise in explaining how the focus of experience (what constitutes feedback, in his terms) is determined. He explains his model as follows:

> Recognition of these problems [of what constitutes feedback] has led social systems theorists to attempt to deal with them by postulating two orders of feedback over and above goal-directed feedback (Deutsch, 1966; Mills, 1965). Goal-directed feedback is referred to as first-order feedback. Its function is to redirect a system as it negotiates its outer environment towards a specific goal. The goals and boundaries of the system are assumed to be defined, so feedback is also defined. . . . The two higher orders of feedback can be viewed as explaining how goals and boundaries come to be defined. Second-order feedback has been named "learning" by Deutsch. Its function is to alert the system to changes it needs to make within its own structure to achieve its goal. The change in structure may lead to a redefinition of what the goal is and always leads to a redefinition of the units of feedback (Buckley, 1967). Third-order feedback is called "consciousness" by Deutsch. Its function is to scan all system-environment interactions immediately in order to maintain a sense of the overall, lifetime, autonomous purpose and integrity of the system.

The terms "purpose" and "integrity," critical to the meaning of "consciousness," can be elaborated as follows: The "inner" conscious purpose can be contrasted to the "external" behavioral goal. Goals are subordinate to one's purpose. Goals are related to particular items and places, whereas purpose relates to one's life as a whole, one's life as act. Purpose has also been termed "intention" (Husserl, 1962; Miller, Galanter, and Pribram, 1960) and can be related to the literary term "personal destiny."

The concept of integrity can be related to Erikson's (1959) life-stage that has the same name. A sense of integrity embraces all aspects of a person, whereas the earlier life-stage in Erikson's sequence, named "identity," represents the glorification of certain elements of the personality and the repudiation of others (Erikson, 1958, p. 54). The distinction between a system's identity and a system's integrity can be sharpened by regarding identity as the particular quality of a system's structure, whereas integrity reflects the operation of consciousness. In this sense, consciousness provides a system with "ultrastability" (Cadwallader, 1968). Ultrastability gives the system the possibility of making changes in its structure because the system's essential coherence and integrity are not dependent upon any given structure. [Torbert, 1972, pp. 14–15]

A simple example will illustrate these three levels of feedback and their interrelationship in determining behavior. The classic example of first-order feedback is the household thermostat. The setting of the thermostat represents the goal, and the built-in thermometer is the sensory receptor that starts the furnace when the reading is below the setting and stops it when the set temperature is reached. A similar thermostat inside the human body performed this same registrative function of consciousness in our earlier time, when feeling cold led our ancestors to throw another log on the fire. Second-order feedback is created by the structure that governs how we set the thermostat. One person may set the thermostat at 70°F. The decision is based on a structure designed to maximize personal comfort. Another person may set the thermostat at 65°F. Her decision is based on a structure designed to save money. The units of feedback here are dollars. Thus, second-order feedback structures are interpretive, governing both goals and the meaning (units) of feedback. Most of us share in some degree both these personal-comfort and economic structures, as well as others based on patriotic energy conservation, concern for one's health, and so on. Third-order feedback provides the integrative perspective or integrity that allows for consistent choice about which structure or combination of structures to apply to this particular problem. It governs the process whereby we trade off the values and units of feedback defined by noncompatible structures and answer such questions as, how much will I pay to avoid feeling chilly at times? and, how much personal comfort will I sacrifice for the good of the planet?

The thermostat is a good model for registrative consciousness. Events are registered in consciousness on the basis of a structure that defines goals and units of feedback, but at this first level of consciousness we have no awareness of the higher level structure that governs the process of registering experience. We respond automatically in terms of that structure, just as a thermostat would respond by turning on the furnace when it got dark if we replaced the thermometer with a light sensor. We undoubtedly share this first level of consciousness with the higher animals, whose second-order interpretive structures are largely instinctively determined. At this level of consciousness, the hierarchic integration of the four learning modes is low. Concrete experience is limited to stimulus-bound sensations and feelings. The emergence of enduring sentiments that exist in the absence of their referent sets the stage for the beginning of interpretive consciousness. Similarly, reflective observation, abstract conceptualization, and active experimentation are all immediate and bound up in the stimulus situation in the first stage of registrative consciousness, and they move toward a constancy of images, concepts, and actions as interpretative consciousness begins.

With the hierarchic integration of the four learning modes and increasing affective, perceptual, symbolic, and behavioral complexity come the emergence of interpretative consciousness and second-order "learning" feedback.[2] This is the distinctively human consciousness that most of us associate with the term. In addition to the simple registration of experience, there is an awareness of an "I" who is doing the registering and guiding the choice and definition of a focal experience. As we have seen, this control of the choice and definition of our experiences is achieved by the development of higher-order sentiments, observations, concepts, and actions that interpret experience selectively. These highest-order structures can be seen as learning heuristics that control the definition and elaboration of experience by giving *a priori* preference to some interpretations over others.

An example of how learning heuristics operate to interpret consciousness is found in Adriaan de Groot's (1965) research on how chess masters and novices perceive game situations and formulate chess strategy. It was originally thought that chess masters were more skilled than novices because they thought further ahead and examined more possible moves. It turns out that masters do not think further ahead and, in fact, examine only a few possible moves. Instead, they think about the game at a higher level than novices do, perceiving grouped patterns of pieces that act as a kind of filter to ignore "bad" moves, much as an amateur might use similar but simpler patterns in order not to perceive illegal moves, such as moving the rook diagonally. These higher-level learning heuristics serve to simplify and refine moves in the game by eliminating from consideration a vast array of potential moves that are of little value in viewing the game. Harry Harlow (1959) has argued that all learning is based on this process of inhibiting incorrect responses, creating internalized programs or learning sets that selectively interpret new experiences.

With specialized development, each learning mode organizes clusters of learning heuristics based upon that particular learning orientation. With increased affective complexity comes a self-aware system of sentiments and values to guide one's life, a system that at higher levels becomes differentiated from a growing awareness of the values and sentiments of others. Increasing perceptual complexity is reflected in the development of perspectives on experience that have personal meaning and coherence. At higher levels of interpretative consciousness, one develops the ability to observe experience from multiple perspectives. Increasing symbolic complexity results first in Piaget's stage of concrete symbolic operations and later in formal hypothetico-deductive reasoning. Increased behavioral complexity results in achievement/action schemes—longer-term goals with complex action strategies to reach them. At higher

---

2. The reason that other animals do not develop the higher levels of consciousness may lie in the fact that they lack the symbolic comprehension powers associated with the left brain and thus cannot participate in the triangulation of experience that results from the dialectic between apprehension and comprehension producing hierarchic integration of experience.

levels of behavioral complexity, these action schemes are combined and traded off in a process that recognizes the necessity of risk taking.

Integrative consciousness based on third-order feedback represents the highest level of hierarchic integration of experience. In Torbert's view, it is a level of consciousness that few achieve in their lifetime. The reason that integrative consciousness is so difficult to achieve is that interpretative consciousness has a self-sealing, self-fulfilling character that deceives us with the illusion of a holistic view of an experience when it is in fact fragmented and specialized (see Argyris and Schon, 1978). Precisely because interpretative consciousness selects and defines the flow of experience by excluding aspects of the experience that do not fit its structure, interpretative consciousness contains no contradictions that would challenge the validity of the interpretation. The person highly trained in, say, the symbolic interpretation of her experience rests at the center of that interpretative consciousness confident of the certainty and sufficiency of her view of the world. It is only at the margins that this view seems shaky, as with logical analysis of personal relationships; and only the most advanced forms of symbolic inquiry, such as Gödel's theorem in logic, call its comprehensive application into question.

To achieve integrative consciousness, one must first free oneself from the domination of specialized interpretative consciousness. Jung called this transition to integrative consciousness the process of individuation, whereby the adaptive orientations of the conscious social self are integrated with their complementary nonconsciousness orientations. In *Psychological Types,* he gives numerous examples of the power of the dominant conscious orientation (interpretative consciousness, in our terms) in thwarting this integration and of the strong measures needed to overcome it:

> For there must be a reason why there are different ways of psychological adaptation; evidently one alone is not sufficient, since the object seems to be only partly comprehended when, for example, it is either merely thought or felt. Through a one-sided (typical) attitude there remains a deficit in the resulting psychological adaptation, which accumulates during the course of life; from this deficiency a derangement of adaptation develops which forces the subject towards a compensation. But the compensation can be obtained only by means of *amputation* (sacrifice) of the hitherto one-sided attitude. Thereby a temporary heaping up of energy results and an overflow into channels hitherto not consciously used though already existing unconsciously. [Jung, 1973, p. 28]

Jung's prescription for the amputation of the dominant function is dramatized by his illustrative example of Origin, a third-century Christian convert from Alexandria, who marked his conversion by castration so that, in Origin's words, "all material things" could be "recast through spiritual interpretation into a cosmos of ideas." Betty Edwards, in her system for learning to draw by using the right side of the brain, suggests a less drastic approach for getting around the dominance of the specialized left-brain interpretative consciousness.

Since drawing a perceived form is largely a right brain function, we must keep the left brain out of it. Our problem is that the left brain is dominant and speedy and is very prone to rush in with words and symbols, even taking over jobs which it is not good at. The split brain studies indicated that the left brain likes to be boss, so to speak, and prefers not to relinquish tasks to its dumb partner unless it really dislikes the job—either because the job takes too much time, is too detailed or slow or because the left brain is simply unable to accomplish the task. That's exactly what we need—tasks that the dominant left brain will turn down. [Edwards, 1979, p. 42]

Because we are ensnared by our particular specialized interpretative consciousness and reinforced for this entrapment through the specialized structure of social institutions, we know little of the nature of integrative consciousness. Most descriptions of this state have come from the mystical or transcendental religious literature, descriptions that fall on deaf ears for those at the interpretative level of consciousness who find the rapturous prose about "golden flowers" and the "Clear Light" to be so much baloney. The problem, of course, is that *integrative* consciousness by its very nature cannot be described by any single *interpretation*. Thus, all these descriptions have an elusive and even contradictory quality, such as that which characterizes Zen Koans. For example:

> Jōshū asked the teacher, Nansen, "What is the true Way?"
> Nansen answered, "Everyday; way is the true Way."
> Jōshū asked, "Can I study it?"
> Nansen answered, "The more you study, the further from the Way."
> Jōshū asked, "If I don't study it, how can I know it?"
> Nansen answered, "The Way does not belong to things seen: Nor to things unseen. It does not belong to things known: Nor to things unknown. Do not seek it, study it, or name it. To find yourself and it, open yourself wide as the sky. [Zen Buddhism, 1959, p. 22]

The transcendent quality of integrative consciousness is precisely that, a "climbing out of" the specialized adaptive orientations of our worldly social roles. With that escape come the flood of contradictions and paradoxes that interpretative consciousness serves to stifle. It is through accepting these paradoxes and experiencing their dialectical nature fully that we achieve integrative consciousness in its full creative force. This state of consciousness is not reserved for the monastery but is a necessary ingredient for creativity in any field. Albert Einstein once said, "The most beautiful and profound emotion one can feel is a sense of the mystical. . . . It is the dower of all true science."

In accepting and experiencing fully the dialectic contradictions of experience, one's self becomes identified with the process whereby the interpretative structures of consciousness are created, rather than being identified with the structures themselves. The key to this sense of self-as-process lies in the reestablishment of a symbiosis or reciprocity between the dialectic modes of adaptation such that one both restricts and establishes the other, and such that each in its own separate sphere can reach its highest level of development by the activity of the other. Carl Rogers, in his description of the peak of human functioning, describes as well as anyone the process-centered nature of integrative consciousness:

> There is a growing and continuing sense of acceptant ownership of these changing feelings, a basic trust in his own process. . . . Experiencing has lost almost completely its structure bound aspects and becomes process experiencing—that is, the situation is experienced and interpreted in its newness, not as the past. . . . The self becomes increasingly simply the subjective and reflexive awareness of experiencing. The self is much less frequently a perceived object, and much more frequently something confidently felt in process. . . . Personal constructs are tentatively reformulated, to be validated against further experience, but even then to be held loosely. . . . Internal communication is clear, with feelings and symbols well matched, and fresh terms for new feelings. There is the experiencing of effective choice of new ways of doing. [Rogers, 1961, pp. 151–52]

The development of integrative consciousness begins with the transcendence of one's specialized interpretative consciousness and continues with, first, the exploration of the previously nonexpressed adaptive orientations and, later, the full acceptance of the dialectic relationship between the dominant and nondominant orientation. This embrace of the dialectic nature of experience leads to a self-identification with the *process* of learning. As can be seen in the description of the highest levels of hierarchic integration in the four learning modes (Figure 6.5), this process orientation is reflected in the incorporation of dialectic opposites in each of the modal descriptions. The integrative levels of affective complexity begin with the relativistic appreciation (in the fullest sense of the term) of value systems and conclude with an active value commitment in the context of that relativism (compare Perry, 1970). Integration in perceptual complexity begins with a similar relativistic appreciation of observational schemes and perspectives and concludes with intuition—the capacity for choosing meaningful perspectives and frameworks for interpreting experience. With integrative consciousness, symbolic complexity achieves first the ability to match creatively symbol systems and concrete objects and finally the capacity for finding and solving meaningful problems. Behavioral complexity at the integrative level begins with the development of an experimental, hypothesis-testing approach to action that introduces new tentativeness and flexibility to goal-oriented behavior—a tentativeness that is tempered in the final stage by the active commitment to responsible action in a world that can never be fully known because it is continually being created.

In his 1955 lithograph entitled "Liberation," M. C. Escher captures the essence of the three developmental stages of experiential learning. The bottom third of the figure (Figure 6.5) shows the emergence of figures from an undifferentiated background, as in the acquisition stage of development. The middle third of the figure shows the articulation of form in tightly locked interaction between figure and ground, much as development in the specialization stage is achieved by finding one's "niche" in society. The top of the figure shows the birds in free flight, emphasizing the process of flying over the content of their form, symbolizing the freedom and self-direction of integrative development.

Figure 6.5 *Liberation,* by M. C. Escher (lithograph, 1955)

Update and Reflections

I believe that when human beings are inwardly free to choose whatever they deeply value, they tend to value those objects, experiences and goals which make for their own survival, growth and development and development of others. . . . Instead of universal values "out there," or a universal value system imposed by some group—philosophers, rulers, priests, or psychologists—we have the possibility of universal human value directions emerging from the experiencing of the human organism.

—Carl Rogers

The experiential learning theory of adult development described in Chapter 6 starts with the premise that development occurs through the process of learning from experience viewed as transactions between individual characteristics and external circumstances—between personal knowledge and social knowledge. Vygotsky's zone of proximal development is outlined as an example of how these transactions integrate personal knowledge and social knowledge (see p. 198). Developmental progression in the theory is viewed as increasing differentiation and hierarchic integration of functioning, with the former preceding the latter in successive cycles of increasing integrative complexity. The Gestalt theorist Heinz Werner provides the basis for the multilinear experiential learning theory developmental model (Figure 6.3) which differentiates it from the Piaget-based unilinear models of adult development—e.g., Kohlberg, Perry, Kegan, and Loevinger. Unlike the Piagetian approaches, experiential learning theory considers individual differences in development, allows for the influence of culture and context, and recognizes development as multidimensional, encompassing affective, perceptual, and behavioral dimensions in addition to the exclusive Piagetian focus on cognitive development. Foregoing the detailed structural stages of the Piagetian models, development is broadly divided into three stages inspired by Jung—acquisition, specialization, and integration. The model then describes three levels of consciousness—registrative, interpretive, and integrative—and three levels of adaptation—performance, learning, and development—corresponding to the three stages respectively (Table 6.1). Since the publication of *Experiential Learning,* research has added support to the experiential learning theory development framework in some areas and suggested modifications in others. The update will review some of these insights.

Culture and Context

Piaget's structural genetic epistemology was a bold effort to describe the child's development toward the internalized logic of scientific rationality solely as an internal developmental process independent of culture and context. But unfortunately his reach exceeded his grasp. As much as his structuralism illuminated how the mind works, as Jerome Bruner notes, there is much his structural approach does not explain:

> Even from within the Piagetian fold, the research of Kohlberg, Colby, and others point to the raggedness and irregularity of the so-called stages of moral development. Particularly, localness, context, historical opportunity, all play so large a role that it is embarrassing to have them outside Piaget's system rather than within. But they cannot fit within. . . the system failed to capture the particularity of Everyman's knowledge, the role of negotiations in establishing meaning, the tinkerer's way of encapsulating knowledge rather than generalizing it, the muddle of ordinary moral judgment. As a system it. . . failed to yield a picture of self and of individuality. [Bruner, 1986, p. 147]

Vygotsky provided a strong counterpoint focusing as he did on the cultural tools, particularly language, and contexts that influence development; though still on a unilinear cognitive track. For Vygotsky language influenced thought giving new meanings and ideas, whereas for Piaget thought develops through its own internal, logic that is not determined by language; language is the medium for the expression of thought. For both men the relationship between thought and language is interactional, not transactional as is the enactivist learning spiral described in Chapter 2 Update and Reflections. Vygotsky's famous example of how Marxist ideas improve the conceptual development of the mind and even his proximal zone of development where a more developed consciousness aids a lesser developed consciousness seem one-way and unilateral. Compare this with the transactional emergence of Gadamer's (1965) conversation, which is larger than the consciousness of any player, or of Freire's (1970) dialogue among equals.

Bruner argues that theories of development are more than descriptions of human growth; they acquire a normative influence that gives a social reality to the principles of the theory. He states, ". . . the truths of theories of development are relative to the cultural contexts in which they are applied. . . a question of congruence of values that prevail in the culture. It is this congruence that gives development theories—proposed initially as mere descriptions—a moral face once they have become embodied in the broader culture" (1986, p. 135). Barbara Rogoff (2003) gives a striking example in her research comparing educational practices in indigenous communities of the Americas with those of Western European heritage societies. In the Western societies children are organized by tight age grades and segregated from the mature activities of the community, spending their time in institutions such as schools where they are taught generalized abstract knowledge to prepare them for their later life in the society. This system is supported and justified by models of development based on reason and abstract universal knowledge from the Enlightenment to Piaget. In the indigenous communities children of all ages have wide access to community activities in which they will be expected to engage. They engage in direct learning from ongoing experience, through observation, collaboration, and ongoing support from others. Ethnographic studies of these communities suggest that children are more attentive and collaborative than Western middle-class children.

Individual Differences and Multilinear Development

In Piagetian schemes, individuality is manifest only in differential progression along the single yardstick of development—progression toward the internalized logic of scientific rationality. In experiential learning theory individuality is manifest not only in the stage of development but also in the course of development. Studies of gender differences in adult development and the ontological, being dimensions of development, tend to support the experiential learning theory view.

Gender Differences in Development

Carol Gilligan's (1982) theory of moral development, which studied 29 women considering abortions, challenged Kohlberg's unidimensional rational moral development theory by showing that women emphasize caring to deal with moral dilemmas in contrast to men's focus on justice. In *Women's Ways of Knowing*, Belenky, Clinchy, Goldberger, and Tarule (1986) challenged Perry's (1970) model of intellectual development in the same way. Their research identified two different dimensions of development—connected knowing and separate knowing. Women tended to use connected knowing, an empathetic approach that takes others' perspectives to understand their ideas. Men on the other hand tend to detach themselves from others in an attempt to objectively challenge and doubt their ideas. Similarly, Baxter-Magolda (1992), in a replication of Perry's model, found an overlap between men and women in their positions in Perry's system but also found receptivity and interpersonal patterns of reasoning in women and impersonal mastery-oriented reasoning in men.

Knight and colleagues (1995, 1997) developed a measure of separate and connected knowing and related it to scores on the Kolb Learning Style Inventory, predicting that separate knowing would be related to abstract conceptualization and connected knowing would be related to concrete experience. Concrete experience was significantly related to connected knowing but primarily for men. However, men who scored lower on concrete experience had lower scores than female low-scorers on connected knowing. In other words, high concrete experience men had connected scores equal to women who scored higher on connected knowing regardless of learning style. The interaction of gender and concrete experience was a strong predictor of connected knowing, but only gender predicted separate knowing.

These studies tracing development in women show that they tend to develop connected knowing in affective and perceptual complexity dimensions of the experiential learning theory developmental model (see Figure 6.3), while men develop separate knowing on symbolic and behavioral dimensions of integrative complexity though with considerable overlap between the genders and individual differences in profiles of the relative strength of the four modes.

Epistemological and Ontological Dimensions of Development

Piagetian inspired adult development models are epistemological; concerned with developmental differences in how one knows about oneself, the world, and their awareness of how they know. In "Is Epistemology Enough?" Vandenberg (1991) argues that theories based on epistemology fail to consider fundamental existential concerns such as the meaning of life and anxiety about death. This is particularly significant in the social world and in relationships with others who we know to be living beings who share these existential concerns. Disagreeing with Piaget's claim that the reaction of intelligence to the social environment is "exactly parallel" to that of the physical environment, he suggests that our awareness of "being here" with fellow humans is fundamentally different. This suggests a different perspective on morality that goes beyond issues of rational judgment to existential issues of guilt and will and the freedom to choose to be moral (see Kohlberg's theory of moral development below).

Ya-hui Su suggests that the epistemological approach to lifelong learning is focused on "having," which is based on acquisition, storing, abstracting, and deferring rather than an ontological "being" approach of constructing, substantiating, and responding. "Lifelong learning as authentic being is not simply based on thought and action but must also concern willingness or affect. . . . Through the affective dimension. . . learners experience themselves as a willing cause of their own learning. When intuitive feeling is placed at the core of learning, a deeper, more primordial understanding is attained, where the learner and his or her world meet at the pre-conceptual level" (2011, p. 65). The experiential learning theory developmental model portrays both ontological and epistemological directions of development. Through being with direct concrete experiences, intuitive affective knowing occurs while through abstract conceptualization, generalized knowledge is created. "Accordingly, experiential learning shapes people epistemologically and existentially" (Malinen 2000, p. 99).

Integration and Advanced Stages of Adult Development

In the experiential learning theory model of development the integrative phase highlights the importance of integrating the multiple dimensions of development. The transition from specialization to integration is a move from identification with a specialized approach to learning shaped by socialization into a particular career path that defines the self as its content: the abilities, knowledge, and values that it "has." Integration, following Jung, brings the emergence of non-dominant approaches to learning into a holistic self-fulfillment that identifies with the process of learning, not *what* is learned.

In contemporary constructive adult development research and theory this is described as a move from conventional to post-conventional stages of development. In the conventional stages people are operating at Piaget's stage of concrete and formal operations, conforming to the norms and values of their culture and context, introjecting these as their own with little self-conscious reflection and choice. In the post-conventional stages meaning-making becomes more reflective, choiceful, and voluntary, questioning beliefs and assumptions acquired during socialization.

At the time *Experiential Learning* was published, the major Piagetian adult development theories—Loevinger's ego development theory, Kegan's subject-object theory, and Kohlberg's moral development theory—all described the highest integrative stage of development as guided by internal, autonomous capacities for integrative reasoning and action—to choose responsibly one's own social role and action. Contemporary constructive adult development research and theory by these scholars and others has focused on still higher stages of adult development focusing on post-formal stages of development that move beyond the rational linear logic of formal operations to a holistic dialectic way of knowing that integrates experiencing and conceptualizing ways of knowing (Alexander and Langer, 1990). While thought based on formal operations is dualistic, choosing one pole over another, post-formal thought is dialectic and holistic, where opposites are seen as poles of one concept that contains contradiction and paradox in movement and process. "This construction allows the self to see others and the self equally as expressions of a larger community to which both belong. . . . No longer can cause and effect or two opposing sides of a conflict be identified within separable systems" (Souvaine, Lahey, and Kegan, 1990, p. 250; see also Basseches, 1984, 2005). The highest level of post-conventional stages of thought is consistent with the self-as-process integrative stage in experiential learning theory, while the lower stage based on formal operations is an integrative process at the experiential learning theory specialization stage.

Kolhberg's 7th Stage of Moral Development

The most dramatic example of the addition of a post-formal stage of development that goes beyond epistemological stages of knowing to a stage that integrates epistemological and ontological perspectives is the seventh stage of moral development proposed by Kohlberg. This stage goes beyond his six-stage Piagetian stage model of moral development that shows how individuals at increasing levels of maturity address the question of *how* to be moral. The six stages describe the progression from self-interest to conventional morality to stage six where individuals rationally define their values and principles in a universal way. The framework, however, does not address the question of *why* one should be moral. Kohlberg goes on to say, "The answer to this question entails the further question, 'Why live?', thus, ultimate moral maturity requires a mature solution to the question of the meaning of life. This, in turn, is hardly a moral question per se; it is an ontological one. Not only is the question not a moral question, but it is a question not resolvable on purely logical or rational grounds, as moral questions are" (Kohlberg and Ryncarz, 1990, p. 192).

To address the ontological question, he proposes a seventh stage that involves experiencing in a non-egoistic and non-dualistic way that involves being part of the whole of life and nature with a cosmic perspective. He goes further, linking his seventh stage to Fowler's (1981) highest stage of faith development, Universalizing Faith; suggesting that the correlation between stages of faith development and moral development shows the intertwining of the ontological and epistemological, the *why* and the *how*, operating at all levels of moral maturity.

Of the seventh stage he says it can be achieved temporarily, "such as when on a mountaintop or before the ocean. At such a time, what is ordinarily background becomes foreground and the self is no longer figure to the ground. We sense the unity of the whole and ourselves as part of that unity. . . one may argue that the crisis of despair precipitated by the recognition of one's finite character from the perspective of the infinite, when thoroughly and courageously explored, leads to a figure-ground shift that reveals the positive validity of the cosmic perspective implicit in it" (Kohlberg and Ryncarz, 1990, pp. 193–195). What is particularly poignant about Kohlberg's recognition of the ontological dimension, and particularly this last sentence, is that it appears in his last publication before his suicide resulting from the chronic pain of an incurable disease. We can only hope that this seventh-stage awareness gave him peace and transcendence.

Kegan's Subject Object Theory

Robert Kegan (1982, 1994; Kegan and Lahey, 2009) in the course of his career has defined and refined a five-stage theory of adult development that traces qualitative changes in how one makes meaning from experience in the cognitive affective, interpersonal, and intrapersonal realms. The system is an elegant and persuasive theory based on subject-object relations that describes how the subjective framework in which one is embedded to view the object at one level becomes the object of a new more encompassing subjective framework at the next level. Kegan describes this growth as making what was subject into object so that we can "have it" rather than "be had" by it. Like Kohlberg, he describes a stage operating at the highest conventional formal operations level, which he calls "the self-authoring mind" (or modern mind), and a highest level stage, "the self-transforming mind" (or post-modern mind), that operates at the post-formal or post-conventional level.

The self-authoring mind describes individuals who see themselves as autonomous independent selves who are responsible for their actions and in control of their lives. Operating in the formal operations stage they rationally analyze variables to determine cause and effect and solve problems. Kegan says these individuals "can coordinate, integrate, act upon or invent values, beliefs, convictions, generalizations, ideals, abstractions, interpersonal loyalties and intrapersonal states. It is no longer *authored* by them, it *authors them* and thereby achieves a personal authority" (1994, p. 185). Cook-Greuter says of them, "It is no exaggeration to say that people with a formal operations worldview quite often look at life itself as a task to be accomplished or as a technical problem to be solved" (1999, p. 24). Weighing the pluses and minuses she says, "On one hand, symbol use and abstract thought have freed human being from direct experience of what is and thus allow for hypothetical reasoning and independent manipulation of mental objects. By reifying and objectifying experience, humans exert a measure of control over their environment. On the other hand, formal operational thought is often perceived as inappropiately detached from feelings, overly abstract or 'too much in the head.' By only granting reality to rational, waking consciousness, it demotes whole realms of human experience to a lesser status" (1999, p. 28).

Baxter-Magolda advocates for the self-authoring mind as the foundation of higher education, "Twenty-first century learning outcomes require self-authorship: the internal capacity to define one's belief system, identity and relationships" (2007, p. 69). Based on her extensive research, including a 21-year longitudinal study of young adults from ages 18 to 39 (2001), she has identified three components of self-authorship—trusting one's internal voice, building an internal foundation of beliefs, and securing internal commitments to strengthen personal identity (2008). The self-authoring mind seems a good fit for the challenges of living in a highly individualistic society such as the United States where responsibility for the course of one's life including health care, retirement, and education is left to the individual; and, as Bruner pointed out, the developmental ideal itself gives justification for the policies that enact these systems.

Kegan's self-transforming mind describes a qualitative development beyond the formal operations of the self-authoring mind, a development that he sees as necessary to meet the challenges of the emerging post-modern world. The self-transforming mind is able to step back from the relatively closed system and self sufficient self-authored self and view it as one form of self-organization that is not necessarily complete or ultimate. It is more open to contradictions and other perspectives. It recognizes that any way of knowing when viewed from the point of view of another way is incomplete and flawed. It operates through dialectic reasoning where opposites are seen as one pole of a larger concept, as apprehension and comprehension are seen as poles of the transformation dimension in experiential learning theory. Identity lies not with a particular form but with transformation through the process of change itself. Relationships are a context for sharing and interacting in which both parties experience and share their multiplicity.

Loevinger and Cook-Greuter's Ego Development

Jane Loevinger's (1976, 1993, 1998) theory of ego development encompasses nine stages—three at the pre-conventional level, three at the conventional level, and three at the post-conventional level—describing growth in maturity of the ego in impulse control, character development, interpersonal style, conscious preoccupations, and cognitive style that develop together. While based in psychoanalytic ego psychology, the developmental stages follow the logic of Piaget's theory. Her highest stages based on formal operations are the individualistic and autonomous, while her integrated stage describing self-actualized persons with complex self-identities is not well-defined. For her the autonomous stage is the highest stage of development achieved by most people. This is probably because her approach emphasizes an empirical, as opposed to theoretical, methodology and very few people can be identified at the integrated level. Indeed, her system has a large body of empirical research using the Sentence Completion Test (SCT) which assesses the different stages. Like Kegan's self-authoring mind, the central issues at the autonomous stage are self-determination, self-actualization, and self-definition. They want to achieve their ideal self. They approach interpersonal relationships in an interdependent way and are able to control impulses to manage conflict.

Suzanne Cook-Greuter (1999) studied a sample of post-conventional SCT protocols from 440 SCTs scored over 17 years. Using this data she redefined the integrated stage into two stages, the construct aware and the unity. Individuals in the construct aware stage come to recognize their fundamental egocentricity as a limit on their growth and awareness, often perceiving the previous autonomous stage as self-centered and self-important, while still yearning for a stable self-identity. Many have had peak experiences where they witness themselves as experiencing beings. They come to see their concepts of the world as relative and arbitrary interpretations of the flow of experience and begin to embrace present, immediate experience as a way of knowing. In the unity stage individuals have a being orientation, let go of conscious mental activity, and immerse themselves in the immediate ongoing flow of experience. They see the permanent self and object world as illusory; everything is changing. Peak experiences are no longer rare but habitual ways of being. They have a universal perspective feeling themselves as part of the cosmos.

Rogers' and Gendlin's Process Conception of Growth

A fourth developmental model, written in 1956 before Piaget's work was widely known in the United States, offers a contrast to the three Piaget inspired frameworks described above. Carl Rogers' (1961, 1964) process conception of growth in psychotherapy, unlike those above that emphasize growth in cognitive meaning making, emphasizes growth in experiencing and its integration with conceptualization, as further developed by Gendlin

(1961, 1962, 1978). It also differs in that the model is not linear but curvilinear, describing a process whereby the child's pure experiencing process is blocked by the cultural intro-jections of significant others only to emerge later as the person matures. For the adults he sees in therapy the process is about recapturing the child's capacity to experience directly. The "continuum is from fixity to changingness, from rigid structure to flow, from stasis to process. . . it is unlikely that in one area of his life the client would exhibit complete fixity and in another area complete changingness. He would tend, as a whole, to be at some stage in the process" (Rogers, 1961, p. 131). He describes this as a process of "let-ting oneself down into the immediacy of what one is experiencing, endeavoring to sense and to clarify all its complex meanings. . . the process is much more complex than it is in the infant. . . . For there is involved in the present moment of experiencing the memory traces of all the relevant learnings from the past. . . . Likewise the moment of experiencing contains, for the mature adult, hypotheses about consequences. . . . Past and future are both in this moment. . ." (Rogers, 1964, p. 164).

The two highest levels of Rogers' (1961) experiencing process continuum directly paral-lel the highest stages proposed by Kohlberg, Kegan, and Cook-Greuter. At stage six any present feeling is directly experienced with immediacy and richness. This immediacy of experiencing and the feeling which constitutes its content are accepted. This is something which *is*, not something to be denied, feared, struggled against. Self as object tends to disappear. The self at this moment, *is* the feeling. A physiological loosening accompanies this process type of experiencing. Any relevant personal construct is dissolved in the experiencing moment and as one feels loose from his previously stabilized framework. . . there are no longer "problems," external or internal. The person is living subjectively, a phase of his problem. It is not an object. The best description seems to be that he neither perceives his problem nor deals with it, but is simply living some portion of it knowingly and acceptingly.

At stage seven new feelings are coming into awareness and are experienced with imme-diacy and richness of detail both in the therapeutic relationship and in the outside. There is a growing sense of acceptant ownership of these changing feelings, a basic trust in one's own inward process. This trust is not primarily in the conscious process which goes on, but rather in the total organismic process. Experiencing has lost almost completely its structure-bound aspects and becomes pure process experiencing—that is the situation is experienced and interpreted in its newness, not as the past. The self becomes increasingly simply the subjective and reflexive awareness of experiencing, is much less frequently a perceived object, . . . and much more frequently something felt in the process. Personal constructs, after disappearing, are tentatively reformulated, to be submitted to validation against further experience, but even then to be held loosely. Internal communication is clear with feelings and symbols well matched; there is an experiencing of effective choice of new ways of thinking . . . and a sensing of a possibility of an effective choice.

Implications for Experiential Learning Theory Development Theory

I chose in the experiential learning theory developmental model to define three broad stages of life—acquisition, specialization, and integration—based on Jung's theory of development toward individuation and Werner's orthogenetic principle that describes development as proceeding from an embedded lack of differentiation to a state of increasing differentiation and articulation to hierarchic integration. These stages parallel the pre-conventional, conventional, and post-conventional phases of the adult development models described above. The above adult development models define two clear and consistent levels in the integrative stage; the autonomous self-authoring self and the integrating processual self. The theorists have developed marvelously meticulous qualitative scoring systems to reliably describe these developmental stages.

Yet their claims of a hierarchy of stages, however compelling they are theoretically, are problematic in a number of respects. The standards necessary to prove these stage models impose a pretty high bar. Loevinger herself states, "There is an underlying assumption that the types found in adult life represent the trace of developmental stages. This assumption is not easily subject to proof" (1993, pp. 6–7).

Hard, Soft, and Functional Stages

Flavell (1971) argues that to define a stage change more than just a couple of discrete variables must differ between stages; the stages must differ as a holistic system of cognitive organization that is qualitatively, not quantitatively, different. It must be an abrupt jump to proficiency in the higher stage for all aspects of the total system. Kohlberg and his colleagues have suggested that there are *functional, hard,* and *soft* stages that differ in how well they meet these criteria (Alexander and Langer, 1990, p. 159). Only hard stages meet Flavell's criteria, being developmental sequences that reorganize cognitive frameworks universally.

Kohlberg and Ryncarz argue that soft stages are optional, not necessary, tracks of development. "Movement in these stages is an option for individuals who are induced by their own personalities and a life circumstance into those forms of reflection on life's meaning that soft stages represent" (1990, p. 204). While hard stages involve only an abstract *epistemic* subject, soft stage theories involve a concept of the self and self-awareness, a psychological concept that is at present not well-developed compared to cognitive functioning. They argue that Kohlberg's seventh stage of post-formal development is a soft stage of reflective meaning making, unlike the formal six stages that precede it. Functional stages are environmentally influenced, referring to stages that emerge to perform new tasks or functions.

The experiential learning theory developmental stages by this analysis are soft or functional stages determined by one's individual life course. For example, the studies of accountants and engineers described in *Experiential Learning* (Chapter 7, pp. 272–273) suggest that movement from specialization to integration for individuals in these two professions is influenced by changes in their work roles. Engineers, who remain in technical jobs, for example, retain their specialized converging learning style and skills while those who move into management integrate these skills with a more accommodating style and skills. As described previously (Chapter 2 Update and Reflections), development occurs not as an isolated, internal individual process, but through the spiraling of the learning cycle in the co-evolution of mutually transforming transactions between ourselves and the world around us.

Is Up the Only Way?

Stages models are unidirectional indicating hierarchical integration of increasing complexity; requiring an explicit logic of what makes one position higher and more mature than another (Noam, 1993, p. 45). Kegan and colleagues show admirable humility at the difficulty of this task, ". . . the plausibility of an argument for a post-formal state also casts a shadow on the likelihood of unexceptional people like ourselves to describe with anything approaching completeness the systematicity of that state. . . Since. . . we spend the vast majority of our lives embedded in the *formal*-operational rational systems. . . The authors come by their modesty honestly" (Souvaine, Lahey, and Kegan, 1990, p. 230). Others in the field are more comfortable in claming the superiority of higher stages. Loevinger claims that "people can understand thinking at their own level or at levels below their own, but not at levels above their own" (1998, p. 33). Cook-Greuter seems to agree, "Paradoxically, these rarer perspectives on life produce types of knowledge that are incomprehensible to those who have not themselves asked the epistemological questions and experienced the self-transformations occurring in this inquiry process" (1999, pp. 1–2).

The claim may or may not be true, but it nonetheless produces uncomfortable claims of superiority by those who see themselves at higher levels of maturity. My social constructionist and critical theorist friends often speak of physical scientists operating in the formal operations stage as "modernists," "positivists," "realists," "empiricists," "reductionists," and the like implying a somewhat lower form of thought that just doesn't "get it." My physical and natural science friends, to the extent that they pay any attention to this "post-modern" stuff at all, say that the social constructionists just don't know what they are talking about when they dismiss logical empiricism and reductionism. My own view is that of Stephen Pepper (Chapter 5) and Stephen J. Gould (2003) who see the two modes of inquiry as co-equal and complementary—qualitatively different ways of knowing.

The unilinear and unidirectional assumption of the models must also be questioned for its upward orientation. Developmental advances are seen as higher, more all-encompassing abstractions that release us from our embeddedness in the ground and grind of daily existence. Yet Gilligan's refinement of Kohlberg's model introduces an ethic of care and compassion that more appropriately seems like a downward embracing of the cares and concerns of others. Mother Theresa's *Total Surrender* (1993) is a testament to this ideal of downward development. Cook-Greuter (2000) has recently proposed a modification in the ego development model suggesting that it is not an upward and linear progression but curvilinear. Early development from the preconventional through the conventional stage of conscientiousness is an upward separation from the ground of being, while post-coventional development is a return to the ground with higher awareness or conscious unity. This is similar to Rogers' curvilinear model of development in experiencing described previously.

Stages or States?

In recent years we have begun to depart from stage models of development to a view that recognizes the states described by the stage models but sees these states as *modes of adaptation* that are not necessarily hierarchical. Differentiation and integration are not primarily broad life stages but continuous processes of development occurring throughout life. Working with many hundreds of individuals over the years we have received pushback on the hierarchical stages of development, particularly from younger students who ask why they can't be at the integrative stage at their age. In some cases, when we talked with them in depth, it seemed that their primary concerns were developmental and holistic rather than specialized. Recently millennial's have suggested that their generation in general frequently operates at the integrative developmental level. Richard Boyatzis and I (Boyatzis and Kolb, 1999) have redefined the three stages as modes of adaptation that differ in their framing of time and space. *Performance* is an adaptive mode of learning confined to immediate time/space situations, while the *learning* mode extends the time/space frame to include similar specialized environments. The *development* mode extends to the total lifespan and all life situations. Individuals may be in any one of these modes at varying times and situations in their life driven by personal choice or the challenges of context.

Applied to the current focus on stages of integrative development, viewing the autonomous self-authoring and integrating processual selves as modes of adaptation that are states rather than stages recognizes that these states are determined partially by culture, context, and one's life situation. For example, Nisbett, Peng, Choi, and Norenzayan (2001) found that East Asians tend to be holistic in their cognition like the integrating processual self, while Westerners are more analytic in their cognition like the autonomous self-authoring self.

Such states may be more prevalent in the population than the low frequency of occurrence of higher stages in Kegan and Loevinger's work, which are defined by the stringent criteria for a stage described earlier. Cook-Grueter (1999, 2000) estimates that about 10 percent of adults are in the pre-conventional stages, 80 percent are in the conventional stages, and 10 percent are in the post-conventional stages. Less than 1 percent of Kegan's (2009) sample achieve the highest level of self-transforming mind, and fewer than 2 percent score in Cook-Greuter's construct aware and unitive stages (Loevinger's integrated stage).

They also may be subject to deliberate development and flexible adaptation to meet different situational challenges (see Chapter 8 Update and Reflections). Langer and colleagues suggest that adult development models have a conservative view of change, "There is too easy an understanding of what the next stage is going to be. 'Development' is perceived as a time dependent continuity where the articulation of later stages 'follows through' from participation in earlier stages. And there is all too definite an idea of what stages and possibilities lie ahead as persons make their way through development" (Alexander and Langer, 1990, pp. 135–136). Temporary states like Kohlberg's unity experience on the mountaintop may prove beneficial for gaining a new perspective on the life challenges we face and may be helpful in framing effective action.

7

Learning and Development in Higher Education

. . . the ways in which we believe and expect have a tremendous effect on what we believe and expect. We have discovered at last that these ways are set, almost abjectly so, by social factors, by tradition and the influence of education. Thus we discover that we believe many things not because the things are so but because we have become habituated through the weight of authority, by imitation, prestige, institution, and unconscious effect of language, etc. We learn, in short, that qualities which we attribute to objects ought to be imputed to our ways of experiencing them, and that these in turn are due to the force of intercourse and custom. This discovery marks an emancipation; it purifies and remakes the objects of our direct or primary experience.

—John Dewey, Experience and Nature

From the perspective of experiential learning theory, educational institutions are the curators of social knowledge. Chief among the responsibilities of their curatorship is the creation of conditions whereby social knowledge is made accessible to individual learners for their development. Jerome Bruner has underscored the importance of this task:

> Perhaps the task of converting knowledge into a form fit for transmission is, after all, the final step in our codification of knowledge. Perhaps the task is to go beyond the learned scholarship, scientific research, and the exercise of disciplined sensibility in the arts to the transmission of what we have discovered. Surely no culture will reach its full potential unless it invents ever better means for doing so. [Bruner, 1971, p. 19]

This responsibility includes the individual development of participants in these institutions in all three developmental stages of experiential learning: (1) acquisition, the preparation of individual learners in basic skills so that they can access and utilize the tools of social knowledge; (2) specialization, the selection and socialization of learners into specialized areas of knowledge that suit their talents and meet societal needs; and (3) integration, the development of the unique capabilities of the whole person toward creativity, wisdom, and integrity. The first of these responsibilities has traditionally been the province of primary and secondary education, although the increased knowledge necessary to function effectively in modern society, coupled with the general decline in the public educational system, has caused considerable overflow of this responsibility into the system of higher education.

The third educational responsibility of integrative fulfillment has for many years been suffering at the expense of the second, specialized occupational training. The selection of Charles Eliot as president of Harvard in 1869 marked the end of classical education in American colleges whereby all students took the same courses in Greek, Latin, and mathematics. By introducing electives and "majors" in the Harvard curriculum, he began what, considering the rapid growth of knowledge, was the inevitable specialization and fragmentation that characterizes the modern university. In the system that has emerged in the last 100 years, students have been increasingly free to select their courses and to define programs suited to their needs, interests, and abilities. Academic disciplines have enjoyed a corresponding freedom to choose those students who best fit their requirements. This trend toward specialization and vocationalism in higher education has recently gained momentum from post-"baby-boom" demographics, a tight job market, and the multifaceted financial crises of institutions of higher learning. College and universities are thus increasingly specialized and fragmented, held together by little more than Robert Hutchins's central heating system, Warren Bennis's parking authority, and a few distribution requirements. In a highly complex and specialized society, the pressures toward specialization in education feed on themselves. Higher education is increasingly called upon to deliver the specialized knowledge, skills, and attitudes needed for students to find their niche in society, and to service that niche as well. Institutions, in turn, become increasingly dependent on these "social niches" for their own survival, and lend further support to the forces of knowledge specialization, usually at the expense of integrative education. Speaking of the specialized formal educational requirements required for entry in occupations, Robert Hutchins said:

> The great bulk of the students in American universities are there in order to meet these requirements. The public acquiesces in them, first, because it is accustomed to acquiesce in the demands of pressure groups, and second because it has a vague feeling that the members of certain occupations at least should be certified, or sanctified, in some way before they are let loose upon the public. The public is unwilling, often for good reasons, to trust these occupations to certify their own

members. The universities acquiesce in these arrangements because they wish to increase their enrollments; students bring in income, and anyway there is a general feeling that excellence in educational institutions, as in most other things, increases in proportion to size. The trades, occupations, businesses, and professions promote these arrangements in order to restrict competition and enhance their prestige. [Hutchins, 1953, p. 31]

Before we return to a consideration of integrative development, it is important to understand first the consequences of this specialized emphasis of higher education on student learning and development. In considering the student careers that are spawned and shaped in the university community and the university's responsibility for the intellectual, moral, and personal development of its members, we have often emphasized the unitary linear trend of human growth and development at the expense of acknowledging and managing the diverse developmental pathways that exist within different disciplines and professions. These paths foster some developmental achievements and, as we shall see, inhibit others. The channels of academic specialization are swift and deep, the way between them tortuous and winding. Many years ago, I served as a freshman advisor to undergraduates in a technological university. Two or three of my students in each group faced the awkward realization near the end of their freshman year that a career in engineering was not quite what they had imagined it to be. What to do? Transfer to a liberal arts school and possibly lose the prestige of a technological education? Endure the institute's technological requirements and "bootleg" a humanities major? Switch to management? Most decided to wait and see, but with a distinct loss of energy and increase in confusion. I felt powerless about what to advise or even how to advise.

It was only later that I was to discover that these shifts represented something more fundamental than changing interests—that they stemmed in many cases from fundamental mismatches between personal learning styles and the learning demands of different disciplines. That disciplines incline to different styles of learning is evident from the variations among their primary tasks, technologies, and products, criteria for academic excellence and productivity, teaching methods, research methods, and methods for recording and portraying knowledge. Disciplines, as we have seen, show sociocultural variation—differences in faculty and student demographics, personality, and aptitudes, as well as differences in values and group norms. For students, education in an academic field is a continuing process of selection and socialization to the pivotal norms of the field governing criteria for truth and how it is to be achieved, communicated, and used, and secondarily, to peripheral norms governing personal styles, attitudes, and social relationships. Over time, these selection and socialization pressures combine to produce an increasingly impermeable and homogeneous disciplinary culture and correspondingly specialized student orientations to learning. This chapter will explore the dynamics of this specialized developmental process in undergraduate and professional education.

Specialized Development and the Process of Accentuation

The major developmental dynamic in specialized education is the selection and socialization of students into specialized areas of social knowledge commensurate with their interests and talents. This development takes place through a process of *accentuation*. In their comprehensive review of the effect of college on students, Feldman and Newcomb describe the accentuation process as it affects the college experience:

> Whatever the characteristics of an individual that selectively propel him toward particular educational settings—going to college, selecting a particular one, choosing a certain academic major, acquiring membership in a particular group of peers—these same characteristics are apt to be reinforced and extended by the experiences incurred in those settings. [Feldman and Newcomb, 1969, p. 333]

Thus, if students with a particular learning style choose a field whose knowledge structure is one that prizes and nurtures their style of learning, then accentuation of that approach to learning is likely to occur. The result is an educational system that emphasizes specialized learning and development through the accentuation of the students' skills and interests. Students' developmental pathways are a product of the interaction between their choices and socialization experiences in academic fields such that choice dispositions lead them to choose educational experiences that match these dispositions, and the resulting experiences further reinforce the same choice disposition for later experiences.

Some examples will serve to illustrate this process of specialization in learning style as a result of accentuation. In a first attempt to examine the details of this process, Plovnick (1971) studied a major university department using the concept of convergence and divergence defined by Hudson (1966). He concluded that the major emphasis in physics education was on convergent learning. He predicted that physics students who had convergent learning styles would be content with their majors, whereas physics majors who were divergent in their learning styles would be more uncertain of physics as a career and would take more courses outside the physics department than would their convergent colleagues. His predictions were confirmed. Those students who were not fitted for the convergent learning style required in physics tended to turn away from physics as a profession, while those physics students having a convergent style tended to continue to specialize in physics, both in their course choices and their career choices.

In another unpublished study, we examined the accentuation process as it operated at the molecular level of course choice. This research examined the choice of sensitivity training by graduate students in management. When we gathered the Learning Style Inventory (LSI) scores of students who chose a voluntary sensitivity-training laboratory, we found that they tended to be more concrete and reflective than those who chose not to attend the lab. When those with divergent learning styles completed the training sessions, their LSI scores became even more concrete and reflective on a post-test, accentuating their disposition toward divergent learning experiences.[1]

Witkin and his associates (Witkin, 1976) have shown that global (field-dependent) students choose specializations that favor involvement with people—such as teaching, sales, management, and the humanities—whereas analytical (field-independent) students choose areas that favor analysis, such as the physical sciences, engineering, and technical and mechanical activities. Clinical-psychology graduate students tend to be global, and experimental-psychology graduate students are analytical. In addition, Witkin found that when cognitive style matches the demands of a given career specialization, higher performance results.

It is important to note not only that the content of choices is associated with cognitive style, but also that there is an association between the choice process and cognitive style. Thus, global students make choices preferred by their peer group, whereas analytical students are more likely to use systematic planning and goal setting. Plovnick (1974) found a similar pattern when he used the LSI to study medical students' choice of medical specialty. There were significant relationships between the LSI scores and specific choices made: accommodators chose medicine and family care; assimilators chose academic medicine; divergers chose psychiatry; and convergers chose medical specialties. In addition, LSI scores were related to the process of choosing: concrete students tended to base their choices on role models and acquaintances, abstract students relied on theoretical material and interest in subject matter.

---

1. Another set of questions is raised by the choice/experience cycle in development. Although the results of these studies show that the majority of students seem to be involved in a series of choices and experiences that accentuate their learning-style tendencies, many students deviate from this dominant trend. If we are to understand the role of learning styles in the development process, we need to understand not only dominant trends but also the causes for deviation from these trends. More specifically, we may gain from this kind of analysis more insight into the relative importance of choices and experiences in human change and development. Until now, much emphasis has been placed on the primary importance of experience as the cause of change. This orientation has given rise to countless research studies seeking to measure with before-after change measurements the effects of various educational experiences. But suppose that a person was changed as much by his choices of experiences as by the experiences themselves. Take, for example, a person interested in mathematics. His interests and aptitudes in mathematics may lead him to seek educational experiences that will enhance these dispositions. In addition, he may be screened formally and informally for admission to this educational program, gaining entry only if he has mathematical aptitude. Thus, by the time his choice has been realized, he will already (1) have gone through a process of consciously recognizing an aspect of himself that he wanted to develop (i.e., his mathematical ability); (2) have done some planning about how to develop this aspect; and (3) perhaps have begun learning mathematics in order to pass selection tests. All these processes will have occurred before the "before" measurement in the typical study designed to assess the effects of an educational experience. Yet they may be as important in determining the directions of development.

Robert Altmeyer (1966) has dramatically illustrated the result of the accentuation process on cognitive abilities in his comparative study of engineering/science and fine-arts students at Carnegie Tech. In a cross-sectional study, he administered two batteries of tests to students at all levels in the two schools; one battery measured analytical reasoning, the other creative thinking. As predicted, engineering/science students scored highest on analytic reasoning and fine-arts students highest on creative thinking; and over the college years, these gaps widened: engineering/science students became more analytical and fine-arts students more creative. The surprising finding was that engineering/science students decreased in creative thinking and fine-arts students decreased in analytic reasoning over the college years. Thus, educational processes that accentuated one set of cognitive skills also appeared to produce loss of ability in the contrasting set of skills.

The corollary to the accentuation process of development in which skills and environmental demands are increasingly matched is the alienation cycle that results when personal characteristics find no supportive environment to nurture them. In this emerging information society, severe alienation can result when there is an incongruity between personal knowledge and social knowledge. This is illustrated most dramatically by the alienation of the poor, whose streetwise way of learning doesn't fit with the symbolic/technological knowledge of the university; or more subtly, it is illustrated by the creative writer who is "turned off" by the pedantic critical climate of her English literature department, or the adult who returns to college and finds little recognition for a lifetime of learning by experience.

Undergraduate Student Development in a Technological University

Thus far we have seen that experiential learning theory characterizes differences in the learning/inquiry norms of different academic fields and that student development and learning are shaped by these fields through a process of accentuation. To examine in greater detail the role of student learning styles in the educational process and to explore the consequences of matches and mismatches between learning styles and the knowledge structure of academic disciplines, let us now examine a case study of undergraduate students in a well-known technological university (TECH).[2]

Data for the study (except for cumulative grade averages, which were obtained from the registrar's office) were collected by means of a questionnaire that was sent to the 720 TECH seniors two months before graduation. Four hundred and seven students (57 percent) responded to the questionnaire. Of these responses, 342 (43 percent) were complete enough to test the hypotheses in this study. The questionnaire included the

---

2. For a detailed report, see Kolb and Goldman, 1973.

Learning Style Inventory, two scales measuring political alienation and anomie, questions about plans for next year, career choice, degree of commitment to that career, undergraduate major, perception of academic workload, and involvement with peers. These variables will be described in detail as the results are presented.

Figure 7.1 shows the LSI scores of students with different departmental majors in those departments with ten or more students. Analysis of variance for the six learning-style dimensions by departmental major shows that reflective observation, active experimentation, and the combination score active-reflective all vary significantly by departmental major. Differences on the abstract-concrete dimensions show no significance. This lack of significant differentiation may well be because of more uniform selective and normative pressures toward abstraction that operate across all the university departments. TECH's reputation as a scientific institution is strongly based on scholarship and the advancement of scientific knowledge. Humanities, architecture, and management are the most concrete departments in the university, and our observations would indicate that these are all quite scholarly in comparison with more concrete programs in other, less "academic" schools such as fine arts, drafting, or business administration. Selective and normative forces on the active-reflective dimension are more diverse, representing the tension in the university between basic science and practical application. With the

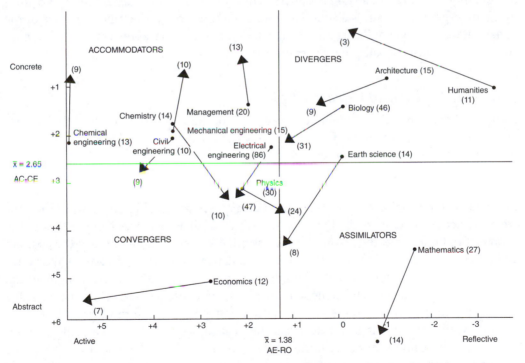

Figure 7.1   Mean LSI Scores for TECH Seniors on Abstract/Concrete and Active/Reflective by Departmental Major

exception of electrical engineering, the engineering departments are the most active in the university. With the exception of chemistry, the basic sciences and mathematics are more reflective.

When the pattern of relationships among departments at TECH is compared with the Carnegie Commission data representing colleges and universities of all types (Figure 5.4), one is immediately struck by the fact that with the exception of architecture and humanities, the concrete disciplines in Figure 5.4 are not represented at this university (there are philosophy, political science, and psychology departments, but they had only two or three students each in our sample). Otherwise, there is a general correspondence with previous studies. Humanities falls in the diverger quadrant, mathematics is assimilative, and management is clearly accommodative. Although the engineering departments all fall on the lower edge of the accommodator quadrant rather than the converger quadrant as predicted, this is most likely a function of the general abstract bias of the university as a whole. Physics and chemistry are not as abstract and reflective as predicted, although if the LSI scores of only those students planning to attend graduate school are used (as indicated by the arrowheads in Figure 7.1), the pattern is more consistent with prediction. Economics is somewhat more abstract and active than the Carnegie data, although, as we will describe later, this is probably a function of the unique nature of the TECH department. The architecture department's position in the divergent quadrant is also to some extent a function of the unique nature of the department, with its emphasis on creative design and photography as well as the more convergent technical skills of architecture.

Learning Styles and Career Choice

Figure 7.1 gives an indication about career paths of the students in each of the departments. The arrowheads indicate for each department the average LSI scores for those students who are planning to attend graduate school. We would predict that those who choose to pursue a given discipline further through graduate training should show an accentuation of the learning style characteristic of that discipline. That is, the arrows for those departments falling in the accommodative quadrant should point toward the concrete and active extremes of the LSI grid, the arrows for divergent departments toward the concrete and reflective, the arrows for the assimilative departments toward the abstract and reflective, and the arrows for the convergent departments toward abstract and active extremes of the LSI grid. The actual results are not so clear-cut. Chemical engineering, mechanical engineering, management, humanities, mathematics, and economics all show in varying degrees the predicted accentuation pattern. Potential graduate students in chemistry, civil engineering, and electrical engineering score in the convergent quadrant rather than becoming more accommodative. Architecture, biology, and earth science potential graduate students move toward the convergent rather than becoming more divergent. Physics moves into the assimilative quadrant.

The results above should be viewed as only suggestive, since several measurement problems prevented a more accurate test of the accentuation hypothesis. The first problem was that it was difficult to determine whether or not a mathematics student planning graduate work in artificial intelligence would continue studying mathematics. Even though most students clearly planned graduate training in the field of their major, the few borderline cases do contaminate the results. A second measurement problem lies in the fact that graduate study in general for TECH students is associated with an abstract and active orientation. Since all six of the departments that did not follow the accentuation prediction showed a tendency toward abstractness, and four of the six showed a tendency toward the active orientation, this general tendency for graduate study may well have overshadowed the accentuation process in those departments. The final measurement problem has to do with the prediction of learning demands for those departments like electrical engineering whose students score close to the middle of the LSI grid.

To deal with these problems in the measurement of the accentuation process, four departments were selected for more intensive case study. Several criteria were used to choose departments whose learning-style demands matched the four dominant learning styles. The first criterion used the average learning-style scores of the students in a given department as an indicator of the learning-style requirements of that department. This criterion assumes that *on the average*, students will over their college careers select themselves and be selected into fields that match their learning styles. The criterion clearly identified three TECH departments that matched three of the learning types—humanities was divergent in its learning demands, mathematics was assimilative, and economics was convergent (see Figure 7.1).

The fourth department that was ultimately chosen, mechanical engineering, was accommodative but was not clearly different from other departments in the accommodative quadrant. To pick the most representative accommodative department, three other criteria were applied. The first was to pick a department whose students going to graduate school showed an accentuation of the departmental learning style. Three departments in the accommodative quadrant showed this accentuation process—chemical engineering, mechanical engineering, and management—as did the three departments already chosen to represent the other styles. Of these three accommodative departments, chemical engineering seemed most representative, but we had to eliminate it because all but two of the students in the department had accommodative learning styles. This made impossible comparisons between students who matched the departmental norms and those who did not. The other candidate, management, was eliminated because a closer examination of students in that department showed that it comprised two separate and distinct groups: behavioral-science and management/computer-science majors. Thus, students would not be reacting to a single set of departmental learning-style demands.

As a final check, the educational objectives and curricula of the four departments selected by the criteria above were examined for indications of their learning-style demands.

Humanities and mathematics showed strong indications of divergent and assimilative orientations, respectively, as our previous data and theory would predict. For example, course descriptions in humanities often emphasize "different perspectives" of a literary work. In mathematics, the emphasis is on basic theory and research, as this quote from the *TECH Bulletin's* description of the undergraduate mathematics program indicates:

> The immediate educational aims are to provide an understanding of a substantial part of the existing body of mathematical knowlede and an ability to impart this knowledge to others. But most important, the department hopes to inspire a deep interest in the discovery or invention of new mathematics or interpretation of mathematics to a new field.

By indication of the learning styles of its students, the economics department at TECH is considerably more convergent—abstract and active—than economics majors in our previous research (Kolb, 1973). This convergent emphasis is borne out, however, by the objectives and curricula of the department. The department places a very strong emphasis on the quantitative/theoretical and policy-formation aspects of economics and considerably less on the more liberal-arts approach (for example, economic history).

Although our previous work showed that engineers on the average fall in the convergent quadrant of the LSI, we were able to obtain no differentiation among the various forms of engineering. One advantage of studying a technical institute like TECH is that we can begin to differentiate among these types. One would expect, for example, that mechanical engineering, with its relatively small theory base, would be more concrete than electrical engineering, where theory plays a larger role. The concrete orientation of mechanical engineering can be illustrated by the following quote, excerpted from the *TECH Bulletin* description of undergraduate study in mechanical engineering:

> . . . the student must experience the ways in which scientific knowledge can be put to use in the development and design of useful devices and processes. To teach this art, largely by project-oriented work of creative nature, is the primary object of subjects in laboratory and design.

To study the career choices of the students in the four departments, we used each student's LSI scores to position him/her on the LSI grid with a notation of the career field he/she had chosen to pursue after graduation. If the student was planning to attend graduate school, the career field was circled (the results of this analysis are shown in Figures 7.2 through 7.5). If the accentuation process were operating in the career choices of the students, we should find that those students who fall in the same quadrant as the norms of their academic major should be more likely to pursue careers and graduate training directly related to that major, while students with learning styles that differ from their discipline norms should be more inclined to pursue other careers and not attend graduate school in their discipline. Although the sample size is small and most students

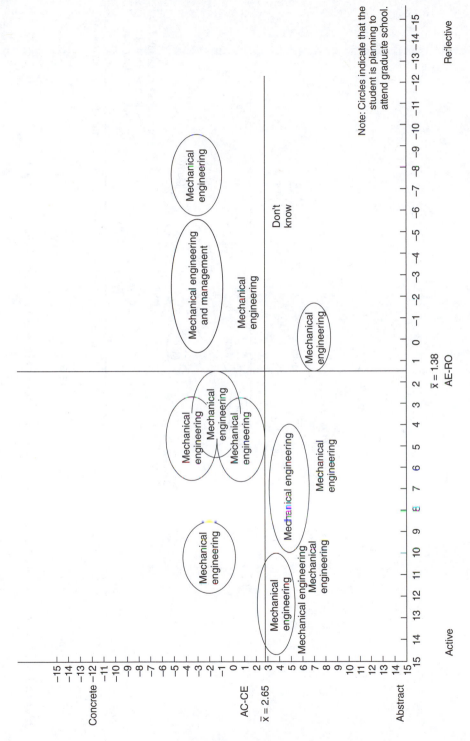

Figure 7.2 Career-Field and Graduate-School Plans for Mechanical-Engineering Majors as a Function of Their Learning Style

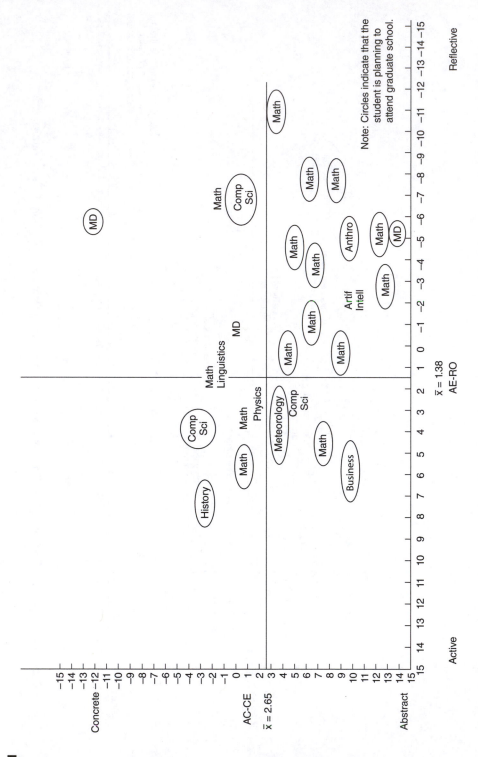

Figure 7.3 Career-Field and Graduate-School Plans for Mathematics Majors as a Function of Their Learning Style

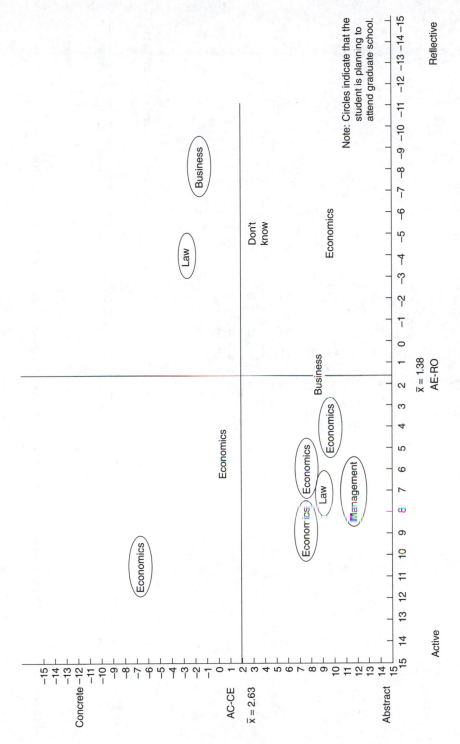

Figure 7.4 Career-Field and Graduate-School Plans for Economics Majors as a Function of Their Learning Style

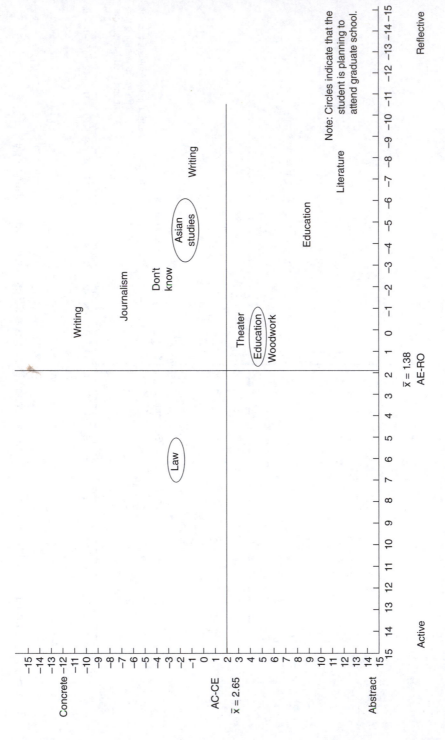

Figure 7.5   Career-Field and Graduate-School Plans for Humanities Majors as a Function of Their Learning Style

plan some form of mechanical-engineering career, this career-choice pattern can be seen in the mechanical-engineering department (Figure 7.2). All four of the students in the accommodator quadrant (100 percent) plan careers in mechanical engineering and graduate training as well. Only four of the ten students (40 percent) whose learning styles do not fit mechanical engineering are committed both to straight engineering careers and graduate training. The pattern is more clear in the mathematics department, where we have a somewhat larger sample (Figure 7.3). Ten of the thirteen mathematics students (80 percent) whose learning styles are congruent with departmental norms choose careers and graduate training in mathematics. Only two of the thirteen students (15 percent) whose learning styles are not congruent plan both careers and graduate training in math (these differences are significant using the Fisher Exact Test, $p < .01$). Figure 7.4 shows the same trend in the economics department, although to a lesser degree. Three of the six economics students (50 percent) with congruent learning styles plan graduate training and careers in economics, but only one of the six (17 percent) with different learning styles has such plans.

The pattern in the humanities department (Figure 7.5) is somewhat more difficult to interpret. One is immediately struck by the fact that only three of the eleven students (27 percent) in the humanities department plan to attend graduate school. This is in contrast to the fact that 63 percent of all TECH seniors plan graduate training. In addition, all of the humanities students' career choices are somewhat related to the humanities but are definitely unrelated to the core curricula of TECH. In this sense, the humanities department as a whole seems not to fit with the learning demands of the rest of the institution. The concrete/reflective orientation of humanities seems in conflict with the abstract and active orientation of a technical school. We will explore this hypothesis further in the next section of results on performance and adjustment at TECH.

To further test the accentuation process in the four departments, we examined whether the student's choice-experience career-development cycle, indeed, operated as an accentuating positive feedback loop. If this were so, then those students whose learning-style dispositions matched and were reinforced by their discipline demands should show a greater commitment to their choice of future career field than those whose learning styles were not reinforced by their experiences in their discipline. As part of the questionnaire, students were asked to rate how important it was for them to pursue their chosen career field. They expressed their answers on a 1-5 scale, where 5 equaled "great importance." The average ratings for students whose learning styles matched discipline demands and those whose styles did not match the norms of their discipline are shown for the four departments in Figure 7.6. In all four departments, the average importance rating was higher for the students with a match between learning style and discipline norms (the differences being statistically significant in the mechanical-engineering and economics departments). Thus, it seems that learning experiences that reinforce learning-style

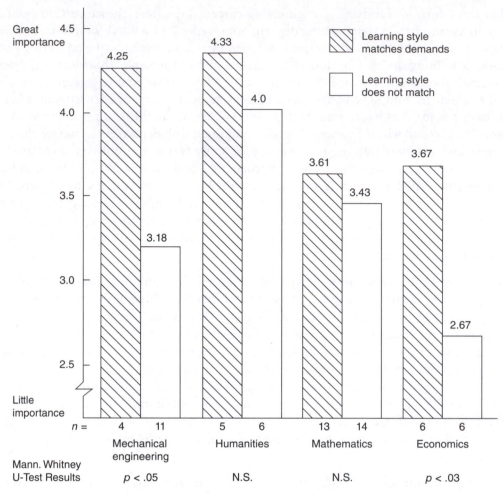

Figure 7.6 Students' Rating of How Important It Is for Them to Pursue Their Career Choice as a Function of Match between Discipline Demands and Learning Style in Four Undergraduate Departments

dispositions tend to produce greater commitment in career choices than those learning experiences that do not reinforce learning-style dispositions.

Taken as a whole, these data present enticing, if not definitive, evidence that career choices tend to follow a path toward accentuation of one's specialized approach to learning. Learning experiences congruent with learning styles tend to positively influence the choice of future learning and work experiences that reinforce that particular learning style. On the other hand, those students who find a learning environment incongruent with their learning styles tend to move away from that kind of environment in future learning and work choices.

Learning Styles, Academic Performance, and Adaptation to the University

The final question to be explored in this research study was whether a student's learning style was an important determinant of social adaptation and performance in the university. To answer this, we compared, on a number of variables, the students whose learning styles fit their discipline demands with the students whose learning styles did not fit in the four departments mentioned above. To begin with, student cumulative grade averages were examined (see Figure 7.7). The mechanical-engineering and economics departments both showed results consistent with predictions; accommodative students

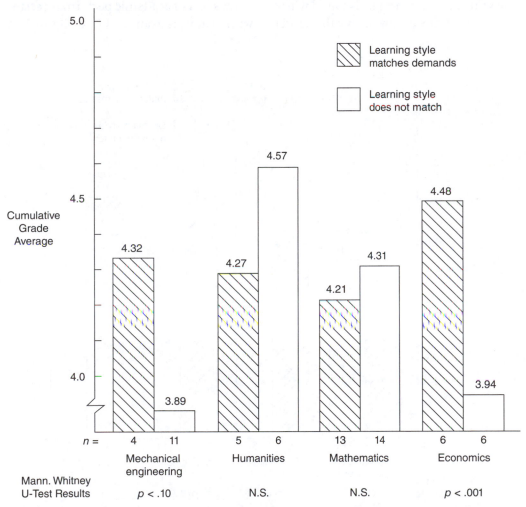

Figure 7.7 Cumulative Grade Average as a Function of Match between Discipline Demands and Learning Style in Four Undergraduate Departments

in mechanical engineering had higher grades ($p < .10$) than mechanical-engineering students with other learning styles, and convergent students in economics had much higher grades ($p < .001$) than economics students with other learning styles. In the mathematics department, however, there was no difference between the two groups of students, and in humanities, the six students whose learning style was not divergent had somewhat higher grades. Although the humanities department results represent a reversal of our original prediction, they offer further evidence for the hypothesis that humanities and the divergent learning style associated with it are incongruent with the abstract and active norms of TECH as a whole. This latter hypothesis would suggest that humanities students who are not divergers should perform better academically.

The same pattern of results is found when another aspect of academic performance, student perceptions of how heavy the academic workload is, is examined (see Figure 7.8).

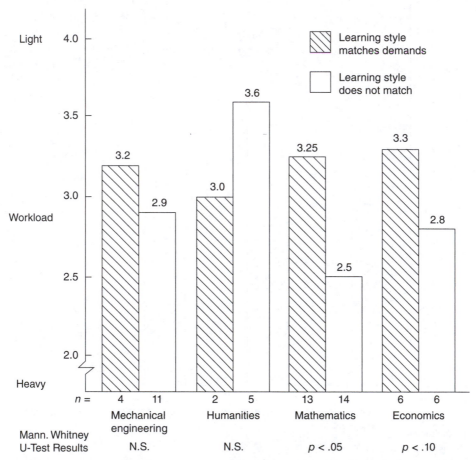

Figure 7.8 Students' Perception of Academic Workload as a Function of Match between Discipline Demands and Learning Style in Four Undergraduate Departments

Students rated their perception of academic workload on a 1-5 scale, where 1 equaled "very great" and 5 equaled "light." In mechanical engineering, mathematics, and economics, those students whose learning styles were congruent with their discipline norms felt the workload to be lighter than did those students whose learning styles did not "fit." (Statistical significance levels in mathematics and economics are $p < .05$ and $p < .10$ respectively.) Again, the humanities department showed a trend in the opposite direction.

Mismatches between learning styles and discipline demands are apt to affect a student's social adaptation to the university. An incongruence between a student's learning style and the norms of his or her major might well undermine feelings of belonging to the university community and alienate him or her from the power structure (faculty and administration). To test these hypotheses, we used a version of Olsen's political alienation scale (1969) and McCloskey and Schaar's anomie scale (1963) that were adapted to apply specifically to the TECH environment (see Kolb, Rubin, and Schein, 1972, for complete details of these scales). These scales measure two uncorrelated aspects of alienation that influence student adaptation. Political alienation results from the failure of authorities, teachers, administrative officials, and the system as a whole to meet the student's needs. The politically alienated student feels that the authority structure of the university is not legitimate because it is unconcerned about students, because it does not involve them in its decision procedures, because it allows its priorities to be set by vested interests, and because it is incapable of solving the problems it faces. Anomie stems not from dissatisfaction with the formal authority system but from a lack of contact with the norms and values that determine and direct behavior of individuals in the university. These norms and values are communicated most directly through contact with one's peers. We have found, for example, that feelings of anomie among TECH students are strongly associated with lack of involvement in a personally important group of peers (Kolb et al., 1972). Anomie students feel lonely, isolated, and out of place at TECH. They have difficulty determining what is expected of them and what they believe.

Figures 7.9 and 7.10 show the anomie scores and political alienation scores respectively in the four departments for students whose learning styles are congruent and incongruent with their discipline demands. The results are generally consistent with the prediction that there would be higher anomie and political alienation among those students whose learning style is incongruent with their discipline norms. (None of the political-alienation differences are significant statistically, however. Anomie significance levels for humanities and economics were $p < .10$ and $p < .01$, respectively.) One interesting fact in Figure 7.10 is the very high political alienation scores of all students in the humanities department. Humanities, in fact, scored highest on this variable of all the departments in the institute. This further develops the pattern of humanities as a deviant learning environment at TECH.

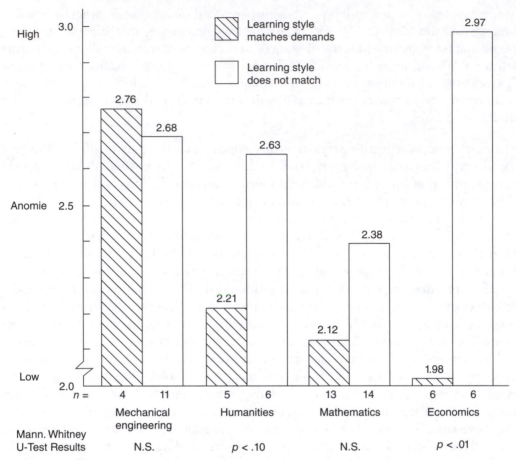

Figure 7.9 Students' Feelings of Anomie as a Function of Match between Discipline Demands and Learning Style in Four Undergraduate Department

Further insight into the effect of learning styles on social adaptation can be gained by examining student involvement with an important peer group (Figure 7.11). Students were asked to rate on a 1-to-5 scale (5 = very involved) how involved they were with their most important peer group. As has already been noted, previous research showed high involvement with peers to be associated with low anomie. As Figure 7.11 shows, in all four departments, students with learning styles matching departmental norms tended to be highly involved with their peers. This pattern was most pronounced in the humanities ($p < .05$) and economics ($p < .01$) departments. These results suggest that student peer groups may be an important vehicle for the communication of the learning-style requirements of a department, although, as we already know from many studies of formal and informal organizations, peer-group norms may sometimes run counter to the formal organizational requirements. Some evidence for this special role of the peer

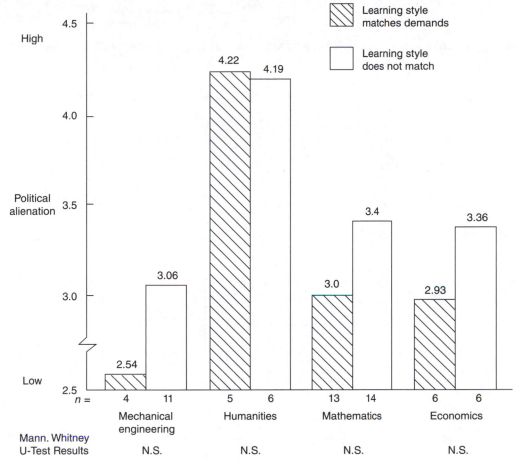

Figure 7.10 Students' Feelings of Political Alienation as a Function of Match between Discipline Demands and Learning Style in Four Undergraduate Departments

group can be seen in a comparison of the economics and humanities departments. In both these departments, students whose learning style fits with the discipline demands are very involved with their peers; and both groups of students score very low in anomie, as we would predict. Yet the convergent economics students score very low in political alienation, whereas the divergent humanities students feel extremely politically alienated from the university. Thus, in humanities, student peer-group solidarity among divergers is based on norms of alienation and rebellion from the university, and in economics, the convergent peer-group norms support the goals and procedures of the formal authorities. This may in part account for the fact that the grades of the divergent humanities students are poor relative to those of other humanities students, while the grades of the convergent economics students are far better than those of other students in economics.

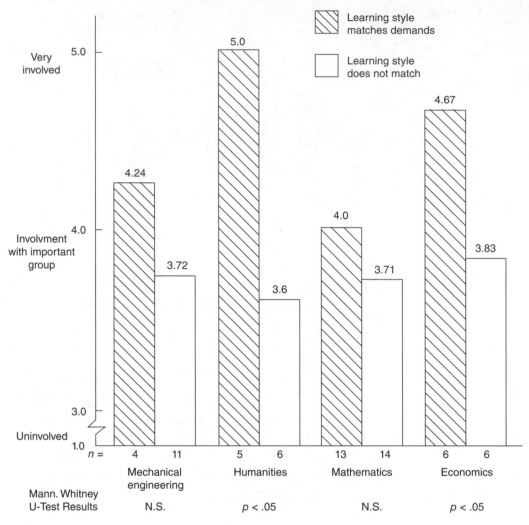

Figure 7.11 Students' Involvement with an Important Peer Group as a Function of Match between Discipline Demands and Learning Style in Four Undergraduate Departments

The research above illustrates the usefulness of experiential learning theory for describing specialized developmental processes in undergraduate education by describing variations in the ways people learn, and corresponding variations in the learning demands of different academic disciplines. This study of TECH undergraduates shows that, at least in this one institution, the experiential learning theory typology is useful for describing the learning-demand characteristics of different academic departments and for predicting the direction of student career choices; and through examination of the matches and mismatches between student learning styles and departmental learning demands, the typology helps to explain variations in academic performance and adaptation to the university. These results suggest that the experiential learning model may well provide a useful framework for the design and management of learning experiences. As was already noted, the dominant trend in research on the "climate" of learning environments has been to focus on the effect on performance and adaptation of social-emotional variables such as motivation, attitudes, participation, liking for the teacher, and social isolation. Many of these variables have been shown to be important. However, the results of this study suggest that the climate of learning environments might as productively be examined in terms of its effect on the learning process itself and, in particular, on the learning styles of students. Rather than being a cause of successful academic performance, motivation to learn may well be a result of learning climates that match learning styles and thereby produce successful learning experiences. Similarly, the sources of student alienation may lie as much in failures to achieve the university's central mission—learning—as they do in its social milieu.

Professional Education and Career Adaptation

Specialization through the process of accentuation is a major force in undergraduate university education in general, but there is reason to suspect that this process is even more central to professional education. From a social control point of view, professions seem to have originally emerged in the areas of human activity—medicine, religion, law—where it is not feasible to judge performance on the basis of outcomes. Since one cannot judge a doctor on whether or not a specific patient dies or a lawyer on whether a specific case is won or lost, the emphasis in professions is on controlling the means of performance rather than the outcomes. One is therefore professionally competent if he or she performs the accepted professional activities or methods adequately, regardless of their results. As professions have expanded into other areas of human activity, this emphasis on means and methods has been retained. One result of this emphasis on means of performance is that schools of professional education have the primary responsibility for the development and certification of professional competence. Although programs of peer review, periodic licensing, and continuing education are now appearing in some professions, for the most part the professional student on graduation is presumed competent for life. This responsibility causes professional schools to make every possible effort to incorporate the appropriate knowledge, skills, and attitudes deemed necessary for professional competence.

As a result, the process of socialization into a profession becomes an intense experience that instills not only knowledge and skills but also a fundamental reorientation of one's identity. We refer to this orientation as a professional mentality. This mentality is pervasive throughout all areas of the professional's life; it includes standards and ethics, the appropriate ways to think and behave, the criteria by which one judges value, what is good or bad. Learning style is an important part of professional mentality. It represents the generic learning competencies that facilitate the acquisition of the specific performance skills required for effectiveness in the core professional role. Through processes of selection and socialization, professional schools make every effort to ensure the proper professional mentality in their graduates. This education is a major social control on the quality of the professional service.

A problem arises, however, when we consider the nature of professional careers in a rapidly changing society. As Whitehead observed, "The fixed person for the fixed duties, who in older societies was such a godsend, in the future will be a public danger" (1926, p. 282). Few professionals remain for a lifetime in the core professional role for which they were trained. In engineering, for example, the typical career path requires a transition to management, a job role requiring a different portfolio of competencies and a different learning style from the convergent professional mentality so suited to engineering work. This lifelong career perspective poses a serious dilemma for professional education. Should it continue to emphasize intensive socialization in the specialized role requirements of the profession, or should some of this rigorous specialized training give way to the broader development of learning competencies required for lifelong learning? The choice for broader development may mean less specialized education at a time when the knowledge required for professional competence is increasing. The specialized choice may result in professional deformation—in the intensive overlearning of a specialized professional mentality that actively hinders adaptation to the changing requirements of one's career.

The dilemma has been central to much of the self-examination, social criticism, and student/alumni evaluation of professional education. Schein, for example, has outlined eight problems of professional education, all of which are related to the dilemma of specialized vs. integrative education:

1. The professions are so specialized that they have become unresponsive to certain classes of social problems that require an interdisciplinary or interprofessional point of view—e.g., the urban problem.

2. Educational programs in professional schools, early career paths, and formal or informal licensing procedures have become so rigid and standardized that many young professionals cannot do the kind of work they wish to do.

3. The norms for entry into the professions have become so rigid that certain classes of applicants, such as older people, women, and career switchers, are in effect discriminated against.

4. The norms of the professions and the growing base of basic and applied knowledge have become so convergent in most professions that it is difficult for innovations to occur in any but the highly specialized content areas at the frontiers of the profession.

5. Professionals have become unresponsive to the needs of many classes of ultimate clients or users of the services, working instead for the organization that employs them.

6. Professional education is almost totally geared to producing autonomous specialists and provides neither training nor experience in how to work as a member of a team, how to collaborate with clients in identifying needs and possible solutions, and how to collaborate with other professionals on complex projects.

7. Professional education provides no training for those graduates who wish to work as members of and become managers of intra- or interprofessional project teams working on complex social problems.

8. Professional education generally underutilizes the applied behavioral sciences, especially in helping professionals to increase their self-insight, their ability to diagnose and manage client relationships and complex social problems, their ability to sort out the ethical and value issues inherent in their professional role, and their ability to continue to learn throughout their careers. [Schein, 1972, p. 59]

A Comparative Study of Professional Education in Social Work and Engineering

To explore this dilemma and its attendant problems, we examined the effect of professional education on career adaptation by surveying the alumni of two professional education programs from a single university.[3] The alumni from the university's social-work and engineering schools in the graduating classes of 1975, 1970, 1965, 1960, and 1955 were studied by means of questionnaires, tests, and interviews (see Kolb and Wolfe et al., 1981, for detailed methodologies). The professions of social work and engineering were chosen for study because they typify the social and science-based professions respectively. Thus, we could examine specialized education in two different professions with different knowledge structures and learning styles—the contextualist/accommodative orientation

---

3. The research reported in this section is part of a larger research program on professional education and career development (see Kolb and Wolfe et al., 1981). The data reported here were analyzed in collaboration with Ronald Sims.

in social work and the formist/convergent orientation in engineering—and examine the consequences of this education on later career development.

The science-based professions, and especially engineering, require a highly developed capacity for working with abstract conceptualizations in the utilization of advanced technology for solving real-world problems. The work itself results not so much in further conceptualization (the province of the basic sciences) but rather in action taken to solve practical problems and to develop and construct physical structures, products, and technical processes. Thus, a well-developed competence in active experimentation is equally essential for effective work in the science-based professions. The adaptive competencies—symbolic complexity and behavioral complexity—combine to make up the convergent style that is the forte of the professional engineer.

Career advancement for engineers often involves a promotion to managerial positions that generally require a substantially different mix of competencies. Much less of these managers' time is devoted to the direct application of scientific knowledge. Although there is a continuing concern for action, the focus is much more on the concrete realities of managing people, planning for various contingencies, setting priorities, and handling administrative tasks. The emergent need, in this transition to management, is for increased competence in handling the complexities and vagaries of concrete experience. The convergent modality must give way to an accommodative style of adaptation, based on competencies in affective complexity (concrete experience) coupled with behavioral complexity (active experimentation). Evidence for this transition in engineering careers is seen in the current job roles of engineering alumni in our study. Of new engineers three years on the job (the 1975 alumni), only 31 percent are managers. This percentage rises steadily over time to the 1955 alumni group, where 76 percent are managers.

Professional work in human-services fields (such as social work) is predicated on highly developed accommodation skills. The emphasis is on dealing with the social and emotional complexities of people in need. The helping process calls for heightened sensitivity to the concrete realities of the human condition, matched with active problem solving. These generic competencies are required for the effective delivery of services to the disadvantaged, the troubled, and the needy.

Career advancement for human-service professionals may also involve taking on managerial responsibilities, but in this case, a change in basic adaptive style may or may not be required. Although a newly appointed director of a social agency generally has many new things to learn, his or her accommodative style is generally appropriate for most of the developmental agenda in this transition. Nonetheless, for many who are promoted from direct-service delivery to administrative or policy-formation assignments, some increase in abstract analytic competencies is called for. One must back away from some of the concrete details of casework with individuals in order to gain a larger perspective.

The basic accommodator style begins to require a backup of converger skills or perhaps even assimilator (social-planning) skills. The study of social-work alumni shows a less clear picture of career transition in that field. The percentage of managers in all five alumni groups ranges from 43 to 63 percent, with no clear transitional pattern. These data, along with observations of individual career histories, suggest that careers in social work are primarily of a dual-track nature. People enter the profession with an orientation to management or direct service and tend to stay in that job role more than is the case in engineering.

Thus, engineering and social work seem to have very different career paths. In engineering, there is a definite general progression from direct engineering work to managerial positions over the cohort years, whereas social work appears to have two tracks, administrative and direct service, which begin in graduate school and continue equally in early and late career with less distinct progression from one role to the next. Since professional education must prepare people not only for early career demands but also for the often quite different demands of later career responsibilities, the different structure of career paths in these two fields offers contrasts of great interest for the study of career adaptation.

Professional Mentality and Professional Deformation

When we examine the Learning Style Inventory scores of social-work and engineering alumni (Figure 7.12), we see that the difference between the two professions in adaptive orientation is dramatically illustrated, particularly in their emphasis on abstractedness (knowing via comprehension) versus concreteness (knowing via apprehension). Engineering alumni fall mostly in the convergent learning style (41 percent); social-work alumni fall in the divergent (34 percent) and accommodative (29 percent) quadrants. The science-based profession of engineering and the social profession of social work are thus markedly different in the way they acquire and use knowledge, at least as measured by the learning styles of alumni educated in these two professions.

Equally relevant to our consideration of specialized professional education and its effect on career adaptation is the degree of variation in learning style among social workers and engineers within their professional specialties. In engineering, we were surprised to find a great deal of homogeneity in learning style. There was significantly less variance in LSI scores than in social work. More important, there were no significant differences among alumni cohort years (note that the averages for the five cohort years are all tightly grouped about the engineering mean in Figure 7.12) or among the three major job roles currently held by engineering alumni—manager, technical manager, and "bench" engineer. Insofar as learning style is a part of the professional mentality of engineering, we see here a very consistent professional mentality that varies little even in the face of age, years of work experience, and different job demands. The social-work professionals

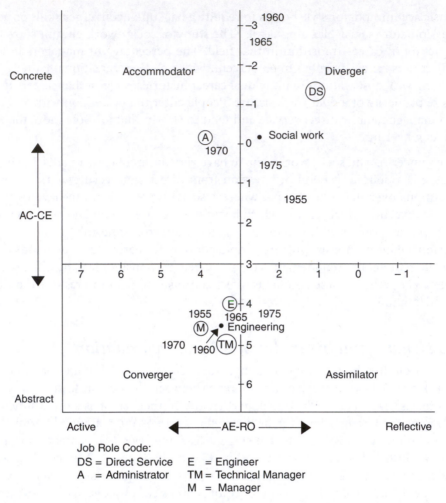

Figure 7.12 Learning Style Inventory Scores for Engineers and Social Workers by Alumni Year and Job Role

show much greater variation in learning style. There is wide (although not statistically significant) variation among cohort-year averages, and the two major job roles in social work, administration and direct client service, are significantly differentiated on the active-reflective dimension of the LSI ($p < .02$), as one might predict from an analysis of demands of these jobs. Administrative job holders are primarily accommodative in their approach to learning, whereas direct-service personnel emphasize the divergent learning style.

Taken together, the results above portray engineering as a field with a highly paradigmatic, coherent professional mentality shaped by the selection and socialization forces of accentuation. A paradigm refers to the body of theory about cause and effect that is subscribed to by all members of the field (Kuhn, 1962). This paradigm serves two important organizing functions: It provides a consistent account of most of the phenomena of interest in a particular area, and it defines those problems that require further research. From these data we would also infer that the social-work profession is a less established and paradigmatic profession than engineering. Schein (1972) identified three trends of maturing professions: (1) They become more convergent in their knowledge base and standards of practice; (2) they become more highly differentiated and specialized; and (3) they become more bureaucratized and rigid with respect to the career alternatives they allow. On all three criteria, the social professions, including social work, are less mature and paradigmatic than are the science-based professions.

Adaptive Competence and Career Adaptation

Given these differences in the maturity and paradigmatic nature of social work and engineering, we would expect different problems of career adaptation in the two fields. To the extent that the specialized professional mentality inculcated in the student becomes a central part of his or her identity, that student may become inflexible and intolerant toward styles that conflict with that mentality. This rigidity may actively inhibit one's ability to adapt to changing career demands. This problem would seem to be most serious for the established paradigmatic professions that have clearly identified "ways of doing things" and the most intensive selection/socialization processes. Less paradigmatic professions would appear to allow for greater flexibility and variability in their graduates, but in many cases this advantage may be offset by the lack of powerful models, tools, and technologies for achieving the core mission of the professions.

One way to assess career adaptation is to measure how well the competencies of the individual professional meet the demands of his or her current job. On the alumni questionnaire, respondents were asked to describe the demands of their current job and their corresponding level of ability to meet these job demands. The technique used was an earlier version of the competency circle described in Chapter 4 (pp. 131–134 and Figure 4.10). Although, as was indicated earlier, these self-ratings of job demand and personal competence would obviously be enhanced by objective independent assessments, the responses of social work and engineering professionals nonetheless reveal interesting patterns of career adaptation. To begin with, differences in job demands were analyzed. The different job roles making up careers in engineering and social work require different portfolios of performance competencies. Engineering jobs require predominately convergent competencies associated with the symbolic and behavioral learning competencies. Managerial jobs in engineering require more affective and behavioral competencies. Direct-service social work requires highly developed affective competencies, and administrative jobs emphasize behavioral competencies more strongly.

To test this hypothesis, one-way analyses of variances were done between the job demands of the different job roles in social work and engineering, and the mean scores were plotted on the competency-circle graphs (Figures 7.13 and 7.14). Figure 7.13 shows great differences in the different job roles comprising engineering careers. Using a Scheffe procedure at .05 level, the significant subsets between job roles are circled. As can be seen in Figure 7.13, professional engineers in the job roles of engineer, technical manager, and manager do perceive their jobs as having different demands in the competencies of dealing with people, being personally involved, and being sensitive to people's feelings, seeking and exploiting opportunities, making decisions, and setting goals, designing experiments, testing theories, and gathering information. Generally, managerial jobs require greater affective and behavioral competencies, and direct engineering work requires greater symbolic and perceptual competencies.

For social workers, the analysis of variance procedures showed significant differences between job roles on making decisions, seeking and exploiting opportunities, analyzing quantitative data, sensitivity to people's feelings, and testing theories and ideas (Figure 7.14). Direct-service social workers and administrators perceive their jobs as having different job demands. Direct-service professionals see their jobs as more demanding affectively than do administrators. Administrators perceive their jobs as more demanding behaviorally—for instance, seeking and exploiting opportunities, committing themselves to objectives, and making decisions.

By comparing alumni's self-ratings of their work abilities with their descriptions of the demands of their current jobs, it is possible to determine the percentage of alumni in different job roles who see themselves as being underqualified in each of the four clusters of performance competencies. These data are shown in Table 7.1.

The data for engineers suggest problems in career adaptation. One-third or more of the technical managers and managers in the engineering alumni sample report that they are underqualified in affective and behavioral competencies. These percentages are greater than the corresponding percentages of bench engineers who are underqualified in affective and behavioral competencies, suggesting that the larger number of underqualified managers in these areas results from a failure to learn how to respond to the increased affective and behavioral demands characteristic of managerial jobs (Figure 7.13). The fact that the number of affectively and behaviorally underqualified managers is greater than symbolically and perceptually underqualified managers suggests that professional education more adequately prepares professionals in symbolic and perceptual competencies than in affective and behavioral competencies (see the following section on learning at school and at work).

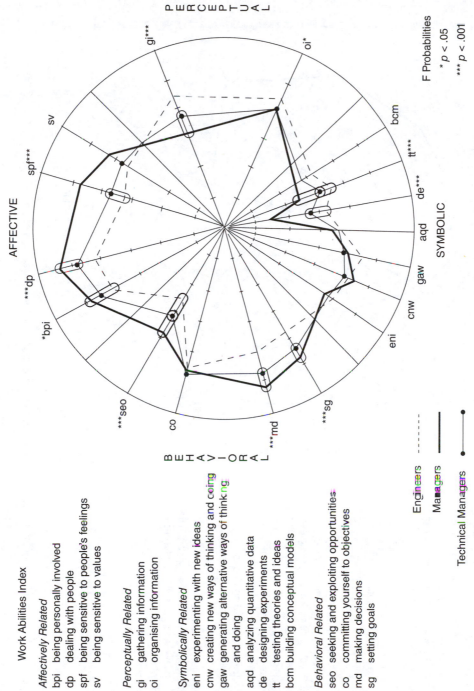

Work Abilities Index

Affectively Related
bpi being personally involved
dp   dealing with people
spf being sensitive to people's feelings
sv   being sensitive to values

Perceptually Related
gi   gathering information
oi   organising information

Symbolically Related
eni experimenting with new ideas
cnw creating new ways of thinking and doing
gaw generating alternative ways of thinking
     and doing
aqd analyzing quantitative data
de   designing experiments
tt   testing theories and ideas
bcm building conceptual models

Behavioral Related
seo seeking and exploiting opportunities
co   committing yourself to objectives
md   making decisions
sg   setting goals

Figure 7.13 Comparison of Job Demands for Engineers, Technical Managers, and Managers

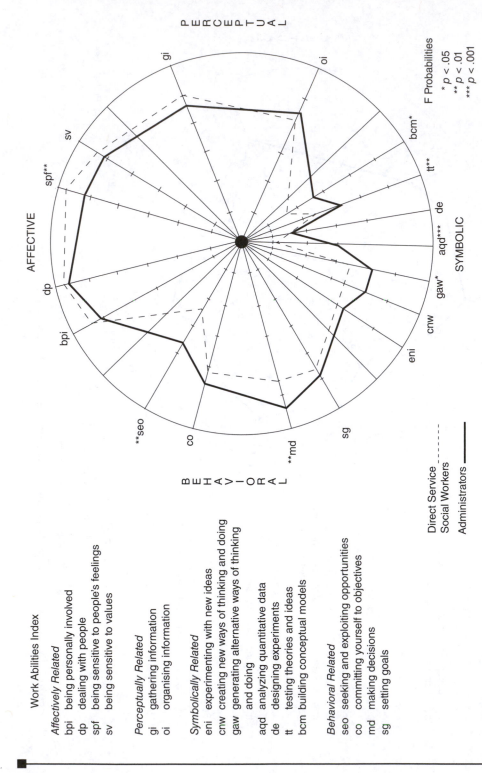

Work Abilities Index

Affectively Related
bpi being personally involved
dp dealing with people
spf being sensitive to people's feelings
sv being sensitive to values

Perceptually Related
gi gathering information
oi organising information

Symbolically Related
eni experimenting with new ideas
cnw creating new ways of thinking and doing
gaw generating alternative ways of thinking and doing
aqd analyzing quantitative data
de designing experiments
tt testing theories and ideas
bcm building conceptual models

Behavioral Related
seo seeking and exploiting opportunities
co committing yourself to objectives
md making decisions
sg setting goals

F Probabilities
* *p* < .05
** *p* < .01
*** *p* < .001

Direct Service
Social Workers - - - - - - -
Administrators ———

Figure 7.14 Comparison of Job Demands for Administrators and Direct-Service Social Workers

Table 7.1 Percentage of Those in Different Job Roles Whose Work Abilities Do Not Meet Job Demands

Job Roles	Job Demands			
	Affective	Behavioral	Symbolic	Perceptual
Engineering:				
Engineer	24%	20%	18%	43%
Technical manager	33%	35%	6%	34%
Manager	42%	31%	22%	15%
Social work:				
Direct service	45%	29%	15%	27%
Administrator	33%	44%	30%	40%

In social work, 44 percent of the administrators report that they are underqualified in the behavioral competencies. The increase in the number of behaviorally underqualified administrators over behaviorally underqualified direct-service workers would seem to result from a failure to learn how to respond to the increased behavioral demands of administrative jobs (see Table 7.1). However, a large percentage of administrators see themselves as underqualified in the other three areas of competence, as well as in the behavioral area that appears to be neglected in professional social-work education (Figure 7.16). This suggests that failures of career adaptation in social work are as much a result of a generalized lack of competencies to deal with the professional tasks in the administrative role that are often nearly impossible, as they are a result of professional deformation.

Thus we see differences in how professionals in social work and engineering adapt to the changing demands of their careers. The job roles in engineering and social work require quite different portfolios of performance competencies. Engineering jobs require strong capabilities in symbolic and perceptual areas; direct-service social work emphasizes affective and perceptual competencies. Administrative and managerial jobs across the two professions are very similar, requiring highly developed affective and behavioral competencies.

Both professions seem to have problems of career adaptation, although for different reasons. In social work, it appears that many incumbents of jobs at all levels feel somewhat overwhelmed by the requirements of their jobs. The challenge for professional education would seem to lie in the development of more powerful "social technologies" and educational methods for responding to our country's increasing social problems in a time of scarce resources.

The problem in engineering may more properly be considered one of professional deformation. The scientific technologies of the various engineering fields with their attendant scientific problem-solving mentality have proven their potency repeatedly. Career adaptation problems in engineering stem more from overspecialization in these learning competencies, often to the point where professionals in the field have difficulty performing in managerial job roles that require greater affective and behavioral competence.

Learning in School and at Work

The specialized development that characterizes most higher educational experiences usually carries forward into one's early career. First jobs often are continuing apprenticeships for the refinement of the specialized skills and knowledge acquired in preparatory education. The acquisition of the knowledge, skills, and values that began in school is carried forward in the workplace, as successful performance in a specialized area of expertise is rewarded by the assignment of increasingly complex challenges in that area. Yet, as has been noted, there is a transition point in most career paths where the demands of job roles change, requiring an increasingly integrative perspective on learning. A study of the accounting and marketing professions conducted by Clarke et al. (1977) illustrated this change in learning style in the later stages of one's career. Their study compared cross-sectional samples of accounting and marketing students and professionals in school and at lower-, middle-, and senior-level career stages. The learning styles of marketing and accounting MBA students were similar, being fairly balanced on the four learning modes.

Lower-level accountants had convergent learning styles, and this convergent emphasis was even more pronounced in middle-level accountants, reflecting a highly technical emphasis in the early and middle stages of accounting careers. The senior-level accountants, however, were accommodative in their learning style, reflecting a greater concern with client relations and administration than with technical functions. Marketing professionals at the lower level also were convergent in learning style but became highly concrete at middle-level responsibilities, reflecting a shift from technical to creative concerns. The senior marketing personnel had accommodative learning styles similar to those of senior accountants, probably reflecting the same client and management concerns.

There is a similar transition in the learning orientations of engineers and social workers over the course of their careers. In a selected interview study of the engineering and social-work alumni, Gypen found that:

> As engineers move up from the bench to the management positions, they complement their initial strengths in abstract conceptualization and active experimentation with the previously non-dominant orientations of concrete experience and reflective observation. As social workers move from direct service into administrative positions, they move in the opposite direction of the engineers. [Gypen, 1980, p. ii]

Furthermore, Gypen found that these changes in learning style were directly related to the changing demands of one's current job.

These results give a somewhat more optimistic picture of professional career adaptation than the just-reported data showing that large numbers of professionals describe themselves as underqualified for their current job demands (see Table 7.1). From this perspective, the developmental "glass" appears half full rather than half empty. Some change in the direction of career adaptation does occur after professional education, most likely through *learning on the job*.

To explore how the social-work and engineering alumni developed their current portfolios of competencies, the alumni questionnaires asked respondents to rate how much their professional education had contributed to the development of each of the performance competencies described in the last section and how much their work experience had contributed to the development of these competencies. Their responses are plotted on the competency circle for engineering alumni in Figure 7.15. The dark shaded area represents contributions of professional education to competencies, and the lined area shows contributions of work experience to the development of competence. The dark line shows the average current job demand for each competence. The figure shows dramatic differences in the competencies acquired in education and work. Engineering education seems to prepare or, in several cases, overprepare people for the demands of their jobs in symbolic and perceptual competencies but makes little contribution to the development of affective and behavioral competencies. These seem to be acquired primarily in the work setting.

Figure 7.16 shows the same analysis for social-work alumni. Here, the shaded area representing the contribution of social-work professional education is larger than in engineering, but it is still biased toward the development of perceptual and symbolic skills. Work experience contributes more to the development of affective and particularly behavioral skills, as in the engineering figure.

Surprisingly, these patterns were not significantly different for different alumni years; alumni only three years out of school (the class of 1975) showed the same pattern as alumni 23 years out (the class of 1955). Engineering alumni in all cohort groups reported that their professional education emphasized the development of symbolic and perceptual skills while neglecting affective and behavioral skills. Social-work alumni in all cohort groups felt that their professional education had developed required competencies in the affective, perceptual, and symbolic areas but had neglected the development of behavioral competencies. Both social-work and engineering alumni consistently felt that they had made up for these deficits as well as supplemented their strengths through experiential learning on the job. In another study, Sims (1981) found that this on-the-job learning is facilitated in those organizations with a strong growth climate characterized by good supervision, advancement potential and autonomy, and a chance

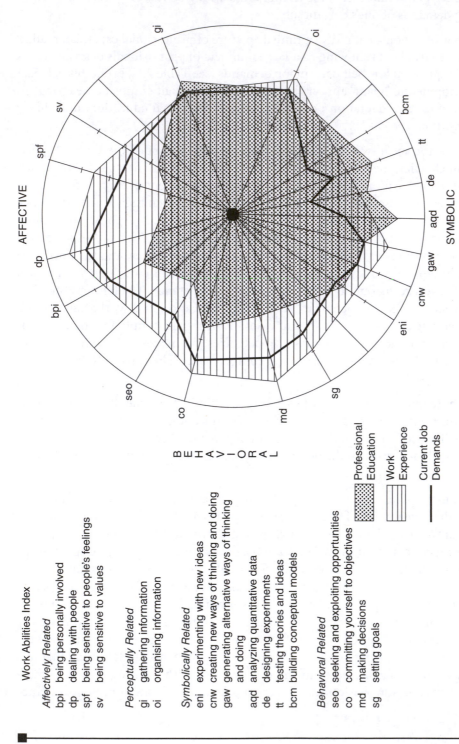

Work Abilities Index

Affectively Related

bpi   being personally involved
dp   dealing with people
spf   being sensitive to people's feelings
sv   being sensitive to values

Perceptually Related

gi   gathering information
oi   organising information

Symbolically Related

eni   experimenting with new ideas
cnw   creating new ways of thinking and doing
gaw   generating alternative ways of thinking
      and doing
aqd   analyzing quantitative data
de   designing experiments
tt   testing theories and ideas
bcm   building conceptual models

Behavioral Related

seo   seeking and exploiting opportunities
co   committing yourself to objectives
md   making decisions
sg   setting goals

Figure 7.15 Contributions of Work Experience and Professional Education to the Development of the Performance Competencies of Engineering Alumni

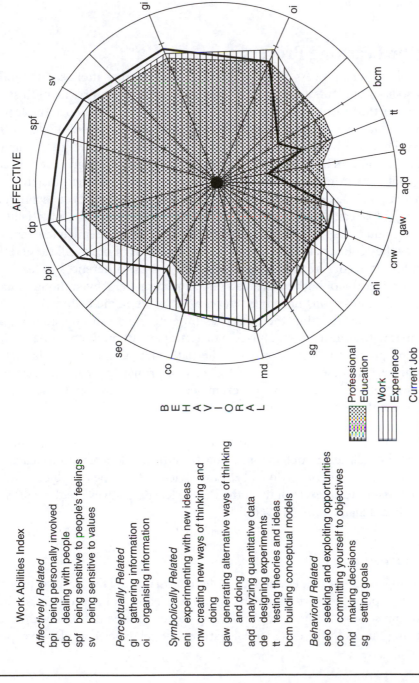

Figure 7.16 Contributions of Work Experience and Professional Education to the Development of the Performance Competencies of Social-Work Alumni

Work Abilities Index

Affectively Related
bpi being personally involved
dp dealing with people
spf being sensitive to people's feelings
sv being sensitive to values

Perceptually Related
gi gathering information
oi organising information

Symbolically Related
eni experimenting with new ideas
cnw creating new ways of thinking and doing
gaw generating alternative ways of thinking and doing
aqd analyzing quantitative data
de designing experiments
tt testing theories and ideas
bcm building conceptual models

Behavioral Related
seo seeking and exploiting opportunities
co committing yourself to objectives
md making decisions
sg setting goals

to grow and develop, and is inhibited in organizations whose climate is not supportive of learning and development. These results showing the critical role of organization climate have been independently replicated by Margulies and Raia (1967). Lifelong learning is not automatic but must be nurtured in a supportive learning environment, both in school and at work.

Managing the Learning Process

To conduct the educational process in universities in a manner that attends to the individual learning styles of students and fosters student development requires identification and management of those aspects of the educational system that influence the learning process. Such a management system must be soundly built on a valid model of the learning process. There has been a great burgeoning of educational techniques designed to assist the learning process in recent years: computer-aided instruction; experienced-based learning materials in math, science, and psychology; programmed instruction; games; multimedia curricula; open classrooms; and so on. Although these techniques tend to be highly sophisticated and creative applications of their own particular fields of expertise, be it computer science, psychology, or architecture, they are much less sophisticated about how they enhance human learning. The weakness of nearly all these techniques is the failure to recognize and explicitly provide for the differences in learning styles that are characteristic of both individuals and subject matters. Even though many of these educational innovations have been developed in the name of individualized education and self-directed learning, there has been little attempt to specify along which dimensions individualization is to take place. For example, although computer-aided instruction and programmed learning provide alternative learning routes or branches for the individual learner, these branches tend to be based primarily on various elaborations of the subject matter being taught (for example; a wrong answer puts the learner on a branch giving him more information about the question). Little has been done to provide the individual learner with branches that provide alternative learning methods (such as pictoral versus symbolic presentation) based on the person's learning style. In addition, there has been little research to assess how the effectiveness of various teaching methods is contingent on either individual learning styles or the type of subject matter being taught. (Two significant exceptions in the case of learning styles are the works of David Hunt, 1974; and Liam Hudson, 1966.)

Learning Environments

Experiential learning theory provides one such system for managing the learning process in Fry's (1978) concept of the learning environment. Any educational program, course design, or classroom session can be viewed as having degrees of orientation toward each of the four learning modes in the experiential learning model, labeled as affective, perceptual, symbolic, and behavioral, to connote the overall climate they create and the particular learning skill or mode they require (Kolb and Fry, 1975). Thus an affective environment emphasizes the experiencing of concrete events; a symbolic environment emphasizes abstract conceptualization; a perceptual environment stresses observation and appreciation; a behavioral environment stresses action taking in situations with real consequences. Any particular learning experience can have some or all of these orientations, to differing degrees, at the same time. A typical lecture obviously has perceptual and symbolic orientations, because it requires students to listen to and interpret the presentation (reflective observation skills) and to reason and induce conceptual relationships from what they hear (abstract conceptualization skills). But there may be an affective orientation as well. Some students may be experiencing the teacher doing the lecturing as a role model. Or if we direct questions or pose dilemmas to the class, we increase the behavioral orientation by urging students to take action by speaking up and testing their ideas out in public.

Fry has found that each type of environmental orientation can be measured by observing the following variables in the context of a course: the purpose of the major activities, the primary source or use of information, the rules guiding learner behavior, the teacher's role, and the provision for feedback. These are useful cues, because to a great extent they are controlled by the instructor, faculty, or administration, independently of the learner. Most decisions affecting these aspects of learning environments are made before learner-classroom interactions take place. Using these variables, the following pictures of different types of environments result.

Affectively complex learning environments are ones in which the emphasis is on experiencing what it is actually like to be a professional in the field under study. Learners are engaged in activities that simulate or mirror what they would do as graduates, or they are encouraged to reflect upon an experience to generate these insights and feelings about themselves. The information discussed and generated is more often current/immediate. It often comes from expressions of feelings, values, and opinions by the learner in discussions with peers or the teacher. Such expressions of feelings are encouraged and seen as productive inputs to the learning process. The learner's activities often vary from any prior schedule as a result of the learner's needs. The teacher serves as a role model for the field or profession, relating to learners on a personal basis and more often as a colleague than an authority. Feedback is personalized with regard to each individual's needs and goals, as opposed to comparative. It can come from both peers and the teacher. There is accepted discussion and critique of how the course is proceeding, and thus, specific events within a single class session are often more emergent than prescribed.

Perceptually complex learning environments are ones in which the primary goal is to understand something: to be able to identify relationships between concepts, to be able to define problems for investigation, to be able to collect relevant information, to be able to research a question, and the like. To do this, learners are encouraged to view the topic or subject matter from different perspectives (their own experience, expert opinion, literature) and in different ways (listen, observe, write, discuss, act out, think, smell). If a task is being done or a problem is being solved, the emphasis is more on how it gets done, the process, than on the solution. Success or performance is not measured against rigid criteria. Learners are instead left to conclude, answer, and define criteria of success for themselves. Individual differences in this process are allowed and used as a basis for further understanding. Learners are thus free to explore others' ideas, opinions, and reactions in order to determine their own perspective. In this process, the teacher serves as a "mirror" or "process facilitator." He or she is nonevaluative, answers questions with questions, suggests instead of critiquing, and relates current issues to larger ones. The teacher creates a reward system that emphasizes methodology of inquiry versus getting a particular answer. In class sessions, there is planned time spent on looking back at previous steps, events, or decisions in order to guide the learner in future activities.

Symbolically complex learning environments are ones in which the learner is involved in trying to solve a problem for which there is usually a right answer or a best solution. The source of information, topic, or problem being dealt with is abstract, in that it is removed from the present and presented via reading, data, pictures, lecture inputs, and so on. In handling such information, the learner is both guided and constrained by externally imposed rules of inference, such as symbols, computer technology, jargon, theorems, graphical keys, or protocols. There is often a demand on the learner to recall these rules, concepts, or relationships via memory. The teacher is the accepted representative of the body of knowledge—judging and evaluating learner output, interpreting information that cannot be dealt with by the rules of inference, and enforcing methodology and the scientific rigor of the field of study. The teacher is also a timekeeper, taskmaster, and enforcer of schedules of events in order that the learner can become immersed in the analytical exercise necessary to reach a solution and not worry about having to set goals and manage his or her own time. Success is measured against the right or best solution, expert opinion, or otherwise rigid criteria imposed by the teacher or accepted in the field of study. Decisions concerning flow and nature of activities in the class session are essentially made by the teacher and mostly prior to the course.

Behaviorally complex learning environments are those in which the emphasis is upon actively applying knowledge or skills to a practical problem. The problem need not have a right or best answer, but it does have to be something the learner can relate to, value, and feel some intrinsic satisfaction from having solved. This would normally be a "real-life" problem, case, or simulation that the learner could expect to face as a professional. In the attack on the problem, the focus is on doing. Completing the task is essential. Although there may be an externally imposed deadline or periodic checkpoints for which reports or other information are required, most of the learner's time is his to manage.

He is thus concerned with what effect his present behavior will have vis-à-vis the overall task to be done. The next activity he engages in will not occur independent of the one he is presently in. In this way, the learner is always left to make decisions/choices about what to do next or how to proceed. The teacher can be available as a coach or advisor, but primarily in the learner's request or initiative. Success is measured against criteria associated with the task: how well something worked, feasibility, sellability, client acceptance, cost, testing results, aesthetic quality, and so on.

Learning environments vary in the degrees to which they are oriented to any of the four pure types described above. In a study of a landscape-architecture department (Fry, 1978), ten courses were measured to determine the degree of environmental complexity or the tendency of a course to be oriented in one or more ways. The results indicated that all the courses had degrees of orientation in each area and that it was even possible for a given course to be very affectively and symbolically oriented at the same time. Consistent patterns of environmental orientation showed up in the following combinations: perceptual and symbolic—an "investigative" or "inquiry" climate with the emphasis on inductive theory building and on understanding why things happen (this was most characteristic of lecture and seminar course sessions in this setting); symbolic and behavioral—a "mastery" climate where emphasis was on mastering techniques by practice in problem solving (this was most characteristic of laboratory and recitation sections of courses in this study); behavioral and affective—a "simulative" climate where situations were created to put the learner in the role expected of a graduate in a work setting (this was most characteristic of courses requiring field experience, site visits, and interaction with others outside the classroom in this setting).

Learner-Environment Interactions

When experiential learning theory is used to view the learner and instructional environment in the terms discussed above, useful relationships begin to emerge concerning the design of learning situations. Studies of the preferences of MBA students and graduate students in architecture (Fry, 1978; Kolb, 1976) suggest that what we considered to be characteristics of affective, perceptual, symbolic, and behavioral orientations in the environment do relate to and require learner skills in concrete experience, reflective observation, abstract conceptualization, and active experimentation, respectively (see Table 7.2).

The students who scored high in concrete experience as a preferred learning mode indicated that their ability to learn was enhanced by affectively related factors such as personalized feedback, sharing feelings, teachers behaving as friendly helpers, activities oriented toward applying skills to real-life problems, peer feedback, and the need to be self-directed and autonomous. An environmental factor that hindered their learning ability was theoretical reading assignments.

Table 7.2   Learning Environment Characteristics that Help or Hinder Learners with Different Learning Styles

Learning Environment Characteristics	Learning Styles			
	Concrete Experience	Reflective Observation	Abstract Conceptualization	Active Experimentation
"Typical" educational events: (Harvard MBAs)	Theory readings—*not helpful* (−.21[b]) Peer feedback helps (.15[a]) When:	Lectures help (.18[a]) When:	Case studies help (.22[b]) Theory readings help (.34[c]) Exercises & simulations—*not helpful* (−.15) Thinking alone helps (.17[a]) Expert talks—*not helpful* (−.15) When:	Lectures—*not helpful* (−.25[c]) Small-group discussions help (.16[a]) Projects help (.18[a]) Peer feedback helps (.20[b]) Homework helps (.19[a]) When:
Situational factors: (Architecture grad. students)	Feedback is personalized (.45[c]) Feelings are shared (.20) Purpose of activities is to apply skills (.24[a]) Teacher is coach/helper (.36[b]) Learner expected to be self-directed, autonomous (.37[b])	Teacher provides expert interpretation (.23[a]) Info. focused on task—*not helpful* −.33[b] Performance judged by external criteria of field (.23[a]) Teacher serves as taskmaster/guide (.20)	Learner is expected to be self-directed/autonomous—*not helpful* (−.39[b]) Teacher is coach/helper—*not helpful* (−.22[a]) Purpose of activity to apply skill to solve problem—*not helpful* (−.23[a]) Personalized feedback—*not helpful* (−.47[c]) Teacher is model of profession—*not helpful* (−.21[a]) Sharing feelings—*not helpful* (−.43[b]) Info, source is "here and now"—*not helpful* (−.29[a]) Purpose of activity is to experience being a professional—*not helpful* (−.26[a])	Teacher is a model of profession (.22[a]) Learner left to determine own criteria of relevance (.21[a]) Purpose of activity to apply skills to solve problem (.37[b]) Info, focused on task completion (.37[b]) Performance judged right or wrong—*not helpful* (−.25[a]) Teacher serves as taskmaster/guide—*not helpful* (−.37[b])

[a] p < .05 Pearson Correlation
[b] p < .01 Pearson Correlation
[c] p < .001 Pearson Correlation

The learners scoring highest in reflective observation reported perceptually related environmental factors as being helpful. These included teachers providing expert interpretations and guiding or limiting discussions, output being judged by external criteria of field or discipline, and lecturing. Reflective learners are not helped by task-oriented situations where information generation was focused on getting some job done.

The learners scoring highest in abstract conceptualization cited symbolically related factors such as case studies, thinking alone, and theory readings as contributing to their ability to learn. They also felt that several elements of affectively and behaviorally oriented environments hindered their ability to learn. These included group exercises and simulations, the need to be self-directed or autonomous, personalized feedback, teachers being models of the profession, sharing personal feelings about subject matter, dealing with "here-and-now" information, and activities oriented toward experiencing being a professional in the field.

Finally, the learners with the strongest active-experimentation tendencies identified several factors as helpful that one would associate with a behaviorally oriented learning environment. These included small-group discussions, projects, peer feedback, homework problems, the teacher behaving as a model of the profession, being left to judge one's work by oneself, and activities designed to apply skills to practical problems. Things these students reported as hindrances to their ability to learn included lectures, teachers serving as taskmasters, and having their work evaluated as simply right or wrong.

People enter learning situations with an already-developed learning style. Associated with this learning style will be some more or less explicit theory about how people learn, or more specifically, about how they themselves learn best. Learning environments that operate according to a learning theory that is dissimilar to a person's preferred style of learning are likely to be rejected or resisted by that person. Many students, for example, resist required courses designed to broaden their interests. One way to deal with this problem is for teacher and student to share explicitly their respective theories of learning. From this discussion, the student can gain an insight into why the subject matter is taught as it is and what adjustments he need make in his approach to learning this subject. The discussion can help the teacher to identify the variety of learning styles presented in the class and to modify his/her approach to accommodate these differences. A third benefit from explicit discussion of the learning process as it applies to the specific subject matter at hand is that both teacher and students are stimulated to examine and refine their learning theories. Learning becomes a skill that can be improved and coached. Perhaps the most important implication of the interaction between learning styles and learning environments is that empathy and communication are central to the teaching process. To educate means literally "to draw out." This requires an ability on the part of the teacher to make contact with the students' inner resources, attitudes, and ideas and through dialogue to develop and refine their knowledge and skills.

A second practical concern that emerges from our research on learner-environment transactions is the need to individualize instruction. Most traditional classroom teaching methods are too homogeneous as learning environments, appealing to only a single learning style while handicapping those who would prefer to learn another way. Approaches that individualize the learning process to meet the student's goals, learning style, pace, and life situation will pay off handsomely in increased learning. One key to this individualization is a shift in the teacher role from dispenser of information to coach or manager of the learning process. The widespread use of e-learning innovations is facilitating this role transition by providing alternative modes for delivery of content.

Specialized vs. Integrative Developmental Goals

Matching student learning styles with corresponding learning environments seems an easy and practical way to improve the learning process. But does this mean we should alter our course designs to accommodate the type of learner that comes into them, and/or require specialized learning skills that typify the inquiry norms of a given profession or field of study?

To answer this question, it is necessary to consider the goals of the educational program. In curriculum design, three classes of learning objectives must be considered: content objectives, learning-style objectives, and growth and creativity objectives. Very often in the design of curricula, it is only the content objectives that are explicitly considered: What material should be covered? What concepts should be introduced? What facts does the student need to know? Yet in most academic disciplines, there are also important norms about learning style. Students are expected to adopt certain perspectives on their work. They must learn to think like a mathematician or feel like a poet or make decisions like an executive. Thus, the learning style that is felt to be appropriate for a given area of study must also be considered when educational objectives are set.

To complicate matters further, the third class of objectives must be considered, objectives for growth and creativity. In addition to specialized developmental training, teachers often have objectives concerning the growth and creativity of their students. In making students more "well-rounded," the aim is to develop the weaknesses in the students' learning style to stimulate growth in their ability to learn from a variety of learning perspectives. Here, the goal is something more than making students' learning styles adaptive for their particular career entry job. The aim is to make the student self-renewing and self-directed; to focus on integrative development where the person is highly developed in each of the four learning modes: active, reflective, abstract, and concrete. Here, the student is taught to experience the tension and conflict among these orientations, for it is from the resolution of these tensions that creativity springs.

The dilemma in making choices among these three levels of objectives is illustrated by Plovnick's study, cited earlier, which concluded that the major emphasis in physics education was on convergent learning, and that physics students who had convergent learning styles were more content with their majors than students whose learning styles did not match the inquiry norms of physics. The dilemma for the physics department is this. To contribute in physics today, one must know many facts, so content learning is important and takes time, time that might be spent developing the convergent skills of divergers. So isn't it simpler to select (implicitly or explicitly) people who already possess these convergent experimental and theoretical skills? Perhaps, but in the process, what is lost is the creative tension between convergence and divergence. The result of this process may be a program that produces fine technicians but few innovators. Kuhn put the issue this way: "Because the old must be revalued and reordered when assimilating the new, discovery and invention in the sciences are usually intrinsically revolutionary. Therefore they do demand just that flexibility and open-mindedness that characterize and indeed define the divergent" (1962, p. 112). It just may be that one of the reasons that creative contributions in the sciences are made primarily by younger persons (Lehman, 1953) is that the learning styles of older adults have been shaped by their professional training and experience, so that they adapt well to the inquiry norms of their profession but the creative tension is lost.

Implications for Higher Education

As we have seen, higher education today encourages early specialization, which necessarily accentuates particular interests and skills. Should we continue to follow the trend toward increasingly specialized education, or should we be creating new educational programs that reassert the integrative emphasis lost in the demise of classical education? Recently, Derek Bok's *President's Report* for Harvard University (Bok, 1978) outlined a revised undergraduate curriculum plan—a plan that some have characterized as a return to classical education, with its compulsory core courses in science and mathematics, literature and the arts, history, philosophy and social analysis, and foreign cultures. The pendulum swing toward specialization that Charles Eliot began in 1869 with the modest introduction of electives and the concept of a major may have reached its peak in the late 1960s in the course proliferation that came with students' demands for relevance and participation in the educational decisions that affected their lives. The "back-to-basic-skills" climate that seemed to permeate American education at all levels in the 1970s may signal, among other things, the reassertion of an integrative emphasis in the educational process.

There is little question that integrative development is important for both personal fulfillment and cultural development. It appears essential for growth and mastery of the period of adult development that Erikson has called the crisis of generativity versus stagnation. The educational issue is how and when to intervene in a way that facilitates this development. The "hows" are not easy. Bok compared the introduction of the new core curriculum to "reorganizing a graveyard." Specialization in the university is greatly reinforced by faculty reward systems, selection and evaluation criteria, and disciplinary values. The result of these organizational processes is brought into sharp focus when we examine the difficulties and obstacles that attend the establishment of truly inter-disciplinary programs of research or teaching, or the struggles for survival and viability that face "deviant" disciplines in an institution where attention, resources, and prestige are focused on the dominant academic culture. Even at a scientific institute like TECH, where the humanities are firmly established with a distinguished faculty, we see intense student alienation, departmental evaluation standards that appear more attuned to the inquiry norms of engineering than to the humanities, and a subtle but powerful impe-rialism of the dominant scientific culture on research and teaching activities. However useful scientific analyses of the humanities (for example, computer models of Greek myths) may be in their own right, one must ask how well such activities serve to broaden the worldview of the science or engineering specialist.

In the words of Robert Hutchins:

> The reverence that natural science has inspired is in large part responsible for the steady narrowing of education that the progress of specialization has caused during the last thirty years. The progress of specialization has meant that the world and ourselves have been progressively taken apart, and at no point have they been put together again. As the progress of the scientific method has dis-credited the methods of history, philosophy, and art, so the specialism essential to science has discredited a generalized approach to history, philosophy, art and all other subjects, including science itself. This means that comprehension has been discredited, for it cannot be attained by splitting the world into smaller and smaller bits. [Hutchins, 1953, p. 25]

The Institutional Context and Integrative Development

So far, this discussion has focused primarily on the course-level units of learning environ-ments. It is more difficult to conceptualize the effect of the larger institutional context on student learning, although the effect is considerable. Included here is the organization and management of departments, including such things as student and faculty interac-tion patterns, emphasis on research, teaching or practical application, the structure and number of required courses, emphasis on grades, and so on. Beyond departments, one must consider the university structure, its mission and philosophy of education, the alternative learning environments available, the selection/evaluation criteria for faculty and students, social networks outside of classes, campus atmosphere, and the like. Some evidence suggests that these large-system phenomena may be particularly connected with the affective and behavioral orientations. For example, faculty members in engineering have suggested to us that concrete experience and active experimentation skills in their students may be developed not as part of their formal curriculum of courses but rather in social groupings in fraternities, one-on-one relationships with faculty mentors, summer work experiences, and other extracurricular campus activities.

Liam Hudson has examined the effect of relationship between departments and larger organizational processes on the educational process:

> At the pragmatic level, for instance, one makes no sense of a certain course in the behavioral sciences, until one sees it as a compromise reached between a number of university departments, each of which has a legitimate interest in its content. The curriculum, simply, is a by-product of a process that is starkly political. And at the conceptual level we find ourselves continually confronting mysterious notions, like that of a "discipline." To begin to grasp what happens inside universities, we find ourselves compelled to grapple with the boundary rules which surround bodies of knowledge like history, medicine, chemistry or psychology, and to make interpretative sense of their function. We need, too, to come to terms with what one might describe as the politics of knowledge—that territory in which such disciplines take shape, in which schools of thought do battle with one another, and in which certain views of mankind are rendered legitimate, while others are cast beyond the pale. [Hudson, 1976, p. 219]

Thus, it would seem that a central function for the larger university organization is to provide the integrative structures and programs that counterbalance the tendencies toward specialization in student development and academic research. Continuous lifelong learning requires learning how to learn, and this involves appreciation of and competence in diverse approaches to creating, manipulating, and communicating knowledge.

To assume that this integrated appreciation and competence can be achieved solely by distribution requirements or other legislative approaches is highly questionable. As with racial integration, we must closely scrutinize any strategy that requires students to do what we ourselves cannot or will not do. To build integrative programs of teaching and research requires that reward systems, selection and evaluation criteria, and inquiry values be confronted and adjusted to sustain interdisciplinary activity. In addition, some kind of focal point may be required for successful integrative education. Successful interdisciplinary programs I have seen have had a common reference point for integrative activity. At Alverno College, a common reference point is the student's development as a self-directed learner. The faculty have reconceptualized their liberal arts curriculum to focus on developing abilities, and have created classroom and off-campus learning experiences with sharp attention to the principles of experiential learning theory and practice (Doherty, Mentkowski, and Conrad, 1978). Results from longitudinal studies (Mentkowski and Strait, 1983) confirm that while students as a group enter college with predominant preferences for some learning styles over others, they show equal preferences for the four styles two years later. They shift in their preferences from more concrete to more abstract and from more reflective to more active. These changes have been directly linked to student performance in the curriculum. This suggests that the environmental press of a college dedicated to experiential learning concepts can cause students to be more balanced in their learning style preferences, and when they are ready to enter their specialized professional programs, they have already experienced multiple learning modes. Further, students as a group maintain their more balanced preferences during the last two years of college, even though practically all of them enter a particular career track. Type of major does not contribute to change. Further, alumnae report having to learn in a variety of modes at work, and being able to adapt to continued and unguided learning situations in a variety of settings (Mentkowski and Much, 1982). In the professions, this reference point is often the professional role itself, in which critical functions and tasks emphasize the need for specialized knowledge from various disciplines. In the "pure" academic disciplines, this focus can come through the broad application of a methodology such as systems analysis or through a research problem that requires multiple perspectives. In the humanities, this reference point may be experiential learning, a focus on the "common experiences of life," reversing a trend toward theorizing and formal specialization that has, in the opinion of W. Jackson Bates, nearly destroyed the field. Bates calls this trend:

> . . . the most serious liability that literary study has been gradually creating for itself: the autonomous nature of literature (and the arts) as a separate preserve apart from the common experiences of life. Hazlitt had a point when he said that the arts resembled Antaeus in the fable, who was invincible as long as his feet touched his mother Earth, but who was easily strangled by Hercules once he was lifted from the strength-giving ground. [Bates, 1982, p. 52]

The "when" question may suggest even more fundamental changes. The continuing knowledge explosion and the corresponding rapid rate of change raise serious questions about the current strategy of "front-loading" educational experience in the individual's life cycle. When, as current labor statistics indicate, the average person will change jobs seven times and careers three times during his or her working life, it makes more sense to distribute educational experiences throughout adult life in order to assist in the preparation for and mastery of these changes. Younger students will need to intersperse more life/work experience between their years of preparation in formal education. Existing programs of field-experience education (internships, work/study, and so on) give testimony to the learning/development payoff of such a mix of academic and practical training (Hursh and Borzak, 1979). The older generation will need the adult work/study version of what used to be called a "liberal arts education" with fresh opportunities to harvest the many fruits of knowledge left behind on their respective climbs to the top. In this model, the university becomes a center for lifelong learning. Integrative learning experiences take on new meaning and vitality when they are directly connected with the integrative challenges of adult life. Discussions of human values and the quality of life are very different with high school graduates than they are with managers of an oil refinery. Quality patient care has one connotation to the idealistic premed student and quite another to the harried medical specialist. Perhaps the richest resources for integrative development lie in the dialogue across age levels that the university for lifelong learning can provide.

Update and Reflections

Becoming an Experiential Educator

> *"To be a teacher in the right sense is to be a learner. Instruction begins when you, the teacher, learn from the learner, put yourself in his place so that you may understand what he understands and in the way he understands it."*

—Kierkegaard

My career as an educator, nearly fifty years since beginning as an assistant professor at MIT's Sloan School of Management in 1965, has in a sense been a journey to become an experiential educator. After an inglorious and painful beginning, lecturing engineering management students about organizational psychology in my first semester, I began searching for a better way to teach and help students learn. As I mentioned in the introduction, the powerful learning I had experienced in Lewin's experiential T-groups stood in sharp contrast to the bored and disinterested audiences I had faced that first semester. With my colleagues Irv Rubin and Jim McIntyre we began an exciting process of experimenting with experiential learning methods, first using T-groups but soon modifying our approach to use the experiential learning cycle to create more structured experiential exercises that focused on the subject matter topics of organizational psychology. This resulted in the first management textbook based on experiential learning (Kolb, Rubin, and McIntyre, 1971b) that is now in its eighth edition (Osland, Kolb, Rubin, and Turner, 2007). The workbook provides simulations, role plays, and exercises (concrete experiences) that focus on central concepts in organizational behavior, providing a common experiential starting point for participants and faculty to explore the relevance of behavioral concepts for their work. Each chapter is organized around the learning cycle providing the experience, structured reflection and conversation exercises, conceptual material, and personal application assignments.

Our success with this work began what, for me, has been a lifelong fascination with how people learn and how as an educator I can facilitate their learning. Unlike most educators who have a primary subject matter interest other than learning and education, for me how people learn was my primary focus in both my research and practice of teaching. Thus my career has been a lifelong series of action research projects. Three concepts have become central for me in my quest to become an experiential educator:

- Creating spaces for learning

- Dynamic matching of individual learning style and subject matter requirements by "teaching around the learning cycle"

- Focusing on the development of learning skills

Learning Spaces

In experiential learning theory, learning is conceived as a transaction between the person and the environment. To learn means to learn *something* that exists *somewhere*. While, for most, the idea of a learning space conjures up the image of the physical classroom environment, the concept of learning space is much broader and multidimensional (Figure 7.17). Dimensions of learning space include physical, cultural, institutional, social, and psychological aspects.

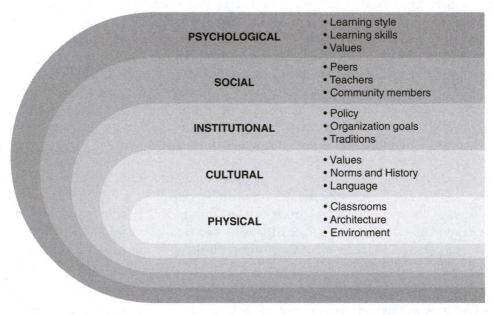

Figure 7.17 Dimensions of Learning Space

In experiential learning theory these dimensions of learning space all come together in the experience of the learner. This concept of learning space builds on Kurt Lewin's (1951) field theory and his concept of life space. For Lewin, the person and the environment are interdependent variables, a concept Lewin translated into a mathematical formula, $B = f(p, e)$ where behavior is a function of person and environment. As Marrow puts it, "the life space is the total psychological environment which the person experiences subjectively" (1969, p. 35). Life space includes all facts which have existence for the person and excludes those which do not. It embraces needs, goals, unconscious influences, memories, beliefs, events of a political, economic, and social nature, and anything else that might have a direct effect on behavior. To take time as an example, in many organizations today employees are so busy doing their work that they feel that there is no time to learn how to do things better. This feeling is shaped by the objective conditions of a hectic work schedule and also the expectation that time spent reflecting will not be rewarded. Teachers objectively create learning spaces by the information and activities they offer in their course; but this space is also interpreted in the students' subjective experience through the lens of their learning style. One's position in a learning space defines their experience and thus defines their "reality." Lewin stresses the importance for education of defining the learning space in terms of the learner's experience: "One of the basic characteristics of field theory in psychology, as I see it, is the demand that the field which influences an individual should be described not in 'objective physicalistic' terms, but in the way that it exists for that person at that time. . . . A teacher will never succeed in giving proper guidance to a child if he does not learn to understand the psychological world in which that child lives. . . . To substitute for that world of the individual the world of the teacher, of the physicist, or of anybody else is to be, not objective, but wrong" (Cartwright, 1951, p. 62).

The various factors in a given life space are to some degree interdependent, and Lewin strongly maintains that only the dynamic concepts of tension and force can deal with these sets of interdependent facts. This is what led him to define psychological needs as tension systems and their topological representation as vectors to denote motion. He postulates that the particular organization of a person's life space is determined by a field of forces, both internal needs and external demands that position the individual in a life space composed of different regions. Using map-like representation, the life space could be depicted topologically. Life spaces can vary in a number of dimensions including extension, differentiation, integration, and level of conflict. Lewin introduced a number of concepts for analysis of the life space and a person's relationship to it that are applicable to the study of learning spaces, including position, region, locomotion, equilibrium of forces, positive and negative valence, barriers in the person and the world, conflict, and goal.

Urie Bronfrenbrenner's (1977, 1979) work on the ecology of human development has made significant sociological contributions to Lewin's life space concept. He defines the ecology of learning/development spaces as a topologically nested arrangement of structures each contained within the next. The learner's immediate setting such as a course or classroom is called the *microsystem*, while other concurrent settings in the person's life such as other courses, the dorm, or family are referred to as the *mesosystem*. The *exosystem* encompasses the formal and informal social structures that influence the person's immediate environment, such as institutional policies and procedures and campus culture. Finally, the *macrosystem* refers to the overarching institutional patterns and values of the wider culture, such as cultural values favoring abstract knowledge over practical knowledge, that influence actors in the person's immediate microsystem and mesosystem. This theory provides a framework for analysis of the social system factors that influence learners' experience of their learning spaces.

Another important contribution to the learning space concept is situated learning theory (Lave and Wenger, 1991). Like experiential learning theory, situated learning theory draws on Vygotsky's (1978) activity theory of social cognition for a conception of social knowledge that conceives of learning as a transaction between the person and the social environment. Situations in situated learning theory, like life space and learning space, are not necessarily physical places but constructs of the person's experience in the social environment. These situations are embedded in communities of practice that have a history, norms, tools, and traditions of practice. Knowledge resides, not in the individual's head, but in communities of practice. Learning is thus a process of becoming a member of a community of practice through legitimate peripheral participation (e.g., apprenticeship). Situated learning theory enriches the learning space concept by reminding us that learning spaces extend beyond the teacher and the classroom. They include socialization into a wider community of practice that involves membership, identity formation, transitioning from novice to expert through mentorship, and experience in the activities of the practice, as well as the reproduction and development of the community of practice itself as newcomers replace old-timers.

Finally, as I described earlier (Chapter 5 Update and Reflections) in their theory of knowledge creation, Nonaka and Konno introduce the Japanese concept of *ba*, a "context that harbors meaning," which is a shared space that is the foundation for knowledge creation. "Knowledge is embedded in *ba*, where it is then acquired through one's own experience or reflections on the experiences of others" (1998, p. 40). Knowledge embedded in *ba* is tacit and can only be made explicit through sharing of feelings, thoughts, and experiences of persons in the space. For this to happen, the *ba* space requires that individuals remove barriers between one another in a climate that emphasizes "care, love, trust, and commitment." Learning spaces similarly require norms of psychological safety, serious purpose, and respect to promote learning.

Assessing Experiential Learning Spaces
with the Kolb Learning Style Inventory 4.0

In experiential learning theory the experiential learning space is defined by the attracting and repelling forces (positive and negative valences) of the poles of the dual dialectics of action/reflection and experiencing/conceptualizing, creating a two-dimensional map of the regions of the learning space. The regions of the experiential learning theory learning space offer a typology of the different types of learning thereby emphasizing some stages of the learning cycle over others. The process of experiential learning can be viewed as a process of locomotion through the learning regions that is influenced by a person's position in the learning space. Research on learning flexibility (Chapter 4 Update and Reflections, and Figure 4.16) has shown that individuals vary in their ability to move about the learning space.

The experiential learning theory learning space concept emphasizes that learning is not one universal process but a map of learning territories, a frame of reference within which many different ways of learning can flourish and interrelate. It is a holistic framework that orients the many different ways of learning to one another. As Lewin put it, "Actually, the term learning refers to a multitude of different phenomena. The statement 'Democracy, one has to learn, autocracy is imposed on the person' refers to one type of learning. If one says that the spastic child has to learn to relax, one is speaking of a different type of learning. Both types probably have very little to do with learning French vocabulary, and this type again has little to do with learning to like spinach. Have we any right to classify learning to high-jump, to get along with alcohol, and to be friendly with people under the same terms, and to expect identical laws to hold for any of these processes?" (Cartwright, 1951, p. 65).

One's position in the learning space defines their experience and thus defines their "reality." Since a learning space is in the end what the learner experiences it to be, it is the psychological and social dimensions of learning spaces that have the most influence on learning. From this perspective learning spaces can be viewed as aggregates of the characteristics of the people in them since the people in a particular environment are arguably the dominant feature of it. "Environments are transmitted through people, and the dominant features of a particular environment are partially a function of the individuals who inhabit it" (Strange and Banning, 2001). An individual's learning style (Chapter 4 Update and Reflections) positions him/her in one of these regions based on their unique equilibrium of forces among acting, reflecting, experiencing, and conceptualizing. A number of studies of learning spaces in higher education have been conducted using the human aggregate approach by showing the percentage of students whose learning style places them in the different learning space regions (Kolb and Kolb, 2005a; Eickmann, Kolb, and Kolb, 2004).

Comparing Learning Spaces in Management and the Arts   To illustrate the concept of learning space, the distribution of student learning styles in two institutions of higher education that are engaged in longitudinal institutional development programs to promote learning—the Case Weatherhead School of Management (CWRU) MBA program and the Cleveland Institute of Art (CIA) undergraduate program—are shown in Figures 7.18 and 7.19. The Case Weatherhead institutional development program, reported in *Innovation in Professional Education: Steps on a Journey from Teaching to Learning* (Boyatzis, Cowen, and Kolb, 1995), focused on curriculum development, student development, and longitudinal outcome assessment (Boyatzis, Stubbs, and Taylor, 2002). MBA student learning style data is from Boyatzis and Mainemelis (2000). The program at the Cleveland Institute of Art is part of a longitudinal study of artistic learning conducted by the Ohio Consortium on Artistic Learning involving a longitudinal study of artistic learning styles, student development workshops, and faculty development seminars Eickmann, Kolb, and Kolb, 2004).

Figures 7.18 and 7.19 show how the learning styles of management and art students are distributed in the learning regions. Art students are concentrated in the experiencing-oriented northern regions of the learning space while management students are concentrated in the thinking southern regions. The figures show that 42.1 percent of art students are in the northern regions while 23.6 percent are in the south, contrasted to 45.7 percent of management students located in the southern regions with 21.2 percent in the north. There are more art students in the eastern reflecting regions than in the western acting regions (35.2 percent to 26.3 percent) and more management students in the western acting regions than the eastern reflecting regions (36.3 percent to 30.4 percent). Among art students the Deciding region is the least populated (3.7 percent) while the least populated region for management students is Imagining (5.1 percent). While 12.5 percent of art students are in the Balancing central region, only 10.2 percent of management students

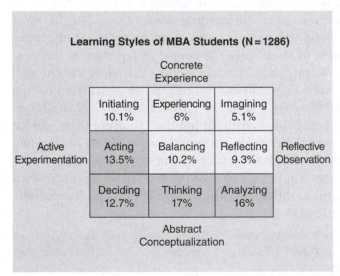

Figure 7.18 Management Student Learning Styles

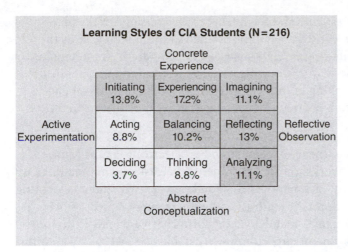

Figure 7.19 Art Student Learning Styles

are found there. Boyatzis and Mainemelis found significant correlations between abstract learning styles and grades and GMAT (full-time MBA sample, r = .16; part-time sample, r = .19), indicating a bias toward abstraction in evaluation and selection practices. For BFA graduates there was no relationship between grades and learning style.

The way the educational process is conducted in art schools and management schools reveals some striking differences that give insight into the nature of learning in the different learning regions. Dewey's distinction between artistic and scientific learning helps us understand the difference between the kinds of learning that occur in art education and in management education:

> The rhythm of loss of integration with environment and recovery of union not only persists in man, but becomes conscious with him; its conditions are material out of which he forms purposes. Emotion is the conscious sign of a break, actual or impending. The discord is the occasion that induces reflection. Desire for restoration of the union converts mere emotion into interest in objects as conditions of realization of harmony. With the realization, material of reflection is incorporated into objects as their meaning. Since the artist cares in a peculiar way for the phase of experience in which union is achieved, he does not shun moments of resistance and tension. He rather cultivates them, not for their own sake but because of their potentialities, bringing to living consciousness an experience that is unified and total. In contrast with the person whose purpose is esthetic, the scientific man is interested in problems, in situations wherein tension between the matter of observation and of thought is marked. Of course he cares for their resolution. But he does not rest in it; he passes on to another problem using an attained solution only as a stepping stone on which to set on foot further inquiries.

The difference between the esthetic and the intellectual is thus one of the places where emphasis falls in the constant rhythm that marks the interaction of the live creature with his surroundings. . . . Because of the comparative remoteness of his end, the scientific worker operates with symbols, words and mathematical signs. The artist does his thinking in the very qualitative media he works in, and the terms lie so close to the object that he is producing that they merge directly into it. [Dewey, 1934, pp. 15–16]

A first awareness of differences in the management and arts learning spaces came as we were preparing a learning style workshop for art students. We asked what readings we should give, and the Provost, Paul Eickmann, said, "You know, for art students learning is not text driven." This stood in dramatic contrast with management education which is almost entirely organized around texts that deliver an authoritative scientific discourse. The scientific basis of the management curriculum was established in 1959 by an influential Carnegie Foundation report that sought to improve the intellectual respectability of management education by grounding it in three scientific disciplines: economics, mathematics, and behavioral science.

The text-driven approach of management education contrasts with the experiential learning process of demonstration-practice-production-critique that is used in most art classes. This process is repeated recursively in art education, while management education is primarily discursive with each topic covered in a linear sequence with little recursive repetition. Management education focuses on telling, while art education emphasizes showing. Management education tends to emphasize theory, while art education emphasizes integration of theory and practice. Art education focuses on the learners' inside-out expression, while management education spends more time on outside-in impression. Most of the time in management classes is spent conveying information, with relatively little time spent on student performance, most of which occurs on tests and papers. In art classes the majority of the time is spent on student expression of ideas and skills. Art education tends to be individualized, with small classes and individual attention, while management education is organized into large classes with limited individualized attention. An assistant dean at the Columbus College of Art and Design who majored in music as an undergraduate and later got an MBA contrasted the three hours a week he spent in individual tutorial with his mentor with the shock he experienced in entering a tiered MBA classroom of 200 students. Finally, art education tends to be represented by faculty members with diverse learning styles, whereas management education tends to favor specialized faculty members with a primarily abstract learning orientation (see Figure 7.20).

The comparison between the observed educational programs and teaching methods of CIA arts education and Case MBA education seems consistent with respective student LSI distributions in the nine-region learning space, with MBA students primarily in the southern thinking and western acting regions and arts students falling mainly in the northern feeling and eastern reflecting regions. The corresponding discursive, telling

Comparison of Arts Education and Management Education	
Arts Education	**Management Education**
Aesthetic	Scientific
Demo-practice-production-critique	Text driven
Recursive	Discursive
Theory and practice	Theory
Showing	Telling
Expression	Impression
Individualized	Batched
Diverse faculty	Abstract faculty

Figure 7.20 Differences between Arts Education and Management Education

educational methods of the MBA program and the recursive, showing techniques of the art school recall Dewey's description of the scientific worker who "operates with symbols, words and mathematical signs" and the artist who "does his thinking in the very qualitative media he works in."

Creating Learning Spaces for the Enhancement of Experiential Learning

From the very beginning, our work to introduce experiential learning in the educational systems has been a struggle to make the space for learning to take place. Educational institutions, with their classrooms, credit hours, and time-blocked schedules, are learning spaces; but spaces constructed with a very different model of learning than experiential learning theory. Based on an information transfer model from teacher to student, classroom learning spaces are usually designed and often bolted down with seats in concrete tiers. Students face the teacher in front in a structure that makes student-to-student interaction difficult. The university *exosystem* learning space of courses, broken down into block-scheduled bits of content that award credit hours for completion, supports the information transfer model. When Alice and I were teaching at CWRU, we used to joke that we were more furniture movers than teachers because we always had to arrive an hour early to move the tables aside and arrange chairs in a circle with books, materials, flowers, music, and other "show and tell" items in the center for everyone to see and interact with. Our goal was to create an experiential learning space based on the principles described below (Kolb and Kolb, 2005a).

Making Space for Engagement in the Learning Cycle   The first step in creating an experiential learning space is to make a space for learners that enables deep learning (Border, 2007) by allowing them to fully engage in all four modes of the experiential learning cycle—experiencing, reflecting, thinking, and acting. Learning effectiveness is increased when one can move from one learning mode to the other in the learning cycle entering the different corresponding regions of the learning space. Lewin used the term loco-motion to describe this movement through the regions. He spoke of boundaries of the learning regions and how they can act as barriers to entering a region. Fazey and Martin (2002) have argued that learning leads to understanding with greater retention and transfer when an "experiential space of variation" is created through repeated practice from different perspectives and under different conditions. This space of variation can be portrayed as the number of learning regions that a person engages in the learning process. Another popular way of representing this idea is a learning pyramid where learning retention is increased from 20 percent when one learning mode is engaged to 90 percent when all four modes are engaged (Reese 1998; Dale 1969). Although we have seen no studies that have assessed these retention percentages by learning mode empiri-cally, Specht and Sandlin (1991) have shown that retention of accounting concepts after six weeks was 84 percent for students in a course taught using a learning method that followed the experiential learning cycle and only 46 percent in a course taught using the traditional lecture method.

We have seen a polarization between experiencing and thinking in the contrast between the feeling-oriented learning space of CIA arts education and the thinking-oriented learning spaces of the Case MBA program. It seems that educational institutions tend to develop a learning culture that emphasizes the learning mode most related to their edu-cational objectives and devalues the opposite learning mode. Yet, Damasio (1994, 2003), LeDoux (1997), Zull (2002), and others offer convincing research evidence that reason and emotion are inextricably related in their influence on learning and memory. Indeed, it appears that feelings and emotions have primacy in determining whether and what we learn. Negative emotions such as fear and anxiety can block learning, while positive feelings of attraction and interest may be essential for learning. To learn something that one is not interested in is extremely difficult.

Learning is like breathing; it involves a taking in and processing of experience and a putting out or expression of what is learned. As Dewey noted, ". . . nothing takes root in mind when there is no balance between doing and receiving. Some decisive action is needed in order to establish contact with the realities of the world and in order that impressions may be so related to facts that their value is tested and organized" (1934, p. 45). Yet many programs in higher education are much more focused on impressing information on the mind of the learner than on opportunities for the learners to express and test in action what they have learned. Many courses will spend 15 weeks requiring students to take in volumes of information and only a couple of hours expressing and testing their learning, often on a multiple-choice exam. This is in contrast to arts education built on the demonstration-practice-production-critique process where active expression and testing are continuously involved in the learning process. Zull (2002) suggests that action may be the most important part of the learning cycle because it closes the learning cycle by bringing the inside world of reflection and thought into contact with the outside world of experiences created by action.

Respect for Learners and Their Experience   We refer to this as the Cheers/Jeers experiential continuum. At one end learners feel that they are members of a learning community who are known and respected by faculty and colleagues and whose experience is taken seriously, a space "where everybody knows your name." At the other extreme are learning environments where learners feel alienated, alone, unrecognized, and devalued. Learning and growth in the Jeers environment "where nobody knows your name" can be difficult if not impossible. While this principle may seem obvious or even "preachy," it is problematic for even the finest educational institutions. President Lawrence Summers of Harvard dedicated his 2003 commencement address to the introduction of a comprehensive examination of the undergraduate program, motivated in part by a letter he received from a top science student which contained the statement, "I am in the eighth semester of college and there is not a single science professor here who could identify me by name." Summers concludes, "The only true measure of a successful educational model is our students' experience of it" (Summers, 2003, p. 64).

Begin Learning with the Learner's Experience of the Subject Matter   To learn experientially, one must first of all own and value their experience. Students will often say, "But I don't have any experience," meaning that they don't believe that their experience is of any value to the teacher or for learning the subject matter at hand. The new science of learning (Bransford, Brown, and Cocking, 2000) is based on the cognitive constructivist theories of Piaget and Vygotsky that emphasize that people construct new knowledge and understanding from what they already know and believe based on their previous experience. Zull (2002) suggests that this prior knowledge exists in the brain as neuronal networks which cannot be erased by a teacher's cogent explanation. Instead, the effective teacher builds on exploration of what students already know and believe, on the sense they have made of their previous concrete experiences. Beginning with these or related concrete experiences allows the learner to re-examine and modify their previous sense-making in the light of new ideas.

Creating and Holding a Hospitable Space for Learning   To learn requires facing and embracing differences, be they differences between skilled expert performance and one's novice status, differences between deeply held ideas and beliefs and new ideas, or differences in the life experience and values of others that can lead to understanding them. These differences can be challenging and threatening, requiring a learning space that encourages the expression of differences and the psychological safety to support the learner in facing these challenges (Sanford, 1966). As Robert Kegan says, ". . . people grow best where they continuously experience an ingenious blend of challenge and support" (1994, p. 42). As Kegan implies by his use of the term "ingenious blend," creating and holding this learning space is not easy. He notes that while educational institutions have been quite successful in challenging students, they have been much less successful in providing support. One reason for this may be that challenges tend to be specific and immediate while support must go beyond an immediate "You can do it" statement. It requires a climate or culture of support that the learner can trust to "hold" them over time. In *Conversational Learning* (Baker, Jensen, and Kolb, 2002) we draw on the work of Henri Nouwen (1975) and Parker Palmer (1983, 1990, 1998) to describe this challenging and supportive learning space as one that welcomes the stranger in a spirit of hospitality where "students and teachers can enter into a fearless communication with each other and allow their respective life experiences to be their primary and most valuable source of growth and maturation" (Nouwen, 1975, p. 60).

Making Space for Conversational Learning   Human beings naturally make meaning from their experiences through conversation, yet genuine conversation in the traditional lecture classroom can be extremely restricted or nonexistent. At the break or end of the class the sometimes painfully silent classroom will suddenly come alive with spontaneous conversation among students. Significant learning can occur in these conversations, although it may not always be the learning the teacher intended. Making space for good conversation as part of the educational process provides the opportunity for reflection on and meaning making about experiences that improves the effectiveness of experiential learning (Keeton, Sheckley, and Griggs, 2002; Bunker 1999). For example, the creation of learning teams as part of a course promotes effective learning when psychologically safe conditions are present (Wyss-Flamm, 2002). *Conversational Learning* describes the dimensions of spaces that allow for good conversation. Good conversation is more likely to occur in spaces that integrate thinking and feeling, talking and listening, leadership and solidarity, recognition of individuality and relatedness, and discursive and recursive processes. When the conversational space is dominated by one extreme of these dimensions, for example talking without listening, conversational learning is diminished.

Making Space for Development of Expertise   With vast knowledge bases that are ever changing and growing in every field, many higher education curricula consist of course after course "covering" a series of topics in a relatively superficial factual way. Yet as the National Research Council in its report on the new science of learning recommends on the basis of research on expert learners, effective learning requires not only factual knowledge, but the organization of these facts and ideas in a conceptual framework and the ability to retrieve knowledge for application and transfer to different contexts (Bransford, Brown, and Cocking, 2000). Such deep learning is facilitated by deliberate, recursive practice on areas that are related to the learner's goals (Keeton, Sheckley, and Griggs, 2002). The process of learning depicted in the experiential learning cycle describes this recursive spiral of knowledge development. Space needs to be created in curricula for students to pursue such deep experiential learning in order to develop expertise related to their life purpose.

Making Space for Inside-out Learning   David Hunt (1987, 1991) describes inside-out learning as a process of beginning with oneself in learning by focusing on one's experienced knowledge: the implicit theories, metaphors, interests, desires, and goals that guide experience. Making space for inside-out learning by linking educational experiences to the learner's interests kindles intrinsic motivation and increases learning effectiveness. Under the proper educational conditions, a spark of intrinsic interest can be nurtured into a flame of committed life purpose (Dewey, 1897). Yet learning spaces that emphasize extrinsic reward can drive out intrinsically motivated learning (Kohn, 1993; Deci and Ryan, 1985; Ryan and Deci, 2000). Long ago Dewey described the trend toward emphasis on extrinsic reward in education and the consequences for the teacher who wields the carrot and stick: "Thus in education we have that systematic depreciation of interest which has been noted. . . . Thus we have the spectacle of professional educators decrying appeal to interest while they uphold with great dignity the need of reliance upon examinations, marks, promotions and emotions, prizes and the time honored paraphernalia of rewards and punishments. The effect of this situation in crippling the teacher's sense of humor has not received the attention which it deserves" (1916, p. 336).

Making Space for Learners to Take Charge of Their Own Learning   Many students enter higher education conditioned by their previous educational experiences to be passive recipients of what they are taught. Making space for students to take control of and responsibility for their learning can greatly enhance their ability to learn from experience. Some use the term self-authorship to describe this process of constructing one's own knowledge versus passively receiving knowledge from others, considering self-authorship to be a major aim of education (Kegan, 1994; King, 2003; Baxter-Magolda, 1999). Others describe this goal as increasing students' capacity for self-direction (Boyatzis, 1994; Robertson, 1988). The Management Development and Assessment course in the Case MBA program aims to develop student self-direction through assessment and feedback on learning skills and competencies and the development of a learning plan to achieve their career/life goals (Boyatzis, 1994). Bransford, Brown, and Cocking (2000) argue for the development of meta-cognitive skills to promote active learning. By developing their effectiveness as learners (Keeton, Sheckley, and Griggs, 2002), students can be empowered to take responsibility for their own learning by understanding how they learn best and the skills necessary to learn in regions that are uncomfortable for them. Workshops on experiential learning and learning styles can help students to develop meta-cognitive learning skills. At CIA and the Case undergraduate programs, student workshops help students interpret their LSI scores and understand how to use this information to improve their learning effectiveness. John Reese at the University of Denver Law School conducts "Connecting with the Professor" workshops in which students select one of four teaching styles based on the four predominant learning styles that they have difficulty connecting with. The workshop gives multiple examples of remedial actions that the learner may take to correct the misconnection created by differences in teaching/learning styles. Peer group discussions among law students give an opportunity to create new ideas about how to get the most from professors with different learning/teaching styles (Reese, 1998).

Educator Roles and Teaching Around the Learning Cycle

In the midst of the multitude of educational theories, learning technologies, and institutional procedures and constraints, it is easy to lose sight of the most important thing—teaching is above all a profound human relationship. We can all think of teachers who have had a major impact on our lives, and in most cases this involved a special relationship where we felt recognized, valued, and empowered by the teacher. Parker Palmer (1998) described the courage necessary for a teacher to fully enter into learning relationships with students as a willingness to expose one's inner world, to honor students as complex, relational beings, and to masterfully weave these worlds together with the course content. Experiential learning theory suggests that educating is not something one does *to* students through implementation of a set of techniques. Rather, it is something educators do *with* learners in the context of meaningful relationships and shared experiences.

Educating is holistic. It is about developing the whole person. Educating the whole person means that the goal of education is not solely cognitive knowledge of the facts, but also includes development of social and emotional maturity. In experiential learning theory terms it is about facilitating integrated development in affective, perceptual, cognitive, and behavioral realms. Rather than acquiring generalized knowledge stripped of any context, learning is situated to the person's life setting and life path (Lave and Wenger, 1991). The experiential educator needs to resolve some fundamental dilemmas of teaching. Do we focus on the learner's experience and interests or subject matter requirements? Do we focus on effective performance and action or on a deep understanding of the meaning of ideas? All are required for maximally effective learning. Experiential education is a complex relational process that involves balancing attention to the learner and to the subject matter while also balancing reflection on the deep meaning of ideas with the skill of applying them. It is important to be learner centered, focusing on the prior knowledge of learners to help them construct new understanding and tapping into their unique interests to increase motivation to learn. It is also important to be subject centered, staying on top of one's field and organizing subject matter in a form that can be communicated effectively. Similarly, it is necessary to explore the deeper meaning of ideas and develop learners' ability to critically evaluate the assumptions that underlie them, while also focusing on performance, the effective application of the ideas.

The simple prescription, made by many learning style approaches to match teaching style to the learning style of learners, is not sufficient to deal with this complexity (Pashler et al., 2008; Willingham, 2005, 2009). Unlike the experiential learning theory process-oriented learning style approach, these style measures see learning styles as fixed traits or personality characteristics. Scott, citing Dweck (2000), argues that this is an entity approach to ability that promotes stereotyping and labeling rather than a process approach that emphasizes developmental potential and contextual adaptation. Also, surprisingly, none are based on a comprehensive theory of learning. The dimensions of individuality that they assess are hypothesized to influence learning, but how the dimension connected to the learning process is not made explicit. An individual may prefer to work alone or in a group, but how is this preference related to learning?

Willingham provides an example of the problems that a trait-based learning style measure that is not related to a theory of learning faces with the matching teaching and learning style approach. The VAK measures individual differences in preferences for visual, auditory, and kinesthetic sense modalities. While there are reliable individual differences in preference/ability for these modalities, "For the vast majority of education, vision and audition are usually just vehicles that carry the important information teachers want students to learn" (2005, p. 3). But the process of learning usually involves storing information in memory in terms of meaning, independent of any modality. His review of studies that match sensory modality with instruction concludes: "We can say that the possible effects of matching instructional modality to a student's modality strength have been extensively studied and have yielded no positive evidence" (2005, p. 3).

The major implication of experiential learning theory for education is to design educational programs in a way that teaches around the learning cycle so that learners can use and develop all learning styles in a way that completes the learning cycle for them and promotes deep learning. Earlier (Chapter 1 Update and Reflections, pp. 26–27) I described Vygotsky's law of internalization and the zone of proximal development where the child's novel capacities begin in the interpersonal realm and are gradually transferred into the intrapersonal realm (Vygotsky, 1978). The key technique for accomplishing this transition is called "scaffolding." In scaffolding the educator tailors the learning process to the individual needs and developmental level of the learner. Scaffolding provides the structure and support necessary to progressively build knowledge. The model of teaching around the cycle described below provides a framework for this scaffolding process. This approach requires competence in relating to learners in complex ways—ways that help them feel, perceive, think, and behave differently. These ways of relating require the educator to play multiple roles in relationship to the learners and the object of the learning endeavor.

In our interviews and observations of experienced, successful educators we find that they tend to "teach around the learning cycle" in this manner. They organize their educational activities in such a manner that they address all four learning modes—experiencing, reflecting, thinking, and acting. As they do this, they lead learners around the cycle, shifting the role they play depending on which stage of the cycle they are addressing. In effect the role they adopt helps to create a learning space designed to facilitate the transition from one learning style to another. Often they do this in a recursive fashion, repeating the cycle many times in a learning program. In effect the cycle becomes a spiral with each passage through the cycle deepening and extending learners' understanding of the subject. When a concrete experience is enriched by reflection, given meaning by thinking, and transformed by action, the new experience created becomes richer, broader, and deeper. Further iterations of the cycle continue the exploration and transfer to experiences in other contexts.

The New Zealand Ministry of Education (2004) has used this spiraling learning process as the framework for the design of middle school curricula. Figure 7.21 describes how teachers use the learning spiral to promote higher level learning and to transfer knowledge to other contexts.

Educator Roles

Teaching around the learning cycle and to different learning styles introduces the need for adjustments in the role one takes with learners. The Educator Role Profile (Kolb, Kolb, Passarelli, and Sharma, 2014) was created to help educators understand their preferred educator role and plan for how they can teach around the learning cycle. The self-report instrument is based on the assumption that preferences for teaching roles emerge from a combination of beliefs about teaching and learning, goals for the educational process, preferred teaching style, and instructional practices. Educator roles are not limited

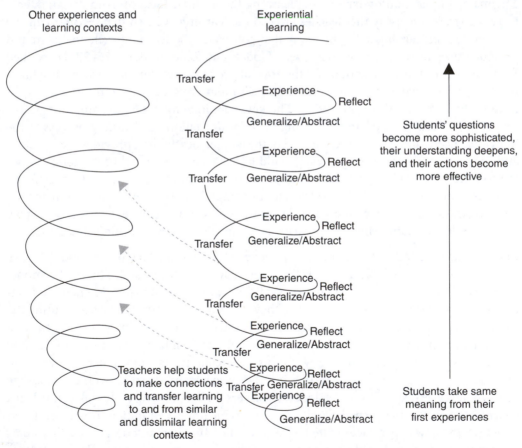

Figure 7.21   Teaching and the Learning Spiral

to individuals in formal classroom teaching situations. The framework can be extended to individuals in all walks of life who "teach" as leaders, coaches, parents, friends, etc.

An educator role is a patterned set of behaviors that emerge in response to the learning environment, including students and the learning task demands. Each educator role engages students to learn in a unique manner, using one mode of grasping experience and one mode of transforming experience. In the facilitator role, educators draw on the modes of concrete experience and reflective observation to help learners get in touch with their own experience and reflect on it. Subject matter experts, using the modes of reflective observation and abstract conceptualization, help learners organize and connect their reflection to the knowledge base of the subject matter. They may provide models or theories for learners to use in subsequent analysis. The standard setting and evaluating role uses abstract conceptualization and active experimentation to help students apply knowledge toward performance goals. In this role, educators closely monitor the quality of student performance toward the standards they set, and provide consistent feedback. Finally, those in the coaching role draw on concrete experience and active experimentation to help learners take action on personally meaningful goals. These roles can also be organized by their relative focus on the student versus the subject and action versus knowledge as illustrated in Figure 7.22.

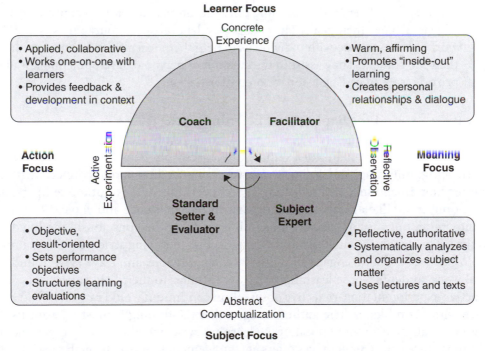

Figure 7.22 Educator Roles and the Learning Cycle

The Educator Role Profile (ERP) describes four role positions—Facilitator, Expert, Evaluator, and Coach. Educators play these roles as they help learners maximize learning by moving through the four stages of the experiential learning cycle.

- *The Facilitator Role.* When facilitating, educators help learners get in touch with their personal experience and reflect on it. They adopt a warm affirming style to draw out learners' interests, intrinsic motivation, and self-knowledge. They often do this by facilitating conversation in small groups. They create personal relationships with learners.

- *The Expert Role.* In their role as subject expert, educators help learners organize and connect their reflections to the knowledge base of the subject matter. They adopt an authoritative, reflective style. They often teach by example, modeling and encouraging critical thinking as they systematically organize and analyze the subject matter knowledge. This knowledge is often communicated through lectures and texts.

- *The Evaluator Role.* As a standard setter and evaluator, educators help learners master the application of knowledge and skill in order to meet performance requirements. They adopt an objective, results-oriented style as they set the knowledge requirements needed for quality performance. They create performance activities for learners to evaluate their learning.

- *The Coaching Role.* In the coaching role, educators help learners apply knowledge to achieve their goals. They adopt a collaborative, encouraging style, often working one-on-one with individuals to help them learn from experiences in their life context. They assist in the creation of personal development plans and provide ways of getting feedback on performance.

Educating Around the Experiential Learning Cycle

Figure 7.23 shows the nine-style experiential learning cycle and the corresponding educator roles that match them; for example, the coach role is most appropriate for the experiencing, initiating, and acting styles, while the facilitator role connects with the experiencing, imagining, and reflecting styles. Learning style is not a fixed personality trait but more like a habit of learning shaped by experience and choices—it can be an automatic, unconscious mode of adapting, or it can be consciously modified and changed. The dynamic matching model suggests that matching style with role is important to connect with and engage learners. Raschick, Mypole, and Day (1998) found that social work students whose learning styles were similar to their field supervisors along the active experimentation-reflective observation continuum would rate their field experience with them higher. The authors suggest that the finding is most relevant for the supervisors at the beginning point of the learning cycle, when matching their teaching techniques to learners' preferences offers encouragement to move through the rest of the

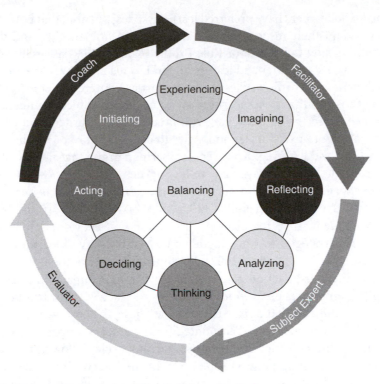

Figure 7.23   Educator Roles and the Nine Style Learning Cycle

learning cycle. Individual learning styles can be an entry point through which learners enter a particular learning space, but most learning requires that they continue to actively move around the learning cycle using other learning styles to acquire increasingly complex knowledge and skills and capacity to adapt to the wider demands of a given learning environment.

While Figure 7.23 depicts an idealized sequential progression through the educator roles and learning styles, in most cases a curriculum design will be based on a sequence of activities and instructional techniques that fits the subject matter and learning objectives that may or may not fit such an orderly progression. In considering a design it is useful to consider for each segment the teaching role to adopt, the learning style that you want to engage, and the choice of instructional technique best suited to the learning style and role.

Educator Role Flexibility

Individuals, however, tend to have a definite preference for one or two roles over the others because of their educational philosophy, their personal teaching style, and the requirements of their particular educational setting including administrative mandates and learner needs. The dynamic matching model recognizes that educators have individual

---

role preferences and learners have preferred learning styles, but also, that both can develop the capacity to adapt their respective roles and styles to one another and the learning situation at hand. Using the Educator Role Profile (Kolb, Kolb, Passarelli, and Sharma, 2014) we find that to some extent educators do tend to teach the way they learn, finding that those with concrete learning styles are more learner-centered, preferring the facilitator role, while those with abstract learning styles are more subject-centered preferring the expert and evaluator roles. However, with practice both learners and educators can develop the flexibility to use all roles and styles to create a more powerful and effective process of teaching and learning. Kosower and Berman argue that faculty members are capable of learning to teach in ways that are incongruent with their own learning styles, "because we all engage in all of the strategies to some degree, it seems to be more a matter of willingness to learn rather than ability" (1996, p. 217). Baker, Simon, and Bazeli (1987) contend that teaching is an art requiring the instructor to select from among a wide variety of instructional strategies to reach students with a diversity of learning preferences. Milne, James, Keegan, and Dudley (2002) developed an observational method to assess mental health trainers' transaction patterns along with their impact on student learning and a training program designed to teach trainers to teach to all learning modes. The results of the study indicate that during the baseline phase, the observed teaching method was primarily didactic in nature and accounted for the greatest impact (46.4 percent) on learner behavior in the reflection mode of the learning cycle, followed by smaller overall impacts on the remaining phases of the cycle. In the intervention phase by contrast, the greatest impact of the trainer's behavior on learners was on the concrete experience (59.5 percent), followed by reflective observation (33 percent), and active experimentation (4.5 percent) phases of the learning cycle. The authors conclude that the intervention phase produced trainer's behaviors that promote learners' ability to take advantage of the full range of the experiential learning cycle thus maximizing their learning outcomes. As education becomes more learner-centered, Harrelson and Leaver-Dunn (2002) suggest that experiential learning requires that teachers assume the facilitator role, which might be a difficult mind-set for some.

Lipshitz (1983) underscores the complexity of roles for an experiential educator who needs to have a firm grasp of the relevant conceptual material and develop sensitivity and skill in managing learners' emotional reactions to the learning process. Learners may also react to the shifting role of the educator from that of a knowledge purveyor to one that creates the learning environment and facilitates the holistic learning process. McGoldrick, Battle, and Gallagher (2000) indicate that the less control instructors exert on the students' experiences the more effective the learning outcome will be. However, instructors may run the risk of losing control over course structure and failing to keep the learning activities bounded within a specific time frame. Most of the risks associated with the experiential method, contend the authors, can be mitigated through careful planning, unambiguous course structure, establishing of clear expectations, and firm deadlines for each class activity.

Learning Style Flexibility

Learners have differing levels of interest as well as difficulties with certain stages of the learning cycle. Studies do show, however, that learners are able to flex their learning styles according to the demand of different learning tasks. Several studies suggest that, in fact, students shift their learning strategies to match the learning demands of a particular discipline (Cornett, 1983; Entwistle, 1981; Kolb, 1984; Ornstein, 1977). Jones, Mokhtari, and Reichard (2003) examined the extent to which community college students' learning style preferences vary as a function of discipline. They found significant differences in students' learning style preference across four different subject-area disciplines: English, math, science, and social studies. The results indicate that 83 percent of the 103 participants switched learning styles for two or more disciplines suggesting that students are capable of flexing their learning strategies to respond to the discipline-specific learning requirements. By understanding the dynamic matching model, they can become more capable of deliberate experiential learning (Kolb and Yeganah, 2016).

Outcome Assessment and Learning Skills

While experiential learning theory emphasizes that learning is an ongoing process, it does not mean that outcomes of learning are unimportant. Rather, it views much assessment in education as problematic because it is overly focused on declarative content knowledge rather than learning skills; and it is not holistic, focused primarily on information and cognitive skills while neglecting interpersonal and action skills. *Experiential Learning* uses the adaptive competency circle to assess outcomes of professional education and their correspondence with current job demands (Chapter 7, pp. 268–276). This instrument was based on relationships established between adaptive comptencies and learning style that arrayed them around the learning cycle (Chapter 4, pp. 131–134). Based on this work Boyatzis and Kolb (1995, 1997) developed and validated the Learning Skills Profile (LSP).

A learning skill is a combination of ability, knowledge, and experience that enables someone to do something well in a specific context. Learning skills can be intentionally developed by practice. Like the adaptive competency circle, learning skills are arrayed around the learning cycle based on their relationship to learning style. The LSP contains 72 learning skills in 12 scales of a "learning cycle clock." The four learning modes encompass three scales each. CE includes interpersonal skills of leadership (11), relationship (12), and help (1). RO includes information skills of sense making (2), information gathering (3), and information analysis (4). AC includes analytical skills of theory building (5), quantitative analysis (6), and technology (7). AE includes behavioral skills of goal setting (8), action (9), and initiative (10). The LSP was validated by a confirmative factor analysis of the scales that determined their fit in the four learning mode categories (Kaskowitz, 1995), examination of scale intercorrelations, relationship to the LSI, and correspondence to supervisor ratings (Boyatzis and Kolb, 1995). The LSP items are rated on a 7-point scale and can be adapted to self ratings of one's skill and job demands and also in a "360" format where the skill and job demands of an individual are rated by supervisors and/or peers.

The LSP has been used extensively for individual personal development and career planning. Figure 7.24 shows the learning skill profiles for two individuals. The woman on the left is a senior human resource development manager who is successful and loves her job. Note the correspondence between her job demands (the solid line) and learning skills (the dashed line) and the high levels of both. The profile on the right is an undergraduate man who is mapping the demands of his prospective major in biomedical engineering with his learning skills. Note the relative match between analytic demands and skills in the southern regions and the mismatch between high interpersonal skills and career demands in the north. This may be why he was questioning whether this major was the right choice. Sometimes when individuals take the LSP, they discover that their job is not using many of their highly developed skills. They are bored and restless, and that is a sign to search for new opportunities. Understanding your learning style and skills and the corresponding demands of different jobs and careers as described in the career chart can help you find that challenging match and a job you love.

The LSP has had a number of educational applications. Baker, Pesut, Mcdaniel, and Fisher (2007) evaluated a new problem-based learning (PBL) curriculum in graduate nursing education and a new PBL MBA program comparing before-and-after LSP results. Kretovics (1999) studied the graduating class of an MBA program in comparison to entering students and a control group finding changes in LSP scores that demonstrated the "added value" of the program. In *Innovation in Professional Education* (Boyatzis, Cowan, and Kolb, 1995) the LSP was used extensively to assess changes from entering to graduating MBA students. The instrument was also used to interview faculty about the learning skill objectives of their courses. Aggregate faculty scores on skill emphasis were related to student outcomes as measured by changes from entering to graduating students.

In health care, Rainey, Heckelman, Galazka, and Kolb (1993) used the LSP as a team-building and faculty development tool in a family medicine department, while Smith (1990) used the LSP to assess the critical competencies of physician executives. The instrument has been used as a framework for describing managerial (Camuffo and Gerli, 2004) and leadership skills (Kolb and Rainey, 2014). Dreyfus (1989) used the LSP to differentiate the learning skills of high-performing and typical managers.

Yamazaki (2010e) and Yamazaki and Kayes (2010) have used the LSP extensively to study cross-cultural differences and ex-patriate cross-cultural adaptation (Yamazaki, 2010a, 2010b, and 2010c; Yamazaki and Kayes, 2004, 2007).

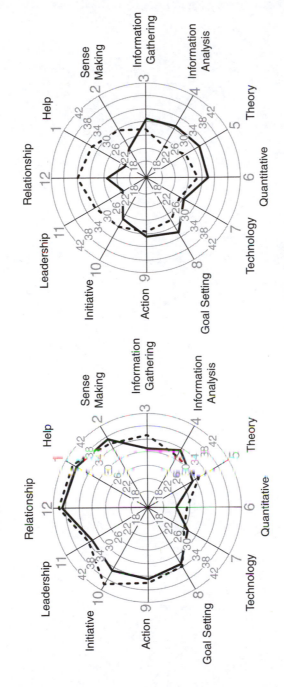

Figure 7.24 Learning Skills Profiles for an HR Manager and Undergraduate Student

8

Lifelong Learning and Integrative Development

But yield who will to their separation,
My object in living is to unite
My avocation and my vocation
As my two eyes make one in sight.
Only where love and need are one,
And the work is play for mortal stakes,
Is the deed ever really done
For Heaven and the future's sakes.

—Robert Frost*

There has been in recent years a dramatic preoccupation with adult development through the later stages of adult life driven by the huge baby boom demographic passing through them. This emphasis on adult learning and development has been labeled by some a "revolution in human development" (Brim and Kagan, 1980), and indeed, one cannot fail to be impressed by the burgeoning of self-development techniques and activities—from bookstores' shelves crowded with self-help books to workshops ranging from AA to TA to TM to Zen. Although some see a dangerous current of narcissism and "me" orientation in these developments, I prefer a more positive interpretation—namely, that the dialectic between social specialization and individual integrative fulfillment is itself reaching toward a higher-level synthesis.

The very diversity and intense specialization that threaten to tear us apart are grist for the integrative mill. Modern communication, the mass media, and the other fruits of

---

* From "Two Tramps in Mud Time" from THE POETRY OF ROBERT FROST edited by Edward Connery Lathem. Copyright 1936 by Robert Frost. Copyright © 1964 by Lesley Frost Ballantine. Copyright © 1969 by Holt, Rinehart and Winston. Reprinted by permission of Holt, Rinehart and Winston, Publishers and Jonathan Cape Ltd.

the information revolution provide an instantaneous cornucopia of fantasies, ideas, perspectives, value conflicts, and crises that challenge and fuel the integrative capacities of us all. We seek to grow and develop because we must do so to survive—as individuals and as a world community. If there is a touch of aggressive selfishness in our search for integrity, it can perhaps be understood as a response to the sometimes overwhelming pressures on us to conform, submit, and comply, to be the object rather than the subject of our life history.

The challenge of lifelong learning is above all a challenge of integrative development. Consider the careers of two great atomic scientists, the American Edward Teller and the Russian Andrei Sakharov, both of whom early in their careers were central in the development of their countries' nuclear capabilities. Teller went on to become one of our country's foremost advocates of nuclear power and a strong defense, whereas Sakharov, who gave his country the hydrogen bomb in the 1950s, was stricken by conscience and became a political dissident and a vigorous defender of human rights. Eventually he was banished from Moscow for his protest against the presence of Soviet troops in Afghanistan.

These moral and ethical decisions to promote or reject one's own inventions, to support or protest against one's own country, are qualitatively different from the specialized problem-solving activities of the working scientist. As Piaget (1970b) and others (such as Kuhn, 1962) have documented, the historical development of scientific knowledge has been toward increasing specialization, moving from egocentrism to reflection and from phenomenalism to constructivism—in experiential learning terms, from active to reflective and concrete to abstract. Yet the careers of highly successful scientists follow a different path. These people make their specialized abstract-reflective contributions often quite early in their careers. With recognition of their achievements comes a new set of tasks and challenges with active and concrete demands. The Nobel prizewinner must help to shape social policy and to articulate the ethical and value implications of his or her discoveries. The researcher becomes department chairperson and must manage the nurturance of the younger generation. So in this career, and most others as well, the higher levels of responsibility require an integrative perspective that can help shape cultural responses to emergent issues.

The challenges of integrative development are great, and not everyone is successful in meeting them, no matter how intelligent the person or how highly skilled in the professional specialty. In fact, as we have seen in Chapter 7, one's professional specialization may inhibit development of an integrative perspective. Charles Darwin, in his autobiography, was puzzled about his lost taste for literature, music, and the fine arts, suspecting that this loss was somehow related to his specialization:

> My mind seems to have become a kind of machine for grinding general laws out of large collections of facts, but why this should have caused the atrophy of that part of the brain alone, on which the highest tastes depend, I cannot conceive. [Darwin, 1958, pp. 138–139]

Several observers have attributed the problems that Jimmy Carter encountered in his presidency to his strong professional identity as a scientist and engineer (Fallows, 1979; Pfaff, 1979) and his difficulties in adapting to the concrete and reflective demands of the presidency (Gypen, 1980). Clark Clifford, who has been a personal consultant and friend to several presidents, said of Carter:

> He prided himself on being an engineer and scientist. . . . And every now and then he would say, "Now, as a scientist I would do this." "As a scientist I would do that." And he had good scientific training. What scientists do is, they start at A. And they go from A to B and B to C and C to D and D is their goal. And they know that if they just stay on the line, unquestionably they will reach D. I saw that in the President from time to time—that he had sufficient knowledge and experience to know that if he proceeded along a certain line the result would be there. The trouble is, it doesn't work in the White House. Because it doesn't take into consideration the House of Representatives, or the Senate of the United States, or the media, or the American people. . . . All these other factors come in. The problems of the President of the United States are not susceptible to scientific treatment. There's a lot more that goes into it. The fact is you almost have to disregard it. . . . President Carter came into the White House and after a while he got settled and began to feel more comfortable and began to look around for problems to solve. Well, one of them was the Panama Canal. . . . And that is a perfect issue for a president to bring up in the third year of his second term when he can be a statesman. And he can say, "This is right." And then he doesn't have to worry about commitments that he has made. But he picked this one out. Now, interestingly enough, he was right. . . . And courageous. But absolutely wrong to bring up at this time. Because he froze a very substantial part of the populace into a position of eternal and permanent enmity, as far as he was concerned. . . . A broader concept on his part of the presidency would have greatly facilitated that decision-making process. Another twenty-two water projects out in the West. . . . He took a look at that and my recollection is he said about 14 of these have no merit and maybe seven or eight have. Well, right about that time out went California, Oregon, Washington, Idaho, Montana, Colorado. [*Bill Moyers Journal*, 1981, pp. 6–7]

President Carter's later successes suggest significant progress toward an integrative response to the demands of his office, particularly in achieving a Mideast agreement through personal diplomacy in the Camp David accords. The early years of his term, however, appear to have suffered because of his specialized scientific perspective.

But the challenges of integrative development are not limited to scientists and presidents. A recent *Wall Street Journal* survey of chief executives asked them to identify the main strengths that determine a manager's potential for advancement (Allen, 1980). At the head of the list (cited by 36 percent of chief executives from large firms) was integrity, followed by an ability to get along with others and industriousness. Specialized technical experience or education was mentioned by only a few as critical for success. In fact, there are integrative developmental challenges in all occupations, at all occupational levels, and in our private lives as well. Many first-line supervisors, for example, have created personal job definitions that transcend the specialized boundaries of their trade to include the development of younger workers and the building of meaningful community and family relationships.

These challenges become particularly acute in midlife, when as adults we face what Erikson has termed the crisis of generativity or stagnation:

> . . . For we are a teaching species. . . . Only man can and must extend his solicitude over the long parallel and overlapping childhoods of numerous offspring united in households and communities. As he transmits the rudiments of hope, will, purpose and skill, he imparts meaning to the child's bodily experiences; he conveys a logic much beyond the literal meaning of the words he teaches; and he gradually outlines a particular world image and style of citizenship. . . . Once we have grasped this interlocking of the human life stages, we understand that adult man is so constituted as to need to be needed lest he suffer the mental deformation of self-absorption, in which he becomes his own infant and pet. I have, therefore, postulated an instinctual and psychosocial stage of generativity. Parenthood is, for most, the first, and for many, the prime generative encounter; yet the continuation of mankind challenges the generative ingenuity of workers and thinkers of many kinds. [Erikson, 1961, pp. 159–160]

In acceptance of the fact that we are a "teaching species" as well as a "learning species," a kind of figure/ground reversal takes place at midlife. Our progressive independence from the care of others, our self-oriented pursuit of individual goals, fades from the foreground of our experience to be replaced by a growing concern for the care of others. In the process, other reversals occur as well. In Jung's terms, the shadow side of personality emerges and claims dominion in consciousness along with the specialized conscious identity of youth. This is a social as well as personal transition, for many forces in the structure of career paths call for personal reassessment and integrative development. For example:

■ The career *cul de sac*—careers that provide advancement and opportunity only to a certain point and then require major adaptation and change, e.g., housewife/mother or engineering.

■ Withdrawal of reward; e.g., up-or-out tenure systems.

■ Withdrawal of opportunity—organizational career paths that have few opportunities for advancement and responsibility at middle and upper levels.

■ The "fur-lined trap" and achievement addiction—organizational and career reward systems that so effectively reward specialized role performance that individuals have little energy remaining for broader development, family, and private life.

- Career demands for integrative development—the extent to which a given career requires and/or allows development beyond specialization. For example, management at top levels requires an integrative perspective and organizations have policies such as job rotation to facilitate the development of this perspective.

- Opportunities for creativity/role innovation (Schein, 1972)—the extent to which a career offers continuing challenges and opportunities for changing roles and job functions.

The developmental model of experiential learning theory holds that specialization of learning style typifies early adulthood and that the role demands of career and family are likely to reinforce specialization. However, this pattern changes in midcareer. Specifically, as people mature, accentuation forces play a smaller role. To the contrary, the approach of the middle years brings with it a questioning of one's purposes and aspirations, a reassessment of life structure and direction. For many, choices made earlier have led down pathways no longer rewarding, and some kind of change is needed. At this point, many finally face up to the fact that they will never realize their youthful dreams and that new, more realistic goals must be found if life is to have purpose. Others, even if successful in their earlier pursuits, discover that they have purchased success in career at the expense of other responsibilities (such as to spouse and children) or other kinds of human fulfillment. Continued accentuation of an overspecialized version of oneself eventually becomes stultifying—one begins to feel stuck, static, in a rut. The vitality of earlier challenges is too easily replaced by routinized application of well-established solutions. In the absence of new and fresh challenges, creativity gives way to merely coping and going through the motions. Many careers plateau at this time, and one faces the prospect of drying up and stretching out the remaining years in tedium. Finding new directions for generativity is essential.

Perhaps it is inevitable that specialization precede integration in development, inevitable that youth be spent in a search for identity in the service of society, until in a last reach for wholeness we grasp that unified consciousness that has eluded us. As William Butler Yeats so eloquently put it, "Nothing can be sole and whole that has not been rent." For wholeness cannot be fully appreciated save in contrast to the experience of fragmentation, compartmentalization, and specialization. Kurt Lewin's observation that pulsation from differentiation to integration is the throb of the great engine of development is writ large as a universal social pattern of socialization.

Adaptive Flexibility and Integrative Development

There is considerable agreement among adult-development scholars that growth occurs through processes of differentiation and hierarchic integration and that the highest stages of development are characterized by personal integration and integrity. From the perspective of experiential learning theory, this goal is attained through a dialectic process of adaptation to the world. Fulfillment, or individuation, as Jung calls it, is accomplished by expression of nondominant modes of dealing with the world and their higher-level integration with specialized functions. With integrative development comes an increasing freedom from the dictates of immediate circumstance and the potential for creative response. This structural potential is expressed behaviorally by the individual's adaptive flexibility. As Werner put it:

> In general, the more differentiated and hierarchically organized the structure of an organism is, the more flexible its behavior. This means that if an activity is highly hierarchized, the organism, within a considerable range, can vary the activity to comply with the demands of the varying situation. [Werner, 1948, p. 55]

Adaptive flexibility and the mobility it provides are the primary vehicles of integrative development. They are the means by which people transcend the fixity of their specialized orientation. Fixity can be inferred from the intrinsic trend of any evolution toward an end stage of maximum stability. Such maximum stability, as the end stage of a developmental sequence, implies the closing of growth—the permanence, for instance, of specialized reaction patterns. But fixity would finally lead to rigidity of behavior if not counter-balanced by adaptive flexibility. As most generally conceived, adaptive flexibility implies "becoming" as opposed to "being."

Assessing Adaptive Flexibility: The Adaptive Style Inventory

One consequence of integrative development for those scientists who wish to predict and control human behavior is a certain amount of frustration, for with integrative development and its attendant adaptive flexibility comes increasing difficulty in the prediction of behavior. It is easy to predict behavior consequences in a low-level system (say, turning on a light switch) but far more difficult to predict behavior of higher-level systems capable of hierarchic integration (as with a computer). This problem is confounded when the attempt is made to characterize individuals as whole persons at a given stage of development. Developmental theorists have recognized this problem and attempted to deal with it in a number of ways—for example, by *ad hoc* concepts, as in Piaget's concept of horizontal *decalage* (variability in cognitive structure from task to task in a given time period; compare Flavell, 1963, p. 23) or by simply averaging this variability and thus ignoring it.[1]

Another approach to these measurement problems is to use the level of adaptive flexibility itself as an indicator of the level of integrative development. Thus, if people show

---

1. This averaging of stage variability is Loevinger's approach: "One must immediately admit that most samples of behavior, e.g., test protocols, contain evidence of functioning on diverse levels. . . . Nonetheless, the first step in bringing the concept within scientific compass is measurement. A probabilistic modification of the hierarchies model both accommodates the complexities and assimilates them to the requirements of measurement" (1966, p. 202).

systematic variability in their response to different environmental demands, we can infer a higher level of integrative development. To accomplish this assessment, however, requires that two conditions be met. First, a holistic system of environmental demands that samples the person's actual and potential life space is required. As Scott (1966) has pointed out, adaptive flexibility is meaningful only if there is some situation or circumstance being adapted to. Variability alone is not necessarily adaptive flexibility; it must be systemic variation in response to varying environmental demands. Second, the dimensions of personal-response flexibility and situation demand should be defined in commensurate terms. Flexibility of response should be measured along a dimension so that situation/person matches or mismatches can be identified that are related to the situation responded to. The theory of experiential learning provides a framework within which these conditions can be met. Toward this end, a modified version of the Learning Style Inventory called the Adaptive Style Inventory (ASI) was created. This instrument profiles the transactions between persons and their environment by providing them with a series of situations in the form of sentence stems (for example, "When I start to do something new"), which they complete by choosing between two responses, each response representing an adaptive mode (such as, "I rely on my feelings to guide me"—concrete experience; "I set priorities"—abstract conceptualization).

The ASI instrument is divided into four situations that the respondent must "adapt" to. These situations correspond to the four learning styles—divergent situations, assimilative situations, convergent situations, and accommodative situations. Each situation is characterized by two sentence stems, each with six pairs of response choices that present the four adaptive-mode responses in paired comparison fashion. The ASI thus yields an adaptive profile for the four different learning-style environments and an average adaptive profile across all four situations.

Responses to the ASI can be portrayed in a way that shows one's adaptive orientations as points on a two-dimensional learning space. One point represents average responses across all situations. It is achieved by noting scores on the abstract-concrete dimension (AC-CE) and scores on the active-reflective dimension (AE-RO) and plotting a point at the juncture of these two points on the learning grid (see Figure 8.1). The same procedure is followed to portray how the person responded in each of the four kinds of situations. Arrows are then drawn from the total score to each of the situational scores. These arrows indicate the direction of the person's response to each kind of situation. *The amount of adaptive flexibility from situation to situation is indicated by the length of the arrows.*

Figure 8.1 shows two sample responses to the ASI. Respondent A has a total score near the center of the grid, indicating a relative balance in the person's average adaptive style. The responses to each environmental press are consonant with the press in three of the four instances. The modal response to the diverger situations is heavily active and does not differ significantly from the total score on the abstract-concrete dimension. It could be said that this person responded to three situational presses—accommodator,

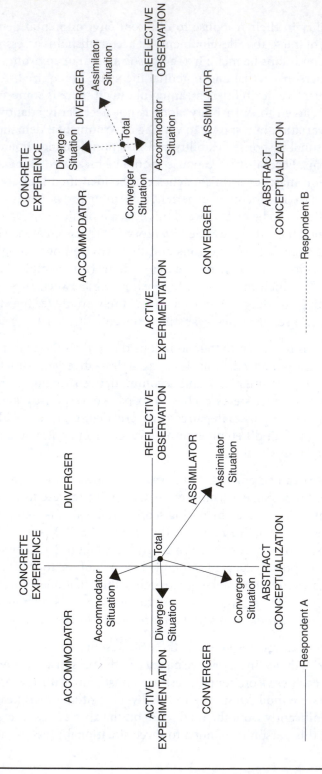

Figure 8.1 Sample Adaptive Style Inventory Scores

converger, assimilator—in terms consonant with those presses; that is, she responded to the situations by increasing emphasis on the adaptive modes "pulled for." However, in diverger situations, the respondent responded primarily in an active mode, acting against the press of the situation.

Respondent B, on the other hand, has a total score well within the diverger quadrant, indicating a tendency to respond to all situations in a concrete and reflective mode. Each of the situational presses was responded to in terms other than conformity to the press of the environment (relative to the total score), except in converger situations. In diverger situations, this person responds to very concrete ways but also responds in slightly more active ways.

The response to diverger situations would be interpreted as more consonant with accommodator situations. (Admittedly, the response in terms of the total grid is still in the diverger quadrant, which makes the response still consonant with the situational press. However, the reference point for each person is not the theoretical center of the grid, but his or her own total score.) In accommodator situations, the person responds in a more abstract way and in a somewhat reflective way, contrary to the accommodator situational press, which demands a concrete and active response. In assimilator situations, respondent B responded in a reflective way, as would be demanded by the situation, but also responded in a concrete way, which is contrary to the assimilator situational press. Finally, this respondent responded to converger situations in ways appropriate to the converger situational press.

To assess the level of adaptive flexibility quantitatively, formulas were devised to determine how much the respondent varied his or her adaptive orientation from situation to situation. Five such variables were created: concrete experience adaptive flexibility (CEAF), reflective observation adaptive flexibility (ROAF), abstract conceptualization adaptive flexibility (ACAF), active experimentation adaptive flexibility (AEAF), and total adaptive flexibility (TAF).[2] CEAF, for example, is the extent to which people vary their concrete experience orientation across the four situations. The total adaptive flexibility score (TAF) is the sum of CEAF, ROAF, ACAF, and AEAF. It should be noted that these scores do not take into account the direction of the person's adaptation to a given situational demand but simply the degree of variation in adaptive modes from situation to situation, since adaptive flexibility is composed of both movement toward the press of a situation and movement in other directions.

---

2. The specific formulas are reported in Kolb and Wolfe, 1981, pp. 117–118. Technical specifications for the ASI, including reliability and validity, are reported in the same publication, pp. 66–86. The study of adaptive flexibility and integrative development was done in collaboration with my friend and colleague, the late Glen Gish. In his life, he exemplified the ideals of integrative development of which we speak here.

The Relation between Adaptive Flexibility and Integrative Development

Armed with this ASI-based operational definition of adaptive flexibility, we can investigate the relation between adaptive flexibility and integrative development empirically. To do so, we studied three samples of midlife adults: a selected sample of 47 professional engineers and 23 professional social workers from the alumni study described in the last chapter, and a group of 39 midlife men and women of varying occupations who were participants in an intensive study of midlife adult development issues (see Kolb and Wolfe, 1981, for details). This latter group participated in an intensive series of self-assessment workshops over a three-year period, thus affording an in-depth assessment of their personalities and life situations.

Ego Development   One widely used measure of integrative development is Loevinger's Sentence Completion Instrument (Loevinger, 1976). In developing her model of the stages of adult ego development, Loevinger drew heavily on the work of Piaget, Kohlberg, and Perry, as well as the psychoanalytic school of ego psychology, most notably Erik Erikson. Scores on the Sentence Completion Test give an indication of a person's level of ego development as defined by her hierarchy of six ego-development stages—impulsive, self-protective, conformist, conscientious, autonomous, and integrated. As can be seen from Table 8.1, these stages are related to the six levels of adaptation defined in the experiential learning theory of development (see Table 6.1). In addition, Loevinger sees adaptive flexibility as a hallmark of development in her framework:

> Flexibility in the exchanges with the environment is no less an important property for survival. Because organisms are dependent on environments and open to them, and because environments can change, organisms need to adjust and accommodate, to substitute a new response for a once successful one. . . . The degree of flexibility . . . may be an indication of the organism's development. [Loevinger, 1976, p. 34]

For these reasons, we predicted a relationship between adaptive flexibility as measured by the ASI and a person's level of ego development. As a test for this relationship, the three samples of midlife adults were given the ASI and the Sentence Completion Instrument, which was scored according to instructions in the Loevinger test manual (Loevinger and Wessler, 1970). Most respondents scored in the middle range of Loevinger's scheme. There were no "impulsive" (level 1) or "self-protective" (level 2) people and no "integrated" (level 6) people in the sample. There was one "autonomous" person. Even with this restricted range of ego development, however, there was a significant positive relationship between total adaptive flexibility and ego-development level ($r = .26$, $p < .003$). Most of this covariation in adaptive flexibility occurred in reflective observation and abstract conceptualization (for instance, ego level with ROAF, $r = .20$, $p < .02$; with ACAF, $r = .22$, $p < .01$). To the extent that the ego-development measure is an indication of integrative development, we can conclude that the ASI measures of adaptive flexibility are also indicative of integrative development. A more detailed analysis of the data suggests, however, that the Loevinger instrument is perhaps more attuned to development of adaptive flexibility in the reflective and abstract adaptive modes than in the concrete and active orientation.

Self-direction Perhaps a more active indicator of integrative development is people's ability to direct their own lives, to be an "origin" rather than a "pawn" (deCharms, 1968) in their life activities. The self-assessment workshops conducted for the group of midlife adults allowed researchers to rate participants on how self-directed they were in their current life situations (see Crary, 1981, for details). The criterion used for these ratings was the extent to which a person's set of life contexts determined that person's behavior as opposed to the behavior's being controlled by the person.

The relationship between total adaptive flexibility and the person's degree of self-directedness was significantly positive ($r = .26, p < .05$) and, as might be predicted, determined primarily by adaptive flexibility in active experimentation (self-directedness with AEAF, $r = .28, p < .05$). This suggests that those at higher levels of integrative development as measured by the ASI are more self-directed and display that self-directedness through choiceful variation of their active behavior in different situations.

Cognitive Complexity in Relationships The experiential learning theory of development describes affective development in concrete experience as a process of increasing complexity in one's conception of personal relationships (see Table 6.1), resulting from integration of the four learning modes. Thus we would predict that increasing adaptive flexibility, particularly in the realm of concrete experience, would be associated with increased richness in construing one's interpersonal world. A major component of internal structural complexity is the constructions, as expressed in the words one uses, which can be called upon to describe and manipulate one's thoughts and interactions with the interpersonal environment. This notion was operationalized in the context of the self-assessment workshops. In the workshops, the midlife adults engaged in a number of exercises in which they portrayed the configuration of their life structures graphically and by analogy. During these exercises, the facilitating researchers noted the words each respondent used to describe his or her life structures. A list of each person's words was later presented to the respondent for verification as the person's own terminology. Each respondent had the opportunity to eliminate or add words in order to make the list truly representative of his or her set of constructs. The final list of constructs became the variable we are using here called "number of constructs."

As predicted, total adaptive flexibility was positively correlated with the total number of constructs a person used to describe his or her interpersonal world ($r = .25; p < .06$). This relationship was most significantly evidenced in the area of concrete experience (CEAF with number of constructs, $r = .28, p < .04$).

Table 8.1 Loevinger's Stages of Ego Development

Ego Level	Impulse Control/Character Development	Interpersonal Style	Conscious Preoccupation	Cognitive Style
I. Impulsive	Does not recognize rules Sees action as bad only if punished Impulsive Afraid of retaliation	Dependent and exploitative; dependence unconscious Treats people as sources of supply	Sex and aggression Bodily functions	Thinks in dichotomous way Has simple, global ideas Conceptually confused Thinks concretely Egocentric
II. Self-protective	Recognizes rules but obeys for immediate advantage Has expedient morality: action is bad if person is caught Blames others; does not see self as responsible for failure or trouble	Manipulative and exploitative Wary and distrusting of others' intentions Opportunistic Zero-sum: I win, you lose Shameless; shows little remorse	Self-protection Gaining control and advantage, dominating Getting the better of others, deceiving them Fear of being dominated, controlled, or deceived by others	As above
III. Conformist	Partially internalizes rules; obeys without question Feels shame for consequences Concerned with "shoulds" Morally condemns others' views Denies sexual and aggressive feelings	Wants to belong to group, to gain social acceptance Feels mutual trust within in-group, prejudice against out-groups Has pleasing social personality: superficial niceness, helpfulness	Appearances Social acceptance and adjustment to group norms Status symbols, material possessions, reputation, and prestige	Thinks stereotypically Uses clichés Sees in terms of superlatives Has sentimental mentality Has little introspection: references to inner feelings are banal and stereotyped

IV. Conscientious	Standards self-evaluated, morality internalized Self-critical, tendency to be hypercritical Feels guilt for consequences	Has sense of responsibility, obligation Has mutual, intensive relationships Concerned with communication, expression of differentiated feelings	Achievement of long-term goals, as measured by inner standards Attaining ideals Motivation, reasons for behavior Self: feelings, traits	Conceptually complex Has sense of consequences, priorities Aware of contingencies, perceives alternatives Sees self in context of community, society
V. Autonomous	Add: [a]Behavior an expression of moral principle Tolerates multiplicity of viewpoints Concerned with conflicting duties, roles, principles Spontaneous, creative	Add: [a]Wants autonomy in relations Sees relations as involving inevitable mutual interdependence Tolerates others' solutions of conflict Respects others' autonomy Open	Individuality and self-fulfillment Conflicting inner needs	Has greater conceptual complexity Tolerates ambiguity Has capacity to see paradox, contradictions Has broad scope of thought (time frame, social context) Perceives human interdependence
VI. Integrated	Add: [a]Reconciles inner conflicts and conflicting external demands Renounces the unattainable Concerned with justice	Add: [a]Cherishes individuality	Add: [a]Integrated sense of unique identity "Precious life's work" as inevitable simultaneous expression of self, principle, and one's humanity	Add: [a]Has sense of self as part of flow of human condition

[a] "Add" means add to the description applying to the previous level.
Source: Adapted from Jane Loevinger, *Ego Development* (San Francisco: Jossey Bass, 1976)

Taken together, the results above suggest that overall adaptive flexibility and adaptive flexibility in the four adaptive modes are meaningful indicators of integrative development. Total adaptive flexibility as measured by the ASI is significantly related to the level of ego development, to self-direction, and to the complexity of one's interpersonal constructs. Ego development, at least as it is measured in the Loevinger model, is most strongly associated with adaptive flexibility in reflection and conceptualization, reflecting the development and manipulation of internalized hierarchical structures for construing the world that characterizes higher levels of cognitive and ego development. Increased self-direction is more associated with flexibility in behavioral actions, and richness in one's constructs about the interpersonal world is associated most strongly with flexibility in concrete experiencing. These results, although limited to one sample, are promising, for they offer a measure of integrative development via the ASI that is sensitive both to development as a unitary process and to specialized development in different adaptive modes.

The Integrated Life Style

What can be said of the nature of the integrated life? How do people cope with the integrative challenges of adult life, and what can we learn from their example? Further results from our ASI study of adaptive flexibility, along with the case-by-case examination of the individual lives in our study of midlife adults, suggest some important characteristics of the integrated lifestyle.

Proactive Adaptation   First, integrated people both adapt to and create their life structures. Their relationship with the world and others around them is transactional, in that they are proactive in the creation of their life tasks and situations and are shaped and molded by these situations as well. Paulo Freire describes this integrative stance toward one's life context as follows:

> *Integration with one's context, as* distinguished from *adaptation*, is a distinctively human activity. Integration results from the capacity to adapt oneself to reality *plus* the critical capacity to make choices and to transform that reality. To the extent that man loses his ability to make choices and is subjected to the choices of others, to the extent that his decisions are no longer his own because they result from external prescriptions, he is no longer integrated. Rather, he has adapted. He has "adjusted." Unpliant men, with a revolutionary spirit, are often termed "maladjusted."

> The integrated person is person as *subject*. In contrast, the adaptive person is person as *object,* adaptation representing at most a weak form of self-defense. If man is incapable of changing reality, he adjusts himself instead. Adaptation is behavior characteristic of the animal sphere; exhibited by man, it is symptomatic of his dehumanization. Throughout history men have attempted to overcome

the factors which make them accommodate or adjust, in a struggle—constantly threatened by oppression—to attain their full humanity.

As men related to the world by responding to the challenges of the environment, they began to dynamize, to master, and to humanize reality. They add to it something of their own making, by giving temporal meaning to geographic space, by creating culture. This interplay of men's relations with the world and with their fellows does not (except in cases of repressive power) permit societal or cultural immobility. As men create, re-create, and decide, historical epochs begin to take shape. And it is by creating, re-creating, and deciding that *men should participate* in these epochs. [Freire, 1973, pp. 3–4]

We found tantalizing suggestions of this proactive stance among integrated people when we examined the ASI adaptive flexibility scores of low- and high-ego-development people in our samples of adult professionals and midlife persons. Low-ego-development people, as we have already seen, showed less flexibility and variation from situation to situation. In addition, a case-by-case examination suggests that most of this variation was toward the press of the situation, such as becoming more active and concrete in accommodative situations or more abstract and reflective in assimilative situations. This pattern is suggestive of adjustment, or what Freire calls adaptation. High-ego-development people, on the other hand, showed greater variation, and much of this variation was counter to the press of the situation, such as responding reflectively in active situations or concretely in abstract situations. Here it appears that integrated people respond more creatively to situations supplying perspectives that from a holistic-learning point of view are missing. Thus, high-ego-development persons may respond to the abstract task of understanding the basic principles of something by seeking and exploring concrete examples, or they may deal with an active task such as completing a task on time by reflectively creating a plan.

This integrated response produces a creative tension between the person and his or her life situations, a tension that may in fact be essential for the creative response that integrative development engenders. Howard Gruber describes the importance of being one's own person in the creative process:

This obligation to move back and forth between radically different perspectives produces a deep tension in every creative life. In the course of ordinary development similar tensions begin to appear. What we mean by such terms as *adaptation* and *adjustment* is the resolution of these tensions. But that is not the path of the creative person. He or she must safeguard the distance and the specialness, live with the tension. [Feldman, 1980, p. 180]

Rich Life Structures   A second characteristic of the integrated life style is seen in the life structures of integrated people. The life structures of integrated persons mirror the integrative complexity of their personalities. It was Kurt Lewin (1951) who first noted the isomorphism between the person's development level and the level of complexity of his or her life space. When we examine the life structures of those who score high on the ASI measures of adaptive flexibility, we see complex, flexible, and highly differentiated life structures. These people experience their lives in ways that bring variety and richness to them and the environment. They engage with their environments by flexibly moving within those environments, by creating highly differentiated life spaces and relationships, and by building networks of relationships and contexts. Marcy Crary has defined these dimensions thus:

> Some people lead lives with a great deal of freedom of movement and variation in involvement within their different contexts. Either through their own person and/or the nature of the contexts they engage within, there is an appearance of a great deal of flexibility in their life structures. The contrasting lifestyle is one in which there is much routine, pre-arranged structuring of day-to-day events, likely leading to much repetition of events, activities, relationships within each of the person's contexts. Low rating on this scale would likely imply a higher degree of role-bounded situations and involvements. A high rating implies a relatively greater amount of "spontaneous" living. [Crary, 1979, p. 20]

A related dimension is that of differentiation within a person's life space. Crary states:

> This dimension relates to the degree of heterogeneity of contexts within a person's life-space. A life-space which is differentiated is multifaceted, containing a variety of components or regions within its boundaries. . . . Applied to the life-space as a whole (within and across contexts) the low end of the scale denotes a life space in which not one of the contexts seem to stand apart from the others in terms of the person's experience of them. The high rating refers to a life style in which the person clearly experiences variation and contrasts within and across their different contexts. [Crary, 1979, p. 10]

When Crary's ratings on these dimensions of life structure were correlated with adaptive-flexibility scores, significant relationships emerged. Flexible life structures were significantly associated with the integrated adaptively flexible people (TAF with flexibility in life structure, $r = .36$, $p < .01$; for AEAF, $r = .41$, $p < .005$; for ACAF, $r = .37$, $p < .01$; N.S. for ROAF and CEAF). Differentiation in life structure was also associated with adaptive flexibility (TAF with differentiation in life structure, $r = .35$, $p < .01$; for AEAF, $r = .34$, $p < .02$; for ACAF, $r = .40$, $p < .005$; for ROAF, $r = .30$, $p < .03$; N.S. for CEAF). The integrated person seems capable of constructing a rich, complex, and flexible life space that sustains him or her and provides new opportunities for growth.

Conflict   A key to the ability to manage complexity lies in a final characteristic of the integrated lifestyle identified in our research—harmony, the constructive management of conflict. We found in our sample of midlife adults no significant difference overall between high-adaptive-flexibility and low-adaptive-flexibility people in the amount of stress and change they had to cope with in their lives. Yet when we measured the amount of conflict these people experienced in their lives, the adaptively flexible, integrated persons experienced much less conflict than those with low adaptive flexibility. A panel of researchers evaluated each respondent on a number of dimensions, including the degree of conflict. Conflict was defined as the extent of "incompatibilities, force and counter-force" (Crary, 1979) a person experiences among the various settings in his or her life, without regard to the number or complexity of the relationships among these settings. This rating was based on various exercises that respondents completed in the self-assessment workshops. These exercises served to portray the respondents' life space, their relationships with others, and a longitudinal view of their past and possible future.

When this rating was correlated with ASI adaptive-flexibility scores, high adaptive flexibility was associated with low conflict. (TAF with degree of conflict, $r = -.34$, $p < .02$; for AEAF, $r = -.30$, $p < .03$; for ACAF, $r = -.24$, $p < .06$; for CEAF, $r = -.27$, $p < .05$; N.S. for ROAF.) Further analysis, controlling for the amount of conflict in each individual life structure, showed that adaptively flexible people experienced the least stress in their lives in spite of the fact that their life structures, as we have seen, are the most complex. This harmony in life structure occurred in the context of the more balanced life structure that characterized most of those in our midlife sample (Kolb and Wolfe, 1981). Early in their lives, people have life structures that are heavily oriented around work (mainly for men) or family (for women). At midlife comes more balance in life investment, a balance that may be the foundation for the harmony and lower conflict in the lives of integrated people.

On Integrity and Integrative Knowledge

The pinnacle of development is integrity. It is that highest level of human functioning that we strive consciously and even unconsciously, perhaps automatically, to reach. The motivation to achieve integrity is a profound gift of humanity—a desire to reach out, understand, become, and grow, a pervasive motivation for mastery that Robert White has called motivation for competence. The *Random House Dictionary of the English Language* (Stein, 1966) offers three definitions of integrity: "1. soundness of and adherence to moral principle and character . . . ; 2. the state of being whole, entire, or undiminished . . . ; 3. sound, unimpaired, or perfect condition" (p. 738). All these usages of the term are essential to define the concept as it is used here, but Warren Bennis's definition of integrity is perhaps more instructive of its meaning for the theory of experiential learning:

> Integrity. Integration. The integral personality. Such permutations are permissible plays on the word, which shares roots with integer, the untouchable (in and tanger) whole number which links the most abstract of endeavors, mathematics, to the human condition. I am talking about the kind of unity—of purpose, goals, ideas, and communication—that makes three musketeers, Three Musketeers.

It's a merging of identities and resolves into a coherent and effective whole. [Bennis, 1981–82, p. 4]

In the theory of experiential learning, integrity is a sophisticated, integrated process of learning, of knowing. It is not primarily a set of character traits such as honesty, consistency, or morality. These traits are only probable behavioral derivations of the integrated judgments that flow from integrated learning. Honesty, consistency, and morality are usually, but not always, the result of integrated learning. One need only reflect on the "immoral" behavior of men like Copernicus and Galileo to realize that integrity is the learning process by which intellectual, moral, and ethical standards are *created*, not some evaluation based on current moral standards and worldviews.

It is misleading to confuse these products of integrity, absolute and reasonable as they appear, with the process that creates them, for creators precede their creations in time and must create with no fixed absolutes to guide them. Integrity as a way of knowing embraces the future and the unknown as well as the codified conventions of social knowledge that are, by their nature, historical record. The prime function of integrity and integrative knowledge is to stand at the interface between social knowledge and the ever-novel predicaments and dilemmas we find ourselves in; its goal is to guide us through these straits in such a way that we not only survive, but perhaps can make some new contribution to the data bank of social knowledge for generations to come.

The knowledge structure of integrity does not comform to any one of the four knowledge structures identified in Chapter 5; it is usually some integrative synthesis of these in the emergent historical moment. As such, integrative knowing is essentially eclectic, if by the term is meant, "not consistent with current forms." It stands with one foot on the shore of the conventions of social knowledge and one foot in the canoe of an emergent future— a most uncomfortable and taxing position, one that positively demands commitment to either forging ahead or jumping back to safety. Stephen Pepper proposes the following guidelines for a reasonable eclecticism:

> In practice, therefore, we shall want to be not rational but reasonable, and to seek, on the matter in question, the judgment supplied from each of these relatively adequate world theories. If there is some difference of judgment, we shall wish to make our decision with all these modes of evidence in mind, just as we should make any other decision where the evidence is conflicting. In this way we should be judging in the most reasonable way possible—not dogmatically following only one line of evidence, not perversely ignoring evidence, but sensibly acting on all the evidence available. [Pepper, 1942, pp. 330–331]

Thus, in integrative learning, knowledge is refined by viewing predicaments through the dialectically opposed lenses of the four basic knowledge structures and then "acting sensibly."

The way in which this process is carried out is in many ways the topic of Pepper's last book, *Concept and Quality*. Here, Pepper proposes a fifth world hypothesis for integrative learning—selectivism—with the root metaphor purposive act. For it is in a single act of purpose that the psychological world of feeling, thought, and desire ("I want that goal") and the physical world (myself and the world as physical/chemical substances) are integrated, that value and fact, quality and concept, are fused. It is here that goal meets reality, "ought" meets "is." Selectivism as a world hypothesis turns out to be very much like contextualism or modern-day pragmatism in its emphasis on novelty and uncertainty as the basic adaptive problem facing the human species. The basic paradigm of selectivism is one where, seeking goals as judgments of value, we pursue realities based on judgments of fact. Reality in this paradigm is "what pushes back," to use E. A. Singer's (1959) apt phrase. Reality allows our conceptions of it, it does not cause them. Von Glasersfeld describes the selectivist paradigm thus:

> Roughly speaking, concepts, theories, and cognitive structures in general are viable and survive as long as they serve the purposes to which we put them. . . .
>
> If we accept this concept of viability, it becomes clear that it would be absurd to maintain that our knowledge is in any sense a replica or picture of reality. . . . [W] hile we can know when a theory or model knocks against the constraints of our experiential world, the fact that it does not knock against them but "gets by" and is still viable, does in no way justify the belief that the theory or model therefore depicts a "real" world. . . .
>
> [W]e must never say that our knowledge is "pure" in the sense that it reflects an ontologically real world. Knowledge neither should nor could have such a function. The fact that some construct has for some time survived experience—or experiments for that matter—means that up to that point it was viable in that it bypassed the constraints that are inherent in the range of experience within which we were operating. But viability does not imply uniqueness, because there may be innumerable other constructs that would have been as viable as the one we created. [von Glasersfeld, 1977, pp. 7–14]

An important implication of this constructionist view of reality is that theories are always combinations of value and fact, since it is value judgments that determine which aspects of reality are selected to be explored and how that exploration will take place. As a result, a primary dialectic that must be resolved in integrative knowledge is that of value and fact. Integrity requires the thoughtful articulation of value judgments as well as the scientific judgment of fact. The essential character of this dialectic integration is one of valuing via apprehension and creating facts via comprehension. The sense in which civilization is a race between such integrated learning and chaos is captured beautifully in Hegel's image of the owl of Minerva, the symbol of wisdom, beginning its flight just as darkness threatens.

> To say one more word about preaching what the world ought to be like, philosophy always arrives too late for that. As thought of the world it appears at a time when actuality has completed its developmental process and is finished. What the conception teaches history also shows as necessary, namely, that only in a maturing actuality the ideal appears and confronts the real. It is then that the ideal rebuilds for itself this same world in the shape of an intellectual realm, comprehending this world in its substance. When philosophy paints its gray in gray, a form of life has become old, and this gray in gray cannot rejuvenate it, only understand it. The owl of Minerva begins its flight when dusk is falling. [Hegel, 1820]

Integrity requires that we learn to speak unselfconsciously about values in matters of fact. We need to develop, in the arena of values, inquiry methods that are as sophisticated and powerful as the methods of science have been in matters of fact.

No less significant for the attainment of integrative knowledge is the resolution of the dialectic between relevance and meaning. Western industrial societies have nearly run amok in their embrace of the extroverted materialism of relevance, ignoring and even actively denying the meaning of religious, humanistic, and spiritual ideals. Cast adrift from any meaningful connection with relevant work in the material world, internal lives can become wastelands of existential *angst* or sensual hedonism. The challenge of integrative knowledge, here, is to reimbue the pragmatic short-term choices and judgments that have given us polluted air and water, the threat of instant nuclear annihilation, the creation of a permanent underclass, and other such harmful side effects of our particular form of technological civilization, with the long-range perspective of meaning that arises from reflection on the human condition and the history of civilization. What we need is a theory of intentional action to guide us through these choices, to lay bare the plan whereby humanity has made these judgments in the past, and to suggest new "rules" for current circumstances.

In resolving the dialectic conflicts between value and fact, meaning and relevance, integrity is the master virtue. In a way that is similar to the identification of learning styles we can see in typical resolutions of these two dialectics, more specialized virtues (see Figure 8.2) whose primary function is to preserve and protect one pole of each dialectic: wisdom, the protector of fact and meaning; justice, the protector of fact and relevance; courage, the protector of relevance and value; and love, the protector of value and meaning. These specialized virtues are counterpress behavioral injunctions: they instruct us to act against the demand characteristic of life situations, to *create,* not adjust. Wisdom dictates that we do not blindly follow the implications of knowledge but that we be choicefully responsible in the use of knowledge. Courage tells us to push forward when circumstance signals danger and retreat. Love requires that we hold our selfish acts in check until we have viewed the situation from the perspective of the other—the Golden Rule. And justice demands fair and equitable treatment for all against the expedience of the special situation.

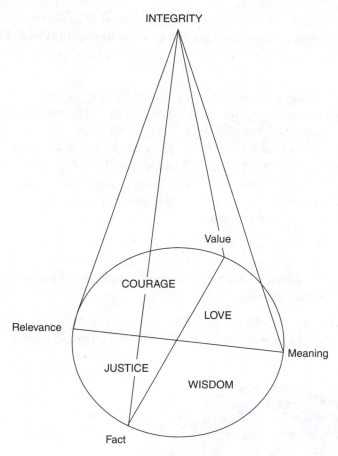

INTEGRITY

Value

COURAGE

LOVE

Relevance

Meaning

JUSTICE

WISDOM

Fact

Figure 8.2 Integrity as the Master Virtue Integrating Value and Fact, Meaning and Relevance, and the Specialized Virtues of Courage, Love, Wisdom, and Justice

The late Niels Bohr once remarked that his interest in complementarity in physics had been stimulated by the thought that one cannot know another human being at the same time in the light of love and in the light of justice. Thus, the specialized virtues have a bias in favor of the dialectic poles they protect. It remains for integrity and integrated knowing to rise above these biases for the truly integrated judgment.

The Experience of Integrity—The Mandala Symbol

The experience of integrity and the characteristics of integrated knowing can be illustrated by the structure of the symbol that has represented them throughout the history of humanity. The mandala symbol is the most important symbol in the Jungian panoply of the symbols and archetypes that populate the human psyche. This symbol of wholeness, unity, and integrity is to be found in most of the world's religions—the Christian cross, the star of David, and the intertwined fishes of *yin* and *yang*. Its value as a tool for meditation is renowned, producing a timeless centering of consciousness in which "you unify the world, you are the world itself, and you are unified by the world." Jung (1931) collected examples of the mandala symbol from paleolithic to modern times, from Eastern religions to Western art and literature. He saw in these symbols the characteristics of individuation, of integrity.

Mandala means a circle, especially a magic circle, signifying the integrity of experience, an eternal process where endings become beginnings again and again. "The mandala form is that of a flower, cross or wheel with a distinct tendency towards quadripartite structures" (Jung, 1931, p. 100). The typical four-part structure of the mandala often represents dual polarities, as in the Tibetan Buddhist Tantric mandala shown here (Figure 8.3). Here, double *dorjes* (*dorje* = "thunderbolt" of knowledge that cuts through confusion with penetrating wisdom) form a cross representing the interconnection of the earth realm (matter) and the realm of heaven (spirit).

It is the integration of these polarities that fuels the endless circular process of knowing. "Psychologically this circulation would be the 'turning in a circle around oneself'; whereby, obviously, all sides of the personality become involved. They cause the poles of light and darkness to rotate. . . ." (1931, p. 104).

The product of this dialectic circulation process is a centering of one's experience. "The mandala symbol is not only a means of expression but works an effect. It reacts upon

Figure 8.3   Tibetan Buddhist Tantric Symbol

its maker. . . . [By meditating on it] the attention or, better said, the interest, is brought back to an inner sacred domain, which is the source and goal of the soul. . . ." [1931, pp. 102–103]. Warren Bennis, in his recent study of effective leaders in all walks of life, has noted that this "centeredness" is a common trait among many of them (1980, p. 20). With centering comes the experience of transcendence, the conscious experience of hierarchic integration where what was before our whole world is transformed into but one of a multidimensional array of worlds to experience. In interviewing the associates of people who are perceived to "have integrity," I have been struck by the awe in which their integrative judgments are held; judgments that, like Solomon's decision to cut the baby in half, appear to rise above the confines of justice to include love; judgments that are seen as not only wise but courageous. The capacity for such integrated judgment seems to be borne out of transcendence, wherein the conflicts that those of us at lower levels of insight perceive as win-lose are recast into a higher form that can make everyone a winner, or can make winning and losing irrelevant. And finally, with centering comes commitment in the integration of abstract ideals in the concrete here-and-now of one's life. When we act from our center, the place of truth within us, action is based on the fusion of value and fact, meaning and relevance, and hence is totally committed. Only by personal commitment to the here-and-now of one's life situation, fully accepting one's past and taking choiceful responsibility for one's future, is the dialectic conflict necessary for learning experienced. The dawn of integrity comes with the acceptance of responsibility for the course of one's own life. For in taking responsibility for the world, we are given back the power to change it.

Update and Reflections

Lifelong Learning and the Learning Way

> "For he had learned some of the things that everyman must find out for himself, and he had found out about them as one has to find out, through errors and through trial, through fantasy and delusion, through falsehood and his own damn foolishness, through being mistaken and wrong and an idiot and egotistical and aspiring and hopeful and believing and confused. As he lay there he had gone back over his life, and bit by bit, had extracted from it some of the hard lessons of experience. Each thing he learned was so simple and so obvious once he grasped it, that he wondered why he had not always known it. . . . Altogether, they wove into a kind of leading thread, trailing backward through his past and out into the future. And he thought now, perhaps he could begin to shape his

life to mastery, for he felt a sense of new direction deep within him, but whither it would take him he could not say."

—Thomas Wolfe, *You Can't Go Home Again*

When I was doing the research for *Experiential Learning*, I was aided immensely by our Organization Behavior Department's project on Lifelong Learning and Development funded by two large grants from the Spencer Foundation (Wolfe and Kolb, 1980) and the National Institute for Education (Kolb and Wolfe, 1981) aimed at increasing understanding of two topics that sparked a lot of national attention at the time: lifelong learning and adult development. Since then "lifelong learning" has steadily moved from an inspiring aspiration to a necessary reality. The transformative global, social, economic, and technological conditions that were envisioned over forty years ago have come to fruition in a way that requires a fundamental rethinking of the relationship between learning and education. From a front-loaded, system-driven educational structure dominated by classroom learning, we are in the process of transitioning to a new reality where individual learners are becoming more responsible for the direction of their own learning in a multitude of learning environments that span their lifetime. This transition parallels other self-direction requirements that have been placed on individuals by the emergence of the global economy such as responsibility for one's own retirement planning and health care. Aspin and Chapman (2000) in their review of these developments identify what they call the triadic nature of lifelong learning encompassing three areas with different learning needs—learning for economic progress and development, learning for personal development and fulfilment, and learning for the development of a just and thriving democracy. The challenge of lifelong learning is not just about learning new marketable skills in an ever-changing economy. It is about the whole person and their personal development in their many roles as family member, citizen, and worker.

The solution is not a world of self-taught autodidacts. Social institutions, government policy makers, and educators face fundamental changes to support lifelong learners. While the individual is primarily responsible for his or her learning, it must happen in an interdependent relationship with others. Hinchcliffe, in his critical rethinking of lifelong learning, describes the situation thusly, "For in embracing the concept of lifelong learning one also embraces a whole pedagogy: one cannot have a lifelong learner without bringing in the associated features of the reflective learner, teaching through facilitation, the emphasis on the transferability of learning and the importance of self-direction and self-management. One cannot be a lifelong learner unless one absorbs a whole discourse of pedagogy. . . a person has to live a whole ideology so that one must 'acquire the self-image of a lifelong learner'" (2006, p. 97). In his rethinking, he emphasizes the organic learner who is an interdependent actor, a becoming self immersed in the contextual world of practices. He emphasizes "the activity-based nature of learning which is experiential, collaborative, and often activated by individual learners rather than trainers or teachers" (2006, p. 99). Su adds the importance of a "being" versus "having" approach to lifelong learning: "The ability that a lifelong learner is expected to demonstrate changes from a focus on how much 'static' knowledge one *has* to the development of a dynamic ability to make sense of knowledge in order to *be* within change. This dynamic ability, which insists on human agency, and thereby on the possibility of flexibility, serves as the foundation for the transformation and development of adult learners into lifelong learners" (Su, 2011, p. 58). Peter Vaill in *Learning as a Way of Being* (1996) makes a similar point stressing the importance of approaching the turbulent change of an emerging world of "permanent white water" with a beginner's mind.

The Learning Way

Experiential learning theory provides a framework for such a program for the lifelong learner; helping learners understand and adapt to these new circumstances through deliberate experiential learning (Passarelli and Kolb, 2011). Learning can have magical transformative powers. It opens new doors and pathways, expanding our world and capabilities. It literally can change who we are by creating new professional and personal identities. Learning is intrinsically rewarding and empowering, bringing new avenues of experience and new realms of mastery. In a very real sense, you are what you learn.

The learning way is about approaching life experiences with a learning attitude. It involves a deep trust in one's own experience and a healthy skepticism about received knowledge. It requires the perspective of quiet reflection and a passionate commitment to action in the face of uncertainty. The learning way is not the easiest way to approach life, but in the long run, it is the wisest. Other ways of living tempt us with immediate gratification at our peril. The way of dogma, the way of denial, the way of addiction, the way of submission, and the way of habit; all offer relief from uncertainty and pain at the cost of entrapment on a path that winds out of our control. The learning way requires deliberate effort to create new knowledge in the face of uncertainty and failure, but opens the way to new, broader, and deeper horizons of experience.

The Learning Way Is a Way of Experiencing   It is a way of being present with the world in the way it is, a way of becoming through being. Opening oneself to experience is necessary for learning and renewal. James March described experience as ambiguous, while William James saw pure experience as having infinite depth, mysterious and even spiritual. The first three quarters of the learning cycle from experiencing to acting all happens in our heads. The last quarter, from after we act to the ensuing experiences, happens in what we naively call "the real world." Here there is novelty, uncertainty, pain and joy, unexpected consequences, and wonderful surprises. D. H. Lawrence describes it as "Terra Incognita":

There are vast realms of consciousness still undreamed of
vast ranges of experience, like the humming of unseen harps,
we know nothing of, within us.
Oh when man escaped from the barbed wire entanglement
of his own ideas and his own mechanical devices
there is a marvellous rich world of contact and sheer fluid beauty
and fearless face-to-face awareness of now-naked life
and me, and you, and other men and women
and grapes, and ghouls, and ghosts and green moonlight
and ruddy-orange limbs stirring the limbo
of the unknown air, and eyes so soft
softer than the space between the stars.
And all things, and nothing, and being and not-being
alternately palpitant,
when at last we escape the barbed-wire enclosure
of Know Thyself, knowing we can never know,
we can but touch, and wonder, and ponder, and make our effort
and dangle in a last fastidious fine delight
as the fuchsia does, dangling her reckless drop
of purpose after so much putting forth
and slow mounting marvel of a little tree. (Lawrence, 1920, p. 1)

Ideally we would live each successive life experience fully—present and aware in the moment, taking it in fully. Yet, many of us live our daily lives making little or no conscious effort to learn from our experiences. While research in many areas has shown that experience alone does not produce much learning, many tend to assume that effective learning happens automatically and give little thought to how they learn or how they might improve their learning capability. Research on automaticity described earlier suggests that many of the activities of our daily lives are conducted on "automatic pilot" without conscious awareness and intention (Bargh and Chartrand, 1999). When I first read about the Theraveda Buddhism concept of moment experiencing as a string of pearls and Kahneman's (Kahneman and Riis, 2005) estimate that we have 20,000 such moments every day, accumulating a half billion moments in 70 years, my spontaneous reaction was, "Wow, I have sure missed a lot in my life!" (Chapter 4 Update and Reflections, pp. 138–139)

The Learning Way Is the Way of Self-Creation   Looking back, your life can be seen as a succession of these experiences, some of which you created for yourself and some that were thrust upon you. These life events are strung together like beads on a string defining that remarkable continuity that determines who you are. Looking forward to the future, the beads are only dreams and distant visions of future experiences. Your experience in *this* present moment is all that actually exists. In it you are fashioning a bead of meaning for the past and choosing the next experience ahead. The next experience offers new potentialities for meaning and choice, and so on in a lifelong process of self-creation and learning. As Oprah Winfrey has said, "With every experience, you alone are painting your own canvas, thought by thought, choice by choice."

The learning way is about awakening the learning life force that lies within all of us. It is a power that we share with all living things, *autopoeisis,* the power of self-making. To open oneself and receive this life energy conveys magical powers of self-transformation. Learning from conscious experience is the highest form of the learning life force. Every human invention and achievement is the result of this process. In some spiritual traditions we humans are thought to be basically "asleep"; going through this process in a semi-conscious way, strangely disengaged from our own lives. The learning way is about awakening to attend consciously to our experience and deliberately choose how it influences our beliefs and how we will live our lives. The spiral of learning from experience is the process through which we consciously choose, direct, and control life experiences. By placing conscious experience at the center of the learning process we can literally create ourselves through learning.

The Learning Way Is a Way of Humility   In the face of the infinite depth and breadth of experience one cannot help but be humbled by our limited partaking of it, drinking from the ocean of experience teacup by teacup, recognizing that our previous conceptions must always be tested by new emerging realities and a desire to learn. Humility is characterized by open-mindedness, a willingness to make mistakes and seek advice (Tangney, 2000). The humble way eschews self-preoccupation and is a process of becoming "unselved" (Templeton, 1997); recognizing our place as one of our 6 billion fellow humans on this small planet in the wider universe.

The Learning Way Is a Moral Way   This last chapter of *Experiential Learning* describes integration and integrity as the culmination of the lifelong process of learning from experience, uniting the virtues of love, justice, courage, and wisdom. Critics have described experiential learning as a self-centered liberal humanism unconcerned about others: "Underneath the avowal that community is indispensable is a longing for a unitary, authentic self, untouched by the demands of human mutuality. . . . Experiential learning encourages psychic growth by freeing us from the oppression of other people's choices" (Michelson, 1999, p. 140). Yet empathy, the deep experiencing of others, must be the motivational source of the emotional compassion that drives the imperative to act morally with others. I have already described (Chapter 6 Update and Reflections) Rogers' theory that morality emerges from the deep experiencing of the human being. It is an inside-out process rather than the outside-in prescription from the imposition of an external moral system or dogma. The experiential learning theory way suggests that abstract moral principles must be integrated into the experience and context of the person in order to guide moral action.

Deliberate Experiential Learning

This process of experiencing with awareness to create meaning and make choices is what we call deliberate experiential learning. Deliberate learning requires mastery of experiential learning, or more particularly, it requires a personal understanding of one's unique way of learning from experience and the ability to intentionally direct and control one's learning. In short, one needs to be in charge of their learning to be in charge of their life. We have identified five metacognitive practices that can awaken and enhance the power of learning that lies within (Kolb and Kolb, 2009; Passarelli and Kolb, 2011; Kolb and Yeganeh, 2015). The five areas of metacognitive regulation are: learning identity, learning spaces, learning relationships, mindful experiencing, and deliberate practice (see Figure 8.4).

Metacognition—The Key to Deliberate Learning

Deliberate experiential learning requires individual conscious metacognitive control of the learning process that enables monitoring and selecting learning approaches that work best in different learning situations. James Zull described metacognition as the culmination of the journey from brain to mind—the mind's ability to reflect on itself and control its own process. "In many ways, a learner's awareness and insight about development of her own mind is the ultimate and most powerful objective of education; not just thinking, but thinking about thinking. It is when our mind begins to comprehend itself that we can say we are making progress. This ability may be the highest and most complex mental

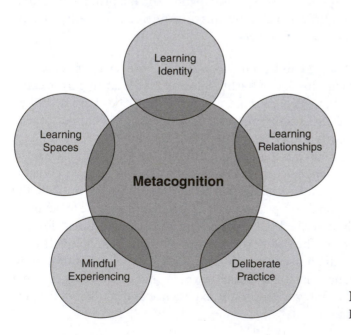

Figure 8.4 The Practices of Deliberate Learning

capability of the human brain. It is the thread that weaves back and forth through the cloth of the mind. . . . Gaining a metacognitive state of mind offers greater possibilities for experiencing the joy of learning than, perhaps, any of the other objectives or goals discussed so far" (2011, Chapter 10).

The concept of metacognition originated in the work of William James in his examination of the role of attention in experience and his ideomotor theory of action described in his two-volume magnum opus, *The Principles of Psychology* (1890). For James, attention plays its focus "like a spotlight" across the field of consciousness in a way that is sometimes involuntary, as when a bright light or loud noise "captures" our attention, but often voluntary. Voluntary attention is determined by one's interest in the object of attention. He defines a spiral of interest-attention-selection that creates a continuous ongoing flow of experience summarized in the pithy statement—"My experience is what I agree to attend to" (1890, p. 403). He defines interest as an "intelligible perspective" that directs attention and ultimately selection of some experiences over others. Selection feeds back to refine and integrate a person's intelligible perspective, serving as "the very keel on which our mental ship is built" (James cited in Leary 1992, p. 157). In his chapter on will, James developed a theory of intentional action which is essential for any metacognitive knowledge to be useful in improving one's learning ability. His ideomotor action theory states that an idea firmly focused in consciousness will automatically issue forth into behavior—"Every representation of a movement awakens in some degree the actual movement which is the object; and awakens it in a maximum degree whenever it is not kept from so doing by an antagonistic representation present simultaneously to the mind" (James, 1890, p. 526).

Flavell (1979) re-introduced the concept of metacognition in contemporary psychology, dividing metacognitive knowledge into three sub-categories: (1) knowledge of person variables referring to general knowledge about how human beings learn and process information, as well as individual knowledge of one's own learning processes; (2) task variables including knowledge about the nature of the task and what it will require of the individual; (3) knowledge about strategy variables including knowledge about ways to improve learning as well as conditional knowledge about when and where it is appropriate to use such strategies. Until recently, research on metacognitive learning has explored the influence of only relatively simple models of learning. For example, a study of fifth grader self-paced learning of stories found that the best students spent more time studying difficult versus easy stories, while there was no difference in study times for the poorer students. The findings suggest that the poorer students lacked a metacognitive model that dictated a strategy of spending more time on difficult learning tasks (Owings, Peterson, Bransford, Morris, and Stein, 1980).

More recently Nelson (1996) and his colleagues have developed a model that emphasizes processes of monitoring and control in metacognition. An individual monitors their learning process at the experience level and relates the observations to a model of their learning process at the meta-level. The results of the conscious introspection are used to control actual learning at the experience level. We (Kolb and Kolb, 2009) have suggested a modification of Nelson's metacognitive model based on experiential learning theory that can help learners gain a better understanding of the learning process, themselves as learners, and the appropriate use of learning strategies based on the learning task and environment (see Figure 8.5). Here an individual is engaged in the process of learning something at the level of direct concrete experience. His reflective monitoring of the learning process he is going through is compared at the abstract meta-level with his idealized experiential learning model that includes concepts such as: whether he is spiraling through each stage of the learning cycle, the way his unique learning style fits with how he is being taught, and the learning demands of what he is learning. This comparison results in strategies for action that return him to the concrete learning situation through the control arrow.

When individuals engage in the process of learning by reflective monitoring of the learning process they are going through, they can begin to understand important aspects of learning: how they move through each stage of the learning cycle, the way their unique learning style fits with how they are being taught, and the learning demands of what is being taught. This comparison results in strategies for action that can be applied in their ongoing learning process.

Learning Identity

A primary metacognitive arena of deliberate learning is one's self-image as a learner, addressing such questions as: Can I learn? How do I learn? How can I improve my learn-

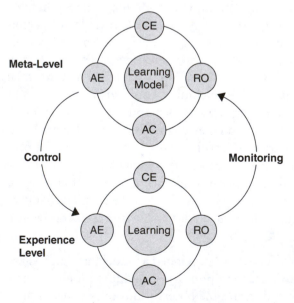

Figure 8.5 Nelson's Metacognitive Model Modified to Include the Experiential Learning Theory Learning Cycle

ing capability? At the extreme, if a person does not believe that they can learn, they won't. Learning requires conscious attention, effort, and "time on task." These activities are a waste of time to someone who does not believe that they have the ability to learn. On the other hand, there are many successful individuals who attribute their achievements to a learning attitude. Oprah Winfrey, for example, has said, "I am a woman in process. I'm just trying like everybody else. I try to take every conflict, every experience, and learn from it. Life is never dull."

People with a learning identity see themselves as learners, seek and engage life experiences with a learning attitude, and believe in their ability to learn. Having a learning identity is not an either/or proposition. A learning identity develops over time from tentatively adopting a learning stance toward life experience, to a more confident learning orientation, to a learning self that is specific to certain contexts, and ultimately to a learning self-identity that permeates deeply into all aspects of the way one lives one's life. This progression is sustained and nurtured through growth-producing relationships in one's life.

In experiential learning theory the concept of learning identity is based on the works of Carl Rogers and Paulo Freire. For both of these foundational scholars of experiential learning, people who see themselves as learners are those who trust their direct personal experiences and their ability to learn from them. Their primary focus is not on immediate performance or goal achievement but on the ongoing process of learning from these experiences. Instead of desiring some fixed goal, they prefer the excitement of being in the process of potentialities being born. In his classic paper on how values are learned, Carl Rogers emphasizes the central role of experiencing in the learning process of the mature person: "He uses his experiencing as a direct referent to which he can turn in forming accurate conceptualizations and as a guide to his behavior" (1964, p. 163). The process of learning values is, "fluid and flexible. . . highly differentiated. . . the locus of evaluation is within the person. . . . There is also involved in this valuing process a letting oneself down into the immediacy of what one is experiencing, endeavoring to sense and to clarify all its complex meanings" (1964, pp. 163–164). Echoing William James' radical empiricism he emphasizes that experiencing includes not only direct sensations and emotions but prior concepts: "For there is involved in the present moment of experiencing the memory traces of all the relevant learnings from the past. This moment has not only its immediate sensory impact, but it has meaning growing out of similar experiences in the past" (1964, p. 164).

He contrasts this approach of a mature learning person with fixed values formed through introjections acquired in youth in order to please loved ones: "These conceived preferences are either not related at all, or not clearly related, to his own process of experiencing. Often there is a wide discrepancy between the evidence supplied by his own experience and these conceived values. Because these conceptions are not open to testing in experience, he must hold them in a rigid and unchanging fashion" (1964, p. 162).

In a very different context, Paulo Freire also has emphasized the critical role that learning centered on one's own personal experience plays in forming a learning identity. In *Pedagogy of the Oppressed* he describes his literacy work with Brazilian peasant farmers helping to liberate them from a self-identity formed through internalized oppression, the incorporation and acceptance by individuals within an oppressed group of the prejudices against them—"So often do (the oppressed) hear that they are good for nothing, know nothing, and are incapable of learning anything—that they are sick, lazy, and unproductive—that in the end they become convinced of their own unfitness" (1970, p. 49). His method for achieving the personal and social transformations necessary to escape this negative, fixed self-identity was to facilitate the creation of critical consciousness in these farmers through his version of the experiential learning cycle which he called praxis, "reflection and action on the world in order to transform it." In a definition echoing metacognition, Leistyna (2004) defines critical consciousness as presence of mind in the process of learning and knowing—the ability to analyze, pose problems, and change the political and cultural realities that affect our lives.

Freire argues that traditional education also promotes a form of internalized oppression and a non-learning identity. It is based on a "banking concept" where all-knowing teachers deposit ideas in students' minds to be received uncritically, mechanically memorized, and repeated. He offers the alternative of "problem-posing education" that empowers a learning self-identity. It is based on a democratic relationship between student and teacher that begins with the here-and-now experience of students' lives and encourages the praxis of critical reflection and action to improve their lives.

If there is a starting point for learning from experience it must be in the belief that one can learn and develop from one's life experiences. In our many years of sharing results from the Kolb Learning Style Inventory with thousands of people, we have discovered to our surprise that not only do most people not understand their unique way of learning, many have not thought about what learning is and themselves as learners. More people than we imagined do not think of themselves as learners at all and have what psychologist Carol Dweck calls a "fixed" view of themselves, in varying degrees believing that they are incapable of learning.

It is possible to develop a learning identity. Research studies have shown that educational interventions can influence the development of a learning identity. Blackwell, Trzesniewski, and Dweck found that eight 25-minute classes for seventh graders focused on the message that "learning changes the brain by forming new connections and that students are in charge of this process" (2007, p. 254) led to increased classroom motivation and reversed a decline in grades experienced by the control group. Similarly, Good, Aronson, and Inzlicht (2003) found that an incremental learning intervention led to significant improvements in adolescents' achievement test scores, and Aronson, Fried, and Good (2002) found that such teaching led to higher grades among college students.

Another example in higher education has focused on the difficult problem of mathematics anxiety and the sense of inferiority many students feel when required to take remedial mathematics education. Hutt (2007) implemented an experiential "learning to learn" course focused on transforming students' math learning identity from one of anxious inferiority ("I don't do math") to one of confident self efficacy ("I can totally do math") as well as improving students' math learning performance in developmental mathematics courses. Results from this research showed that the experiential course content and the teachers' conscious attention to unconscious processes in the learning space, combined with the students' reflections on their learning experiences and self-talk, had a positive impact on learning. Students' mathematics anxiety was reduced, with students in the course feeling safer, more confident, and efficacious about themselves as learners. Students in the "learning to learn" course performed a letter grade better than controls in their developmental math course. Students' learning style preferences played an interesting role in the findings. Typically in mathematics courses, students with an abstract "thinking" learning style preference, which tends to match that of their instructor's teaching style, perform better than students with other learning styles. This learning style difference was erased for students in the experiential course where students of all learning style preferences earned better grades than controls. Hutt maintains that change from a fixed to a learning self-identity requires a safe learning space characterized by unconditional positive regard (Rogers, 1951) from the teacher. This space reduces defensive behavior and allows persons to experience themselves as learners in a new way.

Becoming a learner, someone who can say with confidence "I am a learner," is not accomplished overnight. One's self-identity is deeply held and defended against experiences that contradict it. For the vast majority of us our self-identity is a mix of fixed and learning beliefs. We may feel that we are good at learning some things like sports and not good at others like mathematics. Dweck and her colleagues argue that lay theories are domain specific; for example, one can believe that intelligence is fixed and morality is learned (Levy, Plaks, Hong, Chiu, and Dweck, 2001). Every success or failure can trigger a reassessment of one's learning ability.

Figure 8.6 depicts self-identity as balancing characteristics that reinforce a fixed self—negative self-talk, avoidance of risk and failure, and being threatened by the successes of others—and those that build a learning self—trusting one's ability to learn from experience, seeking new experiences and challenges, persistence, learning from mistakes, and using other's success as a source of learning.

There are a number of metacognitive strategies for developing a positive learning identity that can tip the balance toward becoming a learner.

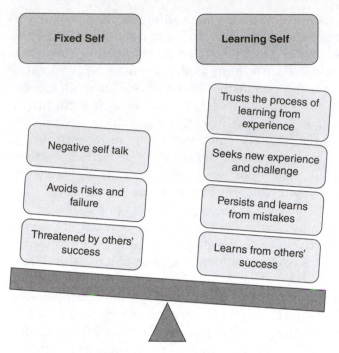

Figure 8.6 Becoming a Learner

Trust Your Experience   Place experience at the center of your learning process, making it the focal point of choices and decisions. This does not mean that you shouldn't learn from experts or the experience of others since this advice is also part of your experience. The key is to own your choices and validate them in your experience. When you do this, you take charge of your learning and your life.

Trust the Learning Process   Avoid an excessive focus on the outcomes of immediate performance and focus instead on the longer-term recursive process of learning by tracking your performance progress over time. Rarely is a single performance test a matter of life and death, and to treat it as such only reinforces a fixed identity. Every performance is an occasion for learning and improvement in future performances.

Redefine Your Relationship to Failure   No one likes to fail but failure is an inevitable part of doing something new. Thomas Edison provided a role model for the learning response to failure when he argued that failure is the most important ingredient for success. James Dyson, the inventor of the Dyson vacuum cleaner and founder of Dyson, Inc, sees Edison as a role model saying he, "achieved great success through repeated failure. His 10,000 failures pale in comparison to his 1,093 U.S. patents. Each one of Edison's inventions, from the Dictaphone to the light bulb came from his inability to give up" (Yang, 2008, p. 28).

Failures can also help focus your priorities and life path on your talents and strengths. In her commencement address to the 2008 graduates of Harvard University, J. K. Rowling

(2008) described the low period in her life after graduation, which was marked by failure on every front, and talked about its benefits as leaving her with a new sense of focus on the only type of work that was important to her. In her address she reflected that if she had not failed, she never would have had the energy and motivation to spend her time writing, an area where she truly belonged. Failure, she found, created a sense of freedom to focus on her area of expertise.

Let Go of Strong Emotional Responses in Order to Learn from Failure   Failures, losses, and mistakes provoke inevitable emotional responses. Yet it is important to learn to regulate emotional reactions that block learning and feed into a fixed identity. Golfers who slam their club and curse themselves and the game after a bad shot lose the opportunity to coolly analyze their mistake and plan for corrections on the next hole. An effective way to deal with the emotions that follow judging oneself a failure is to breathe calmly and intentionally while accepting the current moment as it is. This enables a clearer mind with which to move forward.

Risk Losing   Joel Waitzkin in *The Art of Learning* provides a handbook of his metacognitive learning based on his process of becoming first a chess master and then a martial arts champion. He emphasizes the importance of losing in order to learn how to win. "If a big strong guy comes into a martial arts studio and someone pushes him, he wants to resist and push the guy back to prove that he is a big strong guy. The problem is that he isn't learning anything by doing this. In order to grow, he needs to give up his current mindset" (2007, p. 107).

Reassess Your Beliefs about How You Learn and What You Are Good At   It is important to consciously reflect on and choose how you define yourself as a learner. Often people are unaware of the way in which they characterize themselves and their abilities.

Monitor the Messages You Send Yourself   Pay attention to your self-talk. Saying to yourself, "I am stupid" or "I am no good at. . ." matters and reinforces a negative fixed identity; just as saying, "I can do this" reinforces a positive learning identity. Beware of internalized oppression. Some of these messages are introjections from others that you have swallowed without careful examination.

Balance Your Success/Failure Accounts   Most of us remember our failures more vividly than our successes. For example, in our experience as teachers we both tend to focus on the one or two negative remarks in our course ratings and ignore the praise and positive reactions. The danger of this type of focus is adjusting one's teaching style to suit one or two negative comments and risking losing the majority of positive experiences in the room. A deeper danger is that such a focus will negatively shape longer-term thoughts and behaviors about oneself (Blackwell, Trzesniewski, and Dweck, 2007, pp. 259–260). Sometimes it is useful to make an inventory of learning strengths and successes to balance your accounts.

Learning Style

In addition to believing in ourselves as learners, it is also important to understand how it is that we learn best, our learning style. An understanding of one's unique learning preferences and capabilities, and the match between these and the demands of learning tasks, can increase learning effectiveness. It can suggest why performance is not optimal and suggest strategies for improvement, as well as help explain why some topics and courses are interesting and others are painful. It can also help explain why some develop a non-learning self-identity. Our most gratifying experiences in teaching individuals about their learning style have been when they come up and say, "My whole life I thought I was stupid because I didn't do well in school. Now I realize that it is just because I learn in a different way than schools teach."

Those who use the Kolb LSI to assess their learning style often decide that they wish to develop their capacity to engage in one or more of the four learning modes: experiencing (CE), reflecting (RO), thinking (AC), and acting (AE). In some cases this is based on a desire to develop a weak mode in their learning style. In others it may be to increase capability in a mode that is particularly important for their learning tasks. Because of the dialectic relationships among the learning modes, containing the inhibiting effects of opposing learning modes can be as effective in getting into a mode as actively trying to express it. Overall learning effectiveness is improved when individuals are highly skilled in engaging all four modes of the learning cycle. One way to develop in the learning modes is to develop the skills associated with them. The Learning Skills Profile (Boyatzis and Kolb, 1995, 1997) was created to help learners assess the learning skills associated with the four modes of the learning cycle—interpersonal skills for CE, information skills for RO, analytic skills for AC, and action skills for AE.

Developing the Capacity for Experiencing   Experiencing requires fully opening oneself to direct experience. Direct experience exists only in the here-and-now, a present moment of endless depth and extension that can never be fully comprehended. In fact, the thinking mode, being too much "in your head," can inhibit the ability to directly sense and feel the immediate moment. Engagement in concrete experience can be enhanced by being present in the moment and attending to direct sensations and feelings. This presence and attention are particularly important for interpersonal relationships. Interpersonal skills of leadership, relationship, and giving and receiving help in the development and expression of the experiencing mode of learning.

Developing the Capacity for Reflecting   Reflection requires space and time for it to take place. It can be inhibited by impulsive desires and/or pressures to take action. It can be enhanced by the practice of deliberately viewing things from a different perspective and empathy. Stillness and quieting the mind foster deep reflection. Information skills of sense making, information gathering, and information analysis can aid in the development and expression of the reflecting mode of learning.

Developing the Capacity for Thinking   Thinking requires the ability to represent and manipulate ideas in your head. It can be distracted by intense direct emotion and sensations as well as pressure to act quickly. Engagement in thinking can be enhanced by practicing theoretical model building and the creation of scenarios for action. Analytical skills of theory building, quantitative data analysis, and technology management can aid in the development and expression of the thinking mode of learning.

Developing the Capacity for Action   Acting requires commitment and involvement in the practical world of real consequences. In a sense it is the "bottom line" of the learning cycle, the place where internal experiencing, reflecting, and thinking are tested in reality. Acting can be inhibited by too much internal processing in any of these three modes. Acting can be enhanced by courageous initiative taking and the creation of cycles of goal setting and feedback to monitor performance. Action skills of initiative, goal setting, and action taking can aid in the development and expression of the acting mode of learning.

Increasing Learning Flexibility   The flexibility to move from one learning mode to the other in the learning cycle is important for effective learning. Learning flexibility as assessed in the Kolb Learning Style Inventory 4.0 measures the extent that individuals change their learning style as the demands of context and learning task require. By developing capacities in all four of the learning modes one can increase their ability to flexibly change style to move around the learning cycle (Chapter 4, pp. 146–151).

Learning Relationships

Another important area for the metacognitive monitoring and control of learning is learning relationships. Most learning involves others in some way. Experiential learning theory defines learning relationships as connections between one or more individuals that promote growth and movement through the learning spiral, ultimately inspiring future learning and relationship building. Hunt (1987) suggests that parallel learning spirals are shared between individuals in human interaction. People relate to one another in a pattern of alternating "reading" and "flexing" that mirrors the experiential learning process. When one person is *reading*—receiving feedback (CE) and formulating perceptions (RO)—the other person is *flexing*—creating intentions based on those perceptions (AC) and acting on them (AE). As the exchange continues, their modes of experiencing shift back and forth. However, many interactions take place without mindful awareness of perception and intention, creating a sequence of feedback and action that bypasses key steps in the learning process. Those who seek to support the learning process in others can activate modes of experiencing in others by asking key questions that draw out different learning responses (Abbey, Hunt, and Weiser, 1985).

Teachers, mentors, advisors, family, and friends all can influence learning for better or worse. The key metacognitive strategy for managing learning relationships is to focus on and develop those that are growth-producing and to minimize and contain encounters with those "toxic" relationships that undermine learning and one's learning identity.

Our research (Passarelli and Kolb, 2011) suggests that there is no minimum number of interactions for a learning relationship to take form. When asked who has recently impacted their learning growth and development, some learners told stories of a recent acquaintance making a positive impact on their learning journey. Others, however, were impacted by long-standing, close relationships with individuals such as a spouse, sibling, or mentor. What was common to all of the stories is that learners expressed a baseline level of positive feelings or perceptions of the other, even when the content of the interaction was not positive. Miller and Stiver (1997) suggest that relationships that foster growth are formed through interactions that are characterized by mutual empathy and empowerment. These interactions, or connections, need not always be positive, but they must include reciprocal engagement of both thought and emotion. The tone that arises from mutual empathy and empowerment creates the conditions for mutual growth where individuals experience an increase in their vitality, ability to take action, clarity about themselves and their relationship, sense of self-worth, and desire to form more connections. A connection is constituted by an interaction or series of interactions that build toward a deeper relationship. Similar to Fletcher and Ragins' (2007) description of the development of a mentoring relationship through a series of small "episodes," learning relationships evolve as learning interactions increase in quality and frequency. Each interaction carries with it a sentiment, or emotional charge, that sets the tone for learning. Interactions characterized by compassion, respect, and support build the trust and positive emotional resources necessary to create space for learning—even when learning is challenging.

Learning relationships can have a powerful impact on learning identity for better or worse. Some relationships can reinforce a fixed identity or create a codependency that does not allow for learning flexibility and growth. We have already seen Rogers' description of the lasting power that introjected evaluations from loved ones can have. Evaluations from others can also influence learning identity, sometimes in unexpected and subtle ways. Dweck (2000) has shown that teachers who reward students for successful learning by praising them for being "smart" actually promote a fixed identity and less expenditure of study effort—"I don't need to study because I am smart." Learning identity may be contagious in the sense that those who have a learning identity tend to create relationships that stimulate it in others and those with fixed identities also act in ways that pass on fixed views of others. For example, those with a fixed versus incremental view of themselves show greater stereotype endorsement, perceive greater out-group homogeneity, and show greater intergroup bias and more biased behavior toward out-group members. They are more susceptible to the fundamental attribution error—believing that others' actions indicate the "kind" of person they are, underestimating the influence of situational factors on their behavior (Levy et al., 2001). One of our respondents describes how this contagion may be passed on through generations:

In the introduction I mentioned my Father and the impact that his upbringing has had on my Learning Style. I can recall stories of my Father describing a childhood in which he was shown very little love and was repeatedly told he was stupid. He was told that he wouldn't understand things. To this day, my Grandmother still says to him that she will tell him [confidential things] when he is old enough to understand. He is 63 years old. As a child, I remember my Father's dislike for any kind of game. On the rare occasion when he would play, he got angry and frustrated if he didn't do well and often quit. I now know that my father developed a "fixed" self-concept around learning. He was told he was stupid and wouldn't understand and therefore, in his mind, he was and didn't. He also criticizes educated people, which I can now link to the fixed self-identity. This fixed self-concept has implications beyond his attitude towards games—it impacted my learning development. As a child, I often heard my father ask me "what were you thinking?" when I did something wrong. I believe that contributed to the lack of confidence I have with my decision-making. [Passarelli and Kolb 2011, p. 88]

Learning Times and Spaces

In the previous update and reflection (Chapter 7 Update and Reflections, pp. 288–290) I described the concept of learning space, emphasizing that learning needs a space to happen and the nature of that space can either facilitate or hinder learning. It is a foundational truism of social psychology that we humans are greatly influenced by the situations we are in. Studies show powerful tendencies to conform to social norms and the influence of others (Janis, 1972) while evidence for the influence of individual characteristics shows only modest effects on behavior (Mischel, 1984). It is for this reason that metacognitive monitoring and control of one's learning time and space is so important. With this perspective one can exercise some choice in the learning spaces and times one makes and create the kind of learning space that best facilitates their learning. When embarking on a course of learning, it is useful to consider the learning spaces where this learning will happen and to customize these spaces for yourself based on your learning style and the particular subject matter of your learning. When teachers plan their courses, they may or may not explicitly consider the kind of learning spaces they are creating and the appropriateness of these spaces for the students in their course and/or for the material being taught. For example, John and Tanya Reese (1998) created "Connecting with the Professor" workshops to help law students bridge the differences between the learning spaces created by law school professors and their own learning space preferences resulting from their individual learning styles. Recognizing that law school professors were unlikely to change their course and learning style, they worked with students to develop the learning skills needed to succeed in the learning spaces created by their professors. Another strategy is to supplement the learning space that is given with other spaces that suit your style. For example, a person who learns best by imagining may want to form a group of classmates to talk about the material in the course, or a thinking-style person may want to prepare in advance by reading about material to be covered in the course.

The principles for the creation of an effective space for experiential learning described in the previous chapter (Chapter 7 Update and Reflections, pp. 295–299) can serve as a metacognitive guide to assess one's current learning space or to create a new one. For a learner to engage fully in the learning cycle, a space must be provided to engage fully in the four modes of the cycle—experiencing, reflecting, thinking, and acting. It needs to be a hospitable, welcoming space that is characterized by respect for all. It needs to provide an optimal balance of support and challenge, reminding us of Vygotsky's (1978) concept of the proximal zone of development where the learner is supported in incremental learning by models that set challenging but achievable goals. It must allow learners to be in charge of their own learning and allow time for the repetitive practice that develops expertise.

Mindful Experiencing

I spoke earlier in this chapter of awakening to experience and James' reminder that we create our experiences by the choices we make, "My experience is what I agree to attend to" (1890, p. 403). I have also described two techniques for awakening to present experience, focusing based on Rogers and Gendlin's experiencing method and mindfulness (Chapter 2 Update and Reflections). These metacognitive practices for mindful experiencing are aimed at helping the individual to focus on present and direct experience by being intentionally aware and attentive and accepting life as an emergent process of change. Our research on mindfulness and experiential learning (Yeganeh, 2006; Yeganeh and Kolb, 2009) suggests that the practice of mindfulness can help individuals learn from experience by enhancing presence and intentional attention.

Yeganeh (2006) studied two predominant streams of mindfulness research and practice: meditative mindfulness and socio-cognitive mindfulness. Meditative mindfulness is the core of Buddhist meditation, advocating the development of mindfulness through a discipline of anchoring the mind in the present moment. This is often accompanied with a practice of awareness and acceptance through breathing. Kabat-Zinn (1994, 2003) defines mindfulness as "paying attention in a particular way: on purpose, in the present moment, and non-judgmentally" (1994 p. 4). Non-judgment, in mindfulness theory, is accepting the current state as part of a constant flow of changing experiences. This paradigm suggests that letting go of judgment strengthens the mind, and it challenges the illusion that over-thinking something gives one control over it. Authors who discuss mindfulness within these parameters also talk about the antithesis of mindfulness, which is mindlessness, or a state of autopilot and lack of intention.

Socio-cognitive mindfulness emphasizes cognitive categorization, context, and situational awareness. Ellen Langer relates mindfulness to learning: "When we are mindful, we implicitly or explicitly (1) view a situation from several perspectives, (2) see information presented in the situation as novel, (3) attend to the context in which we perceive the information, and eventually (4) create new categories through which this information may be understood" (1997, p. 111). Mindfulness, from the socio-cognitive perspective, requires broadening one's repertoire of cognitive categories. The idea of creating new categories was influenced by Langer's earlier studies in bias and prejudice. Explaining the practical benefits she illustrates that "If we describe someone we dislike intensely, a single statement usually does it. But if, instead, we are forced to describe the person in great detail, eventually there will be some quality we appreciate" (1989, p. 66). One of the reasons Langer's work is so compelling is that it thoroughly supports the notion that simple labels (e.g., good and evil) do not accurately reflect the complexity of the world. Instead, they allow for mindless rationalizations that justify a broad range of dysfunctional behaviors, from ineffective to criminal.

One way to distinguish the two schools of thought is that meditative mindfulness, with its focus on present-centered awareness, describes an internal process required to maintain a mindful state of present experiencing, whereas socio-cognitive mindfulness focuses on cognitive applications of mindfulness to more effectively sort out experiences and make sense of the world based on new mental categories/models. Furthermore, meditative mindfulness authors offer techniques in practicing mindfulness through breathing, acceptance, and present-centered awareness. Socio-cognitive mindfulness deemphasizes meditation, suggesting supplemental practices such as placing a value on doubt, looking for disconfirming data, and producing new ways of thinking and acting. Yeganeh (2006) offers a multidimensional definition of mindfulness that encompasses both approaches. Mindful experiencing is a state in which an individual focuses on present and direct experience, is intentionally aware and attentive, and accepts life as an emergent process of change. Supporting these links between learning from experience and mindfulness, his research found that individuals who scored high on Langer's mindfulness scale emphasized direct concrete experience in their learning style while also scoring lower on reflective observation, suggesting that they were not "lost in thought" or rumination but were attentive to their experiences. The results suggest two mindful experiencing practices to help individuals learn from experience.

Encouraging a Focus on Here-and-Now Experience Uncluttered by Preconceptions and Bias   To be present and engaged in direct experience, one must anchor in present-centered awareness by attending to the five senses. One of the strongest ways to attend to the present moment is through calm and aware breathing. Attending to the present moment serves to quiet the mind; reducing automatic, habitual patterns of thinking and responding. This presence enhances concrete experience and allows the learning cycle to begin. In a sense, we cannot learn from experience if we do not first *have* an experience, and, often, automatic routines make it difficult for direct experiencing in the moment to occur.

Intentionally Guiding Their Learning Process by Paying Attention to How They Are Going through the Phases of the Learning Cycle   By intentionally guiding the learning process and paying attention to the process of one's progression through the phases of the learning cycle, we can make ourselves through learning. How and what we learn determines the way we process the possibilities of each new emerging experience, which in turn determines the range of choices and decisions we see. The choices and decisions we make, to some extent, determine the events we live through, and these events influence our future choices. Thus, we create ourselves through the choices of the actual occasions we live through. For many, this learning style choice is relatively unconscious, an autopilot program for learning. Mindful experiencing can put the control of our learning and our life back in our hands.

Deliberate Practice

We all know that learning involves repeated practice. However, time spent practicing does not necessarily lead to learning and improved performance. Practice is not just the amount of time doing something, so experience with something alone is not a good predictor of performance. Going to the golf practice range and hitting bucket after bucket of balls doesn't necessarily improve your game and in fact may make it worse by ingraining bad habits. Expert performance research initiated in the early 1990s by K. Anders Ericsson (Ericsson, Krampe, and Tesch-Römer, 1993; Ericsson and Charness, 1994; Ericsson, 2006; Baron and Henry, 2010) teaches a great deal about learning from practice. The good news from this work is that greatness, for the most part, is not a function of innate talent; it is learned from experience. The not-so-good news is that it involves long-term commitment (ten years or 10,000 hours for many top experts) and a particular kind of practice that is hard work, called deliberate practice.

The basic techniques of deliberate practice are useful for improving our ability to learn from experience. Essentially, deliberate practice involves intense concentrated, repeated performance that is compared against an ideal or "correct" model of the performance. It requires feedback that compares the actual performance against the ideal to identify "errors" that are corrected in subsequent performance attempts. In this sense deliberate practice can be seen as mindful experiencing with the addition of focused reflection on a concrete performance experience that is analyzed against a metacognitive ideal model to improve future action in a recurring cycle of learning. Learning relationships can be of great help in deliberate practice by providing expert models, feedback, and support for the focused effort required. Daniel Coyle (2009) emphasizes that this kind of practice is difficult work requiring focused attention, thoughtful analysis, and continuous repetition to eliminate mistakes and reach goals. He argues that most can only engage in this deep learning activity for a couple of hours at a time. Yet, little of importance is learned in one sitting. In *Mastery,* George Leonard describes the master's journey as a path that follows a recurring cycle of brief spurts of progress followed by dips of performance and a plateau of performance that is slightly higher than before where nothing seems to be happening until the next spurt. For many this path, particularly the long plateaus, proves frustrating and efforts to learn and develop are abandoned. Leonard advises, "To put it simply, you practice diligently, but you practice primarily *for the sake of practice itself.* Rather than being frustrated while on the plateau, you learn to appreciate and enjoy it as much as you do the upward surges" (1991, p. 17).

Ongoing deliberate practice can be seen as a learning spiral of recursive progression through the learning cycle over time. A key to learning success is the establishment of the appropriate time frame expectation for its achievement. The most common time-framing error is the expectation of a "quick fix" and instant mastery. When it doesn't happen, the learning effort is abandoned. Learning to control one's weight is perhaps the best example. To embark on a "Lose 10 pounds in 10 days" diet is to limit oneself to one turn through the learning cycle; while weight control is a long-term process with spirals of learning around many issues (calorie intake, exercise, etc.) and many contexts. The inertia of old habits takes time to change, and setbacks and failures are inevitable. By framing the learning process correctly as one that will happen with slow progress over time, quitting and negative fixed self-attributions can be avoided.

Self-Making and the Development of Interest   The deliberate practice spiral of learning is applicable not only to the development of specific skills and subject matter, but it also applies to self-development in general. Self-development proceeds through the identification and development of a person's interests. It occurs through an ongoing spiral of learning that refines, deepens, and extends an initial interest in something. Interest is the spine of the learning spiral; the result of the self-referential *autopoeitic* process. The spine of the learning spiral represents interest in James' spiral of interest-attention-selection which, as he says using another metaphor, is "the very keel on which our mental ship is built" (Leary 1992, p. 157). We attend to those things which draw our interest and select those experiences which allow our interests to be explored and deepened in a continuing spiral of learning. John Dewey, James' colleague, describes the developmental aspects of this process, "I believe that interests are the signs and symptoms of growing power. I believe that they represent dawning capacities. . . showing the state of development which the child has reached (and) the stage upon which he is about to enter" (1897, p. 79). To trust these signs of growing power and nurture the growth of one's interests is to follow the learning way.

Learning How to Learn

Finally, let us examine how the above metacognitive skills of deliberate learning can be developed increasing the ability to learn how to learn. Returning to Figure 8.5, I have emphasized thus far two cycles of learning shown in the illustration. The cycle of learning at the experience level represents the learner's actual concrete learning experience. The cycle at the meta-level describes the learner's normative model of how his learning should be. A closer look at Figure 8.5 reveals that the monitoring and control arrows between one's metacognitive model of experiential learning and his/her learning experience complete another cycle of experiential learning. This third learning cycle describes how individuals develop their meta-level model of learning, that is, how they learn about their learning process.

Current metacognitive research suggests that these three cycles do not operate simultaneously but sequentially. For example, judgments of how well one has learned something are less accurate when they are made immediately than when they are delayed for some time (Nelson, 1996). When one is immersed in a learning task like solving math problems, they may not be thinking much about their meta-model of how they should be going about the task and not at all about perfecting that meta-model. The meta-model of learning may be most useful prior to engagement in learning and for "after-action review." It can be used to plan strategies for engaging and mastering the immediate learning task.

The learning about learning cycle requires a longer time perspective and reflection on previous learning experiences and their fit with the metacognitive normative learning model. We have already seen that educational interventions can facilitate this process and improve learning effectiveness (Blackwell, Trzesniewski, and Dweck, 2007; Good, Aronson, and Inzlicht, 2003; Hutt, 2007; Reese, 1998). Supportive learning relationships and learning spaces are often essential to explore and change a deeply held learning identity and unconscious learning habits. Ultimately, however, it is the learner who manages their learning about learning and takes control of their learning process through metacognitive monitoring and control. Learners can chart their path on the learning way by developing their metacognitive learning capacities and educators can pave the way by placing learning about learning on the agenda of their educational programs.

Bibliography

Abbey, D. S., Hunt, D. E., and Weiser, J. C., "Variations on a Theme by Kolb: A New Perspective for Understanding Counseling and Supervision," *The Counseling Psychologist, 13*(3) (1985), 477–501.

Akrivou, K., *Differentiation and Integration in Adult Development: The Influence of Self-Complexity and Integrative Learning on Self-Integration.* VDM Verlag, 2009.

Alexander, C. N., and Langer, E., eds., *Higher Stages of Human Development.* New York: Oxford University Press, 1990.

Allen, Frank, "Bosses List Main Strengths, Flaws Determining Potential of Managers," *The Wall Street Journal,* November 14, 1980.

Allinson, C. W., and Hayes, J., "The Cognitive Style Index: A Measure of Intuition-Analysis for Organizational Research." *Journal of Management Studies, 33*(1) (1996), 119–135.

Allport, Gordon, *Pattern and Growth in Personality.* New York: Holt, Rinehart & Winston, 1961.

Altmeyer, Robert, "Education in the Arts and Sciences: Divergent Paths," Ph.D. dissertation, Carnegie Institute of Technology, 1966.

American College Testing Program, "Survey of Prior Learning Assessment Programs at American Colleges and Universities," a report to the Council for the Advancement of Experiential Learning, 1982.

Arbaugh, J. B., Dearmond, S., and Rau, B. L., "New Uses for Existing Tools? A Call to Study Online Management Instruction and Instructors," *AMLE, 12*(4) (2013), 635–655.

Arbeiter, S., Aslanian, C. S., Schnerbaur, F. A., and Brickell, H. M., *40 Million Americans in Career Transition: The Need for Information.* New York: College Entrance Exam Board, 1978.

Argyris, Chris, *Interpersonal Competence and Organizational Effectiveness.* Home-wood, Ill.: Dorsey, 1962.

————, "On the Future of Laboratory Education," in G. Golembiewski and P. Blumberg, eds., *Sensitivity Training and the Laboratory Approach. Readings about Concepts and Applications.* Itasca, Ill.: Peacock, 1970.

————, *Theory in Practice: Increasing Professional Effectiveness.* San Francisco: Jossey-Bass, 1974.

————, **and Donald Schon,** *Organizational Learning: A Theory of Action Perspective.* Reading, Mass.: Addison-Wesley, 1978.

Arlin, P. K., "Cognitive Development in Adulthood: A Fifth Stage," *Developmental Psychology,* XI (1975), 602–6.

Aronson, J., Fried, C. B., and Good, C., "Reducing Stereotype Threat and Boosting Academic Achievement of African-American Students: the Role of Conceptions of Intelligence," *Journal of Experimental Social Psychology, 38* (2002), 113–125.

Aspin and Chapman, "Lifelong Learning: Concepts and Conceptions," *International Journal of Lifelong Education, 19*(1) (2000), 2–19.

Bakan, D., *The Duality of Human Experience.* Chicago, IL: Rand McNally, 1966.

Baker, A. C., Jensen, P. J., and Kolb, D. A. and Associates, *Conversational Learning: An Experiential Approach to Knowledge Creation.* Westport Conn.: Quorum Books, 2002.

Baker, C. M., Pesut, D. J., Mcdaniel, A. M., and Fisher, M. L., "Learning Skills Profiles of Master's Students in Nursing Administration: Assessing the Impact of Problem-Based Learning," *Nursing Education Perspectives, 28*(4) (2007), 190–195.

Baker, R. E., Simon, J. R., and Bazeli, F. P., "Selecting Instructional Design for Introductory Accounting Based on the Experiential Learning Model," *Journal of Accounting Education, 5* (1987), 207–226.

Bandura, Albert, "The Self System in Reciprocal Determinism," *American Psychologist,* vol. 33 (1978), 344–57.

Bargh, J. A., and Chartrand, T. L., "The Unbearable Automaticity of Being," *American Psychologist, 54*(7) (1999), 462–479.

Baron, R. A. and Henry, R. A., "How Entrepreneurs Acquire the Capacity to Excel: Insights from Research on Expert Performance," *Strategic Entrepreneurship Journal, 4* (2010), 49–65.

Barron, F., "Threshold for the Perception of Human Movement in Ink-Blots," *Journal of Consulting Psychology, 19* (1955), 3-3-38.

Bash, K. W., "Einstellungstypus and Erlebnistypus: C.G. Jung and Hermann Rorschach," *Journal of Projective Techniques, 19* (1955), 236–42.

Basseches, M. A., *Dialectical Thinking and Adult Development.* Norwood, NJ: Ablex Publishing Corp., 1984.

————, "The Development of Dialectical Thinking as an Approach to Integration," *Integral Review 1* (2005), 47–63.

Bates, W. Jackson, "The Crisis in English Studies," *Harvard Magazine,* September–October 1982.

Baumeister, R. F., and Sommer, K. L., "Consciousness, Free Choice, and Automaticity," in R. S. Wyer, Jr., ed., *Advances in Social Cognition.* vol. X, pp. 75–81. Mahwah, NJ: Erlbaum, 1997.

————, Bratslavsky, E., Muraven, M., and Tice, D. M., "Ego Depletion: Is the Active Self a Limited Resource" *Journal of Personality and Social Psychology, 74* (1998), 1252–1265.

Baxter-Magolda, M. B., *Knowing and Reasoning in College: Gender-related Patterns in Students' Intellectual Development.* San Francisco: Jossey-Bass, 1992.

————, *Creating contexts for learning and self-authorship.* Nashville: Vanderbilt University Press, 1999.

————, *Making Their Own Way: Narritives for Transforming Higher Education to Promote Self-Development.* Sterling, VA: Stylus, 2001.

————, "Self-Authorship: The Foundation for Twenty-First Century Education," *New Directions for Teaching and Learning 100* (2007), 69–83.

————, "Three Elements of Self-Authorship," *Journal of College Student Development, 49*(4) (2008), 269–284.

Becher, T., *Academic Tribes and Territories.* Milton Keynes, UK: Open University Press, 1989.

————, "The Counter-Culture of Specialisation," *European Journal of Education*, 25 (1990), 333–346.

————, "The Significance of Disciplinary Differences," *Studies in Higher Education, 19*(2) (1994), 151.

Belenky, M. F., Clinchy, B. M., Goldberger, N. R., and Tarule, J. M., *Women's Ways of Knowing: The Development of Self-Voice and Mind.* New York: Basic Books, 1986.

Bell, A. A., *The Adaptive Style Inventory: An Assessment of Person-Environment Interactions,* unpublished manuscript, Department of Educational Leadership, University of Connecticut, 2005.

Benne, Kenneth, "History of the T Group in the Laboratory Setting," in Leland Bradford et al., eds., *T Group Theory and Laboratory Method.* New York: John Wiley, 1964.

Bennet, Nancy, "Learning Styles of Health Professionals Compared to Preference for Continuing Education Program Format," unpublished Ph.D. dissertation, University of Illinois College of Medicine, 1978.

Bennis, Warren G., "Interview," *Group and Organization Studies,* 5 (1980), 18–34.

———, "A Goal for the Eighties: Organizational Integrity," *New Jersey Bell Journal,* 4(4) (Winter 1981–82), 1–8.

Benton, Arthur L., "The Neuropsychology of Facial Recognition," *American Psychologist,* 35 (1980), 176–86.

Bereiter, C., and M. Friedman, "Fields of Study and the People in Them," in N. Sanford, ed., *The American College,* pp. 593–96. New York: John Wiley, 1962.

Bethell, S., and Morgan, K., "Problem-Based and Experiential Learning: Engaging Students in an Undergraduate Physical Education Module," *Journal of Hospitality Leisure Sport & Tourism Education,* 10(1) (2011), 128–134. doi: 10.3794/johlste.101.365.

Bieri, J., and Susan Messerley, "Differences in Perceptual and Cognitive Behavior as a Function of Experience Type," *Journal of Consulting Psychology,* 21 (1957), 217–21.

Biglan, A., "The Characteristics of Subject Matter in Different Academic Areas," *Journal of Applied Psychology,* 57 (1973a), 195–203.

———, "Relationships between Subject Matter Characteristics and the Structure and Output of University Departments," *Journal of Applied Psychology,* 51 (1973b), 204–13.

"Bill Moyers Journal," "A Conversation with Clark Clifford," Show No. 712–713. New York: WNET/Thirteen, 1981.

Blackwell, L. S., Trzesniewski, K. H., and Dweck, C. S., "Implicit Theories of Intelligence Predict Achievement Across an Adolescent Transition: A Longitudinal Study and an Intervention," *Child Development,* 78(1) (2007), 246–263.

Block, J., "Ego Identity, Role Variability and Adjustment," *Journal of Consulting Psychology,* 25(5) (1961), 392–397.

Bogen, J. E., "Some Educational Aspects of Hemispheric Specialization," *UCLA Educator,* 17 (1975), 24–32.

Bohm, D., *Physics and Perception in the Special Theory of Relativity.* New York: Benjamin, 1965.

Bok, D., "The President's Report," *Harvard Magazine,* May–June 1978.

Border, L. L. B., "Understanding Learning Styles: The Key to Unlocking Deep Learning and In Depth Teaching," *NEA Higher Education Advocate,* 24(5) (2007), 5–8.

Boud, D., Keogh, R., and Walker, D., *Reflection: Turning Experience into Learning.* London: Nichols Publishing Company, 1985.

———, **and Miller, N.,** *Working with Experience. Animating Learning.* London and New York: Routledge, 1996.

Bourdieu, P., *Homo Academicus.* Paris: Minuit, 1984.

———, *The Logic of Practice.* Stanford, CA: Stanford University Press, 1990.

Boyatzis, R. E. "Stimulating self-directed change: A required MBA course called Managerial Assessment and Development," *Journal of Management Education,* 18(3) (1994), 304–323.

Boyatzis, R. E., Cowen, S. S., and Kolb, D. A., *Innovation in Professional Education: Steps on a Journey from Teaching to Learning.* San Francisco: Jossey-Bass, 1995.

———, **and Kolb, D. A.,** "From Learning Styles to Learning Skills: The Executive Skills Profile," *Journal of Managerial Psychology,* 11 (1995, March-April).

———, **and Kolb, D. A.,** "Assessing Individuality in Learning: The Learning Skills Profile," *Educational Psychology,* 11(3–4) (1997), 279–295.

———, **and Kolb, D. A.,** "Performance, Learning, and Development as Modes of Growth and Adaptation throughout Our Lives and Careers," in M. Peiperl et al., eds., *Career Frontiers: New Conceptions of Working Lives.* London: Oxford University Press, 1999.

———, **and Mainemelis,** "An Empirical Study of the Pluralism of Learning and Adaptive Styles in an MBA Program," paper presented at the 60th annual meeting of the Academy of Management, Toronto, 2000.

————, Stubbs, E. C., and Taylor, S. N., "Learning Cognitive and Emotional Intelligence Competencies through Graduate Management Education," *Academy of Management Learning and Education, 1*(2) (2002), 150–162.

————, Rochford, K., and Jacks, A. I., Antagonistic Neural Networks Underlying Differentiated Leadership Roles," *Frontiers in HumanNeuroscience,* www.frontiersin.org, (March 2014). vol. 8, Article 114.

Bradford, Leland, "Membership and the Learning Process," in Bradford et al., eds., *T Group Theory and Laboratory Method.* New York: John Wiley, 1964.

Bransford, J. D., Brown, A. L., and Cocking, R. R., *How People Learn: Brain, Mind Experience, and School.* Washington D. C.: National Academy Press, 2000.

Brehmer, B., "In One Word: Not from Experience," *Acta Psychologicia, 45* (1980), 223–241.

Brew, C. R., *Exploring the Learning Experience in a First Year Biology Laboratory,* unpublished doctoralthesis, Monash University, Australia, 1996.

Bridges, Katherine, "Emotional Development in Early Infancy," *Child Development,* 3 (1932), 340.

Brim, Orville, and Jerome Kagan, *Constancy and Change in Human Development.* Cambridge, Mass.: Harvard University Press, 1980.

Bronfenbrenner U., "Toward an Experimental Ecology of Human Development," *American Psychologist,* July, (1977), 513–530.

————, *The Ecology of Human Development.* Cambridge, MA: Harvard University Press, 1979.

Brookfield, S. D., *Developing Critical Thinkers: Challenging Adults to Explore Alternative Ways of Thinking and Acting.* San Francisco: Jossey Bass, 1987.

————, *Becoming a Critically Reflective Teacher.* San Francisco: Jossey-Bass, 1995.

————, "The Concept of Critical Reflection: Promises and Contradictions," *European Journal of Social Work, 12*(4) (2009), 293–304.

Broverman, D., Klaiber, E., Kobayashi, Y., and Vogel, W., "Roles of Activation and Inhibition in Sex Differences in Cognitive Abilities," *Psychological Review,* 75 (1968), 23–50.

Brown, K. W., and Ryan, R. M., "The Benefits of Being Present: Mindfulness and Its Role in Psychological Well-Being," *Journal of Personality and Social Psychology,* 84 (2003a), 822–848.

————, and Ryan, R. M., Why We Don't Need Self-Esteem: On Fundamental Needs, Contingent Love, and Mindfulness," *Psychological Inquiry, 14* (2003b), 27–82.

Bruner, Jerome S., *The Process of Education.* New York: Vintage Books, 1960.

————, "The Course of Cognitive Growth," *American Psychologist,* 19 (1964), 1–15.

————, *On Knowing: Essays for the Left Hand.* New York: Atheneum, 1966a.

————, *Toward a Theory of Instruction.* New York: W.W. Norton, 1966b.

————, R. Oliver, and P. Greenfield, *Studies in Cognitive Growth.* New York: John Wiley, 1966.

————, *The Relevance of Education.* New York: W.W. Norton, 1971.

———— *Actual Minds, Possible Worlds.* Cambridge, MA: Harvard University Press, 1986.

Brunswick, Egon, "Organismic Achievement and Environment Probability," *Psychological Review,* 50, (1943), 255–72.

Buchmann, M., and Schwille, J., "Education: The Overcoming of Experience," *American Journal of Education, 92*(1) (1983), 30–51.

Buckley, W., *Sociology and Modern Systems Theory.* Englewood Cliffs, N.J.: Prentice-Hall, 1967.

Bunker, S. S. "Constructing curriculum: Creating a teaching-learning space," *Nursing Science Quarterly, 12*(4) (1999), 297–298.

Burtt, E. A., "The Status of World Hypotheses," *Philosophical Review,* 6 (1943), 590–604.

Cadwallader, M., "The Cybernetic Analysis of Change in Complex Social Systems," in W. Buckley, ed., *Modern Systems Research for the Behavioral Scientist.* Chicago: Aldine, 1968.

Campus News. (February 6, 2003) "Edward M. Hundert Inaugural" pp. 1–2.

Camuffo, A., and Gerli, F., "An Integrated Competency Based Approach to Management Education: An Italian MBA Case Study," *International Journal of Training and Development, 8*(4) (2004), 240–257.

Capra, F. *The Web of Life.* New York: Anchor Books 1996.

Carlsson, B., Keane, P., & Martin, J. B. "R & D Organizations as Learning Systems. *Sloan Management Review, 17,* 1–15, 1976.

Carrigan, Patricia, "Extraversion-Introversion as a Dimension of Personality: A Reappraisal," *Psychological Bulletin, 57* (1960), 329–60.

Cartwright, D., ed., *Field Theory in Social Science: Selected Theoretical Papers by Kurt Lewin.* New York: Harper Torchbooks, 1951.

Certo, S., and S. Lamb, "Identification and Measurement of Instrument Bias within the Learning Style Instrument through a Monte Carlo Technique," *Southern Management Proceedings,* 1979.

Chickering, Arthur, *Experience and Learning: An Introduction to Experiential Learning.* New Rochelle, New York: Change Magazine Press, 1977.

Christensen, M., C. Lee, and P. Bugg, "Professional Development of Nurse Practitioners as a Function of Need Motivation Learning Styles and Locus of Control," *Nursing Research, 28* (January–February 1979), 51–56.

Churchman, C. West, *The Design of Inquiring Systems.* New York: Basic Books, 1971.

Clarke, D., Oshiro, S., Wong, C., and Yeung, M., "A Study of the Adequacy of the Learning Environment for Business Students in Hawaii in the Fields of Accounting and Marketing," unpublished paper, University of Hawaii, 1977.

Clifford, Clark, *Bill Moyer's Journal,* 1981.

Cohen, Morris, and Nagel, Ernest, *Introduction to Logic and Scientific Method.* New York: Harcourt Brace, 1934.

Cole, M., et al., *The Cultural Context of Learning and Thinking.* New York: Basic Books, 1971.

————, **V. John-Steiner, S. Scribner, and E. Souberman,** eds., *L. S. Vygotsky: Mind in Society.* Cambridge, Mass.: Harvard University Press, 1978.

Cook, T. A., *The Curves of Life.* London: Constable and Company, 1914.

Cook-Greuter, S. R., *Post-Autonomous Ego Development: A Study of Its Nature and Measurement,* Doctoral dissertation, Cambridge, MA: Harvard Graduate School of Education, 1999.

————, Mature Ego Development: A Gateway to Ego Transcendence?, *Journal of Adult Development, 7*(1) (2000), 227–240.

Corballis, Michael, "Laterality and Myth," *American Psychologist,* March 1980, pp. 284–95.

Cornett, C. E., *What You Should Know about Teaching and Learning Styles.* Bloomington, IN. Phi Delta Kappa Educational Foundation, 1983.

Coyle, D., *The Talent Code.* New York: Bantam Books, 2009.

Craik, F. I. M., Moroz, T. M., Mocovitch, M., Stuss, S. T., Winocur, G., Tulving, E., and Kapur, S., In Search of the Self: A Positron Emission Tomography Study, *Psychological Science, 10*(1) (1999), 26–34.

Crary, Laura M., "Assessment of Patterns of Life Structure," unpublished manuscript, Department of Organizational Behavior, Case Western Reserve University, 1979.

————, "Patterns of Life Structure: Person-Environment Designs and Their Impact on Adult Lives," unpublished Ph.D. dissertation, Case Western Reserve University, 1981.

Dale, E., *Audio-Visual Methods in Teaching.* 3rd ed. New York: Holt Rinehart & Winston, 1969.

Damasio, A., *Decartes Error: Emotion, Reason and the Human Brain.* New York: Grosset/Putnam, 1994.

————, *Looking for Spinoza: Joy, Sorrow and the Feeling Brain.* New York: Harcourt, Inc., 2002.

Darwin, Charles, *The Autobiography of Charles Darwin: 1809–1882.* London: Collins, 1958.

Davis, B., and Sumara, D. J., "Cognition, Complexity and Teacher Education," *Harvard Educational Review, 67*(1) (1997), 105–125.

Davis, E., "Big Mind Science," *Shambhala Sun* (September 1995), 27–33.

Davis, J., *Undergraduate Career Decisions.* Chicago: Aldine, 1965.

deCharms, Richard, *Personal Causation.* New York: Academic Press, 1968.

Deci, E., and Ryan, R., *Intrinsic Motivation and Self-Determination in Human Behavior.* New York: Plenum, 1985.

De Ciantis, S. M., and Kirton, M. J., "A Psychometric Reexamination of Kolb's Experiential Learning Cycle Construct: A Separation of Level, Style and Process," *Educational and Psychological Measurement, 56*(5) (1996), 809–820.

de Groot, Adriaan, *Thought and Choice in Chess.* The Hague: Mouton, 1965.

Dennett, D., *Consciousness Explained.* Boston: Little-Brown, 1991.

Deutsch, K., *The Nerves of Government.* New York: Free Press, 1966.

Dewey, John, *My Pedagogic Creed.* New York: E.L. Kellogg & Co., 1897.

————, "My Pedagogic Creed," *The School Journal,* LIV(3) (1897), 77–80.

————, "The Postulate of Immediate Experience," *Journal of Philosophy, Psychology and Scientific Methods, 2* (1905), 353–357.

————, *How We Think.* New York: D.C. Heath, 1910.

————, *Democracy and Education.* New York: Macmillan Company, 1916.

————, *How We Think: A Restatement of the Relation of Reflective Thinking to the Educative Process,* New York: D.C. Heath and Company, 1933.

————, *Art as Experience.* New York: Perigee Books, 1934.

————, *Education and Experience.* New York: Simon and Schuster, 1938.

————, *Experience and Nature.* New York: Dover Publications, 1958.

DeWitt, Norman, "Organism and Humanism: An Empirical View," in D. B. Harris, ed., *The Concept of Development: An Issue in the Study of Human Behavior.* Minneapolis: University of Minnesota Press, 1957.

Diekman, Arthur, "Biomodal Consciousness," *Archives of General Psychiatry, 25* (1971), 481–89.

Doherty, A., M. Mentkowski, and K. Conrad, "Toward a Theory of Undergraduate Experiential Learning," *New Directions for Experiential Learning, 1* (1978), 23–35.

Dreyfus, C., "Scientist and Engineer Managers: A Study of Managerial Effectiveness," unpublished paper, Department of Organizational Behavior, Case Western Reserve University, 1989.

Dweck, C. S., *Self-Theories: Their Role in Motivation, Personality, and Development.* Great Britain: Psychology Press, Taylor & Francis Group, 2000.

Dweck, C. S. "The Promise and Perils of Praise" *Educational Leadership, 65* (2008), 34–39.

Eagleton S., and Muller A., "Development of a Model for Whole Brain Learning of Physiology," *Adv Physiol Educ, 35* (2011), 421–426, doi:10.1152/advan.00007.2011.

Eaves, Lindon, and Hans Eysenck, "The Nature of Extraversion: A Genetical Analysis," *Journal of Personality and Social Psychology, 32* (1975), 102–12.

Edwards, Betty, *Drawing on the Right Side of the Brain.* Los Angeles: J.P. Tarcher, 1979.

Eickmann, P., Kolb, A. Y., and Kolb, D. A., "Designing Learning," in Collopy, F., and Boland, R. (Eds.), *Managing as Designing: Creating a New Vocabulary for Management Education and Research.* Stanford University Press, 2004.

Eisenstein, E. M., and Hutchinson, J. W., "Action-Based Learning: Goals and Attention in the Acquisition of Market Knowledge," *Journal of Marketing Research* XLIII (May, 2006), 244–258.

Elkind, David, *Children and Adolescence: Interpretative Essays on Jean Piaget.* New York: Oxford University Press, 1970.

Elliot, T. S., "Little Gidding," Harcourt Brace Jovanovich, Inc. and Faber and Faber Ltd., London, England.

Elms, A., "Skinner's Dark Year and Walden Two," *American Psychologist, 36*(5) (1981), 470–79.

Entwistle, N., *Styles of Learning and Teaching: An Integrated Outline of Educational Psychology for Students, Teachers, and Lecturers.* New York: Wiley, 1981.

Ericsson, K. A., Krampe, R. T., and Tesch-Römer, C., "The Role of Deliberate Practice in the Acquisition of Expert Performance," *Psychological Review 100* (1993), 363–406.

————, **and Charness, L.,** "Expert Performance: Its Structure and Acquisition," *American Psychologist, 49*(8) (1994), 725–747.

————, "The Influence of Experience and Deliberate Practice on the Development of Superior Expert Performance," in K.A. Ericsson, N. Charness, R. Hoffman, and J. Feltovich, eds., *The Cambridge Handbook of Expertise and Expert Performance,* pp. 683–703. New York: Cambridge University Press, 2006.

Erikson, Eric, *Young Man Luther.* New York: W.W. Norton, 1958.

————, "Identity and the Life Cycle," *Psychological Issues,* 1 (1959).

————, "The Roots of Virtue," in Julian Huxley, ed., *The Humanist Frame.* New York: Harper & Row, 1961.

Evans, J. St. B. T., "Dual-Processing Accounts of Reasoning, Judgment, and Social Cognition," *Annu. Rev. Psychol, 59* (2008), 255–278.

Fallows, J., "The Passionless Presidency: The Trouble with Jimmy Carter's Administration," *The Atlantic Monthly,* May and June 1979.

Fazy, J. A., & Martin, F. "Understanding the Space of Experiential Variation," *Active Learning in Higher Education, 3* (2002), 234–250.

Feigl, Herbert, "The "Mental" and the "Physical," in Feigl et al., eds., *Concepts, Theories and the Mind-Body Problem,* pp. 370–497. Minneapolis: University of Minnesota Press, 1958.

Feldman, David, *Beyond Universals in Cognitive Development.* Norwood, N.J.: Ablex Publishing, 1980.

Feldman, Kenneth, and Theodore Newcomb, *The Impact of College on Students,* Vols. I and II. San Francisco, Jossey-Bass, 1969.

Feldman, S., *Escape from the Doll's House.* New York: McGraw-Hill, 1974.

Fenwick, T. J., "Expanding Conceptions of Experiential Learning: A Review of Five Contemporary Perspectives on Cognition," *Adult Education Quarterly, 50*(4) (2000), 243–272.

————, "Reclaiming and Re-embodying Experiential Learning through Complexity Science," *Studies in the Education of Adults, 35*(2) (2003), 123–141.

Ferrary, Jeannette, "On First Looking into Heisenberg's Principle," *Harvard Magazine,* November–December 1979.

Flavell, John, *The Developmental Psychology of Jean Piaget.* New York: Van Nostrand Reinhold Co., 1963.

————, Stage Related Properties of Cognitive Development," *Cognitive Psychology, 2* (1971), 421–453.

————, Meta-Cognition and Cognitive Monitoring," *American Psychologist, 34*(10) (1979), 906–911.

Fletcher, J. K., and Ragins, B. R., "Stone Center Relational Cultural Theory: A Window on Relational Mentoring," in B. R. Ragins, and K. E. Kram, eds., *The Handbook of Mentoring at Work: Theory, Research, and Practice,* pp. 373–399. Thousand Oaks, CA: Sage, 2007.

Follett, M. P., *Creative Experience.* N.Y.: Longmans, Green and Company, 1924.

Fook, J., *Social Work. Critical Theory and Practice.* London: Sage, 2002.

Forrester, Jay W., *World Dynamics.* Cambridge, Mass.: Wright-Allen Press, 1971.

Fowler, J., *Stages of Faith: The Psychology of Human Development and the Quest for Meaning.* New York: Harper Row, 1981.

Frankfurt, H., "Descartes on the Creation of the Eternal Truths," *Philosophical Review,* 86 (1977), 36–57.

Freire, Paulo, *Pedagogy of the Oppressed.* New York: The Seabury Press, 1970.

————, *Education for Critical Consciousness.* New York: Continuum, 1973.

————, *Pedagogy of the Oppressed.* New York: Continuum, (1974), pp. 58, 62, 75–76.

Fry, Ronald E., "Diagnosing Professional Learning Environments: An Observational Framework for Assessing Situational Complexity," unpublished Ph.D. thesis, Massachusetts Institute of Technology, 1978.

Gadamer, H-G., *Truth and Method.* New York: Crossroad, 1965.

Gardner, R. G., and Beatrice Gardner, "Teaching Sign Language to a Chimpanzee," *Science,* 165 (1969), 644–72.

Garner, I., "Problems and Inconsistencies with Kolb's Learning Styles," *Educational Psychology, 20*(3) (2000), 341–49.

Geertz, C., *Local Knowledge: Further Essays in Interpretive Anthropology.* New York: Basis Books, 1983.

Gemmell, R. M., *Socio-Cognitive Foundations of Entrepreneurial Venturing,* unpublished Ph.D dissertation, Weatherhead School of Management, Case Western Reserve University, 2012.

Gendlin, E. T., "Experiencing: A Variable in the Process of Therapeutic Change," *American Journal Of Psychotherapy,* 15 (1961), 233–245.

_____, *Experiencing and the Creation of Meaning.* Glencoe, IL: Free Press, 1962.

_____, "A Theory of Personality Change," in P. Worschel and D. Byrne, eds., *Personality Change,* pp. 100–148. New York: John Wiley, 1964.

_____, *Focusing.* New York: Bantam Books, 1978.

Gerholmm T., "On Tacit Knowledge in Academia," *European Journal of Education, 25*(3) (1990), 263–271.

Germer, C. K., Efran, J. S., and Overton, W. F., "The Organicism-Mechanism Paradigm Inventory: Toward the Measurement of Metaphysical Assumptions," paper presented at the 53rd Annual Meeting of the Eastern Psychological Association, Baltimore, MD, 1982.

Giddens, A., *The Constitution of Society: Outline of the Theory of Structuration.* University of California Press, 1984.

_____, *Modernity and Self-Identity,* p. 256. Stanford University Press, 1991.

Gilligan, C., *In a Different Voice: Psychological Theory and Women's Development.* Cambridge, MA: Harvard University Press, 1982.

Goldstein, K., and M. Scheerer, "Abstract and Concrete Behavior: An Experimental Study with Special Tests," *Psychological Monographs, 53*(239) (1941).

Good, C., Aronson, J., and Inzlicht, M., "Improving Adolescents' Standardized Test Performance: An Intervention to Reduce the Effects of Stereotype Threat," *Journal of Applied Developmental Psychology* 24 (2003), 645–662.

Gould, S. J., *The Hedgehog, the Fox, and the Magister's Pox: Mending the Gap between Science and the Humanities.* New York: Harmony Books, 2003.

Grochow, J., "Cognitive Style as a Factor in the Design of Interactive Decision-Support Systems," Ph.D. dissertation, Massachusetts Institute of Technology, Sloan School of Management, 1973.

Guilford, J. P., "Some Changes in the Structure of Intellect Model," *Educational and Psychological Measurement, 48* (1988), 1–4.

Guisinger, S., and Blatt, S. J., "Individuality and Relatedness: Evolution of a Fundamental Dialectic," *American Psychologist, 49*(2) (1994), 104–111.

Gypen, Jan, "Learning Style Adaptation in Professional Careers: The Case of Engineers and Social Workers," unpublished doctoral dissertation, Case Western Reserve University, 1980.

Hall, D., "The Impact of Peer Interaction During an Academic Role Transition," *Sociology of Education,* 42 (Spring 1969), 118–40.

Hannaford, C., *Smart Moves: Why Learning Is Not All in Your Head.* Arlington, VA: Great Ocean Publishers, 1995.

Harland, L. K., *Forced-Choice Personality Tests in Management Development Contexts: An Experimental Study of Test-Taker Reactions,* paper presented at Midwest Academy of Management Meetings—HR and Careers Division, 2002.

Harlow, Harry, "Learning Set and Error Factor Theory," in S. Koch, ed., *Psychology: A Study or a Science,* vol. 2. New York: McGraw Hill, 1959.

Harrelson, G. L., and Leaver-Dunn, D., "Using Experiential Learning Cycle in Clinical Instruction," *Human Kinetics, 7*(5) (2002), 23–27.

Harris, M., Fontana, A. F., and Dowds, B. N., "The World Hypotheses Scale: Rationale, Reliability and Validity," *Journal of Personality Assessment, 41*(5) (1977), 537–547.

Harvey, O. J., David Hunt, and Harold Schroder, *Conceptual Systems and Personality Organization.* New York: John Wiley, 1961.

————, "System Structure, Creativity and Flexibility," in O.J. Harvey, ed., *Experience, Structure and Adaptability,* pp. 39–65. New York: Springer, 1966.

Hayward, J., "A Rdzogs-chen Buddhist Interpretation of the Sense of Self," *Journal of Consciousness Studies, 5*(5–6) (1998), 611–626.

Hegel, George F., "Philosophy of Right and Law 1820," in Carl Friedrich, ed., *The Philosophy of Hegel.* New York: Modern Library, 1953.

Helson, R., "Commentary: Reality of Masculine and Feminine Traits in Personality and Behavior," in S. Messick, ed., *Individuality in Learning.* San Francisco: Jossey-Bass, 1976.

Hickey, Joseph, and Peter Scharf, *Democratic Justice and Prison Reform.* San Francisco: Jossey-Bass, 1980.

Hinchcliffe, G., "Re-Thinking Lifelong Learning," *Studies in Philosophy and Education, 25* (2006), 93–109, doi: 10.1007/s11217–006-0004–1.

Hofstadter, Douglas, *Gödel, Escher, Bach: An External Golden Braid.* New York: Basic Books, 1979.

Holman, D., Pavlica, K., and Thorpe, R., "Rethinking Kolb's Theory of Experiential Learning in Management Education: The Contribution of Social Constructionism and Activity Theory," *Management Learning, 28*(2) (1997), 197–215.

Hoover, J. D., Giambatista, R. C., and Belkin, L. Y., "Eyes On, Hands On: Vicarious Observational Learning as an Enhancement of Direct Experience," *Academy of Management Learning & Education, 11*(4) (2012), 591–608.

Hopkins, R., "David Kolb's Experiential Learning-Machine," *Journal of Phenomenological Psychology, 24*(1) (1993), 46–62.

Huber, L., "Disciplinary Cultures and Social Reproduction," *European Journal of Education, 25*(3) (1990), 241–261.

Hudson, Liam, *Contrary Imaginations.* Middlesex, England: Penguin Books, Ltd., 1966.

————, "Commentary: Singularity of Talent," in S. Massick, ed., *Individuality in Learning.* San Francisco: Jossey-Bass, 1976.

Humphrey, C., "By the Light of the Tao," *European Journal of Social Work, 12*(3) (2009), 377–390.

Hunt, David E., *Matching Models in Education.* Toronto: Ontario Institute for Studies in Education, 1974.

————, *Beginning with Ourselves in Practice, Theory and Human Affairs.* Cambridge, MA: Brookline Books, 1987.

————, *The Renewal of Personal Energy.* Toronto: Ontario Institute for Studies in Education, 1991.

Hursh, B., and L. Borzak, "Toward Cognitive Development through Field Studies," *Journal of Higher Education, 50* (January–February 1979), 63–78.

Husserl, E., *Ideas.* New York: Collier, 1962.

Hutchins, Robert M., *The University of Utopia.* Chicago: University of Chicago Press, 1953.

Hutt, G. K., "Experiential Learning Spaces: Hermetic Transformational Leadership for Psychological Safety, Consciousness Development and Math Anxiety Related Inferiority Complex Depotentiation," PhD dissertation, Department of Organizational Behavior, Case Western Reserve University, 2007.

Illich, Ivan, *Deschooling Society*. New York: Harrow Books, 1972.

Jacques, Elliott, "Taking Time Seriously in Evaluating Jobs," *Harvard Business Review,* September–October 1979, pp. 124–32.

James, William, *The Principles of Psychology,* Vols. I and II. New York: Holt, Rinehart and Winston, 1890.

————, Does "Consciousness" Exist? *Journal of Philosophy, Psychology, and Scientific Method, 1* (1904), 477–491.

————, *Pragmatism*: *A New Name for Some Old Ways of Thinking*. New York: Longmans, Green and Company, 1907.

————, *Essays in Radical Empiricism*. New York and London: Longmans, Green and Co., 1912, 2010.

Janis, I. L., *Victims of Groupthink*. Boston: Houghton Mifflin, 1972.

Jarvis, P., *Adult Learning in the Social Context*, London: Croom Helm, 1987.

————, *Adult and Continuing Education. Theory and Practice,* 2nd ed., London: Routledge, 1995.

Johnson, J. A., Germer, C. K., Efran, J. S., and Overton, W. F., "Personality as a Basis for Theoretical Predilections," *Journal of Personality and Social Psychology, 55*(5) (1988), 824–835.

————, **Howey, R. M., Reedy, Y. B., Gibble, H. A., and Ortiz, J. M.,** "Extending the Construct Validity of the Organicim-Mechanism Paradigm Inventory," poster presented at the First Annual Convention of the American Psychological Society, June 11, 1989, Alexandria, VA.

Jones, C., Mokhtari, K., and Reicherd, C., "Are Students' Learning Styles Discipline Specific?" *Community College Journal of Research and Practice, 27*(5) (2003), 363–375.

Jung, Carl, Foreword and Commentary in R. Wilhelm, trans., *The Secret of the Golden Flower*. New York: Harcourt, Brace & World, 1931.

————, *The Structure and Dynamics of the Psyche*. New York: Bollingen Foundation, 1960.

————, *Letters*. Princeton, N.J.: Princeton University Press, 1973.

————, *Psychological Types*. R.F.C. Hull, trans., Collected Works of C.G. Jung, Vol. 6. Bollingen Series XX, Princeton University Press (1977), pp. 12–13, 28, 68.

————, "The Symbolic Life," in H. Read, M. Fordham, G. Adler. and W. McGuire. eds., R.F.C. Hull, trans., *Collected Works of Carl Jung,* Vol. 18. Princeton, N.J.: Bollingen Series XX, Princeton University Press, 1977.

————, *The Red Book: Liber Novus*. New York: W.W. Norton & Company, 2009.

Kabat-Zinn, J., *Wherever You Go There You Are*. New York: Hyperion, 1994.

————, "Mindfulness-Based Interventions in Context: Past, Present and Future," *Clinical Psychology: Science and Practice, 10* (2003), 144–156.

Kagan, Jerome, Rosman, B., Day, D., Alpert, J., and Phillips, W., "Information Processing in the Child: Significance of Analytic and Reflective Attitudes," *Psychological Monographs, 78*(1) (1964).

————, **and Kogan, Nathan,** "Individual Variation in Cognitive Processes," in P.H. Musser, ed., *Carmichael's Manual of Child Psychology,* vol. 1. New York: Wiley, 1970.

Kahneman, D., and Riis, J., "Living and Thinking about It: Two Perspectives on Life," in F.A. Huppert, B. Kaverne, and N. Baylis, eds. *The Science of Well-Being*. London: Oxford University Press, 2005.

————, *Thinking, Fast and Slow*. New York: Farrar, Straus and Giroux, 2011.

Kapur, S., Craik, F. I. M., Tulving, E., Wilson, A. A., Houle, S., and Brown, G. M., "Neuroanatomical Correlates of Encoding in Episodic Memory: Levels of Processing Effect," *Proceedings of the National Academy of Sciences, USA, 91* (1994), 2008–2111.

Kaskowitz, G., "Factor Analysis of the Model Constructs Suggested by Kolb's Learning Skills Profile," *Perceptual and Motor Skills, 80*(2) (1995), 479–486.

Kayes, D. C., "Experiential Learning and Its Critic's: Preserving the Role of Experience in Management Learning and Education," *Academy of Management Learning and Education, 1*(2) (2002), 137–149.

Keeton, Morris, and Pamela Tate, eds., *Learning by Experience—What, Why, How.* San Francisco: Jossey-Bass, 1978.

_____, **Sheckley, B. G., and Griggs, J. K.,** *Efficiency and Effectiveness in Higher Education.* Dubuque, IA: Kendall/Hunt Publishing Company, 2002.

Kegan, R., *The Evolving Self: Problem and Process in Human Development.* Cambridge, MA: Harvard University Press, 1982.

_____, *In Over Our Heads: The Demands of Modern Life.* Cambridge, MA: Harvard University Press, 1994.

_____, **and Lahey, L. L.,** *Immunity to Change.* Boston, MA: Harvard Business Press, 2009.

Kelly, George, *The Psychology of Personal Constructs,* Vols. I and II. New York: W.W. Norton, 1955.

King, P. M., "Student Learning in Higher Education," in S. R. Komives, D. B. Woodward, Jr., and Associates, eds., *Student Services: A Handbook for the Profession,* pp. 234–268. San Francisco: Jossey Bass, 2003.

Klemke, E. D., *The Epistemology of G.E. Moore.* Evanston, Ill.: Northwestern University Press, 1969.

Kluckholm, C., and Murray, H., *Personality in Nature, Society and Culture.* New York: Alfred Knopf p1, 1948.

Knight, K. H., Elfenbein, M. H., and Messina, J. A., "A Preliminary Scale to Measure Connected and Separate Knowing: The Knowing Style Inventory," *Sex Roles, 33* (1995), 499–513.

_____, **Elfenbein, M. H., and Martin, M. B.,** "Relationship of Connected and Separate Knowing to the Learning Styles of Kolb, Formal Reasoning and Intelligence," *Sex Roles, 37* (1997), 401–414.

Knowles, Malcolm S., *The Modern Practice of Adult Education: Andragogy vs. Pedagogy.* New York: Association Press, 1970.

Kohlberg, L., "Stage and Sequence: The Cognitive-Developmental Approach to Socialization," in D. A. Goslin, ed., *Handbook of Socialization Theory and Research.* Chicago: Rand McNally, 1969.

_____, *Essays in Moral Development: The Philosophy of Moral Development,* vol. 1. New York: Harper & Row, 1981.

_____, *Essays in Moral Development: The Psychology of Moral Development—Moral Stages Their Nature and Validity,* vol. 2. New York: Harper & Row, 1984.

_____, *Essays in Moral Development: Ethical Stages—Moral Development through the Life Cycle,* vol. 3. New York: Harper & Row, 1987.

_____, **and Ryncarz, R. A.,** "Beyond Justice Reasoning: Moral Development and the Consideration of a Seventh Stage," in C. N. Alexander, and E. Langer, eds., *Higher Stages of Human Development.* New York: Oxford University Press, 1990.

Kohn, A., *Punished by Rewards.* Boston: Houghton Mifflin, 1993.

Kolb, A. Y., and Kolb, D. A., "Learning Styles and Learning Spaces: Enhancing Experiential Learning in Higher Education," *Academy of Management Learning and Education, 4*(2) (2005a), 193–212.

_____, **and Kolb, D. A.,** *The Kolb Learning Style Inventory 3.1: Technical Specifications.* Boston, MA: Hay Resources Direct, 2005b.

_____, **and Kolb, D. A.,** "Learning Styles and Learning Spaces: A Review of the Multidisciplinary Application of Experiential Learning in Higher Education," in R. Sims, and S. Sims, eds., *Learning Styles and Learning: A Key to Meeting the Accountability Demands in Education,* pp. 45–91. New York: Nova Publishers, 2006.

_____, **and Kolb, D. A.,** "The Learning Way: Meta-Cognitive Aspects of Experiential Learning," *Simulation and Gaming: An Interdisciplinary Journal, 40*(3) (2009), 297–327.

————, and Kolb, D. A., *Learning Style Inventory Version 4.0*. Boston, MA: Hay Resources Direct, 2011.

————, and Kolb, D. A., *The Kolb Learning Style Inventory 4.0: A Comprehensive Guide to the Theory, Psychometrics, Research on Validity and Educational Applications*. Boston, MA: Hay Resources Direct, www.haygroup.com/leadershipandtalentondemand, (2013a).

————, and Kolb, D. A., *Learning Style Inventory Version 3.2*. Boston, MA: Hay Resources Direct, 2013b.

————, and Kolb, D. A., *Experiential Learning Theory Bibliography: Volume 1–4 1971–2014*. Cleveland, OH: Experience Based Learning Systems, Inc., www.learningfromexperience.com, (2014).

————, and Kolb, D. A., Passarelli, A., and Sharma, G., "On Becoming an Experiential Educator: The Educator Role Profile," *Simulation and Gaming, 45*(2) (2014), 204–234. doi: 10.1177/1046878114534383.

Kolb, David A., *Individual Learning Styles and the Learning Process*. Working Paper #535–571, Sloan School of Management, Massachusetts Institute of Technology, 1971.

————, Rubin, I. M., and McIntyre, J., eds., *Organizational Psychology: An Experiential Approach*. Englewood Cliffs, NJ: Prentice Hall, 1971.

————, I. Rubin, and E. Schein, "The TECH Freshman Integration Research Project: A Summary Report," unpublished report, M.I.T., 1972.

————, "On Management and the Learning Process," M.I.T. Sloan School Working Paper No. 652–73, 1973.

————, and Marshall Goldman, "Toward a Typology of Learning Styles and Learning Environments: An Investigation of the Impact of Learning Styles and Discipline Demands on the Academic Performance, Social Adaptation and Career Choices of M.I.T. Seniors," M.I.T. Sloan School Working Paper No. 688–73, 1973.

————, and Ronald E. Fry, "Toward an Applied Theory of Experiential Learning," in C. Cooper, ed., *Theories of Group Processes*. London: Wiley, 1975.

————, *Learning Style Inventory*. Boston, MA: McBer & Company, 1976a.

————, *Learning Style Inventory: Technical Manual*. Boston, MA: McBer & Company, 1976b.

————, "On Management and the Learning Process," *California Management Review, 18*(3) (1976c), 21–31.

————, *The Learning Style Inventory: Technical Manual*. Boston: McBer and Company, 1976.

————, "Applications of Experiential Learning Theory to the Information Sciences," paper delivered at the National Science Foundation Conference on contributions of the behavioral sciences to research in information science, December 1978.

————, "Experiential Learning Theory and the Learning Style Inventory: A Reply to Freedman and Stumpf," *Academy of Management Review,* April 1981.

————, and Donald Wolfe, with collaborators, "Professional Education and Career Development: A Cross-Sectional Study of Adaptive Competencies in Experiential Learning," final report NIE grant no. NIE-G-77–0053, 1981. ERIC no. ED 209 493 CE 030 519.

————, "Experiential Learning Theory and the Learning Style Inventory: A Reply to Freedman and Stumpf," *The Academy of Management Review, 6* (1981a), 289–296.

————, "Learning Styles and Disciplinary Differences," in A. Chickering, ed., *The Modern American College*. San Francisco, CA: Jossey Bass, 1981b.

————, and Wolfe, D., *Professional Education and Career Development: A Cross-Sectional Study of Adaptive Competencies in Experiential Learning,* Final report NIE grant no. NIE-G-77–0053, ERIC no. ED 209 493 CE 030 519, 1981.

————, "Problem Management: Learning from Experience," in S. Srivastva & Associates, *The Executive Mind*. San Francisco: Jossey-Bass, 1983.

_____, *Experiential Learning: Experience as the Source of Learning and Development.* New Jersey: Prentice-Hall, 1984.

_____, *Learning Style Inventory, Revised Edition.* Boston, MA: McBer & Company, 1985a.

_____, *Learning Style Inventory: Technical Manual.* Boston, MA: McBer & Company, 1985b.

_____, "Integrity, Advanced Professional Development, and Learning," in S. Srivastava, ed., *Executive Integrity: The Search for High Human Values in Organizational Life,* pp. 68–88. San Francisco, CA: Jossey-Bass, 1988.

_____, "The Challenges of Advanced Professional Development," in L. Landon ed., *Roads to the Learning Society.* Chicago, IL: Council for Adult & Experiential Learning, 1991.

_____, *Learning Style Inventory, Version 3.* Boston, MA: Hay Resources Direct, trg_mcber@haygroup.com, 1999a.

_____, *Learning Style Inventory, Version 3: Technical Specifications.* Boston, MA: Hay Resources Direct, trg_mcber@haygroup.com, 1999b.

_____, **Boyatzis, R., and Mainemelis, C.,** "Experiential Learning Theory: Previous Research and New Directions," in R. Sternberg, and L. Zhang, eds., *Perspectives on Cognitive Learning, and Thinking Styles.* Mahwah, NJ: Lawrence Erlbaum Associates, 2001.

_____, *Learning Style Inventory Version 3.1.* Boston, MA: Hay Resources Direct, 2005.

_____, **and Rainey M. A.,** "Leading in a Learning Way: A 21st Century Perspective on Leadership Using Experiential Learning Theory," *The NTL Handbook of Organization Development and Change: Principles, Practices, and Perspectives.* Arlington, VA: NTL Institute, 2013.

_____, **and Peterson, K.,** "Tailor Your Coaching to People's Learning Styles," *HBR Guide to Coaching Your Employees.* Cambridge, MA: Harvard Business Publishing, 2013.

_____, **and Yeganeh, B.,** "Deliberate Experiential Learning: Mastering the Art of Learning from Experience," in Kim Elsbach, D. Christopher Kayes, and Anna Kayes, eds., *Contemporary Organizational Behavior in Action,* 1st ed. Upper Saddle River, NJ: Pearson Education, 2015.

Koplowitz, Herbert, "Unitary Operations: A Projection beyond Piaget's Formal Operations Stage," unpublished manuscript, University of Massachusetts, 1978.

Kosower, E., and Berman, N., "Comparison of Pediatric Resident and Faculty Learning Styles: Implications for Medical Education," *The American Journal of the Medical Sciences, 312* (5) (1996), 214–218.

Kretovics, M. A., "Assessing the MBA: What Do Our Students Learn?" *Journal of Management Development, 10*(2) (1999), 125–133.

Kuhn, Thomas, *The Structure of Scientific Revolutions.* Chicago: University of Chicago Press, 1962.

Kurtines, W., and E. B. Greif, "The Development of Moral Thought: Review and Evaluation of Kohlberg's Approach," *Psychological Bulletin,* 81 (1974), 8.

Lakoff, G., and Johnson, M., *Metaphors We Live By.* Chicago: University of Chicago Press, 1980.

Langer, E. J., *Mindfulness.* Cambridge, MA: DeCapo Press, 1989.

_____, *The Power of Mindful Learning.* Cambridge, MA: Perseus Publishing, 1997.

Lave, J., and Wenger, E., *Situated Learning: Legitimate Peripheral Participation.* Cambridge, UK: Cambridge University Press, 1991.

Lawrence, D. H. "Terra Incognita"1920 Retreived 10/14/14 at http://www.ralphmag.org/lawrence.html

Leary, D. E. William James and the art of human understanding. *American Psychologist.* 47(2):152–169, 1992.

LeDoux, J., *The emotional brain.* New York: Putnam, 1997.

Lehman, H. C., *Age and Achievement.* Princeton, N.J.: Princeton University Press, 1953.

Leistyna, P., *Presence of Mind: Education and the Politics of Deception.* Boulder, CO: Westview, 2004.

Leonard, G., *Mastery: The Keys to Long-Term Success and Fulfillment.* New York: Dutton, 1991.

Lessor, J., "Cultural Differences in Learning and Thinking," in S. Messick, ed., *Individuality in Learning.* San Francisco: Jossey-Bass, 1976.

Levi-Strauss, Claude, *The Savage Mind.* Chicago: University of Chicago Press, 1969.

Levy, Jerre, "Cerebral Asymmetry and the Psychology of Man," in M. Wittrock, ed., *The Brain and Psychology.* New York: Academic Press, 1980.

Levy, S. R., Plaks, J. E., Hong, Y., Chiu, C., and Dweck, C. S., "Static versus Dynamic Theories and the Perception of Groups: Different Routes to Different Destinations," *Personality and Social Psychology Review 5*(2) (2001), 156–68.

Lewin, Kurt, *Field Theory in Social Sciences.* New York: Harper & Row, 1951.

Lewis, R., and C. Margerison, *Working and Learning—Identifying Your Preferred Ways of Doing Things.* Bedfordshire, England: Management and Organisation Development Research Centre, Cranfield School of Management, 1979.

Linville, P. W., "The Complexity-Extremity Effect and Age-Based Stereotyping," *Journal of Personality and Social Psychology, 42*(2) (1982), 193–211.

―――――, "Self-Complexity and Affective Extremity: Don't Put All of Your Eggs in One Cognitive Basket," *Social Cognition, 3* (1985), 94–120.

―――――, "Self-Complexity as a Cognitive Buffer against Stress-Related Illness and Depression," *Journal of Personality and Social Psychology, 52*(4) (1987), 663–676.

Lippitt, Ronald, *Training in Community Relations.* New York: Harper & Row, 1949.

Lipshitz, R., "Knowing and Practicing: Teaching Behavioral Sciences at the Israel Defense Forces Command and General Staff College," *Journal of Management Studies, 20*(1) (1983), 121–141.

Loevinger, Jane, "The Meaning and Measurement of Ego Development," *American Psychologist, 21* (1966), 195–206.

―――――, *Ego Development.* San Francisco: Jossey-Bass, 1976.

―――――, **and Ruth Wessler,** *Measuring Ego Development,* Vol. 1. San Francisco: Jossey-Bass, 1978.

―――――, "Measurement of Personality: True or False," *Psychological Inquiry,* 4, pp. 1–16. Mahwah, NJ: Lawrence Erlbaum Associates, 1993.

―――――, "Completing a Life Sentence," in P. M. Westenberg, A. Blasi, and L. D. Cohn, eds., *Personality Development: Theoretical, Empirical and Clinical Investigations of Loevinger's Conception of Ego Development,* pp. 347–354. Mahwah, NJ: Lawrence Erlbaum Associates, 1993.

Loo, R., "A Meta-Analytic Examination of Kolb's Learning Style Preferences among Business Majors," *Journal of Education for Business, 77*(5) (2002a), 25–50.

―――――, "The Distribution of Learning Styles and Types for Hard and Soft Business Majors," *Educational Psychology, 22*(3) (2002b), 349–360.

Lyddon, W. J., "Root Metaphor Theory: A Philosophical Framework for Counseling and Psychotherapy," *J. Counsel. Dev., 67* (1989), 442–448.

―――――, **and Adamson, L. A.,** "Worldview and Counseling Preference: An Analogue Study," *J. Counsel. Dev., 71* (1992), 41–47.

Lynch, M., and Ryan, R. M., "On Being Yourself: Consistency versus Authenticity of Self-Concept in Cultural and Interpersonal Contex," Retrieved May 3, 2014, at https://www.researchgate.net/publication/255586808_On_Being_Yourself_Consistency_Versus_Authenticity_of_Self.

Mager, Robert F., *Preparing Instructional Objectives.* Palo Alto, Calif.: Fearon Publishers, 1962.

Mainemelis, C., Boyatzis, R., and Kolb, D. A., (2002). "Learning Styles and Adaptive Flexibility: Testing Experiential Learning Theory," *Management Learning, 33*(1) (1969), 5–33.

Malinen, A. *Toward the Essence of Adult Experiential Learning.* SoPhi: Univrsity of Jyvaskyla, Finland, 2000.

Mann, L., "The Relation of Rorschach Indices of Extratension and Introversion to a Measure of Responsiveness to the Immediate Environment," *Journal of Consulting Psychology, 20* (1956), 114–18.

March, J. G., *The Ambiguities of Experience*. Ithaca, New York: Cornell University Press, 2010.

Margerison, C. J., and R. G. Lewis, *How Work Preferences Relate to Learning Styles*. Bedfordshire, England: Management and Organisation Development Research Centre, Cranfield School of Management, 1979.

Margulies, Newton, and Anthony P. Raia, "Scientists, Engineers, and Technological Obsolescence," *California Management Review*, Winter 1967, pp. 43–48.

Marrow, Alfred J., *The Practical Theorist: The Life and Work of Kurt Lewin*. New York: Basic Books, 1969.

Maturana, H., "The Biology of Cognition," in Maturana and Varela, *Autopoeisis and Cognition*, 1970.

_____, and Varela, F., *Autopoeisis and Cognition*. Dordrecht, Holland: D. Reidel, 1980.

_____, and Varela, F., *The Tree of Knowledge: Biological Roots of Human Understanding*. Boston, MA: Shambala, 1987.

McCloskey, H., and J. Schaar, "Psychological Dimensions of Anomie," *American Psychological Review*, 30(1) (1963), 14–40.

McGoldrick, K., Battle, A., and Gallagher, S., "Service-Learning and the Economics Course: Theory and Practice," *The American Economist*, 44(1) (2000), 43–52.

McNemar, W., *Psychological Statistics*. New York: John Wiley, 1957.

Mead, G., *Mind, Self and Society, from the Standpoint of a Social Behaviorist*. Chicago, IL: University of Chicago Press, 1934.

Mentkowski, M., and N. Much, *Careering After College: Perspectives on Lifelong Learning and Career Development*. Milwaukee, Wisconsin: Alverno Productions, 1982.

_____, and M. J. Strait, "A Longitudinal Study of Student Change in Cognitive Development and Generic Abilities in an Outcome-centered Liberal Arts Curriculum." Paper presented at the annual meeting of the American Educational Research Association, Montreal, Canada, April, 1983.

Mezirow, J., *Transformative Dimensions of Adult Learning*. San Francisco, CA: Jossey Bass, 1990.

_____, "Contemporary Paradigms of Learning," *Adult Education Quarterly*, 46(3) (1996), 158–173.

Michelson, E., "Multicultural Approaches to Portfolio Development," *New Directions for Adult and Continuing Education*, 75 (1997), 41–53.

_____, "Re-Membering: The Return of the Body to Experiential Learning," *Studies in Continuing Education*, 20(2) (1998), 217–233.

_____, "Carnival, Paranoia and Experiential Learning," *Studies in the Education of Adults*, 31(2) (1999), 140–154.

Miettinen, R., "The Concept of Experiential Learning and John Dewey's Theory of Reflective Thought and Action," *International Journal of Lifelong Education*, 19(1) (2000), 54–72.

Miller, G., Galanter, E., and L. Pribram, *Plans and the Structure of Behavior*. New York: Holt, Rinehart & Winston, 1960.

Miller, J. B., and Stiver, I., *The Healing Connection*. Boston: Beacon Press, 1997.

Mills, T., *Sociology of Small Groups*. Englewood Cliffs, N.J.: Prentice-Hall, 1965.

Milne, D., James, I., Keegan, D., and Dudley, M., "Teacher's PETS: A New Observational Measure of Experiential Training Interactions," *Clinical Psychology and Psychotherapy*, 9 (2002), 187–199.

Mintzberg, H., *The Nature of Managerial Work*. New York: Harper & Row, 1973.

Mischel, W., "Convergences and Challenges in the Search for Consistency, *American Psychologist*, 39 (1984), 351–364.

Moon, B. A., "Learning Style Influence on Relationship Sales Success." Unpublished EDM Quantitative Research Report, Weatherhead School of Management, Case Western Reserve University, 2008.

Molden, D. C., and Dweck, C. S., "Finding 'Meaning' in Psychology: A Lay Theories Approach to Self-Regulation, Social Perception and Social Development," *American Psychologist*, 61(3) (2006), 192–203.

Mother Theresa, *Total Surrender.* New York: Walker and Company 1993.

Myers-Briggs, I., *The Myers-Briggs Type Indicator Manual.* Princeton, New Jersey: Educational Testing Service, 1962.

Nelson, E. A., and Grinder, R. E., "Toward an Ex Cathedra Doctrine of Learning," *Contemporary Psychology, 30*(8) (1985), 622–623.

Nelson, T. O., "Consciousness and Meta-Cognition," *American Psychologist, 51*(2) (1996), 102–116.

Neugarten and Associates, *Personality in Middle and Late Life.* New York: Atherton Press, 1964.

New Zealand Ministry of Education, *Making Meaning: Making a Difference.* NZ: Learning Media Limited. Online Version: www.tki.org.nz/r/health/cia/make_meaning/index_e.php, 2004.

Nisbett, R. E., Peng, K., Choi, I., and Norenzayan, A., "Culture and Systems of Thought: Holistic versus Analytic Cognition," *Psychological Review, 108*(2) (2001), 291–310.

Nishida, K., *An Inquiry into the Good* (trans. Maso Abe and Christopher Ives). New Haven, CT: Yale University Press, 1911, 1990.

Noam, G. G., "Ego Development: True or False?" *Psychological Inquiry, 4* (1993), pp. 43–48, Hillsdale, NJ: Lawrence Erlbaum Ass., 1993.

Nonaka, I., and Takeuchi, H. *The Knowledge-creating Company.* New York: Oxford University Press, 1995.

————, **and Konno, N.,** "The Concept of 'Ba': Building a Foundation for Knowledge Creation," *California Management Review, 40*(3) (1998), 40–54.

————, **Toyama, R., and Konno, N.,** "SECI, *Ba* and Leadership: A Unified Model of Dynamic Knowledge Creation," *Long Range Planning, 33* (2000), 5–34.

Nouwen, H., *Reaching Out.* New York: Doubleday, 1975.

Nyirenda, J. E., "The Relevance of Paulo Freire's Contributions to Education and Development in Present Day Africa," *Africa Media Review, 10*(1) (1996), 1–20.

Olsen, M., "Political Alienation Scale," in J. Robinson and P. Shauer, *Measures of Social Psychological Attitudes,* pp. 181–83. Institute for Social Research, University of Michigan, August 1969.

Ornstein, Robert E., *The Psychology of Consciousness.* New York: W.H. Freeman & Company, 1972.

————, *The Psychology of Consciousness.* New York: Harcourt Brace, Jovanovich, 1977.

Orwell, G., "Politics and the English Language," in S. Orwell and I. Angus, eds., *In Front of Your Nose,* Vol. 4, The Collected Essays of George Orwell. New York: Harcourt Brace & World, 1968.

Osipow, Samuel H., *Theories of Career Development,* 2nd ed. New York: Appleton-Century-Crofts, 1973.

Osland, J. S., Kolb, D. A., Rubin, I. M., and Turner, M. E., *Organizational Behavior: An Experiential Approach.* 8th edition. Upper Saddle River, NJ: Prentice Hall, 2007.

Owings, R., Peterson, G., Bransford, J., Morris, C., and Stein, B., "Spontaneous Monitoring and Regulation of Learning: A Comparison of Successful and Less Successful Fifth Graders," *Journal of Educational Psychology, 72* (1980), 250–256.

Palmer, J. O., "Attitudinal Correlates of Rorschach's Experience Balance," *Journal of Projective Techniques, 20* (1956), 207–11.

Palmer, P., *To Know as We Are Known: Education as a Spiritual Journey,* San Francisco: Harper and Row, 1983.

————, *The Active Life: A Spirituality of Work, Creativity and Caring.* San Francisco: Harper and Row, 1990.

————, *The Courage to Teach: Exploring the Inner Landscape of a Teacher's Life.* San Francisco: Jossey-Bass, 1998.

Papaert, S., *Mindstorms: Children, Computers, and Powerful Ideas.* New York: Basic Books, 1980.

Pashler, H., McDaniel, M., Rohrer, D., and Bjork, R., "Learning Styles: Concepts and Evidence," *Psychological Science in the Public Interest, 9*(3) (2008), 105–119.

Passarelli, A. M., and Kolb D. A., "The Learning Way—Learning from Experience as the Path to Life-long Learning and Development," in London, M., ed., *Handbook of Lifelong Learning,* (2011), Chapter 6, 70–90. New York: Oxford University Press.

_____, **and Kolb, D. A.,** "Using Experiential Learning Theory to Promote Student Learning and Development in Programs of Education Abroad, in Michael Vande Berg, Michael Page, and Kris Lou, eds., *Student Learning Abroad.* Sterling, VA: Stylus, 2012.

Pepper, S., *World Hypotheses.* Berkeley, Calif.: University of California Press, 1942.

Perlmutter, S., "Cognitive Complexity and Time Perspective in Hybrid Organizations," unpublished doctoral dissertation Case Western Reserve University, 1990.

Perkins, M., "Matter, Sensation and Understanding," *American Philosophical Quarterly,* 8 (1971), 1–12.

Perry, William, *Forms of Intellectual and Ethical Development in the College Years: A Scheme.* New York: Holt, Rinehart & Winston, 1970.

Peterson, K., Decato, L., and Kolb, D. A., "Moving and Learning: Expanding Style and Increasing Flexibility," *Journal of Experiential Education,* 2014.

Pfaff, W., "Mr. Carter's Slide Rule," *New York Times,* op-ed page, June 6, 1979.

Piaget, Jean, *Play, Dreams and Imitation in Childhood.* New York: W.W. Norton, 1951.

_____, *The Origins of Intelligence in Children.* New York: International University Press, 1952.

_____, *Structuralism.* New York: Harper Torchbooks, 1968.

_____, *Genetic Epistemology.* New York: Columbia University Press, 1970a.

_____, *The Place of the Sciences of Man in the System of Sciences.* New York: Harper Torchbooks, 1970b.

_____, *Psychology and Epistemology.* Middlesex, England: Penguin Books, 1971.

_____, "What Is Psychology?" *American Psychologist,* July 1978, pp. 648–52.

Pigg, K., Busch, L. and Lacy, W., "Individual Learning Styles and the Development of Extension Education Programs," unpublished paper, University of Kentucky, 1978.

Plovnick, Mark, "A Cognitive Ability Theory of Occupational Roles," Working Paper #524–71, M.I.T. School of Management, Spring 1971.

_____, "Individual Learning Styles and the Process of Career Choice in Medical Students," doctoral dissertation, M.I.T. Sloan School of Management, 1974.

_____, "Primary Care Career Choices and Medical Student Learning Styles," *Journal of Medical Education,* vol. 50 (September 1975), 849–855.

Polanyi, Michael, *Personal Knowledge.* Chicago: University of Chicago Press, 1958 and Routledge and Kegan Paul, London, England.

_____, *Socialization Effects in Predicting Medical Career Choices: Some Questions from a Study of Learning Styles,* paper presented at the Academy of Management National Meetings, Detroit, 1980.

Pounds, William, "On Problem Finding," Sloan School Working Paper No. 145–65, 1965.

_____, *The Tacit Dimension.* New York: Doubleday, 1966.

Power, M. J., "The Multistory Self: Why the Self Is More than the Sum of its Autoparts," *Journal of Clinical Psychology,* 63(2) (2007), 187–198.

Rainey, M. A., Heckelman, F., Galazka, S., and Kolb, D. A., "The Executive Skills Profile: A Method for Assessing Development Needs among Family Medicine Faculty," *Family Medicine,* 25 (1993), 100–103.

_____, **and Kolb, D. A.,** "Organization Leadership: Leading in a Learning Way," in B. B. Jones, and M. Brazzel, eds., *The NTL Handbook of Organization Development and Change: Principles, Practices, and Perspectives,* pp. 329–348. Arlington, VA: NTL Institute, 2014.

Rasanen, M., *Building Bridges. Experiential Art Understanding: A Work of Art as a Means of Understanding and Constructing.* Helsink, Finland: Publication Series of the University of Art and Design. Helsink UIAH, 1997.

Raschick, M., Maypole, D. E., & Day, P., "Improving Field Education through Kolb Learning Theory," *Journal of Social Work Education, 34*(1) (1998), 31–43.

Read, H., Fordham, M., and Adler, G., eds., *The Collected Works of C.G. Jung,* Bollingen Foundation, 8, 1961–67.

Reese, J., *Enhancing Law Student Performance: Learning Styles Interventions,* unpublished report. Saratoga Springs, New York: National Center on Adult Learning, Empire State College, 1998.

Reynolds, M., "Learning Styles: A Critique," *Management Learning, 28*(2) (1997), 115–134.

————, "Reflection and Critical Reflection in Management Learning," *Management Learning, 29*(2) (1998), 183–200.

Robertson, D. L., *Self-directed Growth.* Muncie, Indiana: Accelerated Development, Inc., 1988.

Roe, Anne, "Early Determinants of Vocational Choice," *Journal of Counseling Psychology,* Vol. 4, 3, 212–17, 1957.

————, *The Psychology of Occupations.* New York: John Wiley, 1956.

Rogers, Carl, *Client-Centered Therapy: Its Current Practice, Implications and Theory.* London: Constable, 1951.

————, "A Theory of Therapy, Personality, and Interpersonal Relationships, as Developed in the Client-Centered Framework," in S. Koch, ed., *Psychology: A Study of a Science, vol. 3 Formulations of the Person and the Social Context* (1959), 184–256. New York: McGraw Hill.

————, *On Becoming a Person.* Boston: Houghton Mifflin, 1961.

————, "Toward a Modern Approach to Values: The Valuing Process in the Mature Person," *Journal of Abnormal and Social Psychology, 63*(2) (1964), 160–167.

Rogoff, B., *The Cultural Nature of Human Development.* London: Oxford University Press (2003).

Rorschach, H., *Psychodiagnostics,* 5th ed. (trans. P. Lemkau and B. Kronenberg). Berne Switzerland: Verlag Hans Huber, 1951.

Rose, N., and Abi-Rached, J. M., *Neuro: The New Brain Sciences and the Management of the Mind,* NJ: Princeton University Press, 2013.

Rowling, J. K., "A Stripping Away of the Inessential," *Harvard Magazine,* July-August (2008), 55–56.

Rubin, Zick, "Does Personality Really Change after 20?" *Psychology Today,* May 1981, pp. 18–27.

Russell, B., *The Problems of Philosophy.* London: Butterworth, 1912.

Ryan, R. M., and Deci, E. L., "Self-Determination Theory and the Facilitation of Intrinsic Motivation, Social Development, and Well-Being," *American Psychologist, 55*(1) (2000), 68–78.

————, **and Deci, E. L.,** "Autonomy Is No Illusion: Self-Determination Theory and the Empirical Study of Authenticity, Awareness and Will," Chapter 28: pp. 449–479, in J. Greenberg, S.L. Koole, and T. Pyscznski, eds., *Handbook of Experimental Existential Psychology.* New York: Guilford Press, 2004.

Sagan, Carl, *The Dragons of Eden.* New York: Random House, 1977.

Samples, Bob, *The Metaphoric Mind.* Reading, Mass.: Addison-Wesley, 1976.

Samuelson, Judith, "Career Development and Cognitive Styles," unpublished paper, Ohio State University, 1982.

Sanford, N., *Self and Society: Social Change and Individual Development.* New York: Atherton Press, 1966.

Schein, Edgar, and Warren Bennis, *Personal and Organizational Change through Group Methods.* New York: John Wiley, 1965.

————, *Professional Education: Some New Directions.* New York: McGraw-Hill, © The Carnegie Foundation for the Advancement of Teaching, 1972.

Schiller, Friedrich, *Uber Die Asthetischa Erziehung Das Menschen.* Hamburg: Cotta'sche Ausgabe, Bd. xviii, 1826.

Schilpp, Paul A., *Albert Einstein—Philosopher Scientist.* La Salle, Ill.: Library of Living Philosophers, Open Court Publishing, 1949.

Schon, D. A., *The Reflective Practitioner.* New York: Basic Books, 1983.

Schroder, H. M., Driver, M. J., and Streufert, S., *Human Information Processing.* New York: Holt, Rinehart & Winston, 1967.

Scott, William A., "Flexibility, Rigidity, and Adaptation: Toward Clarification of Concepts," in O. J. Harvey, ed., *Experience, Structure and Adaptability,* pp. 369–400. New York: Springer, 1966.

Seaman, J., "Experience, Reflect, Critique: The End of the 'Learning Cycles' Era," *Journal of Experiential Learning, 31*(1) (2008), 3–18.

Sharma, G., and Kolb, D. A., "The Learning Flexibility Index: Assessing Contextual Flexibility in Learning Style," Chapter 5 (pp. 60–77), in S. Rayner, and E. Cools, eds., *Style Differences in Cognition, Learning and Management: Theory, Research and Practice.* New York: Routledge Publishers, 2010.

Signell, K. A., "Cognitive Complexity in Person Perception and Nation Perception: A Developmental Approach," *Journal of Personality,* 34 (1966), 517–37.

Simon, H. A., *Administrative Behavior.* New York: Macmillan, 1947.

Sims, Ronald, "Preparation for Professional Careers and Changing Job Roles: An Assessment of Professional Education," qualifying paper, Department of Organizational Behavior, Case Western Reserve University, 1980.

———, "Assessing Competencies in Experiential Learning Theory: A Person-Job Congruence Model of Effectiveness in Professional Careers," unpublished Ph.D. dissertation, Case Western Reserve University, 1981.

Singer, E. A., *Experience and Reflection.* Philadelphia: University of Pennsylvania Press, 1959.

Singer, J. L., and H. E. Spohn, "Some Behavioral Correlates of Rorschach's Experience-type," *Journal of Consulting Psychology,* 18 (1954), 1–9.

———, **Harold Wilensky, and Vivian McCraven,** "Delay Capacity, Fantasy and Planning Ability: A Factorial Study of Some Basic Ego Functions," *Journal of Consulting Psychology,* 20 (1956), 375–83.

Skinner, B. F., *Walden II.* New York: Macmillan, 1948.

Smith, D., *Physician Managerial Skills: Assessing the Critical Competencies of the Physician Executive,* unpublished doctoral dissertation, Department of Organizational Behavior, Case Western Reserve University, 1990.

Smith, M. K., "Mary Parker Follett and Informal Education," *The Encyclopedia of Informal Education,* http://www.infed.org/thinkers/et-foll.htm. Last Update: May 29, 2012.

———, **and Kolb, D. A.,** "On Experiential Learning," *The Encyclopedia of Informal Education,* 2010. Retrieved [3/11/14] from http://www.infed.org/b-explrn.htm.

Snow, C., *The Two Cultures: On a Second Look.* Cambridge, England: Cambridge University Press, 1963.

Souvaine, E., Lahey, L. L., and Kegan, R., "Life after Formal Operations: Implications for a Psychology of the Self," in Alexander and Langer, eds., *Higher Stages of Human Development.* New York: Oxford University Press, 1990.

Specht, L. B., & Sandlin, P. K., "The differential effects of experiential learning activities and traditional lecture classes." *Simulation & Gaming, 22*(2) (1991), 196–210.

Sperry, R. W., Gazzaniga, M. S., and Bogen, J. E., "Interhemispheric Relationships: The Neocortical Commissures; Syndromes of Hemispheric Disconnections," in P. J. Vinken and G. W. Bruyn, eds., *Handbook of Clinical Neurology.* Amsterdam: North Holland Publishing, 1969, pp. 273–89.

Stabell, C., "The Impact of a Conversational Computer System on Human Problem Solving Behavior," unpublished working paper, Massachusetts Institute of Technology, Sloan School of Management, 1973.

Staude, J., *The Adult Development of C.G. Jung.* Boston, MA: Routledge & Keegan Paul, 1981.

Stein, J. (Ed.) *The Random House Dictionary of the English Language: The Unabridged Edition.* New York: Random House, 1966.

Strange, C. C., & Banning, J. H., *"Educating by Design: Creating Campus Learning Environments that Work"* San Francisco, CA: Jossey Bass, 2001

Su, Y., "Lifelong Learning as Being: The Heideggerian Perspective," *Adult Education Quarterly, 61*(1) (2011), 57–72.

Summers, L. H., "On Undergraduate Education," *Harvard Magazine* (July–August 2003), 63–65.

Super, C. M., and Harkness, S., "The Metaphors of Development," *Human Development, 46* (2003), 3–23.

Super, D. E., Starishevsky, R., N. Matlin, and Jordaan, J. P., *Career Development: Self Concept Theory.* New York: CEEB Research Monograph, No. 4, 1963.

Swartz, D. L., "The Sociology of Habit: The Perspective of Pierre Bourdieu," *The Occupational Therapy Journal of Research, 22* (2002), 61S-69S.

Tangney, J. P., "Humility: Theoretical Perspectives, Empirical Findings and Directions for Future Research," *Journal of Social and Clinical Psychology, 19* (2000), 70–82.

Taylor, E. I., and Wozniak, R. H., *Pure Experience: The Response to William James.* Bristol England: Thoemmes Press, 1996.

Taylor, F. C., "Relationship between Student Personality and Performance in an Experiential Theoretical Group Dynamics Course," Faculty Working Paper #132, Kent State University, 1973.

Templeton, J. M., *Worldwide Laws of Life.* Philadelphia, PA: Templeton Foundation Press, 1997.

Terman, L., and M. Oden, *The Gifted Child Grows Up.* Stanford, Calif.: Stanford University Press, 1947.

Tharpe, R. G., and Gallimore, R., *Rousing Minds to Life: Teaching, Learning and Schooling in Social Context.* Cambridge UK: Cambridge University Press, (1988).

Thompson, L. M., "Love of Learning as the Driver for Self-Directed Learning in the Workplace," unpublished doctoral dissertation, Case Western Reserve University, 1999.

Torbert, William, *Learning from Experience: Toward Consciousness.* New York: Columbia University Press, 1972.

————, "Organizing Experiential Learning," in Douglas E. Wolfe and Eugene Byrne, eds., *Developing Experiential Learning in Professional Education,* No. 8. San Francisco: Jossey-Bass, 1980.

Torrealba, D., "Convergent and Divergent Learning Styles," master's thesis, Massachusetts Institute of Technology, Sloan School of Management, 1972.

Tough, Allen, *Major Learning Efforts: Recent Research and Future Directions.* Toronto: Ontario Institute for Studies in Education, 1977.

Trinh, M. P., and Kolb, D. A., "Eastern Experiential Learning: Eastern Principles for Learning Wholeness," *Journal of Career Planning and Adult Development,* Special Issue, "Recovering Craft: Holistic Work and Empowerment," William Charland (guest editor), *27*(4) (2011), 29–36.

Tulving, E., *Elements of Episodic Memory.* New York: Oxford University Press, 1983.

————, "Episodic Memory and Autonoesis: Uniquely Human?" in Terrace and Metcalfe, eds., *The Missing Link in Cognition: Origins of Self-Reflective Consciousness.* London: Oxford University Press, 2005.

Turner, Terence, "Piaget's Structuralism," *American Anthropologist, 76* (1973), 351–73.

Tyler, Leona, *Individuality.* San Francisco: Jossey-Bass, 1978.

Vail, P. B., *Learning as a Way of Being: Strategies for Survival in a World of Permanent White Water.* San Francisco, CA: Jossey Bass, 1996.

Vandenberg, B., "Is Epistemology Enough: An Existential Consideration of Development," *American Psychologist, 46*(12) (1991), 1278–1286.

Vannoy, J., "Generality of Cognitive Complexity-Simplicity as a Personality Construct," *Journal of Personality and Social Psychology,* 1965, pp. 385–96.

Varela, F. J., Thompson, E., and Rosch, E., *The Embodied Mind: Cognitive Science and Human Experience.* Cambridge, MA: MIT Press, 1991.

Vickers, Geoffrey, *Value Systems and Social Process.* Middlesex, England: Penguin Books, 1968.

Vince, R. "Behind and Beyond Kolb's Learning Cycle." *Journal of Management Education, 22*(3), 304–319, 1997.

von Glasersfeld, E., "The Concepts of Adaptation and Viability in a Radical Constructionist Theory of Knowledge," paper presented at the Theodore Mischel Symposium on Constructivism at the 7th Annual Meeting of the Jean Piaget Society, Philadelphia, May 19–21, 1977.

Vygotsky, L. S., *Mind in Society: The Development of Higher Psychological Processes.* Cambridge, MA: Harvard University Press, 1978.

Waitzkin, J., *The Art of Learning: A Journey in the Pursuit of Excellence.* New York: Free Press, (2007).

Wallas, G., *The Art of Thought.* New York: Harcourt Brace, 1926.

Weathersby, Rita, "A Developmental Perspective on Adults' Formal Uses of Education," doctoral dissertation, Harvard University Graduate School of Education, June 1977.

————, "Life Stages and Learning Interests," in *The Adult Learner.* Washington, D.C.: American Association for Higher Education, 1978.

Weirstra, R. F. A., and DeJong, J. A., "A Scaling Theoretical Evaluation of Kolb's Learning Style Inventory-2," in M. Valcke and D. Gombeir, eds., *Learning Styles: Reliability and Validity.* pp. 431–440. Proceedings of the 7th Annual European Learning Styles Information Network, 26–28 June, 2002, Ghent: University of Ghent.

Weisner, Frank, "Learning Profiles and Managerial Styles of Managers," S.M. thesis, Sloan School of Management, M.I.T., 1971.

Werner, Heinz, *Comparative Psychology of Mental Development.* New York: International University Press, 1948.

————, "The Concept of Development from a Comparative and Organismic Point of View," in D.B. Harris, ed., *The Concept of Development: An Issue in the Study of Human Behavior,* pp. 125–48. Minneapolis: University of Minnesota Press, 1957.

Wheeler, M. A., Stuss, D. T., and Tulving, E., "Toward a Theory of Episodic Memory: The Frontal Lobes and Autonoetic Consciousness," *Psychological Bulletin, 121* (1997), 331–354.

Whitehead, A. N., *Science and the Modern World.* New York: Macmillan, 1926.

————, *Adventures of Ideas.* New York: Macmillan, 1933.

Willingham, D. T., "Do Visual, Auditory and Kinesthetic Learners Need Visual, Auditory and Kinesthetic Instruction?" *American Educator, 29*(2) (2005), 31–35.

————, *Why Don't Students Like School: A Cognitive Scientist Answers Questions about How the Mind Works and What It Means for the Classroom.* San Francisco: Jossey Bass, 2009.

Willingham, Warren, John Valley, and Morris Keeton, *Assessing Experiential Learning: A Summary Report of the CAEL Project.* Columbia, Md.: CAEL, 1977.

Wilson, A. L., and Hayes, E. R., "From the Editors: The Problem of (Learning in-from-to) Experience," *Adult Education Quarterly, 52*(3) (2002), 173–75.

Witkin, H., "Cognitive Styles in Academic Performance and in Teacher-Student Relations," in S. Messick, ed., *Individuality in Learning.* San Francisco: Jossey-Bass, 1976.

Wober, M., "Adapting Witkin's Field Independence Theory to Accommodate New Information from Africa," *British Journal of Psychology,* 58 (1967), 29–38.

Wolfe, D., *America's Resources of Specialized Talent.* New York: Harper Bros., 1954.

Wolfe, Donald, and David Kolb, "Beyond Specialization: The Quest for Integration in Midcareer," in Brooklyn Derr, ed., *Work, Family and the Career: New Frontiers in Theory and Research.* New York: Praeger Publishers, 1980.

————, **and Kolb, D. A.,** "Beyond Specialization: The Quest for Integration in Mid-Life," in B. Derr, ed., *Individuals, Organizations and Careers.* New York: Praeger Publishers, 1980.

————, *Learning Processes in Adult Development: A Study of Cognitive and Social Factors in Mid-Life Transition.* Final Report to the Spencer Foundation, 1982.

Wunderlich, R., and Gjerde, C., "Another Look at Learning Style Inventory and Medical Career Choice," *Journal of Medical Education,* 53 (1978), 45–54.

Wynne, B. E., Abstraction, Reflection and Insight—Situation Coping Style Measurement Dimensions," working paper, University of Wisconsin, Milwaukee School of Business Administration, Winter 1975.

Wyss-Flamm, E. D., "Conversational Learning and Psychological Safety in Multicultural Teams," unpublished Ph.D. dissertation. Case Western Reserve University, 2002.

Yamazaki, Y., and Kayes, D. C., "An Experiential Approach to Cross-Cultural Learning: A Review and Integration of Competencies of Successful Expatriate Adaptation," *Academy of Management Learning and Education, 3*(4) (2004), 362–379.

————, **and Kayes, D. C.,** "Expatriate Learning: Exploring How Japanese Managers Adapt in the United States," *International Journal of Human Resource Management, 18*(8) (2007), 1373–1395.

————, "Expatriate Adaptation," *Management International Review, 50*(1) (2010a), 81–108.

————, "Expatriate Adaptation: A Fit between Skills and Demands among Japanese Expatriates in the United States," *Management International Review, 50*(1) (2010c), 81–108.

————, "Japanese Expatriate Adaptation: A Study of Fits between the Skills and the Demands in Japanese Multinationals," unpublished paper, Graduate School of International Management, International University of Japan, Niigata Japan, 2010b.

————, "Impact of Learning Styles on Learning-Skill Development in Higher Education," working paper Series No. IM-2010–03, Graduate School of International Management, International University of Japan Niigata Japan, 2010d.

————, "Using a Competency Approach to Understand HCN Managers in Asia: A Study of Japanese, Chinese, Malaysian, Thai, and Hong Kong Managers in Japanese MNEs," working paper, Graduate School of International Management, International University of Japan, Niigata Japan, 2010e.

————, **and Kayes, D. C.,** "Learning and Work Satisfaction in Asia: A Comparative Study of Japanese, Chinese, and Malaysian Managers," *International Journal of Human Resource Management, 21*(12) (2010), 2267–2285.

Yang, J. "My Latest Product Launch Was a Failure. How Do I Move on?" *Fortune, 158*(1) (2008), 28.

Yeganeh, B., *Mindful Experiential Learning,* dissertation, Case Western Reserve University, 2006.

————, **and Kolb, D. A.,** "Mindfulness and Experiential Learning," *OD Practitioner, 41*(3) (2009), 8–14.

Zajonc, R. B., "Feeling and Thinking: Preferences Need No Inferences," *American Psychologist,* 35 (February 1980), 151–75.

Zen Buddhism. Mount Vernon, New York: Peter Pauper Press, 1959.

Zull, J., *The Art of Changing the Brain.* Sterling, VA: Stylus, 2002.

————, *From Brain to Mind: Using Neuroscience to Guide Change in Education.* Sterling, VA: Stylus, 2011.

————, "The Brain, Learning and Study Abroad", in Michael Vande Berg, Michael Page, and Kris Lou, eds., *Student Learning Abroad.* Sterling, VA: Stylus, 2012.

Index

Consciousness, 16, 20, 38–39, 53, 74, 160, 199, 208, 211, 217–218, 314
   critical, 199
   integrative, 211–212, 215, 221–223, 225
   interpretative, 156, 211, 214–215, 218, 219–222, 225
   receptive mode of, 84
   registrative, 156, 211, 214, 218, 219, 225
Construct aware, 232, 237
Constructionalism, 34, 36, 50, 54, 321
Constructivism, 26, 54–55
Consulting, 180
Content, 160, 165, 208, 282
Context, 149, 226–227, 290
Contextualism, 99, 165, 170–175, 179, 188–189, 193, 329
Contextualist/accommodative, 263
Contigency, 95
Continuity of self, 139
Conventional development stage, 237
Convergence, 146, 206, 211–214, 242, 246–248, 264–265
   decision skills, 134
   knowledge, 68, 166
   learning style, 36, 43, 114–115, 124, 126, 178, 179, 207, 211, 243, 256, 272, 283
   situations, 317, 319
Convergent learning, 179
Conversation, 64, 298
Conversational learning, 29
Conviction, 155. *See also* Belief
Cook, Theodore, 62
Cook-Greuter, Suzanne, 232, 235, 236, 237
Cooperative Assessment of Experiential Learning (CAEL), 7. *See also* Council for the Advancement of Experiential Learning
Cooperative education, 5
Copernicus, 328
Corballis, Michael, 16
Corpus callosum, 72–73, 86
Correlation, canonical, 119
Correspondence, 167, 173, 174. *See also* Root metaphor
Cortical homunculus, 94
Council for the Advancement of Experiential Learning, 7. *See also* Cooperative Assessment of Experiential Learning (CAEL)
Courage, 330–331
Coyle, Daniel, 352
Crary, Marcy, 321, 326, 327
Creativity, 10, 42–44, 205, 240, 244, 282, 315, 325
Crick, Francis, 20–21
Crisis of generativity, 283–284, 314
Critical consciousness, 16, 342
Critical idealism, 154
Critical reflection, 58
Critical theory, 54
Criticism, 156–157
Culture, xxi, 17, 21, 103, 175, 181, 198–199, 203, 210, 226–227, 283, 298, 307
Culture circles, 22

Cumulative grade average, 244, 255
Curriculum, 13–14, 282, 283–284
   competence-centered, 15
   design of, 15
   development of, 13
   discovery, 19
   experience-based, 13
Curvilinear development, 236

D

Darwin, Charles, 312
Davis, J., 177
de Groot, Adriaan, 220
deCharms, Richard, 321
Deciding style, 145
Decision making, 44–45, 114, 117, 134
Deep experiencing, 28
Default mode network (DMN), 87
Defensiveness, 205
Deliberate learning, 338–340
Deliberate practice, 338, 352–353
Democracy, 9, 334
Democritus, 165, 168
Dennett, Daniel, 94
Departments, 284
Descartes, 154, 155
Development, 45, 197–201, 203–4, 211, 216, 225, 234–236, 311
   cognitive, 16, 199–201
   conventional, 229
   differentiation and integration, 199–201
   dimensions of, 228
   individual, 114
   integrative, 229
   as a lifelong process, 15
   moral, 14
   personal, 42
   post-conventional, 229
   socioemotional, 15–16
      processes of, 12
   specialization stage of, 209, 214
   specialized, 210, 220
   theory, 205–10, 226
   toward a life of purpose and self direction, 17
   unilinear *vs.* multilinear, 201–5
Developmental psychology, 46
Dewey, John, xvii, xviii, xxi, xxii, xxiii, 4–5, 12, 15, 17, 22, 24–25, 33, 44, 46, 47, 48, 53, 54, 55, 57, 59, 99, 153, 159, 161, 170, 171, 197, 293, 296, 353
DeWitt, Norman, 172
Dialetic, 10, 16, 17, 24, 33, 40, 42, 50–51, 56–57, 66, 87, 111, 145, 155–157, 159–163, 199, 205, 209, 212, 215, 222–223, 229, 231, 291, 329–330
Dialogue, 2, 16, 41, 205
Dialoguing ba, 188
Dictatorship, 9
Diekman, Arthur, 84–85
Differentiation, 199–201, 211–213, 236, 326
Digital, 170
Dionysian typology, 98
Discernment, 139

Personal knowledge, 48. *See also* Knowledge
Personal-response flexibility, 317
Personal responsibility, 163
Personality theory, 201
Personality type, 116, 118
Personnel/labor relations, 128
Pessoa, Fernando, 141
Pfaff, W., 313
Phenomenal language, 71
Phenomenalism/constructivism, 34, 50, 51, 66, 85, 312
Phenomenology, xxii, 12, 173, 181, 194
Philosophy, xxii–xxiii, 39, 70, 94, 181, 189, 246, 283, 284. *See also* James
Physical education, 182
Physical sciences, 124, 167, 243
Physics, 156, 177, 179, 242, 246, 247, 283
Physiognomic perception, 156, 204
Physiology, 180, 182
Piaget, Jean, xvii, xviii, 12, 13, 15, 19, 22, 26, 34, 44, 48, 50, 57, 66, 68, 78–79, 85, 86, 153, 155, 156, 198, 203, 207, 226, 312, 316, 320
Pigg, K., 127
Planned change, 13
Plato, 165, 167
Play, 34, 42
Plovnick, Mark, 126, 129, 130, 243, 283
Pneumatici, 98
Polanyi, Michael, 17, 156–158, 163, 170, 187
Political alienation, 244, 257–259
Political science, 124, 178, 179
Politics of knowledge, 285
Positivism, 155, 162–163, 167, 174
Possibility processing structures, 99–100, 114, 135
learning styles, 100–1, 208
Post-conventional development stage, 237
Post traumatic stress disorder (PTSD), 95
Power of self-making, 337
Practice, 352–353
Pragmatism, 12, 17, 168, 171, 329
Praxis, 38, 40–41, 98, 199
Pre-conventional development stage, 237
Precision, 165
Preconceptions, 351
Preferenda, 76
Prehension, 67, 86, 100, 114
apprehension process, 69–71
comprehension process, 69–71
dimension, 66, 85, 111, 155
Present-centered awareness, 351
Presential immediacy, perception by, 71
Prigogene, Ira, 63
Primary qualities, 168, 170
Prior concepts, 341
Prior knowledge, 297
Prior learning experience, 3
Prison reform, 15
Proaction, 1, 197, 199, 205
Proactive adaptation, 324
Problem-based learning (PBL), 308
Problem-posing education, 342

Problem solving, 10, 36, 44–45, 114, 115, 167, 198, 212, 264
process, 33
style, 106
Process, 155, 171–172, 174, 243
Process conception of growth, 232–233
Process experiencing, 233
Professional deformation, 183, 265–267, 271
Professional education, 261–267, 273
Professional mentality, 126, 261–262, 265–267
Professional specialization, 312
Professional training, 283
Professions, 175, 241, 261
Progressive Movement of the 1920s, 22
Provisionalism, 39. *See also* Partial skepticism
Proximal development, zone of, 26, 199, 211, 225, 301, 350
Psyche, 80
Psychiatry, 243
Psychici, 98
Psychoanalysis, 15
Psychological orientation, 116
Psychological time dimension, 216
Psychological types, Jung's, 16, 43, 98, 116–117
extrovert type, 117, 120
feeling type, 117, 120
introvert type, 117, 120
intuition type, 117, 120
judging type, 117, 120
perceiving type, 117, 120
sensing type, 117, 120
thinking type, 117, 120
typology of, 117
Psychology, 48, 124, 178, 179, 181, 243
Psychotherapy, 232
Pure experience, 24, 59–60, 89
Pure sciences, 190
Purpose, 17–18, 197, 218

Q

Qualitative humanistic, 177
Quantitative scientific, 177

R

Racial integration, 285
Radical educators
Freire, Paulo, 16
Illich, Ivan, 16
Radical empiricism, xviii, xxii, 23–24, 59, 60–61, 96, 341
Raia, Anthony P., 276
Rational, 154
Rational controlled doing, 24
Rationalism, 2, 12–13, 154, 155, 168
Reactive, 1
Reading, 247
Real world, 335
Realism, 80, 165, 166, 174
Reality, 69, 173
Reasonable eclecticism, 193–194
Reasoning, hypothetico-deductive, 36